Recognition Struggles and Social M

Recognition Struggles and Social Movements is the first book to look comparatively and cross-nationally at the dynamic interplay between those fighting for a fairer division of economic resources and those struggling for recognition and respect of group differences. Combining theory and empirical research, it decodes the moral grammar of recognition into real struggles of collective actors who contest social hierarchies in arenas of power: From the Roma in Hungary to the Travesti prostitutes in Brazil, from abortion discourse in the USA and Germany to the translation of feminist texts from East and West. Looking through multiple mirrors of gender, race/ethnic and sexual identities, the authors dramatize the competition and conflicts among groups vying for recognition. Written by prominent scholars across disciplinary and geographical borders, this book breaks new ground in social movement studies confronting issues of power and governance, authenticity, and boundary-making.

BARBARA HOBSON is Professor of Sociology and holds a chair in Sociology and Gender Studies at Stockholm University. Her most recent publications include *Making Men into Fathers: Men, Masculinities and the Social Politics of Fatherhood* (Cambridge, 2002), *Gender and Citizenship in Transition* and the co-edited collection (with Jane Lewis and Birte Siim) *Contested Concepts in Gender and Social Politics*.

Recognition Struggles and Social Movements

Contested Identities, Agency and Power

Edited by

Barbara Hobson

Stockholm University

CAMBRIDGE
UNIVERSITY PRESS

PUBLISHED BY THE PRESS SYNDICATE OF THE UNIVERSITY OF CAMBRIDGE
The Pitt Building, Trumpington Street, Cambridge, United Kingdom

CAMBRIDGE UNIVERSITY PRESS
The Edinburgh Building, Cambridge, CB2 2RU, UK
40 West 20th Street, New York, NY 10011–4211, USA
477 Williamstown Road, Port Melbourne, VIC 3207, Australia
Ruiz de Alarcón 13, 28014 Madrid, Spain
Dock House, The Waterfront, Cape Town 8001, South Africa

http://www.cambridge.org

First published 2003

Printed in the United Kingdom at the University Press, Cambridge

Typeface Plantin 10/12 pt.   *System* LATEX 2_ε [TB]

A catalogue record for this book is available from the British Library

ISBN 0 521 82922 4 hardback
ISBN 0 521 53608 1 paperback

Contents

Figures

Notes on contributors

These are given in the order they appear in the book.

BARBARA HOBSON is Professor of Sociology and holds a chair in Sociology with a specialization in Comparative Gender Studies at Stockholm University. She has published articles on social movements, gender and citizenship, and gender and welfare state regimes. Her most recent books include: *Making Men into Fathers: Men, Masculinities and the Social Politics of Fatherhood* (2002); *Contested Concepts in Gender and Social Politics* (with Jane Lewis and Birte Siim); and *Gender and Citizenship in Transition* (2000). She is a founder and a current editor of *Social Politics: International Studies of Gender, State, and Society* (Oxford University Press). Her current research is on the role of supranational institutions and networks in the framing of citizenship.

NANCY FRASER is the Henry and Louise A. Loeb Professor of Politics and Philosophy at the Graduate Faculty of the New School for Social Research, New York. She is also co-editor of *Constellations: An International Journal of Critical and Democratic Theory*. Her books include *Unruly Practices: Power, Discourse, and Gender in Contemporary Social Theory* (English edition: University of Minnesota Press and Polity Press, 1989; German edition: Suhrkamp Verlag, 1994); *Justice Interruptus: Critical Reflections on the "Postsocialist" Condition* (English edition: Routledge, 1997); and *Adding Insult to Injury: Social Justice and the Politics of Recognition*, ed. Kevin Olson (Verso, 2001). Professor Fraser is also a co-author of two books: with Seyla Benhabib, Judith Butler, and Drucilla Cornell, *Feminist Contentions: A Philosophical Exchange* (English edition: Routledge, 1994) and with Axel Honneth, *Redistribution or Recognition? A Philosophical Exchange* (English edition: Verso, 2002). She is a co-editor of *Revaluing French Feminism: Critical Essays on Difference, Agency, and Culture* (Indiana University Press, 1992). Her current research is on globalization.

MYRA MARX FERREE is Professor of Sociology at the University of Wisconsin-Madison. On American feminism, she is co-author, with Beth Hess, of *Controversy and Coalition: The New Feminist Movement* (3nd edition, Routledge, 2000), and co-editor, with Patricia Yancey Martin, of *Feminist Organizations* (Temple, 1995). Recent articles on German feminism include, with Eva Maleck-Lewy, "Talking About Women and Wombs: Discourse About Abortion and Reproductive Rights in the GDR During and After the 'Wende'," in Susan Gal and Gail Kligman (eds.) *Reproducing Gender: Politics, Publics and Everyday Life After Socialism* (Princeton, 2000) and, with Silke Roth, "Gender, Class and the Interaction Among Social Movements: a Strike of West Berlin Daycare Workers" (*Gender & Society*, 1998, 12(6): 626–48). Her most recent work, *Shaping Abortion Discourse* (with William Gamson, Jürgen Gerhards, and Dieter Rucht; forthcoming, Cambridge University Press), compares Germany and the USA in terms of social movements, media, and political discourse.

WILLIAM A. GAMSON is Professor of Sociology and co-directs the Media Research and Action Project (MRAP) at Boston College. He has most recently co-authored *Shaping Abortion Discourse: Democracy and the Public Sphere in Germany and the United States* (2002) and is the author of *Talking Politics* (1992) and *The Strategy of Social Protest* (2nd edition, 1990) among other books and articles on political discourse, the mass media, and social movements. He is a past president of the American Sociological Association and a Fellow of the American Academy of Arts and Sciences.

SUSAN GAL is Professor of Anthropology and Linguistics at the University of Chicago. She is the author of *Language Shift* (1979) and *The Politics of Gender After Socialism* (2000, with G. Kligman); she is co-editor of *Reproducing Gender* (2000, with G. Kligman) and *Languages and Publics: The Making of Authority* (2001, with K. Woolard). Gal writes broadly on the politics of language as well as on gender issues. She is currently a Guggenheim Fellow, working on a project about the semiotics of language ideologies and on the politically contested definitions of truth and trust in mass mediated communication.

FIONA WILLIAMS is Professor of Social Policy at the University of Leeds and Director of the ESRC Research Group on Care, Values and the Future of Welfare. She has written widely on gender, "race," ethnicity, and class in relation to social policy. Her publications also include work on postmodernism and feminism, on learning disability, on masculinities, and on new approaches to researching poverty and social exclusion. Her most recent book, co-edited with Ann Oakley and Jennie Popay, is *Welfare Research: A Critical Review* (UCL Press, 1999).

MARILYN LAKE is Professor in History at Latrobe University, where she was also the founding director of the Program in Women's Studies. Between 2001 and 2002, she held the Chair in Australian Studies at Harvard University. Her publications include studies of the gendered and racialized nature of citizenship and nationalism. In 1994, her co-authored book *Creating a Nation* won the Human Rights Award for Non-Fiction. In 1999, she published *Getting Equal: The History of Feminism in Australia* (Allen and Unwin), who also published her biography of Aboriginal rights activist, Faith Bandler, in 2002. She is currently working on a study of white colonial masculinity "From Wild Colonial Boy to Anxious Colonial Man."

DIANE SAINSBURY is the Lars Hierta Professor of Political Science at Stockholm University. She is author of *Gender, Equality and Welfare States* (1996) and editor of *Gendering Welfare States* (1994) and *Gender and Welfare State Regimes* (1999). Her articles include "Gendering Dimensions of Welfare States," in Janet Fink, Gail Lewis and John Clarke (eds.), *Rethinking European Welfare* (Sage, 2001); "Gender and the Making of Welfare States: Norway and Sweden," *Social Politics* 8(1), 2001; "Social Welfare Policies and Gender," *International Encyclopedia of the Social and Behavioral Sciences* (Elsevier, 2001); "Rights without Seats: The Puzzle of Women's Legislative Recruitment in Australia," in Marian Sawer (ed.), *Elections: Full, Free and Fair* (Federation Press, 2001); and "Welfare State Challenges and Responses: Institutional and Ideological Resilience or Restructuring?," *Acta Sociologica* 44(3), 2001.

JÚLIA SZALAI is the Head of the Department of Social Policy and Social History at the Institute of Sociology of the Hungarian Academy of Sciences, and Professor of Social Policy at ELTE University, Budapest. She is the editor of *East Central Europe/l'Europe du Centre-Est: Eine Wissenschaftliche Zeitschrift (ECE/ECE)*, a trilingual journal of the social sciences and the humanities, addressing issues of the East-Central European region. She is also Chair of the Max Weber Foundation for the Study of Social Initiative (Budapest–Glasgow), and advisor to the Hungarian Ministry of Welfare. Szalai's main research interests are the history of social policy in East Central Europe; "old" and "new" poverty in Central Europe and social exclusion/inclusion amid the postcommunist condition in Central European societies. She is currently writing a book on the deficiencies of the postcommunist embourgeoisement process and their consequences on the new class and ethnic relations in Hungary.

DON KULICK is Professor of Anthropology at New York University and Stockholm University. He is the author of a book on language socialization and language death in Papua New Guinea (*Language Shift and Cultural Reproduction*, Cambridge University Press, 1992), and a book on Brazilian travesti prostitutes (*Travesti*, University of Chicago Press, 1998), in addition to several edited volumes in English and Swedish. His most recent work focuses on prostitution in Sweden and Italy, and he is currently completing a book entitled *Language and Sexuality* (with Deborah Cameron) for Cambridge University Press.

CHARLES KLEIN is a Health Program Planner at the HIV Prevention Section of the San Francisco Department of Public Health. He received his PhD in Anthropology from the University of Michigan in 1996. He has previously published in journals such as *Sexualities*; *Culture, Health and Sexuality*; *AIDS*; and *NACLA Report on the Americas*. His current research focuses on queer sexuality and health movements in Brazil and the USA.

CELIA VALIENTE is Visiting Professor (*Profesora Visitante*) in the Department of Political Science and Sociology of the Universidad Carlos III de Madrid (Spain). Her major area of research is comparative public policy and social movements with an analytical focus on gender. Her publications include "A Closed Subsystem and Distant Feminist Demands Block Women-Friendly Outcomes in Spain," in Amy G. Mazur (ed.), *State Feminism, Women's Movements, and Job Training: Making Democracies Work in the Global Economy* (Routledge, 2001); "Do Political Parties Matter? Do Spanish Parties Make a Difference in Child Care Policies?," in Tricia David (ed.), *Promoting Evidence-Based Practice in Early Childhood Education: Research and its Implications* (JAI Press, 2001); "Gendering Abortion Debates: State Feminism in Spain," in Dorothy McBride Stetson (ed.), *Abortion Politics, Women's Movements, and the Democratic State: A Comparative Study of State Feminism* (Oxford University Press, 2001); "Implementing Women's Rights in Spain," in Jane H. Bayes and Nayereh Tohidi (eds.), *Globalization, Gender and Religion: The Politics of Women's Rights in Catholic and Muslim Contexts* (2001).

ANNE PHILLIPS is Professor of Gender Theory and Director of the Gender Institute at the London School of Economics and Political Science. She is a leading figure in feminist political theory and has written extensively on equality, democracy and difference. Her many publications include *Engendering Democracy* (1991); *Democracy and Difference* (1993); *The Politics of Presence* (1995); and *Which Equalities Matter?* (1999). She also recently edited a collection of readings on *Feminism and Politics* (Oxford University Press, 1998)

CAROL MUELLER is Professor of Sociology at Arizona State University West and past Chair of the Section on Collective Behavior and Social Movements of the American Sociological Association. She has edited three volumes on social movements including *The Women's Movements of the United States and Western Europe*, with Mary Katzenstein (1987); *Politics of the Gender Gap* (1988); and *Frontiers of Social Movement Theory* with Aldon Morris (1992). A fourth edited volume on Mobilization and Repression, with Christian Davenport and Hank Johnston, is currently under review. She has published numerous articles in major sociological journals. An article on the "International Women's Movement" with Myra Ferree is forthcoming in the *Blackwell Handbook on Social Movements*. Her current research is on the role of international conferences as a vehicle for women's mobilization.

Acknowledgments

This book began with a conversation between myself and Nancy Fraser in 1994 about claims and frames, recognition and social movements. Two years later, thanks to the generosity and support of the Bank of Sweden's Tercentenary Foundation, we assembled our first meeting of an extraordinary group of scholars who would meet over the next five years. Although Nancy Fraser was unable to attend the meetings after the first two, her introductory chapter was an inspiration for us all.

The core group in this book, Myra Marx Ferree, Susan Gal, Charles Klein, Don Kulick, Marilyn Lake, Diane Sainsbury, Júlia Szalai, Celia Valiente, and Fiona Williams, were in Stockholm every spring, harnessing their intellect, energy, endurance, and humor for our Herculean labors. They are remarkable people with a passion and intensity that pervades their scholarship and their lives. To call them authors is a misnomer, they were composers, each providing a template, formed from their own wealth of experience and deep theoretical insights, which served as the basis for the genesis of this book. The postulate, the whole is greater than the sum of its parts, needs to be revised in this case: the participants are the product.

Though unable to contribute to the final version of the book, Dave Lewis's research on the Saami in Sweden and Lin Chun's papers on China enriched this book. Both were active and important members of our group (Dave Lewis came to every meeting). Lotta Coniavitis, who also had to drop out of the book to finish her dissertation, introduced her perspectives on corporatism in Greece. Over the years, the participants in this project have become colleagues and friends, and our collaborations continue.

A special thanks is in order to the authors of the epilogues. Carol Mueller came to our last meeting bringing to our discussions a nuanced and multilayered analysis of social movement theorizing, which is found in her penetrating epilogue. Joining our group last, but certainly not least, was Anne Phillips, whose epilogue mirrors her brillance and keen sense of the dilemmas in politics of recognition. Bill Gamson was with us in spirit as co-author with Myra Marx Ferree. Sheila Shaver and Yasmin Soysal were valuable commentators, each attending one of our meetings. I want to acknowledge the contribution of Lis Clemens for her perceptive commentary on several chapters of the book at the Social Science History panel. I made last-minute revisions of the introduction in light of her synthesis.

Three of my doctoral students were invaluable resources for this research project and the final book: Maria Törnqvist, Sanja Magdalenic, and Michelle Ariga. Maria Törnqvist made the arrangements for every meeting and organized everything to the last detail. Michelle Ariga, our editorial assistant for *Social Politics*, put to use her exceptional editorial and computer skills and made ready the entire manuscript on time. Sanja Magdalenic was always there to guarantee that our equipment functioned and all discussions were recorded.

Sarah Caro, my editor for two books, not only recognized the importance of this book but took the care to find the perfect reviewers, analysing the book from different lenses. I want to thank her and them for their valuable comments. Rare in the publishing field these days, Sarah Caro goes to bat for her authors.

Projects like this only happen with large program grants. The Centennial Fund of Sweden awarded me over 4 million crowns for the development of new research fields. Three books and five dissertations came out of this program. I want to express my appreciation to Dan Brändstrom (director of the Bank of Sweden's Tercentenary Foundation) and Kerstin Stigmark (program officer) for supporting us every step of the way. At the end of our research project, they organized a day-long seminar at the Swedish Parliament buildings, where we presented our book to politicians, journalists, and policymakers. This was truly recognition of our work.

Introduction

Barbara Hobson

Over the last decades, multiculturalism, identity politics, and, more broadly, struggles for recognition have dominated the political landscape. We now have a new language to express forms of exploitation that are culturally symbolic, and to describe processes that make invisible racial, ethnic, and gender differences. In popular parlance we refer to this as dissing someone or being dissed. In academic discourse, the terms misrecognition or nonrecognition are applied when members of excluded or marginalized groups find their way of life or status as persons denigrated and devalued. Implicit in this discourse is a new construction of justice, one that goes beyond saying that to non-recognize a group or person can and does inflict harm, but is also a form of oppression (Taylor, 1994).

This has been described as a paradigm shift in which claims for redistribution, those based on a fairer and more equal division of the pie, have been eclipsed by claims for recognition, based on respect and valuation for group differences (Fraser, 1997a; 2003). It is safe to say that the collapse of Soviet-style communism, alongside the ascendancy of neoliberal politics and economic policies, has dampened and delegitimized class-based politics. Nevertheless, as the events of the past years have underscored, this shift has been overblown. One has only to consider the rise of social movements around globalization and its economic consequences for industrialized countries and exploited third-world workers. Not to be forgotten in this discussion of recognition and redistribution is the devastatingly destructive linkage terrorists have made between certain extreme forms of Muslim fundamentalism and the symbolic icon of global economic power, the World Trade Center.

To ask if the cultural is displacing the material, or if identity is replacing class is to ask the wrong question (Phillips, 1997). First, it assumes a very narrow definition of recognition as identity politics (Fraser in this volume). Second, to pose the question that way is to ignore the dynamic interplay between claims to alter maldistribution and challenges to the devaluation of members of a group based on their identities, an interplay that empirical cases in the book so vividly demonstrate. Struggles for recognition involve issues of land rights, equitable distribution of economic resources, and access to social goods. All of these are deeply interwoven into claims for respect and strategies for remedying racial, ethnic, and gender disadvantage and discrimination (Lake, 1994b; Lewis, 2002). Struggles for redistributive justice, cast as class struggles in the past, were and continue to be entwined with appeals for the dignity of workers and respect for working-class culture (Thompson, 1963; Sewell, 1980).

The core question of this book is what shapes the interplay between these dimensions. To understand this interplay, the authors have located claims for recognition in the specific histories, institutional settings, national narratives, and collective memories of various social groups. While social actors often make strategic choices (different kinds of differences require different kinds of strategies) (Fraser, 1997a), in recognition struggles the forms that actions take are more complicated than narrow instrumentalism would predict. The making of political identities and the framing of claims are shaped by national, regional, ethnic, and gender narratives, but also by historical and cultural legacies around citizens' rights and obligations (Steinberg, 1999).

Looking at such specific contexts reveals the complex processes that lay behind strategic choices made by social actors representing social groups and movements; it raises questions about the meanings attached to recognition and the institutional settings and policy logics that connect them to redistribution. When viewed this way, recognition and redistribution become specific lenses for viewing the same struggles, rather than discrete categories.

Most relevant to the emergence of a politics of recognition is the rise of social movements around particularized identities including blacks, women, aboriginals, gays, and the disabled. These movements made similar challenges to the universalist framing of rights and social citizenship that shaded out their values, experiences, and needs, and did not redress particular inequalities and injustices they faced. The salience in these kinds of claims based on particularized identities and the range of claimants and claims-making has spawned much research on what some would call "new" social movements.[1]

Bridging theoretical domains

As our title, *Recognition Struggles and Social Movements*, suggests we are building bridges across two theoretical terrains. On the one side, recognition has been grounded in normative political theories of justice, citizenship, and democracy in which inclusion, rights, and membership are the cornerstones. Variations among theorists in this tradition exist in terms of the way they conceptualize the different outcomes: greater or lesser participation of citizens in political, economic, and social spheres, extent of redistribution of resources, and opening or closing geographic, political, social, and economic borders. National level political institutions play a central role in these outcomes. On the other side, social movement theories are centered on organizations and actors at a subnational level. They often revolve around processes: what generates a movement, its resources and opportunities, what shapes the dynamics of movements, how do they ebb and flow through the cycles of protest, what is their relation to identity formation, and what role do structures play in mobilizing specific forms of collective action? Little attention has been paid to outcomes in terms of shifts in institutional and macro-political structures (McAdam et al., 2001).

Bringing the state and institutions back in is very much on the social movement agenda (see McAdam et al., 1996; Meyer et al., 2002). McAdam, Tarrow, and Tilly make this explicit in their recent book, *Dynamics of Contention* (2001), by addressing the mechanisms underlying revolutionary and nationalist movements, and looking at democratic contention that challenges formal political structures. But they leave out a large segment of "contentious politics" that involves struggles over social politics and social policy, which is a major arena of concern for both political theorists and actors engaged in recognition struggles themselves. One could say that POLITICS in their study is in capital letters, whereas politics in recognition struggles, in the lower case, involves confronting everyday institutionalized patterns and practices that deny social groups participatory citizenship, struggles that challenge the basic coding of rights and obligations in nation states and constitute different varieties of collective "we" than the norms that emerged in the eighteenth and ninteenth centuries when these polities were formed (Yuval-Davis, 1997).

Our focus on social politics paves the way for rebuilding some of the earlier links between social movements and social policy (Amenta, 1998; Lipsky, 1970; Piven and Cloward, 1971). Recognition struggles often involve making claims for resources, goods, and services through state polices: care allowances via women's movements, social security benefits for gay couples, or building access ramps for the disabled. But claims in recognition struggles are also connected to membership and inclusion in the polity.

Our approach to empirical studies of recognition struggles fills a void in the literature on redistribution and welfare regimes, which has focused on the competing interests and the power resources different social actors accumulate (Korpi and Palme, 1999; Esping-Andersen, 1990) and paid insufficient attention to the processes of political identity formation and the framing of claims (Hobson, 2000a). Identity is at the core of the recognition paradigm (Taylor, 1994; Honneth, 1995b), but there has been little attempt to understand the ways in which institutional contexts shape collective identities. It has been social movement studies that have paid attention to the interaction between actors and institutions, and their discursive resources and political opportunities.

Recognition and social movements

Are recognition struggles a subset of social movements? While defining something as a social movement helps to legitimate research in these terms,[2] in the real world of political interaction such labels are both arbitrary and without practical consequence. It is more useful to ask where the struggles we examine fit in this conceptual landscape. Not all social movements are recognition struggles, that is, they do not involve groups that make claims resulting from devalued statuses and misrecognized identities.

For the same reasons that McAdam, Tarrow, and Tilly (2001) refer to their cases as "contentious politics," we use the concept struggles to emphasize that these are not episodes of collective action, but rather unbounded expressions of protest and claims-making in which institutions are the loci of group interaction. Recognition struggles often represent a long durée of struggle, spanning decades and reflecting histories of disrespect and devaluation (see Hobson, Sainsbury, and Lake in this volume). Comparing such struggles across space and time, as the authors in this volume have done, reveals how they are embedded in political cultures, and how they reframe claims and recast strategies in response to new political configurations and institutional change.

Collective identity formation

Constructionist social movement theorists, the main protagonist being Alberto Melucci, have paved the way for studies like ours (see Mueller's epilogue). For Melucci, collective identity formation is a dynamic process involving negotiations among individuals within a movement and with outside competitors, allies, and adversaries in relation to a political system (Melucci, 1996: 78–79). His analysis (Melucci, 1995) of these social processes provides some of the missing links to Axel Honneth's (1995b) sociopsychological interpretation of recognition and social movements. Within Honneth's analysis of the structure of relations of recognition is the idea that the individual must establish a "relation to herself." Thus the cognitive processes involved in the experience of shame and disrespect are "psychological symptoms," from which a person can come to the realization that he or she is being denied social recognition (1995b: 136). Through social movements, these feelings become articulated so that the experience of disrespect can become a source of political motivation (1995b: 139).

My earlier research challenges Honneth's (1995b) disjuncture between an individual's sense of disrespect and harm and the political act of resistance. I have argued that recognition struggles name, interpret, and make visible histories of discrimination and disrespect, and thus not only motivate an aggrieved person to become politically active or to resist, but are a crucial part of the process of self-realization of mis- and nonrecognition. The very framing of grievances as injustices and the articulation of group identity shape cognitive processes, by which individuals understand and interpret personal experiences of disrespect and self-realization, seeing them as shared with others in a devalued and disadvantaged group (Hobson and Lindholm, 1997). To begin with this perspective is to take the analysis of recognition struggles further into the territory of social movement theory, which is often concerned with how identities are contested, negotiated, and mediated through different institutional and discursive universes (Snow and Benford, 1992; Steinberg, 1999; Taylor and Rupp, 1993). Our studies of recognition confirm Melucci's (1996: 69) argument that collective identities are not just a sum of individual motives nor merely expressions of structural preconditions, but a dynamic interplay between structure and meaning. The research projects in this book also highlight the often-neglected fact that this interplay often occurs within enduring political cultures (see Mueller in this volume).

Contested identities

Whereas the thrust of social movement research has been on finding out how shared meanings are generated within groups – on the construction of collective identity – the theorizing on recognition has focused on the contests around identities with others. Charles Taylor (1994) in his pathbreaking essay on the "Politics of Recognition," set the agenda: that identities are not made in isolation but constituted in dialogue "unshaped by a predetermined social script" (1994: 36), which he claims, has made the politics of equal recognition more conflictual. Our studies not only show that this dialogue is between elites and marginalized groups, but also among those engaged in different recognition struggles. White Australian feminists were challenged by Aboriginal women who castigated them for referring to women's oppression by men as colonization

(Lake in this volume). The minority women in the Migrants' Lobby in the European Union confronted the official EU Women's Lobby for their failure to address the inequalities faced by minority, ethnic, and black women (Williams in this volume).

Agency and power

Recognition struggles are boundary-making activities. This is true of all social movements in terms of who is a member/participant and who is not. But in recognition movements, who represents whom over what is embroiled in conflicts around authenticity and political identities (who is an authentic Aboriginal, which groups of women should speak for women). In recognition struggles, boundary-making occurs in different arenas among actors and various institutions, including political parties, government bureaucracies, churches, non-governmental organizations (NGOs), and the media. Such institutions confer agency on certain actors in collectivities by recognizing them as the authorities to represent the group. These actors then become certified spokespersons for a group: asked to serve on government commissions, interviewed in the media, featured as public speakers in political arenas, published in popular and academic journals (see Ferree and Gamson, Gal, Hobson, and Szalai in this volume). The more institutionalized the recognition, the greater the power to shade out other articulations of misrecognition or nonrecognition and the greater the governance that can be exercised.

Political opportunity

Shifting institutional structures (changing elites and elite alliances) or shifts in the ideological disposition of those in power (Tarrow, 1996), classic definitions of political opportunity, do not provide a wide enough lens through which to analyze recognition struggles. First, the usual conceptualization of opportunity structure does not acknowledge its cultural dimensions, and these are often central to recognition struggles. Second, it does not address the growing importance of supranational and global processes on political opportunity, assuming instead that nation states are somehow the "natural" boundaries within which politics occurs. This is particularly untrue in the domain of recognition, but is ever more unrealistic with regard to redistribution, too, as the language of "globalization" reminds us (Guidry et al., 2000).

Considering this first point, inclusion of the cultural dimensions of political opportunity structures is a controversial position in social movement theory.[3] We would suggest that, in recognition struggles, it is difficult to argue otherwise. Recognition struggles take place on symbolic terrains where discourse is of paramount importance in organizing the political arena itself, by defining rights, citizenship, and even what counts as a political resource. Moreover, recognition struggles are encased in a universe of political discourse about persons, groups, and nations, that can limit or expand the framing of claims. Take two examples from authors in this book (Gal and Hobson in this volume). Gender equality was characterized as anachronistic in the former Soviet Union and other orthodox Marxist states in Eastern Europe, the argument being then that the emancipation of women was already complete. Feminism was trivialized by the state then and yet is now attacked for its discursive association with the debunked "accomplishments" of the state. In Swedish political discourse, women were constrained by their successes. UN reports said they were living in the most gender equal society in the world, and that they had achieved parity with men in labor market participation (Hobson in this volume). These "state accomplishments" also serve discursively to marginalize continuing feminist analysis of the inequalities that remain.

Some social movement scholars do view cultural processes as elements of political opportunity (Gamson and Meyer, 1996; Steinberg, 1999; Meyer et al., 2002; Ferree et al., 2002a). Discursive opportunities embedded in institutional pronouncements and ideological resources available to challenging groups affect what it is politically possible to say, and this affects the likelihood of altering policies of mis- and nonrecognition. The media is a crucial field in which frames are transmitted, as well as a site where discursive contests take place over who and what is recognized. Two essays in this book highlight the ways in which media can open up or close down political opportunity. The media brackets who is authorized to speak for women and on behalf of the right to abortion in Germany and the USA, and the focus on certain speakers and on certain ways of making claims is interrelated (Ferree and Gamson in this volume). The translation of feminist texts from West to East creates trajectories in the universe of political discourse (Gal in this volume).

Moreover, nearly all the theorizing on political opportunities has considered opportunities in terms of national structures (McAdam et al., 1996). Keck and Sikkink's (1998) analysis of transnational advocacy groups and their leverage politics is relevant to recognition struggles. International non-government organizations (INGOs), by supporting local groups in their analysis and offering them discursive resources and international recognition, have helped such groups become national power brokers. For example, South African women who gained material resources and prestige through their involvement in the anti-apartheid struggle were reinforced in their desire to participate in the writing of the South African constitution through their participation in transnational conferences and interactions on gender politics, and ended up being able to take a strongly feminist position in this process (Seidman, 1999; 2000). In the new democracies of Eastern Europe, feminist groups who were mis-recognized in their respective countries acquired a sense of legitimacy through their contact with outside organizations, which gave them funding and access to international forums (Gal and Kligman, 2000b).

The European Union (EU) arms national actors with a whip in leverage politics, as its Directives become laws in member states (though implementation involves active mobilization on specific issues in each country) (see Hobson in this volume). Moreover, EU discourse and guidelines in formal and informal documents and policies have opened up a range of political opportunities. The insertion of a new clause in the Amsterdam Treaty on non-discrimination based on ethnicity and race has resulted in mobilizations within nation states across ethnic groups. In many instances, these groups did not represent themselves as an immigrant or minority group experiencing "ethnic and racial discrimination," but as distinct nationalities within a host country – as Turks or Iranians, Pakistanis or Jamaicans.

Institutional political contexts

Our approach underscores the fact that the relation between social actors in recognition struggles and institutional contexts is an indeterminate one (McAdam et al., 2001; Ferree et. al., 2002a). Nevertheless, we acknowledge the centrality of institutional contexts, and the path dependencies in recognition struggles. Recognition politics are dynamic: social actors seize political opportunities, reclaim and refashion public discourses, and reconfigure the politics surrounding recognition and redistribution. But claims and claims-makers exist in political cultures. Sociopolitical context can be seen as a field of constraints and opportunities both in terms of: (a) who and what gets recognized; and (b) where and how cultural identities are embedded.

There are hospitable and inhospitable fields for recognition struggles. Groups claiming rights on the basis of particularized identities in authoritarian regimes may not only be illegal, but violence can be used to repress them. It is almost inconceivable to imagine the mobilization of women in a recognition struggle for gender equality with men in Afghanistan (RAWA, or the Revolutionary Association of Women in Afghanistan, did so, often with transnational resources, even though to articulate such claims meant the risk of torture and death). Recognition struggles were also dampened in the former Soviet Union, where there was political censure against those making claims based on ethnic identities. Gypsy activists, who now serve on local municipal committees representing their communities in Hungary, risked reprisals against themselves and their families if they expressed ethnic identities and norms in the former Soviet regimes (Szalai in this volume).

One institutional form that dampens recognition struggles in democratic welfare states is corporatism. The institutionalized recognition of a tripartite of interests – employers, workers, and governing parties – in bargaining over social policy has facilitated the inclusion of workers' interests and power and their influence over wages, but has left few channels open for recognizing the demands for participatory parity by other groups, such as ethnic and racial groups and women (Åmark, 1992). This was certainly a constraint for Swedish feminists (Hobson in this volume).

Finally, institutional/political contexts also have different capacities for making change, because they vary in terms of economic development and GNP, in the institutions that are in place for altering laws and practices, and in the ideologies underpinning these institutions. To take an example from this book, the Spanish mothers making claims for more resources for their drug-addicted children were confronting a state that did not have a highly developed social welfare regime (Valiente in this volume). Along the same lines, Ferree and Gamson (in this volume) show how, in the USA, where there are few social rights guaranteed, it is harder to make the claim for social support in claiming a formally secured right to abortion, while in Germany, where political liberalism is weak, it is difficult for women to make a claim for rights to individual self-determination that would limit state intervention.

Policy logics shape the redistribution in families as well as the stakes individuals have in perpetuating gendered identities in society, both by limiting the possibilities for making claims to alter the family wage, which would demand expansion of public sector spending (O'Connor et al., 1999), and by not challenging the way markets discriminate in the allocation of jobs and positions, because there is an assumption of naturalized gender difference.

States can make laws and policies that create constituencies (Pierson, 1994). In recognition struggles, laws promoting gender equality or gay rights have led to the forging of collective identities through mobilizations to initiate or implement policy (Meyer, 2002; Bernstein, 2002; Hobson in this volume). State policies, through laws and policing, can also shape the content of recognition struggles by stigmatizing certain identities. Kulick and Klein's chapter in this volume on the scandals of gender-crossing "travestis" in Brazil makes this point.

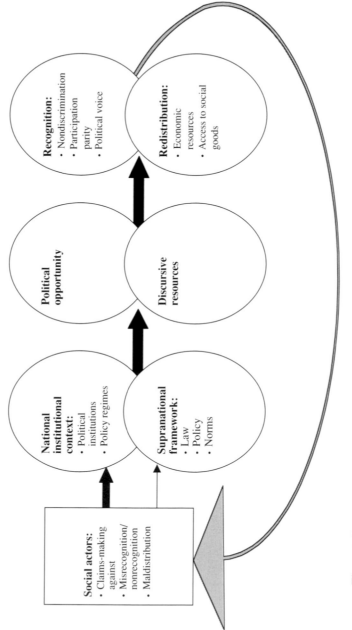

Figure 1 Recognition struggles, national political cultures, and supranational frames

Frames and claims

As Figure 1 illustrates, national institutional contexts not only constrain and enable opportunities for recognition struggles, but can also shape the patterns of solidarity and resistance. This can be understood from two vantage points. First, collectivities construct political identities and conceptions of justice in specific cultural locales, with a shared history, cultural narratives, and daily life experiences (Snow and Benford, 1992; Gamson, 1992b). Second, groups seeking to gain recognition often employ strategic discourses to achieve their ends within a specific policy context.

Supranational frames and political opportunity

Supranational institutions have become more and more important for recognition movements. The United Nations has been an important catalyst for emerging movements, particularly among women's groups, by commissioning governments to make reports for their international publications and forums, which in turn has forced governments to set up delegations to carry out these mandates (Hobson in this volume). International law framed minority rights legislation in Hungary aimed at Hungarians living abroad, which limited the possibilities for the Roma to make claims concerning misrecognized ethnic minorities in Hungary (Szalai in this volume).

The EU has provided alternative framing devices for groups seeking recognition. Recognition politics often include the refrain that certain polices appear anachronistic – out of step with European culture, not modern. This has been a powerful discursive resource for women's movements. In the instance of gender, one could make the claim that the EU provided a master frame of gender equality that has permeated European debates, providing publications with guidelines for good practice (Hoskyns, 1996; Hobson in this volume). For the black, migrant, and minority ethnic women in the Migrants' Forum in the EU, EU resources and legitimation were essential sources of political opportunity (Williams in this volume). Supranational institutions have enabled them to frame their claims as "minorities" within the discursive universe of exclusion. As the above examples suggest, political opportunities for recognition struggles encompass discursive resources.

Discursive resources

Discursive resources are important for providing momentum and sustaining all social movements, but they are critical for those groups involved in a politics of recognition. Theirs are struggles that take place on symbolic terrains and involve disadvantaged groups who have few if any institutional bases for making claims, and thus have little access to non-discursive power-brokering arenas (Hobson, 1999). Groups seeking recognition often reclaim the discursive landscape by invoking the metaphors and narratives of national histories in their own struggles for justice. Sainsbury (in this volume) tracks the ways in which different groups embraced the metaphor of civilization in her study of contesting claims for inclusion in Oklahoma statehood. Discursive arenas are also fields on which opponents resist and foster misrecognition. Susan Gal, in her analysis of feminist texts in Hungarian journals (in this volume), reveals that elite antagonists to feminism selected radical feminist works on pornography to translate that would be most repugnant to a society recently freed from state censorship.

Recognition and redistribution as outcomes

The interplay of claims for redistribution and recognition is highly dependent on the dynamic sets of relations shown in Figure 1 and described above. This is also true of the outcomes of recognition struggles. Greater participation parity and influence on policy-making should be expected to alter redistributive policies and vice versa: greater access to resources can enhance respect and lead to more participation parity, which is illustrated in the two-way arrows in Figure 1. Outcomes in recognition struggles can also have a feedback effect on institutional structures, regimes, and policy logics in states. Recognition politics can also produce unintended consequences. The assertion of cultural rights may lead to the loss of social rights, or the ability to make claims based on them, as was true of the Roma in Hungary. Or in the case of the Saami, the conflicts around who are the authentic representatives of Saami people – persons of Saami heritage or only the reindeer herders – have resulted in deep rifts in the movement concerning different interpretations of recognition, involving competing claims for cultural respect and social justice.[4]

Considering outcomes of recognition struggles, it is important to lodge claims for respect and acknowledgment of histories of devaluation and discrimination within the broader struggles for a politics of presence and membership in the polity. We can see these as dimensions of recognition politics: the visibility of groups in the political arena and media and their voice in political debate and influence in policy-making.

The making of this book

This book evolved over five years of meetings, mostly in the long days of daylight in Stockholm's spring. We were crossing borders – not just across continents (Australia, North America, and Eastern and Western Europe) and not just across disciplinary boundaries (including sociology, political science and political philosophy, anthropology and history), which many of us had done before. But we were also making our way across an uncharted conceptual region of recognition politics. How could we apply a virtual model or moral grammar to real recognition movements? We all had pieces of the map: via research on social movements, comparative research on states and societies, and political theories of social justice, democracy, identities, and citizenship.

We began with a larger group than the published authors, although those not in the book are still authors in the sense of participating in crafting the new set of conceptual tools we use here. Though their contributions are not in the book, we benefited from their discussions. Dave Lewis, in his study of the Saami in Sweden, gave us valuable insights on authenticity and authority in recognition struggles. Though reindeer herders represent a small proportion of the Saami in Sweden, the centerpiece of Saami social claims-making – like that of indigenous political movements elsewhere – is the call for the recognition and protection of land rights (which necessarily includes the right to resources and the right to utilize those resources in a Saami way). At the same time, Lewis in his empirical research revealed that one cannot speak of one Saami community, rather that the Saami case in Sweden suggests competing identity claims that show differences around gender and generation. Lin Chun provided us with a window into how changes in the market economy in China affected recognition of workers, particularly women workers. Hers was a case of an authoritarian regime that permitted a feminist movement that framed its claims in terms of gender equality, but found other claims for worker rights intolerable, and put the lid on movements for extending democratic rights. One author in the book, Celia Valiente, had to abandon her original project on right-wing women's groups in the Franco regime because the archives were not accessible. This case, along with others we discussed, persuaded us that while the recognition paradigm had been formulated as a "moral grammar" and tended to focus on "progressive" movements, our thinking about recognition struggles could and should also embrace right-wing reactionary and intolerant groups. In short, recognition struggles do not have to be politically correct.

Our interest was on the framing of claims (for recognition and redistribution) and what settings were enabling and disenabling for groups to make them. Rather than asking whether multiculturalism was bad or good for women (Okin, 1999), as many of our cases involved gendered struggles for recognition, we were asking what are the contests between different groups within and outside the group; what kinds of resources and opportunities could they mobilize in different sociopolitical contexts and did their exchanges lead to a reformulation of group claims and goals? We shifted our own concern from the normative to the empirical, thus avoiding such morally loaded questions as whether groups have the right to discipline their members to keep the integrity of the group. Was this a violation of minority rights within the minority (Kymlicka, 1995)? Was this intentional or unintentional (Halley, 1999; Kymlicka, 1999)? What we found empirically in our cases of recognition struggles were generalized forms of governance of within-group claims: how boundaries were made, marking who was inside and outside the group; who was given authority to speak for the group, providing legitimacy vis-à-vis others; and what were defined as the sources and remedies of disadvantage and devaluation. And we found such mechanisms in diverse groups espousing multiculturalism, feminism, gay rights, and black and ethnic claims for more inclusionary citizenship (see Ferree and Gamson, Hobson, Kulick and Klein, Lake, and Williams in this volume).

At our first meeting, we opened our discussions with Nancy Fraser's basic premise that most groups make claims involving recognition and redistribution. She was a participant in these discussions. As we began to apply this insight to our empirical cases, we became even more convinced that it was impossible to separate out the bands of difference along the spectrum of claims for cultural justice and claims for economic justice. Where did one form of claims-making end and another begin? Furthermore, we could not find any pure ideal types of either structure of claims-making. Lesbian and gay movements should come closest to "pure recognition struggles" involving anti-discrimination laws, protection from violence, and the right to marry and adopt children (Fraser, 1997a). However, not only do these groups make explicit claims involving access to social benefits and services (redistribution), but the very organization of social rights and privileges is structured around a heterosexual relation and a family unit (Butler, 1997). Workers' movements have traditionally interwoven claims for a greater share of the pie with demands for respect and dignity. It was only through our analytical lens that we become able to separate the chromatic tones of recognition and redistribution from one another in these movements (an optical illusion in the real politics of recognition: see Phillips in this volume).

Considering recognition and redistribution as dimensions of justice, our research tends to support Iris Young's assertion (2000) that much of the ground of conflict between different cultural groups lies in competition over territory, resources, or jobs, that they are rooted in structural inequalities. But our cases also lend credence to Anne Phillips' insight in the epilogue of this volume, that demeaning stereotypes may long outlast demeaning conditions of employment, and racist abuse does not stop when people become millionaires. In all our examples in which redistributive claims were central, lack of access to resources was linked to devaluation and marginalization of their race/ethnicity, gender, or sexual preference.

In applying the recognition paradigm to real struggles, we increasingly viewed recognition as a form of claims-making linked to outcomes of recognition struggles. This meant going beyond the confines of Nancy Fraser's conceptual borders in the opening essay on recognition justice. For Fraser (in Chapter 1, "Rethinking recognition: overcoming displacement and reification in cultural politics"), misrecognition does not mean the depreciation and deformation of group identity, but rather social subordination in the sense of being prevented from participating as a peer in social life. We agreed with her conclusion that today's identity politics tends to reify group identities, counteracting the stigmatizing gaze of the dominant society by creating new self-representations of their own. And that to talk identity politics is to turn misrecognition into a free-floating discourse about culture that abstracts claims for recognition from the institutional matrix that makes them both possible and necessary. Nevertheless, we did not want to throw away the baby with the bath water. We decided that to keep identity and identity formation as a core dimension in the politics of recognition does not inevitably lead to "identity politics." Recognition struggles are about collective representations constructed around a shared identity that contest social hierarchies in arenas of power.

This reformulation extends Fraser's status model of recognition justice on two fronts. First, recognition outcomes are linked to recognition struggles and the mobilization of collective identities. Second, participation parity and citizen inclusion (Fraser's norm for recognition justice) are dependent on political voice (Phillips in this volume). These struggles are about groups seeking to represent the concerns and experiences of their constituents, to make visible histories of discrimination and devaluation. They have lacked voice or power to influence discourse, laws, policies, and practices.

Finally, for Fraser (1997a), the distributive dimension corresponds to the economic structure of society – to property regimes and labor markets. Our cases highlighted the role of state and supranational institutions in the structuring of misrecognition and maldistribution in societies. States not only embody systems of stratification (Esping-Andersen, 1990), but also provide frameworks for the coupling and decoupling of the recognition/redistribution dimensions.

What this book does and does not do

The essays in this volume are provocative contextual studies of recognition struggles that take place in political and social arenas with an elaborate play of social actors and discursive backgrounds. The book is not a collection of country-level studies or essays that seek to cover all types of recognition struggles. Nevertheless, we offer perspectives that are alternately historical, comparative, and transnational. Though our studies range from the center to the periphery of major industrial democracies, we still do not cover many parts of the world where there are recognition struggles. Clearly, we miss the contributions from our original group.

The authors reflect upon the politics of recognition through multiple mirrors of gender, class, race/ethnic, and sexual identities, revealing cross-cutting loyalties as well as competition and conflicts among social groups vying for recognition. Our purpose was to use our rich empirical cases as means of problematizing different aspects of recognition, which are highlighted in three sections of the book.

Authority and voice in recognition struggles   By addressing the dimensions of power, authority, and agency in recognition, the chapters reveal how context shapes and constrains the content of recognition struggles, which are expressed in political and discursive strategies and practices.

Struggles in dialogue: multiple recognizers, audiences, and arena The chapters in this part dramatize the ways in which the politics of recognition involves "struggles in dialogue" across social movements. They underscore the importance of different political arenas: the local, national, and supranational.

Authenticity: Who represents whom on what basis?   In this part, the authors expand upon the issue of who represents the members of a group. The spokespersons for travesti prostitutes engage in a politics of recognition that threatens the individualized micropolitics of scandal and shame in the daily contacts between travesti and customer. Seeking recognition for their drug-addict children, mothers deny them voice and agency.

The book ends with two stimulating chapters that reflect upon the implications of our research in bridging two research fields: democratic theories of citizenship and social movements. Anne Phillips, a central figure in the debates on democracy, difference, and political power focuses on the recognition/redistribution binary. Carol Mueller, a renowned scholar on social movements, locates our studies within the evolution of new theorizing on identity construction in movement mobilization.

Part 1

Shifting paradigms? Recognition and redistribution

1 Rethinking recognition: overcoming displacement and reification in cultural politics

Nancy Fraser

At the turn of our century, social conflicts turn increasingly on questions of "recognition." Throughout the world, claims for recognition fuel campaigns for national sovereignty and subnational autonomy, not to mention "ethnic cleansing" and genocide, as well as movements that have mobilized to resist them. But such claims also occupy center stage in countries whose borders and constitutional frameworks are relatively settled. Thus, claims for the recognition of difference now figure prominently in struggles over multiculturalism within polyethnic and multi-religious states. They have also become salient in many "new social movements," such as feminism, which previously foregrounded claims for redistribution. Finally, claims for recognition are central to newly energized movements for international human rights, which seek to promote both universal respect for shared humanity and difference-regarding esteem of distinct "cultures."

To be sure, these struggles for recognition differ importantly from one another. They run the gamut from the patently emancipatory to the downright reprehensible, with most falling somewhere in between. But putting such differences to one side, temporarily, the recourse to a common grammar is worth considering. Why, today, after the demise of Soviet-style communism and the acceleration of globalization, do so many conflicts take this form? Why do so many movements couch their claims in the idiom of recognition?

To pose this question is also to note the relative decline in claims for egalitarian redistribution. Once the hegemonic grammar of political contestation, the language of distribution is less salient today. Movements that not long ago boldly demanded an equitable share of resources and wealth no longer typify the spirit of the times. They have not, to be sure, wholly disappeared. But thanks to a sustained neoliberal rhetorical assault on egalitarianism, the absence of any credible model of "feasible socialism," and widespread doubts about the viability of state-Keynesian social democracy in the face of accelerated economic globalization, they have ceded pride of place to movements focused chiefly on recognition.

In general, then, we are facing a new constellation in the grammar of political claims-making. In this constellation, the center of gravity has shifted "from redistribution to recognition" (Fraser, 1995). How should one evaluate this shift?

The current situation is disturbing on two counts. First, the shift from redistribution to recognition is occurring despite (or because of) an acceleration of economic globalization. Thus, cultural conflicts have achieved paradigmatic status at precisely the moment when an aggressively expanding capitalism is exacerbating economic inequality. In this context, recognition struggles are serving less to supplement, complicate, and enrich redistribution struggles than to marginalize, eclipse, and displace them. I shall call this the *problem of displacement*.

Second, today's recognition struggles are occurring despite (or because of) increased transcultural interaction and communication. They occur, that is, just as accelerated migration and global media flows are hybridizing and pluralizing cultural forms. Yet they often take the form of a communitarianism that drastically simplifies and reifies group identities. In such forms, struggles for recognition do not promote respectful interaction across differences in increasingly multicultural contexts. They tend, rather, to encourage separatism and group enclaving, chauvinism and intolerance, patriarchalism and authoritarianism. I shall call this the *problem of reification*.

Both the displacement problem and the reification problem are extremely serious. Insofar as the politics of recognition is displacing the politics of redistribution, it risks aiding the forces that promote economic inequality. Likewise, insofar as today's politics of recognition is reifying group identities, it risks sanctioning violations of human rights and freezing the very antagonisms it purports to mediate.

Given these all-too-common tendencies, it is no wonder that many progressive observers have simply washed their hands of "identity politics." Rejecting the politics of recognition as "false consciousness," they have proposed jettisoning cultural struggles altogether. For some, this means (re)prioritizing class over gender, sexuality, and "race"/ethnicity. For others, it means resurrecting economism. For still others, it means rejecting all "minoritarian" claims out of hand and requiring assimilation to majority norms – in the name of secularism, universalism, or republicanism.

Such rejectionist approaches are understandable but deeply misguided. In fact, not all forms of recognition politics are equally likely to encourage displacement and reification. Nor are all versions morally pernicious. On the contrary, some recognition struggles represent genuinely emancipatory responses to serious injustices that cannot be remedied by redistribution alone. Culture, moreover, is a legitimate, even necessary, terrain of struggle. A site of injustice in its own right, it is deeply imbricated with economic inequality. Thus, struggles for recognition, properly conceived, can actually aid struggles for redistribution. And far from necessarily promoting separatism, they can foster interaction across differences.

Everything depends on how recognition is approached. What is needed is an approach that can help to solve, or at least mitigate, the problems of displacement and reification. On the one hand, this means conceptualizing struggles for recognition in ways that can be integrated with struggles for redistribution, instead of in ways that displace and undermine the latter. On the other hand, it means developing an account of recognition that can accommodate the full complexity of social identities, instead of one that oversimplifies and reifies them. This would have to be an account that promotes respectful social interaction across differences, not one that encourages group enclaving and "ethnic cleansing."

Misrecognition as identity distortion?

The usual approach is to view recognition through the lens of identity. From this perspective, what requires recognition is group-specific cultural identity. Misrecognition consists in the depreciation of such identity by the dominant culture and the consequent damage to group members' sense of self. Redressing this harm requires engaging in a politics of recognition. In such a politics, group members join together to refashion their collective identity by producing a self-affirming culture of their own. Thus, on the identity model of recognition, the politics of recognition means "identity politics."

Let me elaborate. The identity model begins with the Hegelian idea that identity is constructed dialogically through a process of mutual recognition. According to Hegel, recognition designates an ideal reciprocal relation between subjects in which each sees the other both as its equal and also as separate from it. This relation is constitutive for subjectivity; one becomes an individual subject only by virtue of recognizing, and being recognized by, another subject. Thus, recognition from others is essential to the development of a sense of self. To be denied recognition is to suffer a distortion in one's relation to one's self and an injury to one's identity.

Proponents of the identity model transpose the Hegelian recognition schema onto the cultural and political terrain. They contend that to belong to a group that is devalued by the dominant culture of one's society is to be misrecognized, hence to sustain damage to one's individual and collective identity. Depreciated in the eyes of the dominant culture, the members of disesteemed groups suffer a collective distortion in their relation to self. As a result of repeated encounters with the stigmatizing gaze of a culturally dominant other, they internalize negative self-images and are prevented from developing a healthy cultural identity of their own.

On the identity model, accordingly, the politics of recognition means "identity politics." Such a politics aims to repair internal self-dislocation by contesting the dominant culture's demeaning picture of one's group. It requires that members of misrecognized groups reject such pictures in favor of new self-representations of their own making. Jettisoning internalized negative self-identities, they must join collectively to produce a self-affirming culture of their own. Having refashioned their collective identity, moreover, they must display it publicly in order to gain the respect and esteem of society at large. The result, when successful, is "recognition," an undistorted relation to oneself.

Without doubt, this identity model contains some genuine insights concerning the psychological effects of racism, sexism, colonization, and cultural imperialism. Yet it is theoretically and politically problematic. By equating the politics of recognition with identity politics, it encourages both the reification of group identities and the displacement of redistribution by recognition.

Consider, first, that identity politics tends to displace struggles for redistribution. Largely silent on the subject of economic inequality, this approach treats misrecognition as a freestanding cultural harm. Many of its proponents, accordingly, simply ignore distributive injustice altogether and focus exclusively on efforts to change culture. Others, in contrast, appreciate the seriousness of maldistribution and genuinely wish to redress it. Yet both subcurrents are engaged in displacement.

The first subcurrent casts misrecognition as a problem of cultural depreciation. Proponents of this approach locate the roots of the injustice in demeaning representations, which they do not, however, view as socially grounded. For them, accordingly, the nub of the problem is free-floating discourses, not *institutionalized* significations and norms. Hypostatizing culture, they abstract misrecognition from its institutional matrix and obscure its entwinement with distributive injustice. They miss, for example, the links, institutionalized in labor markets, between androcentric norms that devalue activities coded as "feminine," on the one hand, and female workers' low wages, on the other. Likewise, they overlook the links, institutionalized in social-welfare systems, between heterosexist norms that delegitimate homosexuality, on the one hand, and the denial of resources and benefits to gays and lesbians, on the other. Obfuscating such links, they strip misrecognition of its social-structural underpinnings and equate it with distorted identity. With the politics of recognition thus reduced to identity politics, the politics of redistribution is displaced.

A second subcurrent, in contrast, does not simply ignore maldistribution. Rather, it appreciates that cultural injustices are often linked to economic injustices. But it misunderstands the character of those links. Subscribing effectively to a "culturalist" theory of contemporary society, proponents of this perspective suppose that maldistribution is merely a secondary effect of misrecognition. For them, accordingly, economic inequalities are simple expressions of cultural hierarchies. Thus, class oppression is a superstructural effect of the cultural devaluation of proletarian identity, or as one says in the USA, of "classism." It follows from this view that all maldistribution can be remedied indirectly by a politics of recognition. When one undertakes to revalue unjustly devalued identities, one is simultaneously attacking the deep sources of economic inequality. Thus, no explicit politics of redistribution is needed.

In this way, culturalist proponents of identity politics simply reverse the claims of an earlier form of vulgar Marxist economism. They allow the politics of recognition to displace the politics of redistribution, just as vulgar Marxism once allowed the politics of redistribution to displace the politics of recognition. In fact, vulgar culturalism is no more adequate for understanding contemporary society than was vulgar economism.

Culturalism *might* make sense if one lived in a society in which there were no relatively autonomous markets. In that case, cultural value patterns would regulate not only the relations of recognition but those of distribution as well. In such a society, economic inequality and cultural hierarchy would be seamlessly fused. Identity depreciation would translate perfectly and immediately into economic injustice, and misrecognition would directly entail maldistribution. Consequently, both forms of injustice could be remedied at a single stroke. A politics of recognition that successfully redressed misrecognition would counter maldistribution as well.

The idea of a purely "cultural" society in which there were no economic relations once fascinated generations of anthropologists, but it is far removed from the current reality. Today, virtually nowhere in the world can one encounter such a society. Rather, marketization has pervaded all societies to some degree, everywhere decoupling, at least partially, economic mechanisms of distribution from cultural patterns of value and prestige. Partially independent of such value patterns and following a logic of their own, markets are neither wholly constrained by, nor wholly subordinate to, culture. As a result, they generate economic inequalities that are not mere expressions of identity hierarchies. Under these conditions, the idea that one could remedy all maldistribution by means of a politics of recognition is deeply deluded. Its net result can only be to displace struggles for economic justice.

Displacement, however, is not the only problem. In addition, the identity politics model of recognition tends to reify group identities. Stressing the need to elaborate and display an authentic, self-affirming, and self-generated collective identity, it puts moral pressure on individual members to conform to group culture. Cultural dissidence and experimentation are accordingly discouraged, when they are not simply equated with disloyalty. So, too, is cultural criticism, including efforts to explore intra-group divisions, such as those of gender, sexuality, and class. Thus, far from welcoming scrutiny of, for example, the patriarchal strands within a subordinated culture, the tendency of the identity model is to brand such critique as "inauthentic." The overall effect is to impose a single, drastically simplified group identity, which denies the complexity of people's lives, the multiplicity of their identifications, and the cross-pulls of their various affiliations. Ironically, then, the identity model serves as a vehicle of misrecognition. In reifying group identity, finally, it obscures the politics of cultural identification, the struggles *within* the group for the authority, and indeed for the power, to represent it. By shielding such struggles from view, it tends to mask the power of dominant fractions and thus to reinforce intragroup domination. Thus, the identity model lends itself all too easily to repressive forms of communitarianism, which promote conformism, intolerance, and patriarchalism.

Paradoxically, moreover, the identity model tends to deny its own Hegelian premises. Having begun by assuming that identity is dialogical, constructed via interaction with another subject, the model ends up valorizing monologism, supposing that misrecognized people can and should construct their identity on their own. It supposes, moreover, that a group has the right to be understood in its own terms, thus that no one is ever justified in viewing another subject from an external perspective or in dissenting from another's self-interpretation. But this runs counter to the dialogical view. It makes cultural identity an auto-generated auto-description, which one presents to others as an *obiter dictum*. Seeking to exempt "authentic" collective self-representations from all possible challenges in the public sphere, this sort of identity politics scarcely fosters social interaction across differences. On the contrary, it fosters separatism and group enclaving.

In general, then, the identity model of recognition is deeply flawed. Both theoretically deficient and politically problematic, it equates the politics of recognition with identity politics. In so doing, it encourages both the reification of group identities and the displacement of the politics of redistribution.

Misrecognition as status subordination

Consequently, I shall propose an alternative analysis of recognition. My proposal is to treat recognition as a question of *social status*. From this perspective, what requires recognition is not group-specific identity but rather the status of individual group members as full partners in social interaction. Misrecognition, accordingly, does not mean the depreciation and deformation of group identity. Rather, it means social subordination in the sense of being prevented from participating as a peer in social life. To redress the injustice requires a politics of recognition, but this does not mean identity politics. On the status model, rather, it means a politics aimed at overcoming subordination by establishing the misrecognized party as a full member of society, capable of participating on a par with other members.

Let me explain. To view recognition as a matter of status is to examine institutionalized patterns of cultural value for their effects on the relative standing of social actors. If and when such patterns constitute actors as *peers*, capable of participating on a par with one another in social life, then we can speak of *reciprocal recognition* and *status equality*. When, in contrast, institutionalized patterns of cultural value constitute some actors as inferior, excluded, wholly other, or simply invisible, hence as less than full partners in social interaction, then we can speak of *misrecognition* and *status subordination*.

From this perspective, misrecognition is neither a psychical deformation nor a freestanding cultural harm. Rather, it is an institutionalized relation of *social subordination*. To be misrecognized, accordingly, is not simply to be thought ill of, looked down on, or devalued in others' attitudes, beliefs, or representations. It is rather to be denied the status of a full partner in social interaction and to be prevented from participating as a peer in social life as a consequence of institutionalized patterns of cultural value that constitute one as comparatively unworthy of respect or esteem.

On the status model, moreover, misrecognition is not relayed through free-floating cultural representations or discourses. It is perpetrated, rather, through *institutionalized patterns of cultural value*. It arises, in other words, through the workings of social institutions that regulate interaction according to parity-impeding cultural norms. Examples include marriage laws that exclude same-sex partnerships as illegitimate and perverse, social-welfare policies that stigmatize single mothers as sexually irresponsible scroungers, and policing practices such as "racial profiling" that associate racialized persons with criminality. In each of these cases, interaction is regulated by an institutionalized pattern of cultural value that constitutes some categories of social actors as normative and others as deficient or inferior: straight is normal, gay is perverse; "male-headed households" are proper, "female-headed households" are not; "whites" are law-abiding, "blacks" are dangerous. In each case, the result is to deny some members of society the status of full partners in interaction, capable of participating on a par with other members.

As these examples suggest, misrecognition can assume a variety of forms. In today's complex, differentiated societies, parity-impeding values are institutionalized at a plurality of institutional sites and in a plurality of qualitatively different modes. In some cases, misrecognition is juridified, expressly codified in formal law; in other cases, it is institutionalized via government policies, administrative codes, and professional practices. Misrecognition is also institutionalized informally – in associational patterns, long-standing customs, and sedimented social practices in civil society. But despite these differences in form, the core of the injustice remains the same. In each case, an institutionalized pattern of cultural value constitutes some social actors as less than full members of society and prevents them from participating as peers.

On the status model, then, misrecognition constitutes a form of institutionalized subordination, hence a serious violation of justice. Wherever and however it occurs, a claim for recognition is in order. But note precisely what this means: aimed not at valorizing group identity, but rather at overcoming subordination, claims for recognition seek to establish the subordinated party as a full partner in social life, able to interact with others as a peer. They aim, that is, *to deinstitutionalize patterns of cultural value that impede parity of participation and to replace them with patterns that foster it.*

In short, redressing misrecognition means changing social institutions. More specifically, it means changing interaction-regulating values that impede parity of participation at all relevant institutional sites. Exactly what this means depends in each case on the mode in which misrecognition is institutionalized. Juridified forms require legal change, policy-entrenched forms require policy change, associational forms require associational change, and so on down the line. Thus, the mode and agency of redress vary, as does the institutional site. But in every case, the goal is the same: redressing misrecognition means replacing institutionalized value patterns that impede parity of participation with patterns that enable or foster it.

Consider, again, the case of marriage laws that deny participatory parity to gays and lesbians. As we saw, the root of the injustice is the institution-alization in law of a heterosexist pattern of cultural value that constitutes heterosexuals as normal and homosexuals as perverse. Redressing the injustice requires deinstitutionalizing that value pattern and replacing it with an alternative that promotes parity. This, however, can be done in more than one way. One way would be to grant the same recognition to gay and lesbian unions as heterosexual unions currently enjoy by le-galizing same-sex marriage. Another way would be to deinstitutionalize heterosexual marriage, decoupling entitlements such as health insurance from marital status and assigning them on some other basis, such as citi-zenship. Although there may be (other) good reasons for preferring one of these approaches to the other, in principle either of them would promote sexual parity and redress this instance of misrecognition.

In general, then, the status model is not committed *a priori* to any one type of remedy for misrecognition. Rather, it allows for a range of possibil-ities, depending on what precisely the subordinated parties need in order to be able to participate as peers in social life. In some cases, they may need to be unburdened of excessive ascribed or constructed distinctive-ness. In other cases, they may need to have hitherto underacknowledged distinctiveness taken into account. In still other cases, they may need to shift the focus onto dominant or advantaged groups, outing the latter's distinctiveness, which has been falsely parading as universality. Alterna-tively, they may need to deconstruct the very terms in which attributed differences are currently elaborated. In every case, the status model tai-lors the remedy to the concrete arrangements that impede parity. Thus, unlike the identity model, it does not accord an *a priori* privilege to ap-proaches that valorize group specificity. Rather, it allows in principle for what we might call *universalist recognition* and *deconstructive recognition*, as well as for affirmative recognition of difference.

The crucial point, once again, is this: on the status model, the politics of recognition does not mean identity politics. Rather, it means a politics that seeks institutional remedies for institutionalized harms. Focused on culture in its socially grounded, as opposed to free-floating, forms, *this* politics of recognition seeks to overcome status subordination by chang-ing the values that regulate interaction. Entrenching new value patterns that constitute previously subordinated persons as peers, it aims to pro-mote parity of participation in social life.

There is a further important difference between the status and iden-tity models. For the status model, institutionalized patterns of cultural value are not the only obstacles to participatory parity. On the contrary, equal participation is also impeded when some actors lack the necessary resources to interact with others as peers. In such cases, maldistribution constitutes an impediment to parity of participation in social life. Like misrecognition, therefore, maldistribution represents a form of social subordination and injustice.

Unlike the identity model, then, the status model understands social justice as encompassing two analytically distinct dimensions.[1] The recognition dimension concerns the effects of institutionalized meanings and norms on the relative standing of social actors. The distributive dimension concerns the allocation by economic systems of disposable resources to social actors. Thus, each dimension is associated with an analytically distinct dimension of social order. The recognition dimension corresponds to the *status order* of society, hence to the constitution, by socially entrenched patterns of cultural value, of culturally defined categories of social actors (status groups), each distinguished by the relative honor, prestige, and esteem it enjoys vis-à-vis the others. The distributive dimension, in contrast, corresponds to the *economic structure* of society, hence to the constitution, by property regimes and labor markets, of economically defined categories of actors (classes), distinguished by their differential endowments of resources.[2] As an issue of status, therefore, recognition concerns the effects of institutionalized value patterns on different actors' capacities for social participation. As an issue of economic class, in contrast, distribution concerns the systemic effects of economic structures on the relative economic position of social actors, which also affects their capacities for participation.

Each dimension, moreover, is associated with an analytically distinct form of injustice. For the recognition dimension, as we saw, the associated injustice is *misrecognition*, in which entrenched patterns of cultural value deny some actors the necessary standing to participate fully in social life. For the distributive dimension, in contrast, the corresponding injustice is *maldistribution*, in which economic structures, such as property regimes and labor markets, deprive some actors of the necessary resources. Each dimension, finally, corresponds to an analytically distinct form of subordination. The recognition dimension corresponds, as we saw, to *status subordination* rooted in institutionalized patterns of cultural value. The distributive dimension, in contrast, corresponds to *economic subordination* rooted in structural features of the economic system.

In general, then, the status model situates the problem of recognition within a larger social frame. From this perspective, societies appear as complex fields that encompass not only cultural forms of social ordering but economic forms of ordering as well. In all societies, these two forms of ordering are imbricated. Under capitalist conditions, however, neither is wholly reducible to the other. On the contrary, the economic dimension becomes relatively decoupled from the cultural dimension, as marketized arenas, in which strategic action predominates, are differentiated from non-marketized arenas, in which value-regulated interaction predominates. The result is a partial uncoupling of economic distribution from structures of prestige. In capitalist societies, therefore, cultural value patterns do not strictly dictate economic allocations, *contra* the culturalist theory of society. Nor do economic class inequalities simply reflect status hierarchies. Rather, maldistribution becomes partially uncoupled from misrecognition. For the status model, therefore, not all distributive injustice can be overcome by recognition alone. A politics of redistribution is also necessary (Fraser, 1998; 2003). Nevertheless, distribution and recognition are not neatly separated from each other in capitalist societies. For the status model, rather, the two dimensions are imbricated and interact causally with each other. Thus, economic issues, such as income distribution, have recognition subtexts, as value patterns institutionalized in labor markets privilege activities coded as masculine and/or "white" over those coded as feminine and/or "black." Conversely, recognition issues, such as judgments of aesthetic value, have distributive subtexts, as diminished access to economic resources impedes equal participation in the making of art (Bourdieu, 1984). The result is often a vicious circle of subordination, as the status order and the economic structure interpenetrate and reinforce each other (Fraser, 1998; 2003).

Unlike the identity model, then, the status model views misrecognition in the context of a broader understanding of contemporary society. From this perspective, status subordination cannot be understood in isolation from economic arrangements. Nor can the recognition dimension of justice be viewed in abstraction from distribution. On the contrary, only by considering both dimensions together can one determine what is impeding participatory parity in any case. And only by teasing out the complex imbrications of status with economic class can one determine how best to redress the injustice (Fraser, 1995; 2003).

In this way, the status model works against tendencies to displace struggles for redistribution. Rejecting the view that misrecognition is a freestanding cultural harm, it understands that status subordination is often linked to distributive injustice. Unlike the culturalist theory of society, however, it avoids short-circuiting the complexity of these links. Appreciating that not all economic injustice can be overcome by recognition alone, it advocates an approach that expressly integrates claims for recognition with claims for redistribution. Thus, it mitigates the problem of displacement.

In addition, the status model avoids reifying group identities. As we saw, what requires recognition on this account is not group-specific identity but the status of *individuals* as full partners in social interaction. This orientation offers several advantages. By focusing on the effects of institutionalized norms on capacities for interaction, the model avoids hypostatizing culture and substituting identity engineering for social change. Likewise, by refusing to privilege remedies for misrecognition that valorize existing group identities, it avoids essentializing current configurations and foreclosing historical change. Finally, by establishing participatory parity as a normative standard, the status model submits claims for recognition to democratic processes of public justification. Thus, it avoids the authoritarian monologism of the politics of authenticity; and it valorizes transcultural interaction, as opposed to separatism and group enclaving. Far from encouraging repressive communitarianism, then, the status model militates against it.

In general, therefore, the status model offers important advantages over the identity model. Resisting pressures to equate the politics of recognition with identity politics, it sets its sights on overcoming institutionalized subordination. As a result, it discourages both the displacement of redistribution and the reification of group identities.

Conclusion

Today's struggles for recognition often assume the guise of identity politics. Aimed at countering demeaning cultural representations of subordinated groups, they abstract misrecognition from its institutional matrix and sever its links with political economy. Insofar as they propound "authentic" collective identities, moreover, such struggles serve less to foster interaction across differences than to enforce separatism, conformism, and intolerance. The results tend to be doubly unfortunate. In many cases, struggles for recognition simultaneously displace struggles for economic justice and promote repressive forms of communitarianism.

The solution, however, is not to reject the politics of recognition *tout court*. That would be to condemn millions of people to suffer grave injustices that can only be redressed through struggles for recognition of some kind. What is needed, rather, is an alternative politics of recognition, a *non-identitarian* politics that can remedy misrecognition without encouraging displacement and reification.

The status model provides the basis for such an alternative. Thus, I have argued that by understanding recognition as a question of status, and by examining its relation to economic class, one can take steps to mitigate, if not fully solve, the displacement of struggles for redistribution. Likewise, by avoiding the identity model, one can begin to diminish, if not fully dispel, the current tendency to reify collective identities.

Part 2

Frames and claims: authority and voice

2   The gendering of governance and the governance of gender: abortion politics in Germany and the USA

Myra Marx Ferree and William A. Gamson

The different conceptions of injustice offered by Nancy Fraser's recognition and redistribution paradigms in her lead essay in this volume include alternative notions of the collectivities who suffer injustice. In her redistribution model, class, race, gender, or other groups are, like Marxian classes, situated in relation to a political economy and have some distinctive relation to the production of goods and people in society. In her recognition model, these same groups are "more like Weberian status groups." The status issue, the lack of respect and prestige within the culture, places some persons by virtue of their group identities in a stigmatized or marginalized position in relation to others. This status inequality, like inequality in economic resources, is regarded as a fundamental social injustice, not because it causes specific psychic harms but because status is an important dimension of ordered social life. Important as these two dimensions of inequality and injustice are, we wonder whether they exhaust the important dimensions on which groups may be seen as politically arrayed.

Taking the connection that Fraser makes to Weber seriously, we raise the question of whether class and status alone define the dimensions of inequality. In the classic Weberian model there is a third dimension, that of *power*. We suggest that abortion conflict is a useful arena in which to examine the implications of justice conceptualized in such power terms. We take injustices of power, and struggles over power, to contain within them moments of both recognition and redistribution, but not to be wholly reducible to them. Thus, in our conclusion, we attempt to suggest how both recognition and redistribution remain entangled in the politics of abortion above and beyond what our analysis of the power dimension can reveal.

We approach the issues of equality and justice from the standpoint of feminist critiques of conventional stratification models. Such critics have pointed to the need to widen the lens on stratification to include more than inequality and injustice expressed in differential access to and control over economic resources, to look at the dimensions of autonomy (freedom to make life choices and freedom of movement) and power (participation in decisions concerning the social group) (Agassi, 1989; Ferree and Hall, 1996). Both autonomy and power as defined above (i.e., as participation in political authority) would fall within the broader domain of power with which Weber was concerned. We therefore think it useful to split the concept of power into its two elements, autonomy and authority. Power, whether expressed as authority or autonomy, is a third dimension that we suggest should join Fraser's two dimensions of redistribution and recognition as a model for understanding justice relations.

From a Weberian perspective, autonomy reflects power as experienced at the level of the individual, power as the expression of self-determination. Thus an ability to act for or express oneself, without or despite constraints from others in the community, is the heart of autonomy. Autonomy can be exercised in resistance to or with the support of society and the state. Familiar limitations on autonomy based on gender include cultural stereotypes defining certain feelings or actions as gender-inappropriate as well as societal and state assaults on bodily integrity (legally allowing marital rape or punishing women who violate the family's honor by their conduct). The positive dimension of power manifested as autonomy often appears discursively as "choice."

Authority is the second dimension of power. Such power involves actual participation in decisions concerning the common life in any society. The exercise of authority is seen in the ability to define the nature of the common good, and also reflects the ability to share in and exercise collective authority in and over the community as a whole. Limitations on authority based on gender include such familiar state exclusions as the denial of the right to vote or to serve on juries, but restrictions of authority may also be informal and social rather than institutionalized as formal political rules. Informal limits on women's authority can be seen, for example, in the social reluctance to place women in positions where they would be supervising men or in the deference given to husbands as family decision-makers. Although denial of authority may be based in issues of cultural value or status (recognition) or lack of economic resources (redistribution), it compounds both with a further injustice of its own.

Both personal autonomy and collective authority reflect Weber's conceptualization of power as relational, as a matter of politically determining how the community and individual relate. The nature of this political relationship between individual and community is itself subject to examination in moral terms as just or unjust. Because we see the political relationship between individual and community as not wholly subsumed in Fraser's understanding of recognition and redistribution, there remain distinctive issues of justice to be considered with regard to struggles over autonomy and authority. These are *power* struggles, and they have implications for both recognition and redistribution.

Using women as the relevant group for our analysis, we suggest that autonomy is about the governance of gender, or the ways in which society and states control the self-determination of women and men as individuals, and authority is about the gendering of governance, or the access that men and women have to making decisions that regulate the common life of social groups, including states and nations. To understand power struggles as such, we need to look both at the political process, how authoritative decisions are reached, as well as at the substantive outcomes of the decision-making process. In relation to this process, contests over the justice of how collective authority is exercised raise distinctive issues about the gendering (or racializing, etc.) of governance. In relation to outcomes, struggles over the justice of the decisions produced include contests over rules governing the collective meaning of gender (or race, etc.), which we here refer to as the governance of gender.

The limitations placed on autonomy and authority have obvious consequences for how systems create and maintain economic injustices. Indeed, power and material injustice are often linked in the concept of political economy. Yet, we believe that it is better to keep the distribution of power and the distribution of goods and services analytically independent. To blur power issues into the distribution of economic resources obscures the extent to which political structures engage not only in the regulation of production but also directly in the regulation of persons and personality. Foucault's conception of disciplinary power diffused through a variety of social institutions reveals more of the political dynamic in which autonomy is contested, and in so doing, highlights the multiplicity of forms of limitations on autonomy that may be considered injustices (such as surveillance, emotional manipulation, and indoctrination).

With regard to the formation of persons who are dichotomized as male and female and regulated both *de jure* and *de facto* as such, we can speak of the *governance of gender* as an arena in which injustice may be experienced directly in regard to autonomy (Brush, 2003; building on Foucault, 1979). In parallel fashion, the structuring of political systems based on social compacts among men, patriarchal assumptions about natural hierarchy, and authoritarian practices grounded in analogies with kinship systems can be seen as expressions of the *gendering of governance*, constructing the state itself as a gendered social institution (Brush, 2003; Smith, 1974).

Both the governance of gender and the gendering of governance connect the actions of the state to the experiences of collective and individual injustice against which people struggle. To define such struggles as being about "recognition," as Fraser does, appropriately highlights the extent to which the stakes of the struggle involve personhood and personality. Of course, a group's increasing participation in the polity implies their greater "recognition" as people entitled to a share in collective power. But contesting the power of the state to make determinations of collective will without the full participation of all its members is also about the "redistribution" of substantive authority, and this is a form of redistribution of material benefits, even if not of narrowly defined economic goods. Conversely, the issue of autonomy can be viewed as a matter of legal rights, subject to state "redistribution," even as it is obviously also about the cultural "recognition" of people as having full status as members of society. Neither recognition nor redistribution can be realized without power, and both autonomy and authority are required to articulate what recognition would encompass and redistribution entail.

Thus, although we are suggesting power as being a third dimension of inequality that would be analytically useful, we do not want to separate it entirely from the other two. As Fraser argues, treating these as lenses or paradigms for viewing the same struggles rather than as discrete classifications for different issues is helpful. Bringing recognition and redistribution together as factually intertwined, as Fraser suggests we should, allows for an examination of the variety of forms that particular contests over gender relations may take in the actual struggles over autonomy and authority in the polity. Similarly, taking recognition and power as interwoven suggests both how status and value in the community permit the exercise of authority and protect autonomy.

In this paper, we look at the discursive contest over legal abortion in Germany and the USA from 1970 to 1994 as a comparative case study of the governance of gender and the gendering of governance. Abortion regulation by the state is a direct expression of the governance of gender through the limitations it places on the autonomy of the female person (Bordo, 1995; Maleck-Lewy, 1995). The participation of women and men as speakers and actors in the political debate over regulation is also a manifestation of the gendering of governance, expressed in the gender inequality of participation in collective decision-making about important social issues. Women's under-representation in politics generally is made particularly unjust in the matter of legally regulating abortion since it is a matter that differentially affects women and men.

We see the power questions in the abortion debate in both countries as having implications both for recognition – of women collectively as political actors and of women individually as full persons – and for redistribution – of positions of political and moral authority and of legal and practical autonomy to make a deeply personal choice. Since this is a book about recognition struggles, we focus here primarily on how recognition is intertwined with women's authority and autonomy. We separate recognition into two parts, corresponding with our dual focus on the gender of governance and the governance of gender. In regard to the former, the gender of governance, recognition implies the extent to which women as a group are acknowledged as having a special stake in the abortion decision and have a greater collective voice in the debate over abortion. Recognition struggles in this case are also power struggles about the collective exercise of authority. In the second instance, the governance of gender, recognition struggles are about limitations of autonomy and self-realization imposed on the individual by the construction and maintenance of stereotyped and limited conceptions of the person. In this latter case, recognition struggles are also power struggles about autonomy.

We argue that German women have achieved greater recognition of abortion as a gendered issue, in this case, as an issue that primarily concerns the full personhood and citizenship of women rather than being about religion or medical care or anything else. They have in this way also achieved greater legitimacy as political actors and speak with greater authority than US women on this issue. They have, in effect, more successfully challenged the gendering of governance, at least within the domain of abortion. However, we also argue that the success of German women in being recognized as speakers in the debate is tempered by state limitations placed on their autonomy as individual decision-makers. US women, by focusing on the pregnant woman as an autonomous individual, have succeeded more than German women in breaking boundaries of what womanhood necessarily entails and thus challenging the governance of gender. Although women in both countries are struggling over recognition of gender as politically meaningful, the alternative forms that their successes have taken illustrate the importance of considering these recognition struggles also as power struggles.

The political context of abortion in Germany and the USA

The choice of Germany and the USA for this analysis reflects a comparison of two countries that are both similar and different in important ways.[1] Fundamentally, both are modern, industrial democracies with a federal structure, independent judiciaries with powers of judicial review, and privately owned, politically independent newspapers. In Germany, there was a lively debate about abortion in the early part of the century that came to an end when the Nazis came to power, while in the USA there was a "century of silence" on the abortion issue that only gradually ended in the 1960s (Luker, 1984). In both countries, the issue of abortion surfaced on the national political agenda in the early 1970s. The political developments from that point both diverged in substance but paralleled each other in timing for the next twenty-five years. This period from 1970 to 1994 is the focus of our attention.

In the USA, the early state efforts to reform abortion law were dramatically accelerated in 1973 when the Supreme Court, in its famous *Roe v. Wade* decision, argued that there was a constitutional right to privacy that extended to cover the autonomous decision of a woman to terminate a pregnancy. Although recognizing the state's right to regulate abortion in the interests of women's health in the first trimesters and concern for developing fetal life in the third, the court's decision swept away existing state laws and ushered in a period of experiments on the part of state legislatures as to how much regulation would be permitted. It also stimulated efforts to pass a constitutional amendment that would give the fetus the status of a child, and other protest actions to overturn or limit the court's decision.

The ensuing years were a period of intense social conflict over abortion, with significant mobilization of social movements on both sides of the issue (Staggenborg, 1991; Blanchard, 1994). Presidents Reagan and, to some extent, Bush lent the moral support of their office to the restrictionist forces, and in particular appointed justices to the Supreme Court who were viewed as likely to overturn *Roe*. In 1989, the Court revisited the principles of the *Roe* decision in hearing the *Webster* case. In the months around the decision, attention to abortion as a political issue rose still further. The Court's decision in *Webster* shifted the principle from a virtually absolute protection of the autonomy of the pregnant woman to a more limited affirmation of the illegality of states imposing restrictions that place an "undue burden" on women's exercise of their right to decide, but it did not overturn *Roe*.

Also in this period, anti-abortion activists increasingly resorted to nonviolent direct action (such as "rescue" protests aimed at closing clinics) and to violence. Since 1992, there have been six murders and numerous attempted murders, arsons, bombings, and assaults on abortion providers and clinic staff. Although practical access to legal abortion became more limited, both through the action of the Court in allowing more state regulation and through the violence and intimidation directed at abortion providers by those protesting against abortion rights, the principle of freedom of choice is still fundamental to US abortion politics.

In Germany, the first post-war Social Democratic government re-opened consideration of the law making abortion a criminal act, known as §218 of the Criminal Code, with the report of an expert commission in 1970. After extensive hearings, parliamentary debates, and public demonstrations, the federal legislature (*Bundestag*) passed a reform of §218 that decriminalized abortion in the first trimester. The Constitutional Court intervened and struck down the law, finding that the general provision in the post-Nazi federal constitution (the Basic Law or *Grundgesetz*) which said that the first duty of the state was the protection of human life extended to cover fetal life as well. Unlike the US Court, which found that there was no scientific or moral consensus on when life began, the German Court explicitly considered this to be a matter on which there was no debate (Riemer, 1993). The *Bundestag* rewrote its reform in 1976, permitting abortion only under special circumstances, the so-called four "indications" – the life or health of the mother, a pregnancy resulting from rape or incest, fetal deformity, or "social need/emergency."

In the following decade, the Catholic Church and other anti-abortion groups attempted to close the "social necessity" loophole through which approximately 90 percent of all legal abortions were done, while feminists and other opponents of restriction encouraged and supported women who sought abortion outside the country (so-called abortion tourism). The conflict remained relatively low-key as a national political issue, despite ongoing but sporadic prosecutions that were seen by both sides (for different reasons) as indicating the inadequacy of the social necessity exception. Attention to this issue increased in 1988 with the prosecution of a doctor in a rural and conservative area (Memmingen in Bavaria) for illegal abortion by inappropriate use of the social necessity indication. The fall of the Berlin Wall and subsequent move towards German unification forced the issue back on the agenda of the *Bundestag*. East Germans, who since 1972 had the right to legal abortion in the first trimester in their own country, strongly resisted the imposition of restrictive West German law. Given two years after unification to arrive at a new law for the unified state, the *Bundestag* in 1992 passed a modified decriminalization of abortion in the first trimester. The law mandated counseling and a waiting period for the woman, and forbade any advertisement of or encouragement to use abortion services. This law, too, was overturned by the Constitutional Court as inadequately protecting life. Under the direction of the Court, the *Bundestag* in 1994 added provisions directing that the counseling be aimed at protecting the life of the unborn child and reaffirming the criminal nature of the act at all times (by denying insurance coverage among other things), even when the state might choose not to punish it in the first trimester. Despite these restrictions, practical access to legal abortion was seen to have improved for West German women, since the risk of arbitrary prosecution diminished.

Thus in both countries there were essentially three chronologically parallel phases of the debate. In the first period, there were reform efforts and a landmark constitutional court decision establishing the fundamental principle defining the legal status of abortion. In the USA, this principle was privacy and the rights of the autonomous individual. In Germany, the principle was the definition of the fetus as a human life subject to the protection of the state. In the second period, there was controversy over the new laws in both countries. The protests were more pronounced and public in the USA, but discontent with the law was articulated in both countries and some restrictions on funding abortion appeared in both. In the third phase, the conflict escalated in both countries as, for different reasons, the constitutional courts returned to re-evaluate their fundamental principles. In both countries, the courts reaffirmed their widely variant original decisions, while practical access became more similar – easier in western Germany and harder in the USA.

The similar time periods and different trajectories of the conflict in the two countries allow us to examine the role of women as political actors in the debate under sharply different conditions. The discursive opportunity structure created by the respective constitutional court decisions favored a pro-life position in Germany and a pro-choice position in the USA. Although favoring a particular side, neither framing of the issue prevented conflict from emerging in both countries. Despite recurrent protests and other actions, the abortion issue never left the legislative and judicial arena in Germany, although overall coverage of and attention to the issue ebbed substantially in the second phase. In the USA, social movement mobilization of both sides of the issue was considerably greater, and the media's attention to abortion as a political issue grew steadily from the 1970s to the 1990s. Social movement actors play a correspondingly larger role in the US abortion debate.

Women's movements in the two countries are also differently situated in the abortion conflict. In the USA, feminist organizations such as the National Organization for Women and the Feminist Majority have a national as well as local structure and are represented in Washington as part of a coalition of interest groups. Other national organizations make the defense of abortion rights their central concern (such as the National Abortion Rights Action League [NARAL]) and some situate abortion as one of a number of fundamental constitutional rights to defend (such as the American Civil Liberties Union [ACLU]). This coalition confronts anti-abortion groups that also have a national presence independent of any church (such as the National Right to Life Committee) as well as national church groups (such as the Catholic Bishops' Secretariat for Pro-Life Activities). American feminist organizations – on abortion as well as on other issues such as welfare reform – are thus national players in a conflict among interest groups and their legislative supporters (Peattie and Rein, 1983; Spalter-Roth and Schreiber, 1995).

Most German feminists, in contrast, resist forming any sort of enduring national organization (Ferree, 1987; Kaplan, 1992). Committed to the principle that non-hierarchical, grassroots organization is the only appropriate means to challenge patriarchy, German feminists center their organizational efforts on local projects and typically temporary networks among such local groups and projects that focus on single issues. The leadership group for feminists on the abortion issue was such a group, the Federal Network for the Repeal of §218.

However, the feminist impulse that revived internationally in the 1970s, giving rise to a plethora of new women's movement organizations around the globe, did not only affect German women who saw themselves as feminists and who limited themselves to working in local projects. The 1970s also saw the formation of new women's organizations within existing political parties (such as the Association of Social Democratic Women, *AsF*), while the 1980s included the involvement of feminists in forming and supporting the new Green political party and participating in campaigns for women's influence in German and European politics. This wider women's movement, of which local feminist groups are only a tiny part, also largely supported abortion rights. Germany's interest group sector centers on the representatives of business and labor, who, with the state, form a widely recognized "tripod" for legitimate policy-making. There are no national level abortion pressure groups for women's movement groups to either work with or oppose. Insofar as women seek a policy voice in Germany, the primary route open to them is the political parties. Since the formation of the Green Party in 1980, which led the way in formalizing representation of women in government, all of the parties have competed to a greater or lesser extent to include women prominently among their spokespeople and candidates (Mushaben, 1989).

In sum, this overview of the political opportunities available to women on the abortion issue indicates that US feminists have more organization, resources, and potential allies outside the formal political structures of parties and legislatures than do German women with feminist inclinations, who have more to draw on inside the parties than outside them. The abortion issue itself is more decentralized in the USA, being governed by state rather than federal law, but the women's movement is more decentralized in Germany, being largely split into local projects and women's groups formed within contending political parties.

Given the differences in the discursive opportunity structure and the trajectory of the abortion issue as well as these differences in institutional opportunity structure for women's movements concerned with abortion rights, we are not likely to be able to advance any single causal argument to account for the differences in outcomes we identify. Here we hope only to be able to describe how the struggles over abortion differ in the way that gender is made relevant, that is, how women's recognition struggles become power struggles and contribute to different problems of authority and autonomy in each country.

Data and methods

The data we discuss here are drawn from a larger study conducted in collaboration with Jürgen Gerhards, Friedhelm Neidhardt, and Dieter Rucht. The research project involved a content analysis of 1,243 American newspaper articles sampled from the *New York Times* and *Los Angeles Times* and 1,423 German newspaper articles sampled from the *Frankfurter Allgemeine* and the *Süddeutsche Zeitung* for the period between 1970 and 1994.[2] In addition, we surveyed organizations involved in contesting abortion rights in the period 1989–92, collected documents from these organizations, and interviewed leaders and media directors of particularly significant groups. The project as a whole thus connects the efforts of the contending groups to use the media with their actual representation in these policy-relevant newspapers. While inclusion of other media, such as radio and television, would have been desirable to get a fuller picture of the public debate, these materials are not archived in both countries for this whole period. In order to have a long time series and a balanced comparison between the two countries, a narrower spectrum of discourse had to be used.

The newspaper articles were analyzed by means of a hierarchical coding scheme. We coded the characteristics of articles themselves, the speakers within articles, and the properties of the utterances of each speaker. We selected only articles that had abortion as a major theme. We considered a speaker to be anyone who was given an opportunity to present a view on abortion, whether or not this opportunity was used. Thus anyone who was directly quoted or paraphrased in the context of the article's coverage of abortion was considered a speaker, even if the speaker merely said "no comment," since such opportunities to present a viewpoint are themselves a recognition by the media of the speaker's legitimate right to have an influence on public opinion. Journalists themselves were also considered speakers, but, unlike other public actors, journalists were only counted as making an utterance on abortion when they used their access to the public to present a statement on what abortion meant. Opportunities to speak afforded to individuals and groups are what we consider *standing*, or the legitimate right to have a voice in the debate on an issue. There were 3,736 speakers in Germany and 4,763 in the USA.[3]

Every utterance, or distinct speech act, by each speaker in an article was also coded for the way that abortion was framed (if it contained any framing at all). By *framing* we mean the context of meaning that was imputed to the act of abortion. We coded eight major frames of meaning in which abortion could be placed.[4] For this paper, we consider only two of these eight frames in any detail, the framing of abortion as a matter of individual rights vis-à-vis the state or state rights vis-à-vis the individual (individual/state frame) and the framing of abortion as a matter of women's rights or gendered roles and responsibilities (women/gender frame). Each of these frames was further subdivided into claims and ideas that advanced or tended to be favorable to a position of greater restriction on the availability of abortion, those that tended to support fewer restrictions and more access, and those claims that were neutral as to whether abortion should be more or less available. Every frame contained both pro-restrictionist, anti-restrictionist, and neutral ideas. For example, the individual/state frame contained arguments that abortion was a matter of individual privacy, an issue of freedom of conscience, and separation of church and state (anti-restriction), that those who opposed abortion should not have to pay for it or perform it (pro-restriction) and that decisions about abortion should be a matter of respecting a democratic majority (ambiguous/neutral, used to support more restrictions or fewer depending on the local majority). In addition, we coded the specific nature of the particular claim within each directional frame group (thus a claim that abortion was about separation of church and state was distinguished from a claim that it was about individual privacy). Each specific different claim, called an idea element, in each utterance was coded. There were 12,323 idea elements in the USA, and 6,932 in Germany.

Overall, the general distribution of standing and framing found in our data reflects the structure of both institutional and discursive opportunity discussed above. In the USA, the proportion of speakers who represent a social movement organization is roughly the same as the proportion who speak for the state in some form (about a third in either case), while in Germany about half of all speakers represent the state and social movements contribute only a tiny fraction of the discourse. In the third phase of the debate in the USA, the proportion of speakers coming from the social movement sector rises while the state share remains fairly stable over time. In Germany, the social movement share falls in phase three, while the proportion coming from state and party actors rises. But from the very beginning, social movements are not nearly as prominent in Germany as in the USA, where weak parties and strong and diverse interest group organizations have long been characteristic (Clemens, 1998).

The framing differences between the two countries are also consistent with the discursive opportunities presented by the courts: in Germany, the single most common frame used is fetal life (25% of all idea elements) and in the USA the single most common frame is the individual and the state (23% of all idea elements). Overall, 46% of German speakers frame the issue in a way that supports a restrictionist understanding, while only 35% of US speakers do. Instead, 50% of American speakers are on balance pro-choice in their framing, compared to only 37% of German speakers. Although these differences are important for understanding the overall shape of the discourse in both countries, for our purposes the comparison that matters is not between pro-life and pro-choice arguments or the various types of arguments offered to defend restrictionist legislation, but *how* the justice claim for less restriction is framed.

We therefore turn to look at the contrast between two of the frames that are most important in arguing against restrictive abortion legislation, the individual/state frame and the women/gender frame. These two different frames have quite different significance in the two countries. In Germany, the most prominent frame with a pro-abortion-rights direction is women/gender (28% of all pro-rights idea elements), which clearly overshadows arguments based on individual autonomy and freedom (12%). In the USA, the reverse is the case: individual/state arguments against restriction (30%) are twice as common as women's rights claims (15%). We turn now to consider why this more strongly gendered form of the argument for abortion rights is so dominant in Germany and what relation it has to the voice that women have gained in the discourse of each country.

Challenging the gender of governance

Over time, the increased global political mobilization of women is reflected in the increasing proportion of speakers in each country who are women. As Figure 2 indicates, the share of women in the discourse at least doubles in each country. It rises from about 20% in the USA in the earliest days of phase one to approximately 40% of all non-journalist speakers by the mid-1990s. In Germany, the picture is a little more complicated, since women are 30% of all speakers during the earliest period, before the legislature begins debating the bills and while feminist protest activity is prominent. Women's share then sinks to only about 20% once the issue becomes a matter for the *Bundestag* and the court before rising to 50% in the 1989–92 period of renewed legislative debate and about 70% in the most recent period. There is clear evidence here that women are considered more relevant speakers on abortion now than they were two decades ago.

This shift in the prominence of women who are given legitimacy to speak to the abortion issue is particularly evident in Germany with regard to the visibility of women within the formal institutions of politics. Between the 1970s and the 1990s, the share of those in state and party roles with a voice in the media who are women rises dramatically in Germany but comparatively little in the USA. While less than 10% of American state and party speakers on abortion were women in the early 1970s, this share climbed to just under 30% by the mid-1990s. Without any comparative data, this might seem a fairly substantial rise. Yet in Germany over the same period, the proportion of women among the state and party speakers rises from about 20% to about 70% (see Figure 3). Even if one just compares the two periods of most intense media debate in Germany, the periods from 1973–76 and 1989–92, the difference in women's share of the official political discourse is strongly evident. Although women were just 20% of the official speakers in the first period of legislative debate they are over half the official speakers when the legislature returned to the issue after unification.

Moreover, while US women in this first period do not offer a markedly different share of the official discourse on abortion than German women do, by the time of the Webster decision the differences in standing between US and German women are profound. German women in official state and party roles enjoy much more visibility and legitimacy in speaking on the abortion question than do their American counterparts (50% vs. 20%).

Some of this difference may have to do with the greater inroads that German women made in official political representation in this period. Between 1980 and 1994, for example, the proportion of members of the German federal legislature, the *Bundestag*, who were women rose from 8% to 26% while in the USA the increase of women in the House of Representatives in the comparable period was only from 7% to 12% (and even less in the Senate). Additionally, in this period all the German political parties adopted affirmative action plans for the greater inclusion of women, including in some cases formal quotas for party offices and candidate positions. Yet it remains true that German women are particularly over-represented among the official speakers on abortion topics relative to their share of seats in the legislature or proportion of office-holders in the executive branch (26% of legislators but 50% of state voices in the media are women).

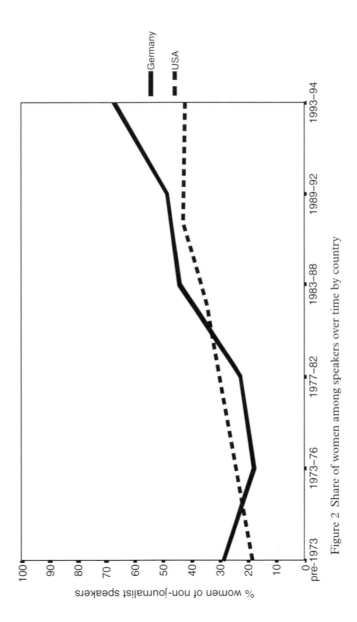

Figure 2 Share of women among speakers over time by country

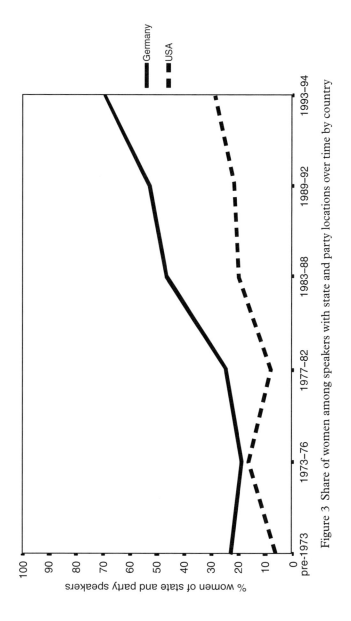

Figure 3 Share of women among speakers with state and party locations over time by country

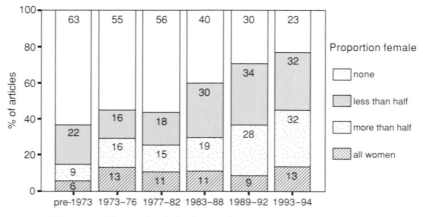

Figure 4a Share of articles by gender composition and period: the USA

Moreover, the gendering of governance is not only expressed by women who hold formal roles in policy-making positions. The ability to speak on this issue that the media selectively accords to some individuals and representatives of organizations is itself a form of governance that can be gendered. The nature as well as extent of women's standing has changed in both countries. The extent to which media discourse on abortion has altered its form to give women a distinctively legitimate voice on this issue can also be captured by the way that articles have become differently constituted as public forums for the debate. To see this, we shift from looking at the shares of speakers to looking at the articles as units, the way that a reader would see them. As Figures 4a–4b indicate, both in Germany and in the USA in the 1970s, most articles on abortion were dominated by male speakers. In the earliest period, about 60% of US articles and 70% of German articles contained only male speakers.

Over time the proportion of articles in both countries that give men alone voice declines steadily until by the most recent period they account for only about a quarter of all articles. Thus the idea that men alone could speak legitimately to the regulation of abortion has eroded, and the public discourse that governs how abortion is to be understood is, as we have seen before, one in which women play an increasingly prominent role. However, the way that the gendering of public discourse governing abortion has changed is very different in the two countries. In the USA, this discourse has become less specifically gendered. It now is much more likely to include both men and women (the majority of articles have become mixed in regard to gender and are about as likely to include

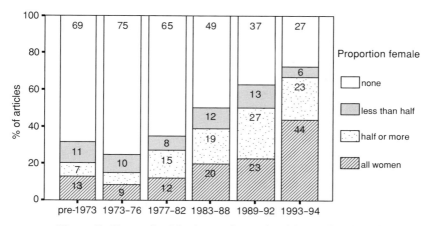

Figure 4b Share of articles by gender composition and period: Germany

more women than men as more men than women). The proportion of
articles that only include men has declined, but the share of articles that
contain only women has not increased. Abortion is presented as an issue
in which both men and women have something legitimate to say.

This is in striking contrast to the situation in Germany. Here the proportion of articles containing only men dropped while the proportion
that contains only women speakers rose dramatically, particularly in the
most recent period. Half of all articles in the recent period dominated
by legislative debate (1989–92) are composed entirely (23%) or mostly
(27%) of women speakers. The proportion of articles containing only
women speakers is even higher (44%) in the last period, even though
the total number of articles has begun to decline again. The shift from
abortion being publicly discussed by men to being a matter discussed
only by women begins to occur even before it re-emerges as a significant
legislative matter, and the trend continues in the period after the reform
of the law is essentially complete. The issue of abortion in Germany is
re-gendered from being a male domain to being one in which women's
voices are increasingly dominant.

Thus, to summarize the shifts in the gendering of governance of abortion, we can see that German women have succeeded more than US
women in exerting a specific claim to standing on this issue. Both in
terms of their role as speakers in the formal halls of government and in
their position in articles that define the nature of the debate, German
women have emerged in a particularly prominent position. While US
women have also succeeded in obtaining more voice in the discourse, this

increase in standing is not so profound among those with formal policy roles as it is in Germany. The public forum, as represented by newspaper articles, has apparently become more de-gendered in the USA as women participate more equally with men in the same discussions, while in Germany it has been re-gendered as more appropriately female than male. German women and men largely appear in separate articles, speaking as it were in separate rooms rather than as part of the same conversation. In the gendering of the process by which abortion is governed discursively, German women have won dominant and more often exclusive standing, while US women are less central among policy-making speakers. US articles on abortion show a remarkable degree of gender balance in the most recent period, but women can hardly be said to enjoy any special standing. German women have to some degree won a recognition struggle that gives them special authority as speakers on abortion, and in doing so have challenged the gendering of governance. This struggle over authority to speak is an important part, but not the entire picture, of what recognition entails.

Challenging the governance of gender

The second aspect of power struggles we identified takes place over autonomy. This includes the practical rights of individual women to make an abortion decision, but also the recognition of the pregnant woman as a person who is not reducible either to her status of mother-to-be or to her gender alone (Bordo, 1995; Sauer, 1995). The diversity of women's needs and expectations becomes flattened into a stereotype when the discourse around abortion assumes that all women are or want to be mothers, and the autonomy of women to define their own needs and demand recognition of their own personalities is overridden by state policies that assume the government knows best. We consider the governance of gender therefore to be expressed in large part by the relative role that personal autonomy plays in the discourse relative to the role played by claims that women need protection.

The formal nature of government abortion policy in the two countries clearly recognizes autonomy as a more central issue in the USA. As we have seen, the Supreme Court placed abortion rights under the rubric of privacy, casting them as a matter of defending the individual from the incursions of the state in this personal domain, and US abortion discourse echoes this priority, making the individual's rights to privacy, religious freedom, and personal self-determination the most common theme in the discourse overall and about 30% of all pro-choice ideas. Even the US arguments that would tend to support limitations on abortion rights are

often cast in terms of limits on the state (for example, freedom of conscience not to perform or pay indirectly for abortion). These arguments,
on both sides, are typically presented as a matter of "being let alone."
For example, when asked in our interview what "the role of government
should be in the abortion issue," one abortion rights activist said, "Get
the hell out of it totally! Obviously. We don't think government or religion
or any group has any role."

US abortion policy as established by *Roe* and *Webster* in fact admits
only such interventions that place "no undue burden" on women who are
attempting to exercise such rights but also offers no support, financial or
otherwise, for women who are pregnant. As feminist critics of US abortion
policy have often pointed out, women who cannot support another child,
or who are being pressured by their families or boyfriends to have an
abortion they do not want, are offered no support to have a child and
thus have little practical ability to exercise their theoretical freedom of
choice. Poor women of color have often faced pressure for abortion and
sterilization, for example. Reflecting such concerns, some pro-abortion-
rights organizations have adopted names that affirm their commitment to
"reproductive rights," at least nominally widening their scope to include
both having and not having a child as a matter of choice to be defended.
Thus, the leading pro-choice social movement organization, NARAL,
officially changed its name in the 1980s from National Abortion and
Reproductive Rights Action League to National Abortion and Reproductive Rights Action League.

German abortion policy reflects a stronger welfare state tradition and
thus is both more actively interventionist and more committed to connecting rights to the economic opportunity to exercise them. Thus, while
the 1993 German court decision affirmed that abortion was always a
criminal act even when it was not to be punished in the first trimester,
it also held that women on welfare who choose to exercise their right to
a non-punished abortion have the right to have it paid for by the state,
since they would otherwise be denied in practice a freedom that others could exercise. The law regulating abortion also included provisions
for expanding the state's supply of public pre-school places as part of its
inducement to women to choose to bear children. At the same time, however, the court authorized mandatory counseling directed at persuading
the woman to have the child, pointing out the benefits that the state provides to mothers as an inducement to do so, and enforcing significant
waiting periods and repeat counseling sessions to ensure that the woman
was obdurate in wanting an abortion before she could exercise her formal
right to choose it. Those in the woman's immediate circle could also be
punished legally for trying to persuade or coerce her to have an abortion.

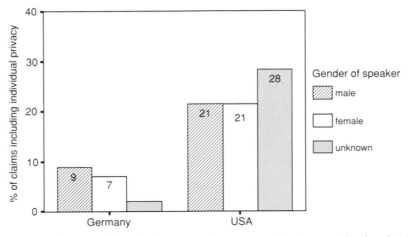

Figure 5a Pro-choice views of government involvement in abortion by gender: issue of individual privacy

Thus, in terms of both positive inducements and negative sanctions, the state takes a more active role in directing women's choices in the way that it considers morally and socially appropriate, thus playing an active role in the governance of gender.

This interventionist stance is reflected in a considerably higher proportion of German than US pro-choice idea elements that affirm a specific moral role for government in the abortion issue. Conversely, the argument against restriction in the USA often takes the form of making a claim for privacy of the individual against the state's intervention. In Figures 5a and 5b, we compare the relative frequency of two specific clusters of idea elements in each country among pro-choice speakers who are identified as male, those who are female and those with no gender identification (e.g., institutional spokespersons and editorial writers who are not named).

As one can readily see, the privacy argument is much more dominant in the USA among speakers of all gender than it is in Germany and, conversely, the pro-choice argument for government taking a moral role of some sort is clearly evident in Germany and virtually invisible in the USA. About a quarter of all pro-choice speakers in the USA include at least one argument about privacy compared to less that 10% of German speakers. By contrast, pro-choice German men especially (14%), but also pro-choice German women (9%), see some affirmative moral role for government in regulating the abortion decision, while virtually no pro-choice US speakers do.

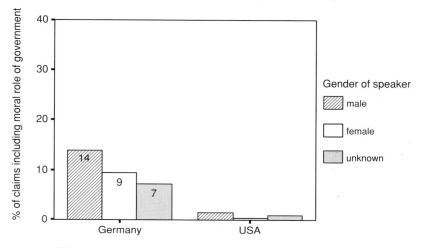

Figure 5b Pro-choice views of government involvement in abortion by gender: issue of the moral role of government

Importantly, the framing of abortion as a right in Germany is also more gender-specific. As noted earlier, claims that abortion is a matter concerning women or gender are 28% of German abortion-rights discourse and only 15% of American pro-choice discourse, while claims that abortion is about an individual right vis-à-vis the state are 30% of all US pro-choice idea elements but only 12% of German ones. Here we shift our level of analysis from counting the number of times a specific idea is used to consider which speakers include which frames overall. In Figures 6a and 6b, we contrast the relative likelihood of a pro-choice German speaker employing any pro-choice idea from the individual/state frame and/or from the women/gender frame with the probability that a US pro-choice speaker will do so.

As we see in Figures 6a and 6b, which look only at pro-choice speakers using specifically pro-choice ideas, German women are by far the most likely group to use the women/gender frame for abortion. Over half of pro-choice German women use the women/gender frame, either alone (51%) or in combination with the individual/state frame (6%). Pro-choice German men are only about half as likely as these German women to frame in gender terms alone (25% of these men). Nonetheless, even German men are more likely than pro-choice US women to be using the gender frame alone (20% of US women). Rather than gender of speaker being the primary correlate of gendered framing, national context plays at least as large a role. US pro-choice speakers all strongly prefer the

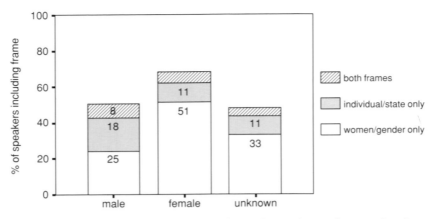

Figure 6a Pro-choice framing of abortion as issue of women/gender, individual/state, or both: Germany

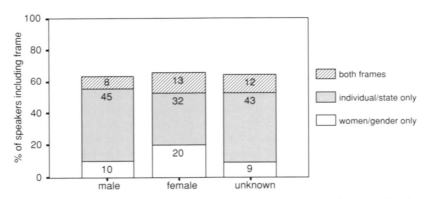

Figure 6b Pro-choice framing of abortion as issue of women/gender, individual/state, or both: USA

individual/state frame to the gendered one. Even US women, who are twice as likely as US men (20% vs. 10%) to use just a gender-based argument, are still more likely to offer only an individual rights argument (32%) than only the gender-based one (20%). US men are more than three times as likely to use just the individual rights framing than just a gender-based claim (45% vs. 10%), while German men actually offer the gender-based framing alone slightly more often than just the individual-rights one (25% vs. 18%).

It is thus clear that the gender-based definition of what abortion rights are, as something particular and special for women rather than an example of a general right that happens to apply to women in this case, is much more strongly established in Germany than in the USA for pro-choice speakers of both genders. Conversely, the general individual rights claim is far more likely to be advanced in the USA by all groups of speakers than by any group in Germany. The specificity of the gender-based claim, however, seems to particularly privilege German women speakers as advocates of abortion rights. Unlike in the USA, where all three groups of speakers are equally likely to make these two rights claims, either separately or together, in Germany women are about 20 percentage points more likely than either men or speakers of unknown gender to do so. Since these are all pro-choice speakers, those who are not making a rights claim here are not arguing against abortion but are offering some different sort of argument against restrictions. Rather than advancing women's autonomy, either as women or as individuals, German men and other speakers defend legal abortion on other grounds.

In order to get a better idea of what those other grounds might be, we constructed two clusters of specific framing arguments. One cluster, which we call autonomy, specifically selects individual idea elements that address the issue of self-determination, whether as women (the gendered form) or as individuals entitled to a right to privacy (the non-gendered form). The other cluster picks up those idea elements that speak of protection, whether specifically emphasizing women as needing protection (the gendered form) or more generally of the state's need to act morally, to offer alternatives to abortion, to consider the reasons that women might have for abortion, and to attempt to address social need (the ungendered form). In other words, when abortion is framed as an aspect of the welfare state and justified in terms of helping those in need, we coded this as part of the protection cluster.

In Figures 7a and 7b we examine the relative share of autonomy claims of both autonomy and protection claims combined. Considering just how pro-choice speakers use these ideas, we see that autonomy outweighs protection as an argument for abortion for all three groups of Americans and for German women, but not for German men or non-gender-identified speakers. Autonomy arguments are about equally dominant for all subgroups of pro-choice American speakers, with their share being about 56% ($\pm$3%). By contrast, German men favor protection over autonomy by two to one (only 32% of their arguments are about autonomy compared to 68% about protection). German speakers for whom no gender is given, typically institutional speakers and non-bylined journalists, are

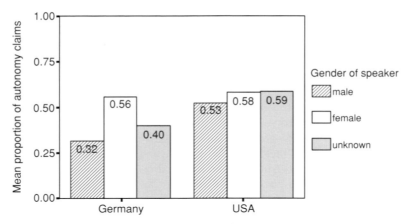

Figure 7a Autonomy as a share of autonomy and protection clusters by gender and country: pro-choice speakers

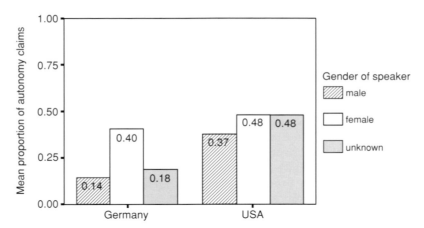

Figure 7b Autonomy as a share of autonomy and protection clusters by gender and country: all speakers

also inclined to favor protection over autonomy, suggesting the extent to which German welfare state thinking is formally institutionalized, not merely a reflection of individual men's tendency to think in protectionist terms about women.

In effect, German women's pro-choice arguments in favor of autonomy, which we have seen tend to be gender-specific arguments, do not carry the rest of the discourse with them. Instead, German women, influential as they are in terms of standing in the discourse, remain isolated as advocates of seeing abortion as a matter of women's autonomy rather than of help for the needy. Indeed, the Social Democratic Party, the largest single institutional advocate for reducing legal restrictions on abortion, framed its approach to abortion with the slogan "Help, don't punish," arguing that women who seek abortion are in need of the state's help rather than criminal prosecution. Thus German women's effort to challenge the governance of gender through an assertion of women's autonomy has largely not succeeded in swaying the balance of the rest of the discourse away from its emphasis on protection.

The pro-choice arguments in favor of autonomy in the USA, by contrast, are equally strong among all three gender groups. US women, who we saw earlier also tend to make their argument for autonomy in non-gender-specific terms, are supported in this argument by both men and institutional speakers. In successfully making a claim for personal autonomy as a rule guiding abortion decision-making, they have challenged the governance of gender. However, this emphasis on individual autonomy also means that US women who are in fact needy and seeking help from the government, whether to have an abortion or to avoid one, are left without any specific group that represents them.

If one were to look at the entire configuration of German and US discourse, the contrast in balance in favor of autonomy in the USA and protection in Germany would be even more pronounced, since as we saw earlier, German discourse on the whole is more tilted towards a pro-life framing of abortion than US discourse is. In addition, the difference between the proportions of men and women who are pro-choice is somewhat greater in Germany than in the USA (26% of German speakers who are men are pro-choice on balance compared to 58% of German women, while 38% of American men are pro-choice compared to 65% of US women speakers).

What this indicates is the extent to which the overall discourse takes up autonomy and self-determination. For Americans, the autonomy theme is a very substantial part of the overall discourse, just about equaling concerns about protection for women that come from both pro-choice and pro-life speakers. In German discourse, the concern for protecting women expressed by pro-choice speakers joins with the concerns expressed for protecting women (from the dangers of legal as well as illegal abortion, from social pressure to have an abortion, etc.) expressed by the pro-life side of the debate to make concern about women's autonomy a very minor part of all but women's own speech. In German discourse, protection is the leading theme in the governance of gender and women's decision-making is regulated more directly by the state in practice as well.

In sum, what we see here is a focus on the state as moral and helpful in Germany and as dangerous and intrusive in the USA. This underlies the concept of the welfare state as a positive construct in Germany but a negative one in US discourse. In addition, German pro-choice speakers, especially but not at all exclusively women, tend to frame abortion as a gender-specific concern rather than as a matter of individual rights that just happen in this instance to be applicable to women. American pro-choice speakers do just the opposite, and tend to downplay the gender-specific arguments in relation to making non-gendered rights claims. The ideas of the welfare state as a benevolent force and of women as having gender-specific claims in regard to abortion then come together to advance the idea of women as being in special need of state protection rather than being autonomous moral agents. Although German women have advanced women's claims to autonomy, largely in gender-specific language, they have found less resonance for this claim among other speakers in the discourse than US women have found for their claim that women's autonomy is a matter of individual rights.

Thus the efforts of women to challenge the governance of gender by asserting a right to self-determination have been more successful in the USA than in Germany. In the USA, broad suspicion of the state and support for an individual right to privacy articulated by the Supreme Court have served to buttress women's claims for autonomy. In Germany, women have instead faced a discursive opportunity structure that privileges the fetus' right to life and views the welfare state positively. Within this framework, women have been more likely to be constructed as needy victims of circumstances who can be "helped" rather than "punished" when they seek abortions. German women have actively contested this definition, making a distinctive plea for considering abortion a matter of women's autonomous choice. Within the welfare state framework of protection advanced by other speakers, however, they have not made much headway in challenging the governance of gender.

Conclusion

The power struggles through which women have attempted to gain control over the abortion issue on their own behalf have taken different courses and led to different victories in these two countries. In Germany, there has been a dramatic change in authority as women have successfully challenged the gendering of governance on the abortion issue. Women have achieved a notable level of standing both in the media and among policy-makers on this issue, and abortion is framed much more as a gendered issue there than in the USA. But in the autonomy dimension of power – the governance of gender – women have been more successful in the USA than in Germany. All speakers in the USA, not only women, are much more likely to frame women as autonomous moral agents compared to those in Germany and to justify abortion in terms of an individual's right to make decisions concerning their own body and life. German abortion law constructs pregnant women as needy victims whom the state is obliged to help, largely by counseling them to have the child and by pointing out the social supports the state makes available for them in that case. German discourse as a whole also follows this model, and women speakers' claims to autonomy, advocating the individual woman's right to decide whether motherhood or abortion is the moral course of action for her, are not echoed by other speakers.

German women have succeeded more than US women in gaining access to political and social authority on the abortion issue. However, US discourse and law both grant women more autonomy in making abortion decisions. Both of these victories in struggles over gendered political power also provide important gains in recognition of women's status and the redistribution of substantive rights. In fact, women in both countries have made progress in winning authority and autonomy in regard to abortion, even if the changes in one dimension or the other are relatively more pronounced in one country or the other. The changes that have occurred both in law and in discourse over these twenty-five years are significant and do reduce injustice for women in regard to social power. Yet, neither victory is without its contradictions. Redistribution and recognition remain issues of justice that are only incompletely addressed through the measurable gains in power that women have made in both countries.

Redistribution is the dominant dimension of continuing inequity in the USA. The practical autonomy that US women can exercise in choosing between abortion and motherhood is limited by the endemic problems of economic maldistribution that constrain US women, particularly women of color. Women who would prefer not to have an abortion are not protected or assisted by the state in realizing that choice. The *de jure* autonomy of women's decision-making, which both the law and the discourse support, is undercut by *de facto* financial and social constraints on women, especially poor women and teenagers, that force them into decisions that do not express their free preferences at all. Indeed, the woman who is left with no choice but to have an abortion that she deeply regrets has become a figure invoked by the anti-abortion side of the debate, and pro-choice forces are therefore reluctant to even acknowledge her existence. The distinctively US focus on women as autonomous individuals with rights under the law has obscured the injustices of access to abortion and to mothering that real women – especially poor women – confront in practice. Both the stigmatization of teen motherhood and the absence of any significant material state support for motherwork in the USA make abortion still a matter of injustice with regard to recognition and redistribution.

While, on the recognition dimension, serious problems of stigmatization remain for some specific groups of US women, the issue of misrecognition is a more general one in Germany. The practical authority of German women is diluted by the devaluation of all women who choose abortion as criminal and immoral actors. Abortion is still defined by the state as a crime and women who abort are thus still criminals, even though the state has decided to help rather than punish them. The state's decision not to punish women in the first trimester is legitimated by the Constitutional Court as a means of inducing women to come for counseling, the prerequisite for a certificate allowing the abortion to be performed, specifically so that state-licensed counselors can try to induce her to change her mind. Because the counseling is defined by law as directed to convincing the woman to bear the child to term, and explicitly justified as reducing the risk that she will leave the country for an abortion elsewhere, the substitution of Foucauldian manipulation and surveillance for direct use of force and punishment is relatively transparent. The coercion of women into motherhood remains legitimated as a state purpose.

In this context, the ability to speak of women as free moral actors who can legitimately choose between abortion and motherhood is greatly limited in practice, even for those women who have gained standing in political parties and in the media to address this issue. Although women speakers in Germany are far more likely than other German speakers to affirm women's right to decide as a principle, even they are likely to disavow the woman who chooses abortion as immoral and unwomanly. Several in-depth analyses of the *Bundestag* debates themselves showed how women legislators distanced themselves from "the woman who would choose an abortion" and affirmed motherhood as women's true calling (Mushaben, Lennox, and Giles, 1997; Sauer, 1995). Their insistence that women would never choose to have an abortion for anything less than grave reasons, because all women want their babies, specifically rebuts the pro-life arguments about the triviality and callousness of women who abort. But ultimately this argument undermines the social recognition of those women who do not want to be mothers or who make free moral choices of which one personally does not approve.

In effect, some women are misrecognized and made invisible in both countries. In the USA, the women who are most unacknowledged are those whose practical choices are not as free, particularly for economic reasons, as the law imagines. In Germany, the women who vanish from the discourse are those who make or wish to make free choices that conflict with the gendered perceptions of women's proper role and responsibilities. In both countries, the victories that have been won in terms of authority and autonomy are significant gains in justice for women, but in neither country has the need for further struggle for recognition and redistribution ended.

3 Recognition struggles in universalistic and gender distinctive frames: Sweden and Ireland

Barbara Hobson

Introduction

·The state and institutions are central to theorizing on redistribution and welfare regimes, yet they are not integrated into theorizing the recognition paradigm. Axel Honneth (1995b: xv), for example, notes that recognition politics is a result of two distinct historical processes: an increase in the number of persons treated as full-fledged citizens and an increase in the actual content of what it means to be a citizen, the emergence of political or welfare rights. However, he does not focus on these institutional processes, but rather on the self-realization of the individual and his motivation to resist exclusion. Nancy Fraser's very definition of misrecognition, "institutionalized patterns that constitute certain actors as inferior and invisible," acknowledges the importance of institutional practices. But the complex and dynamic role of the state and institutions is not elaborated in theorizing the interplay between recognition and redistribution. To understand this interplay, we have to locate recognition politics in specific histories, political structures, policy, and institutions. At the same time, we have to build in the role of agency and power: *who and what gets recognized*. To understand these processes, we have to focus our lens on social actors and the making of collective identities: how groups connect their movements to cultural frames and fit their claims into institutional venues (Snow and Benford, 1992; Gamson, 1992).

To render the dynamic play of actors and institutions in recognition struggles, it is useful to trace recognition struggles over time and across societies. I have chosen two cases of women's recognition struggles, in Sweden and Ireland, which represent paradigmatic cases of responses to different forms of non- or misrecognition: one based on gender distinctiveness, the Republic of Ireland (hereafter referred to as Ireland), in which gender difference is imprinted in the Constitution in the construction of familialism and nationalism. The gender policy logic revolves around a strong male-breadwinner wage. The other, Sweden, exemplifies

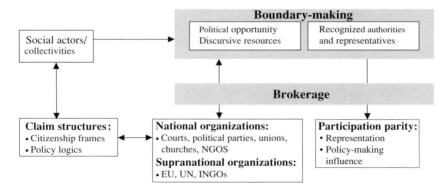

Figure 8 Claims and frames and boundary-making in recognition struggles

the struggle for recognition in reaction to social democratic universalism, which defined inequality and solidarity in terms of class differences, making invisible the devalued status and different positions of women and men. In contrast to Ireland, the Swedish welfare state has developed a policy logic with dual-earner families, and epitomizes the weak male-breadwinner wage society (Jane Lewis, 1992).

Before turning to the two cases, I want to highlight the ways in which recognition struggles are shaped by institutional contexts and in dialogue with specific institutions. When we analyze recognition struggles in specific institutional contexts, we can see the interplay of recognition and redistribution in the framing of claims and the making of collective identities. Recognition struggles also involve contests both among and between movement groups over identities, the meanings attached to emancipation and empowerment, as well as discursive battles in the media over authentic representation: who speaks for whom. Embedding the politics of recognition in different institutional settings also reveals privileging of certain actors over others, in which they are recognized as the authorities for a movement and constituency. Figure 8 illustrates the complex and dynamic processes in which some claims-makers and their claims are recognized and not others.

Gendered recognition struggles take shape from different institutions: state policy-making bodies, political parties, unions, churches, and nongovernmental organizations. They confront different policy logics around the flow of entitlements from the state to the family. The cultural coding of gender, which I call *citizenship frames*, in combination with the policy logics in welfare states, set the terms for collectivities to make claims for recognition, to alter exclusionary practices, and to enhance participatory rights, which in turn can influence the redistribution of resources. In effect, this is to acknowledge the interaction between claims and frames in social movements. What I have called *claim structures* reveals this interchange, which can offer windows of opportunity for gendered recognition struggles or hold at bay feminist movements. They can limit or expand the discursive universe. The Swedish universalistic frame allowed feminists to make gendered claims based on equal treatment of citizens as well as solidarity with weaker parties, in which women were included in the class of vulnerable persons. But this frame has inhibited claims-making that articulates gender differences in power and agency between men and women. Gender distinctiveness in Ireland made visible gender inequalities between men and women, but provided few discursive resources for women's collectivities to contest, reclaim, and reconfigure gender organized around familialism and male breadwinning.

As the recognition struggles in these two societies underscore, this is a dynamic process with windows of political opportunity widening and contracting, in which historical contingencies and the introduction of new social actors create new bases of power. In the past, gendered recognition struggles have been coupled to broader movements, including anti-slavery, suffrage, and nation building, as well as riding on the coattails of debates about demographic decline and labor shortage. The latter was true of Swedish women's activism. In the late twentieth century, not only national but supranational institutions created new bases of power and structures of political opportunity, as well as discursive resources for gendered recognition struggles.

Brokerage, defined in *Dynamics of Contention* (McAdam et al., 2001: 233) as "the linking of two or more unconnected sites," embraces multiple dimensions and processes and it is very diffuse mechanism. I employ brokering to capture a very specific process in my analysis: the pursuit of allies who have different interests and agendas, but gain advantages from their linkages with a movement. In women's movements, brokerage can involve strange bedfellows. Radical feminists in their anti-pornography campaigns in the USA were often joined by right-wing fundamentalist groups. Swedish feminists pressing the state to develop women-friendly policies (for daycare and parental leave benefits) were supported by industrial unions, who typically saw feminism as a divisive strategy against working-class solidarity. Brokerage has been applied to national settings (McAdam et al., 2001), but it also can encompass the role of transnational movements and supranational actors. Irish women brokered with EU bureaucrats, who had been apprehensive about coercing recalcitrant governments, to enforce gender equality directives.

Embedding the politics of recognition in different institutional settings also reveals privileging of certain actors over others – boundary-making – in which they are recognized as the authorities for a movement and constituency. Struggles for recognition in both of these cases involved boundary-making activities that were dependent on evolving institutional environments and their interaction with other national and supranational actors. One might think of boundary-making in ecological and evolutionist terms. Suppose we imagine our two cases as social movements emerging in different habitats, institutional fields in which certain groups dominate. But rather than survival of the fittest, a crude evolutionary metaphor, we can see social actors in collectivities as the most adaptive, able to seize windows of opportunity, broker their claims with powerful allies, and mark their boundaries through discursive and political resources.

In using this evolutionist metaphor, I am not suggesting institutional determinism, because actors and movements in recognition struggles are the key players in defining the meanings and interpretations of rights. They often succeed in creating and extending institutional capacities for dealing with minority rights (ombudsmen, special courts for airing grievances, etc.), as well as opening up new spheres of policy-making. To view recognition in this process-oriented way is to highlight the importance of power in the boundary-making activities of collectivities. Individuals, organizations, and social movement activists author group identity, in the sense of defining what is mis- or nonrecognition, as well as the remedies for inclusion.

These individuals and groups are also given authority to speak for the group in the media, in political debate, in expert commissions, councils, or ministries investigating the unequal distribution of resources and the cultural coding of disrespect and devaluation in law and policy. They become part of the machinery of governance for groups that they represent, often shading out other dissident voices or non-recognizing the marginality and devaluation of others whom they speak for. In this way, they tend to suppress the multiple identities within collectivities. For example, claims-makers for gender equality have tended to make invisible cleavages of race, ethnicity, class, and sexual preference (Yuval-Davis, 1997; Lake, 1994b). This was true in both these cases of recognition struggles, but more pronounced in the more institutionalized Swedish feminism.

In the following sections, I reveal how the cultural coding of gender through policy logics opens up and closes off certain paths for recognition struggles. Here I turn to the questions concerning how context matters in recognition struggles: How are social groups recognized? Who are the specific actors who become authors and spokespersons for women? And finally, I consider how institutional contexts (the gender distinctive and universalistic frames) configure the dynamic interplay between claims for recognition and redistribution.

Sweden

Citizenship frames and policy logics

The framing of citizenship is linked to nationalist projects, constructions based on notions of origin and culture as well as ideologies that define who is to be included in the collective "we" (Turner, 1993; Yuval Davis, 1997). Citizenship frames reflect certain assumptions about what community is if we use T. H. Marshall's (1950) concept of inclusion as full participation, which can be seen in the parameters surrounding rights and obligations (Lister, 1997).

   In universalistic frames of citizenship, legislation based on difference is coded as lesser or inferior, rather than as a form of protection. Advocacy based on special rights has little play in law and policy. In Sweden, the dominance and the long tenure of Social Democratic governments and hegemony of social democracy ideologies set the borders for the discursive landscape in which individuals and groups represented their claims (Åmark, 1992). Universalism in Swedish social democracy was imprinted in the masterframe of the People's Home, a metaphor which embraced community, solidarity, and equality, in which there "were to be no privileged or deprived members or step-children" (Tingsten, 1973: 265). But in this framing of inclusion, inequality was translated into class inequalities and working-class actors became the central figures fighting for the rights of the people. Gendered claims had to fit into this model, in which particularized identities were not made explicit. Policies addressing gender inequalities were nearly always placed within a gender neutral frame – women as workers, women as parents, or women as citizens. None of these considered women as a group with a history of disadvantage or discrimination.

The first wave of recognition struggles

Swedish feminist recognition struggles are path dependent. Therefore it is important to begin with the first wave in the 1930s. This was a crucial period of welfare state formation when women's groups began making claims for greater participation in the "building" of the People's Home

(Hertha, 1938: 4:98). During this era, there was not only a dramatic surge in women's organizations, almost twice the number of organized groups in the suffrage campaign, but also an assertion of women's collective identities and interests (Hobson and Lindholm, 1997). Women cooperated across party and class lines, which represented a movement away from the class antagonism that had dominated women's activism in the past (Hobson and Lindholm, 1997).

There were ideological cleavages among women's groups that revolved around gendered identities. Ellen Key, the voice of maternalism in Sweden, claimed that a woman's power derived from her maternal role and female consciousness, and that feminists who advocated the vote and women's careers were misguided (Key, 1912). She had followers among Swedish feminists, but her ideas had more influence abroad, particularly in Germany and the USA (Hobson, 1993). By the 1930s, a new generation of feminists became the spokespersons for "women," the most prominent being Alva Myrdal, who affirmed that equality between men and women in the labor market was the road to women's emancipation. She put forward a range of policies and programs to free women from the fetters of the home; her proposal for cooperative housing with collective kitchens was the most radical (Hirdman, 1989).

Many feminist groups in this period affirmed that women had collective interests, but they did not assert a politics of difference. Inclusion meant recognizing women's contribution as mothers but also affirming their rights to paid work and equal treatment in employment (Myrdal, 1941). Through their mobilization, in the 1930s women's groups working across party lines obtained rights for working mothers: protection against firing women who were married or pregnant, a paid maternal leave for women in public sector employment, and an income maintenance law in which the state paid benefits to unmarried and divorced mothers when fathers failed to pay their support (Bergman and Hobson, 2002).

Women's activism in the 1930s shaped the contours of future recognition struggles in several important ways. First, social democracy gave recognition to feminists who de-emphasized women's particularized identities and privileged feminists in government commissions and gave policy-making roles to those who did not decouple class equality from gender equality (Hobson and Lindholm, 1997). Second, women's activism was lodged in institutions, including political parties, policy-making bureaucracies, and unions. Sweden is a paradigm case of "femocracy" and institutionalized feminism. Finally, women's claims as citizens became more and more bound to their participation in the labor market. This was to be the case for nearly all of the Nordic welfare states, but most true for Swedish women's claims-making.

The 1970s: claim structures and windows of reform

Called the Golden Age of the Nordic welfare states, the 1960s and 1970s brought to fruition the institutionalized welfare state with its comprehensive policies covering a range of protections and risks and reaching all citizens (Huber and Stephens, 1998). The Swedish welfare state became inclusive among classes and among men and women: high earners were brought into the system through the principle that benefits were related to income loss (Korpi and Palme, 1998). Everyone was entitled to a basic amount for part of their pension, sickness insurance, and, later, parental benefit, but the rest was based on prior work record (Marklund, 1992). Women as housewives became part of the group of marginal persons who lacked permanent jobs, received the lower flat-rate benefits in contrast to the majority of the "working" population who received the more generous benefits and the difference was substantial (Sainsbury, 1996). How would women be integrated into a new expansionist welfare state?

For women's groups, this pivotal period of institutional change opened up policy windows for reform that would shape gender identities and interests. A new policy logic would emerge constructed around individuals rather than male-breadwinner families.

The Swedish model of the worker–parent–citizen came into being during this period. This comprised a set of benefits and policies that were gender neutral that assumed families with children would be dual-earner families. However, the dual-earner model was the result of struggles for recognition among different groups of women and men in political arenas that were inexorably connected to redistributive struggles. By the end of the 1970s, the dual-breadwinner family model became the norm, and by the end of the 1990s, only 4 percent of households had a full-time housewife. General surveys of attitudes reflect the interplay between institutions and gendered identities. In Sweden, women as well as men overwhelmingly reject the idea of the traditional housewife role or the traditional division of unpaid work in the home (Sjöberg, 2000; Takahashi, 2003).

The outcome was not a foregone conclusion. It was the result of contests that on the surface were about redistributive systems that would best benefit women, but in essence these were struggles over women's identities and interests, and which actors and groups would speak for women. For the Center and Liberal Parties, the main issue was freedom of choice, and they proposed a care allowance for mothers[1] that would allow them to choose to continue their caretaking roles (Hinnfors, 1992). For many Social Democratic women, choice was decoded as a bourgeois class privilege, since it was a luxury that many working-class families could not afford (Wachter, 1962; Winkler, 2002). For the younger radical women in both the Liberal and Social Democratic Parties, choice meant the ability to choose not to be housewives.

However, the male-breadwinner norm had strong supporters in the Social Democratic Party Women's Federation. The issues cut across party and gender (Bergqvist, 1999). This was true of the individualized tax reform, which was, in effect, the death knell for the male-breadwinner wage. The system of taxation had been a tax penalty for working wives and a marriage subsidy for households with a single male breadwinner (Montanari, 2000). The proposed reform sparked one of the rare grass-roots campaigns in Swedish politics. Though it was orchestrated by a politically conservative woman, it drew thousands of housewives from across the political spectrum who sent petitions and marched in the streets (Florín, 1999).

Brokerage

There was a long tradition in Swedish social democracy of the right of working men to earn wages that allowed them to support a housewife, even though it was a bourgeois ideal (Florín, 1999: 122). Feminists who argued for women's independence through paid work found allies in the large industrial union (LO). It was the main power block in social democracy. The 1960s was a period of labor shortage and the union, who preferred women's labor to that of immigrants in order to solve the country's labor problems (Kyle, 1979), put pressure on the government to restrict immigration. The preference for married women rather than immigrants was defended: women did not require housing and social services as immigrants did; and an expansion of public day-care would compensate working-class families. LO also saw immigrant labor as a cheap source of industrial labor that would interfere with the Union's agenda of modernizing industry. Xenophobia lay beneath the surface.

Swedish unions have not been strong supporters for women's recognition struggles, seeing feminism as the mantle for bluestockings in the early part of the century. Nevertheless, in the daycare and tax debates, the backing of the industrial unions was crucial. Unions also promoted a wage solidarity policy for low-income earners, which indirectly helped women who were over-represented in low-paid unskilled jobs. However, they were adamantly against gender anti-discrimination law in wages, hiring, and promotion (Ruggie, 1984). These laws undercut the supremacy of the tripartite wage bargaining structures in Sweden among unions, employers, and the state. While LO was a supporter of women's recruitment into unions, they did not recruit women into the union hierarchies until the 1990s (Mahon, 2002: Hirdman, 1998). However, in the daycare and tax debates, their backing of feminist demands was crucial, as they were the main power block in the Social Democrat Party.

The 1990s: articulating gender in a universalist frame

How gender was articulated in a universalist frame can be mapped through the shifting meanings of equality, and the discourses that surrounded them. In the Swedish language, the word for equality (*jämlikhet*), which was used in the sex-role debates of the 1960s, did not recognize women as a social category with a history of discrimination or disadvantage. Equality meant equal treatment along many dimensions: occupation (white- and blue-collar workers), class, gender, and region (Eduards, 1991). A new concept (*jämställdhet*) emerged in public discourse on gender in the latter part of the 1960s and the 1970s, which distinguished gender/sex inequalities from other inequalities. In effect, the discourse on *jämställdhet* acknowledged gender difference: women and men should have equal positions even though they were not the same due to physical differences and sex-role socialization (Florín and Nilsson, 1999). *Jämställdhet*, which translates into English as gender equality, literally means equal positions.

How this concept was integrated into social democratic ideology can be gleaned from Olof Palme's 1972 congress speech: Palme defined gender equality in terms of making "women's economic and social conditions become more like men's. Their experiences in working life create a larger practical community between men and women in working life." Equality also meant increasing employment for both men and women and finally it meant changing attitudes about male and female tasks in the home and a sharing of the division of work at home. Women were to be encouraged to increase their activity in politics and unions but they were not meant to alter the constellations of power. Palme saw women's struggles as part of the labor movement's struggle for a just society, and had claimed that women in the movement viewed it that way themselves (Palme, 1972). During the Golden Age of the welfare state, gender equality was engrafted into the model of the worker citizen.

Different actors decoded the concept of *jämställdhet* differently in the universalist citizenship frame. Its evolution can be traced in two government commissions on power: one on democracy and power in the mid-1980s and one on the division of economic power between men and women in the mid-1990s. Both linked gender equality to recognition and redistribution and challenged the false universalism in gender neutral policies (Hirdman, 1987; Hernes, 1988; SOU, 1997).[2] Most importantly the shifting meanings of *jämställdhet* reflected the power and agency of feminists to represent themselves as a women's constituency to articulate a politics of recognition.

In the 1980s and 1990s, feminists began to reclaim *jämställdhet* with an inflection of power: power to represent women's interests and power to influence policy outcomes. They also broadened its terrain to include spheres of power outside the labor market: power in the family and power to combat violence against women, sexual harassment in the workplace (Gustafsson et al., 1997), and prostitution (Svänström, 2003).

There were formidable constraints against gendered recognition struggles in Sweden. First, it was hard to make claims around gender inequalities since it was argued that Sweden was the most women-friendly society in the Western world (Acker, 1992). Second, class was still the privileged discourse and although women were recognized as workers and as parents, they were not recognized as a social category in policy nor as a distinct constituency in institutionalized politics.

The 1990s witnessed a flowering of organizations on both local and regional levels that embraced a range of issues: health, education, bodily integrity, participation, and representation, which appealed to a broad spectrum of women (Gustafsson et al., 1997).

Mobilization of women's constituency took the form of loosely coordinated organizations that were represented in the public arena as a network that called themselves the Support Stockings, a multilayered symbol. It expressed the strategy of the group to support women in politics – in political parties and policy-making roles. It brought together images of bluestockings, upper-class feminists of the late nineteenth century, and the redstockings of the 1970s (Stark, 1997), which reflected the support from women in both Left and Conservative Parties. The slogan that emerged in the campaign encapsulated both claims for recognition and redistribution: "HALF THE POWER: ALL THE PAY." Swedish feminists made explicit how these dimensions could not be decoupled from one another in a universalistic framing of rights. They also reflected a growing awareness among feminist groups that, during a period of welfare state retrenchment and rising unemployment, recognition politics was crucial for protecting women's gains.

To recognize gender as distinct from class, that women's interests differed from men's, was to challenge Social Democratic hegemony and the blue-collar union's influence in party politics on several levels. First, it called into question the very basis of universalism in policy and discourse, which took for granted that redressing class inequalities would redistribute society's resources in the most equitable way. The framework of universalism embraced the idea that the exclusion of individuals in social categories (women and immigrants) would be included. Finally, to break ranks in the Social Democratic Party was to undermine the highly disciplined party structure – unruly discourses were nipped in the bud at party congresses and consensus was the norm.

Women did not form a separate party, but their strategic discourse enabled them to boost women's voice in policies and policy-making. In comparison to other Western welfare states, Sweden has had a high representation of women in parliament. The immediate catalyst for Swedish feminist mobilization in the 1990s was a dramatic drop in the proportion of women in parliament, which fell from 37.5 percent to 33.5 percent, in the 1991 election when a Conservative Party coalition took power. In past elections women were put on party lists as one of many interests for which the party set nomination quotas by age, region, youth, etc. Women were given token seats. But after women in the network threatened to form a separate party, the Social Democratic Party in the 1994 election made the decision to alternate women and men on all of their party lists. This meant greater representation in real terms. In the campaign, all parties promoted women candidates, and women not only won back their lost seats but also increased their representation to 41 percent. Half the ministers appointed to the Cabinet in the Social Democratic government are now women (Hobson, 1999).

This is a classic example of a social movement capitalizing on political opportunity. The Social Democratic Party had lost the last election to the Conservative coalition, only the second time in its thirty-year hegemony. Women, who had become dependent on services of the welfare state, had become the mainstay of Social Democratic voters. In this shifting power constellation, Social Democratic women had more power resources to make claims and to mark the boundaries around feminist claims and women's interests.

Boundary-making, authority and power

Carers and worker/carers

Contests over women's identities, as carers vs. workers, came to the fore in the recognition struggles of the 1990s. In the 1960s and 1970s, the ability of women's groups to broker with men in political parties and unions shifted the balance of power towards the parent-worker model. In the 1990s, Social Democratic women had the power resources to defeat a reform introduced by the Conservative coalition, which once again revisited the care allowance debate. The main impetus came from the Christian Democratic Party. Different from the proposals in the 1960s for a care allowance, the current law did not imagine that the benefit would replace public daycare but it would limit its use. In effect, one goal of the reform was the downsizing of the public sector since the benefit was a direct transfer based on the number of hours children were in public daycare. Capitalizing on this discontent, the Conservative coalition elected in 1991 passed a bill for a care allowance.

As we look at the discursive battles around the care allowance, it is important to keep in mind that they took place after two decades of boundary-making had shaped women's identities and interests. In the 1990s, women had reached participation parity in terms of numbers in the labor force, and these women were dependent upon daycare services for their participation as well as their source of employment. The majority were in public sector jobs. As was true in the earlier debates of the 1960s and 1970s, the care-benefit debate revived the issue of freedom of choice. The reform sought to reach the current generation of dual-earner families who wanted to have more flexibility and involvement in their children's care and expressed frustration at the rigidity and bureaucratic rules in the state system (Sundström, 1987; Schlytter, 1993).

Within the parliamentary debates, both in the passage and repeal, issues of redistribution were central. The left parties argued that the care allowance was only for high-income families who could afford to live on one income, that the 1,600 crowns a month was not an alternative for most families who needed two earners (Protokoll 1994/95: 10). The parties on the right countered that the freedom to choose one's type of care was an individual and family issue. Christian Democrats cited studies that showed low-income groups gained the most from the allowance, particularly in municipalities with rising daycare costs (*Protokoll*, 1994/95: 10). Whether the care allowance increased or decreased class inequalities was not the heart of the matter, however. In fact both sides recognized that the care allowance was so meager that few families could afford to lose women's earnings in the family income package.[3]

What was really being contested was which women and groups had the authority to speak for women. In essence this was a recognition struggle among different women claiming to represent women. Both the Christian Democrats and Conservatives challenged the assumption that Social Democratic women spoke for all women: one Christian Democrat claimed that "we politicians can moralize all we want, but that many *young* [my emphasis] women with the double burden long for the possibility to have more time with their children." Another spokesperson from the Conservative Party made the point directly: "Young women choose their own definition of gender equality. Not just women who chose the Social Democratic way of gender equality" (*Protokoll*, 1994/95: 43). The Social Democratic women's defense was that the care allowance threatened the basis of gender equality in Sweden, not just the right to be in the labor market but the possibilities to be a full participant, which was threatened by three, four, or five years of absence from one's job (*Protokoll*, 1994/95: 43). One argument made against the care allowance in the original debate was that it was a strategy to get women out of the labor market at a time of retrenchment and unemployment (*Protokoll*, 1994/95: 7). This was considered a dangerous strategy during a period when jobs were at risk.

The repeal of the care allowance was one of the first orders of business after the re-election of the Social Democrats. For Social Democratic women it was a victory and a recognition of their power resources in the party. It reflected the hegemonic framing of gender in the parent-worker model, and the ways in which the recognition of some feminists shaded out the voices of others. One exception challenging this hegemonic frame of the parent-worker model is the recent widows' pension grassroots mobilization. Widows still receiving pensions (under the pre-1989 law) condemned a policy reform which means-tested their benefit and questioned its rationale, that gender equality policies had made widows' pensions unnecessary. Finding little support from women in political parties, they took their case to the streets (a weekly vigil in front of the parliament) and made a claim against the Swedish government for breach of contract in the European Court of Human Rights.[4] The benefits have been reinstated.

Authority and diversity

Nonrecognition of immigrant and ethnic women

Throughout the 1990s, when feminists flexed their muscles, a gender and power discourse dominated policy and research questions. Yet there was a paucity of research analyzing gender equality issues from immigrant women's perspective. In the Government Commission on gender and economic power in the mid-1990s, only two short articles addressed immigrant women. One focused on the restructuring of industry and the loss of jobs for immigrant women from Southern Europe, Asia, and Africa (Wadensjö, 1997). But no analysis was made of discriminatory practices or the consequences of the high rates of unemployment for immigrant women, where their loss of employment disempowers them in their families and weakens their possibilities to exit untenable marriages. Another study focused on Iranian women and divorce (Darvishpour, 1997), and cultural conflict, which in effect highlighted their otherness, as have earlier studies of immigrants and domestic violence (Elman, 1995).

In Sweden, the problems of minority women have been located in the box of immigrant questions rather than gender issues. One rarely finds immigrant or minority women speaking on a gender equality platform, even as a token immigrant or minority representative. In the last election of 2002, only the Left Party had a visible immigrant/minority profile in the public debates.[5]

The role of immigrants in Swedish society became center stage in the 2002 election, framed in terms of "integration." Should immigrants be required to take language tests for citizenship? But the issue went beyond language to embrace cultural differences of groups residing in Sweden but not "living" within Swedish society. The integration debate was fueled by a recent sensationalized case of a Kurdish woman who was murdered by her father, which was justified by many in her community as a restoration of the family honor, referred to as Heder.[6] She had resisted the practice of a pre-arranged marriage to a Kurdish man, choosing to live with a Swedish man in hiding, and surfacing periodically to politicize the plight of fundamentalist Muslim women. This case unleashed a media debate on the rights and protections of Muslim women, once again reflecting the tendency to characterize immigrants as the "other," defining them as a class of people not integrated into Swedish culture and defying Swedish law and norms (Darvishpour, 2002).

The feminist response to the murder and the plight of such immigrant women also opened up a discourse on women's oppression, which was played out in virtual space.[7] Catalyzing the debate, Left Party leader Gudrun Schyman, took up the issue at her party's congress, affirming that abuse and violence of Muslim women are expressions of the same structures and patterns in Swedish families (Schyman, 2002).[8] This triggered a barrage of emails around culture and cultures, which embodied the framing of gender. The basic question addressed among Swedish feminists revolved around the degree to which Swedish democratic traditions and gender politics provide a measuring stick for other cultures. One minority woman responded, who at the time was living in Canada, a society highly sensitized to multiculturalism and ethnic difference. Making the astute point that there is no universal concept of sisterhood, she did not go to the crux of the problem, however, that ethnic/immigrant women are objects and not subjects in the debate.

State feminism and diversity in claims

In Sweden, gender equality has become highly institutionalized in specific ministries and with policy-making advocates, all working within a framework of the parent-worker citizen. Extra parliamentary groups and grassroots organizations and movements tend to be absorbed, often co-opted by the state. There is a Cabinet minister responsible for equality between men and women, an equal opportunities *Sekretariat*, and a gender equality ombudsman, as well as an independent research commission on equality, *Jämo*, which was created in 1983 to initiate and monitor equal opportunities research in the labor market. Recognition politics has mainly revolved around representation in political and policy-making bodies; the major claim in this campaign was that every other seat should be reserved for a woman. The claims addressing misrecognition have been connected to equality in the labor market or access to jobs. Sexuality, rape, and violence against women have been less visible in the debates, though in the 1990s there was some mobilization around these issues. One of the most prominent campaigns concerned the criminalization of prostitution.[9] What began as a campaign of grassroots feminist organizations pressuring to criminalize the client soon flowed into institutional politics and the discursive battles moved to the parliamentary arena. Women's organizations in all of the political parties, except the Conservative Party, rejected the official government commission report to criminalize prostitutes and supported the criminalization of the client. Bucking their own party leaders, the Social Democratic and Left Party women pushed through the legislation. Once again, this case highlights the way in which feminist politics operates in Sweden, through policy entrepreneurs (femocrats) and women's organizations in the political parties.

   Swedish institutional feminism, often called state feminism, allows us to discern the boundary-making process in recognition struggles – which feminists are recognized is connected to the claim structure (see Figure 8, p. 65), as well as linked to the political opportunities and the discursive resources available. That Swedish recognition struggles have been located in institutionalized feminism has had a threefold effect on women's mobilizing and collective identity formation. There is little political space left for grassroots feminism, which one scholar analyzing gender equality in Sweden, mistakenly interpreted as feminism without feminists (Gelb, 1989). Institutionalized feminism within a universalist claim has translated into less diversity in claimants and claims. This has produced hegemonic representations of women's identities, which define the path to emancipation in terms of paid work. It has meant less diversity in claimants, shading out experiences of immigrant and minority women (Mulinari, 2001) and lesbian women (Rosenberg, 2000).

Ireland

Citizenship frames and policy logics

Two key definitions of Irishness emerged in the early period of nation building, which were codified in the 1937 Constitution. Catholic nationalism and familialism were fused in the construction of the family, "the moral institution forming the necessary basis of social order" (quoted in Eileen Connelly, 1999: 76). Divorce,[10] contraception, and abortion were interpreted as challenging the Constitutional protections of the family. Ireland continues to hold one of the most stringent anti-abortion laws. Gender distinctiveness was coded into the Constitution, expressed in two articles that affirmed the centrality of different gender roles in the family for the Irish national project. "In particular the state recognizes that by *her life within the home* [italics added], the woman gives to the state a support without which the common good cannot be achieved." It is important to note that it is a woman's "life" and not her work in the home that is referred to, which in effect naturalizes the woman's function as mother and homemaker (Meaney, 1991). The Constitution explicitly defined the parameters of women's contribution, by stating that women's employment outside the home should be discouraged: "The state shall therefore endeavor to ensure that mothers shall not be obliged by economic necessity to engage in labor to the neglect of their duties in the home" (*Bunreacht NA Heireann*, 1937: Articles 40.1 and 41.2).

The Constitution, attacked as being retrograde by socialists and Republican women who had fought for independence, was ardently defended by the Irish President, De Valera: "I do not think that the words 'equality and inequality' can properly be applied to the (sexes). Each has its own particular and important role to play, just like a back or forward in a football team. Men and women are complementary to each other in society, working out in their own particular spheres the parts for which they are best fitted" (quoted in Reid, 1988: from *Dail* debates De Valera, vol. 67, 1938).

Certain theorists of post-colonial societies argue that the history of colonization is a history of de-masculinization. Colonial powers identify their subjects as passive, incapable of self-government, passionate and unruly (Nandy, 1983; Fletcher, 2001). Nandy reasons that subject people compensate for this history by asserting a traditionally masculine role of power, in which gender roles are strictly differentiated in order to empower male subjects. Meaney (1991: 232–33) analyzes the sexual conservatism of post-independent Ireland from this perspective.

Gender distinctiveness permeated the construction of civil law. Up until the Married Women's Status Act in 1957, women had no rights in the family (Jackson, 1993). The relegation of women to "life" in the home went beyond discouraging women from paid employment, embracing many facets of public life. A wife could not make contracts; her income was considered to be her husband's for purposes of taxation, and she had no rights to share in his income or property. The husband was the legal guardian of the child. A man could disinherit his wife and children, though the wife could not do the same (Anne Connelly, 1993). Property ownership took for granted that the family was a unit of shared interests with a male breadwinner at the helm. The protection for private property ensured by the Constitution denied married women's access to property ownership in marriages and continues to do so in regards to the family farm.[11]

Ireland epitomizes the gender differentiated policy logic around paid and unpaid work. Women were embedded in the system as wives, but not necessarily as mothers unattached to husbands. Not until 1973–74 was there any recognition of, or redistributive policies that addressed the needs of, unmarried, separated, or deserted wives (divorce was not legal in Ireland until 1996). No state provisions for motherhood existed outside the male-breadwinner household. Those women who did not fit the model had to rely on family and friends (Galligan, 1998; Yeates, 1997).

The role of women as homemakers as framed in the Constitution assumed that a women's labor market undermined the family. In the 1920s, married women were barred from public sector employment and a decade later they were excluded from many industrial sectors, policies that also reflected a concern for protecting men's male-breadwinner status during hard economic times (Eileen Connelly, 1999). These policies were in force until 1973, when the government was forced to change the law in order to apply for EU membership.[12]

Claim structures and the family

Feminists organizing to speak for women tend to be less problematic in recognition struggles within gender distinctive frameworks than in universalistic ones since it is already assumed that women are a category with separate identities and interests. However, feminists often must battle with conservative groups of women claiming to represent women. Moreover, they have to find a discursive frame that does not naturalize women's difference. In the following cases, we can see how different individual women and groups sought to exploit the framing of gender difference in law and policy.

Given the prominence of the family as the upholder of social order, it is not surprising that claims for women without male breadwinners were not recognized in policy. Beginning with radical feminist groups in the 1970s, such as Chains of Change, and later liberal feminists in AIM (Action Information Motivation), there have been concentrated campaigns for benefits for women who were excluded from family law. But rather than affirming women's right to form autonomous households or right to exit untenable marriages, the policies that emerged were aimed at shoring up a system of benefits constructed around women's dependency on a male breadwinner (McLaughlin and Yeates, 1999; Galligan, 1998). Unmarried mother's allowance, unmarried mother's benefit, single woman's allowance, and prisoner's wife allowance in one sense represented a break with the past in which women's welfare was assumed to derive from a husband's situation. Still, the basic principle underlying these women-only benefits was to reinforce the notion of familialism by providing for the exceptions, that is, women lacking a male breadwinner.

Attempts to alter the Constitution (Articles 41.1 and 41.2) have engaged many feminists since its passage. However, women seeking to extend their civil and social rights have used these articles as a framework for making claims. Take, for example, a 1973 case that paved the way for more liberal contraceptive use. Mary McGee, a twenty-nine-year-old wife with four children who had experienced many complications in pregnancy, ordered a spermicidal jelly by post. Rather than claim that her inability to have access to contraceptives would threaten her life, her lawyers made the case that by not permitting her to import contraceptives the fear of further pregnancies would make it impossible for her to have full marital relations. The judge in this case recognized this as a valid claim and alluded to the Constitutional protection of the family and marriage (Alpha Connelly, 1999: 25).

Two court cases challenging unequal treatment of married women in tax law and in social security employed the justification of protection of the family more directly. In one case (*Hyland v. Minister*), a woman challenged the law that denied wives unemployment benefits. Here, the lawyers argued that the state favored cohabiting couples relative to married couples and hence undermined the protection of family in the Constitution. The state's attorney countered that a social welfare code should not make the financial position of the working wife, when compared to the wife that stays at home, so attractive as to encourage mothers to take up outside work to the neglect of their work in the home. However, the Court ruled that the law discriminated against married couples (Reid, 1988: 40–43). Similarly, in an earlier case, *Murphy v. Attorney General*, a dual-earner married couple claimed that the joint income tax law disfavored married couples. The Court once again ruled that cohabiting couples should not receive preferential treatment in taxation, saying that it undermined the marital family (Reid, 1988: 40–43).

These cases, which led to a formal acknowledgment of cohabiting couples – non-marital relationships in policy and law – nevertheless did not recognize women as earners in their own right. Rather, the change in the law sought to protect marriage, as seen in the changes devised after this ruling, which not only permitted income splitting among dual-earner married couples, but included single-earner families. These cases benefited married women working outside the home, but did not disturb the notion of women's social function and nonrecognition of women outside the family unit (Reid, 1998: 43).

In 1996, the government created a Constitutional Review Group to consider altering the Constitution and construction of the family was seen as a crucial area. They specifically asked whether the sections on women's special role in the family should be removed from the Irish Constitution. While admitting that the Constitutional formulas relegating women to the home in their "domestic role and as wives" were outdated and did not provide women in the home with any entitlements, the Constitutional Review Committee did not, however, recommend eliminating the article. Rather, the group proposed a gender-neutral formula that still "recognizes that home and family life gives to society a support without which the common good cannot be achieved" (Constitutional Review Group, 1996: 335). Instead of wives, the state should endeavor to support persons caring for others within the home. Considering the interrelationship between claims and frames, it is noteworthy that Ireland is the country that scores highest on traditional gender roles in the family among European countries. In 1997, two fifths of women were in favor of women not having a job (O'Connor, 1998: 142).

Recognition struggles

The ideological compact between the Catholic Church and the state produced a set of laws, institutions, and discourses on caring, reproduction, and familialism that perpetuated a consensual view of womanhood. It left little discursive or political opportunities for frontal challenges (O'Connor, 1998). Though there were women's organizations in the decades after independence (the largest being the Irish Women's Housewives Association), they had small constituencies and were politically marginalized. Aptly, one Irish scholar of women's movements refers to this as the "period of abeyance" (Linda Connelly, 2002).

Nearly all accounts of the Irish women's movement focus on two key events in the late 1960s and early 1970s, one of whose impetus came from an international forum, while the other emerged from a cafe in Dublin, the base for a local action group which helped to launch the Irish Women's Liberation Movement.

A group of long-term Irish feminists who were active in the International Housewives Association, with international links, took up the 1967 United Nations directive issued to NGOs to create official national organizations to lobby governments for gender equality. The Irish section was composed of groups of business and professional women who called a meeting of all women's organizations in Ireland and formed a committee to investigate the status of women in 1968. The report, containing forty-nine recommendations concerned with discrimination against women in employment, taxation, social welfare, law, and public life (Galligan, 1998: 40–45), was presented to the Prime Minister. This led to a national governmental task force and the creation of a Commission on the Status of Women. A crucial demand was the claim for participation in the political process, which mandated permanent funding for an organization recognized as representing women's interests in government. In 1973, the Council for the Status of Women was formed to monitor the implementation of the recommendations in the commission report and to act as an umbrella organization coordinating women's organizations and claims-making. In 1995, it became an official part of the government with a name change, the National Women's Council of Ireland (Smyth, 1993).

The other event was the publication of a manifesto by a group of radical Dublin feminists called *Chains of Change: The Civil Wrongs of Irish Women.* Their manifesto called for:

One Family, One House; Equal Rights in Law, Equal Pay Now, Removal of the Marriage Bar, Justice for Widows, Deserted Wives and Unmarried Mothers, Equal Educational Opportunities, Contraception a Human Right. (Smyth, 1993: 252)

The focus on the lack of rights women had in the family and household responded to constraints in the gender distinctive frame. But the chains also referred to the silence around body politics, particularly contraception and abortion – the challenge for feminists to speak the unspeakable. Alongside claims for equal treatment in education and wages were claims for "recognition of motherhood and parenthood as a social function with special provisions" (see preamble in Smyth, 1993: 258). Throughout the 1970s, autonomous feminist groups held mass meetings and pickets, and repertoires of political actions were aimed at making visible the marginalization, disrespect, and misrecognition of women in Irish society. The most confrontational was the contraceptive train in which feminists en masse purchased condoms in Belfast. They walked through customs waving banners and chanting, in open defiance of the ban on the sale and advertising of contraceptives, an action that more moderate women's rights groups sought to distance themselves from (Linda Connelly, 2002: 120–21).

The Irish women's liberation movement of the 1970s receded, and was replaced by a diffusion of organizations on different issues, including rape, domestic violence, and lesbian rights. Feminist politics moved into more institutionalized settings through the legitimacy of the National Women's Council of Ireland; mainstreaming gender and lobbying have become their main strategies. One interpretation of the mainstreaming gender strategy is that it was a response to the anti-feminist, highly orchestrated successful campaign in 1983 to introduce a specific anti-abortion amendment in the Irish Constitution (Linda Connelly, 2002: 168–69). But not to be forgotten in an analysis of the mainstreaming of feminist politics is the role of the EU, offering legitimacy to national institutionalized feminist actors as well resources for local community-based projects.[13]

Brokerage: supranational allies and windows of political opportunity

If we consider the role of international and supranational institutions in recognition struggles, these cases differ. In Sweden, the EU has been seen as a threat to women's social and participatory rights, since the male-breadwinner wage shaped the policy landscape of many member states. There was a visible gender gap in the higher proportions of women opposed to EU membership in the 1990s referendum vote for membership (Hobson, 2000a). For Ireland, the EU has provided an alternative frame for gender equality claims-making and for challenging the hegemony of the male-breadwinner wage. It has also been a source of leverage politics for body rights.

Gender equality has been accepted as a norm in EU discourse and been acknowledged in law and policy, but both the implementation of the first articles on equal pay in the Treaty of Rome and the passage of the Equality Directives were recognition struggles in themselves, of mobilized women's constituencies, feminist actors lobbying, and pressure groups (Hoskyns, 1996). When analyzing gender equality in the EU, it is important to keep in mind that the basic rationale for including a gender equality clause was to prevent social dumping, that is moving companies to countries where there is low-waged female labor (Hobson, 2000a). Moreover, the market frame of EU law, to promote the free flow of capital, goods, services, and labor, actually shaded out many areas of claims-making around gender equality. Four decades later, the rewriting of gender equality in the Amsterdam Treaty alongside the attachment of structural funds to mainstreaming of gender in policies reflects the relentless efforts of national and supranational feminist actors in lobbying and power brokering (Helfferich and Kolb, 2001). In the 1990s, enforcement of EU gender equality law became easier and women's groups had more leverage to challenge recalcitrant states and employers.

As the evolution of EU law and policy on gender equality reveals, mobilized constituencies at the national level are crucial. They are also essential for ensuring that EU law is implemented (Hoskyns, 1996). Ireland has consistently dragged its feet in implementing EU directives. Rather than imposing change, EU law legitimated, made visible, and in some cases were the power brokers that tipped the balance in gender equality struggles.

In the early struggles over equal pay, EU policy-makers were reluctant brokers. The implementation of the Equal Pay Directive in Ireland was threatened by the negative feedback from craft unions and employers who complained that it would be too costly. With the opposition of two social partners, the Irish government began to get cold feet and sought a derogation from the EU to delay implementation (Galligan, 1998: 86).

A broad coalition of feminists (trade union women and feminists in the Industrial Union) mobilized. Representatives of the National Irish Women's Council on Equality went to Strasbourg to plead their case to the Commissioner for Social Affairs, Patrick Hillary. This resulted in a study group being sent to Ireland to meet with all of the groups including a united women's lobby. The study group recommended refusal of derogation. Through the authority of the EU, the Irish government was forced to implement the Anti-Discrimination Pay Act. However, it was mobilized groups of women that brokered with EU bureaucrats (Galligan, 1998: 72).

The Irish government's response to EU Gender Equality Directives (equal treatment in social security, social benefits, and parental leave) has also been one of passive resistance, which is evident in the long delays in implementation. Implementing the Social Security Directive, the government dragged its feet for years, despite a six-year lead time for all member states. Regarding social assistance, the government sought to circumvent equal treatment. As with social security, social assistance assumed the male-breadwinner logic; benefits were paid to a man regardless of whether his wife had paid work or not. Children were dependants of their father in the social security law, even if he were not the main earner in the family. Interestingly, when this equal treatment principle was applied to Irish families, the state introduced legislation to bypass the law, arranging for a transitional payment between 10 and 20 Irish pounds per week to be paid to the male breadwinner whose income had been reduced, which in effect was the adult dependant allowance men had lost and women were not entitled to (Coakley, 1997). When women successfully challenged this lack of equal treatment under the EU guidelines (they won the right to the transitional benefit),[14] the payment was discontinued. The EU Parental Leave Directive (here again, Ireland was the last country to implement the legislation) has entitled parents to fourteen weeks leave, but it is unpaid leave.[15] Nor has Ireland responded with any real policy response to the EU recommendations for developing daycare facilities, which is part of a general set of guidelines in EU policy on rec-onciling work and family life. Nevertheless, in 1999 the EU requirement that all countries develop an annual employment action plan resulted in the strengthening of gender equal opportunity polices (O'Connor, 1999).

In issues of body politics, the EU's role is complex and reflects the limitations and advantages of the market-derived claim structure. For example, the EU Court rejected a petition by Irish students who were barred from disseminating information about abortion, ruling that the students had no economic partnership with abortion providers and there-fore their claim lay outside its jurisdiction (Judith Taylor, 1999). Yet a counseling service, the Open Door, has argued that informing clients about abortions in other countries is a service/commodity protected by EU law (Fletcher, 2000).

The EU response to contests over abortion in Ireland highlights the difficulty of social movement groups brokering with a supranational in-stitution dependent on the support of a national government. This is ob-vious in the moves and countermoves between Irish conservative forces, the feminist community, and the European Community. Throughout the 1980s, the European Parliament put forward a resolution that constituted abortion as a "normal practice," and recommended that women not be forced to travel to other countries for abortion services (Judith Taylor, 1999: 207). Fearful of the influence of the EU, in 1983 the Catholic Church and many politicians successfully launched an anti-abortion ref-erendum that made abortion illegal in the Irish Constitution (instead of law that had been inherited from the British Constitution). The Irish law was more restrictive in that it denied women the right to travel to other countries for an abortion or the right to provide information on abortion services in other countries. To ensure that Ireland would not be forced to alter its abortion law in light of the Maastricht Treaty pending in 1993–94, the Irish Prime Minister negotiated a special clause in the treaty that allowed Irish law on abortion to be protected from any EU directives surrounding abortion rights.

The wall of protection shattered in 1992 after the High Court ruled that a fourteen-year-old rape victim and her family were not permitted to leave Ireland (referred to as Case X), since the girl was seeking an abortion in England. The day after the High Court's ruling, there was a groundswell of censure from the EU Parliament, and from member states, including Sweden, the Netherlands, the UK, Germany, and France. The

Swedish king cancelled his visit to Ireland. The Dutch parliament raised the possibility of bringing a case against Ireland in violation of human rights. The Committee on Women's Rights of the European Parliament wrote a letter to President Mary Robinson. Newspapers around Europe portrayed Ireland as backward looking and out of step with Europe. One Dutch newspaper put in succinctly: "Is Ireland given its archaic abortion laws, worthy of being a member of the European Community?" (Taylor, 1999). This discourse touched a sensitive chord in Ireland and a way out had to be found. Ten days later, the Irish Supreme Court found such a loophole, that the denial of the right to travel for the abortion was a threat to the girl's life, who might commit suicide.

As the EU has had no jurisdiction over the right to an abortion, the pressure brought to bear from European nation states, the EU parliament, and transnational feminist groups was indirect, what Keck and Sikkink (1998) have called leverage politics. After Case X, liberal advocates of choice and feminist groups were able to mobilize opinion for a referendum that removed the ban on travel and abortion information services. The defeat of the Irish anti-abortion referendum in 2002, which sought to close the loophole that the Supreme Court had opened, not only reflects the weakening of the Catholic Church in steering Irish politics, but also the confidence of feminists who have gained a foothold in the policy-making structure of government.

Authority/diversity

Since the mid-1980s, institutionalized feminism has become more and more dominant in Ireland, though grassroots feminism has existed alongside it. An example of a successful grassroots campaign was that of the lesbian feminist groups who managed to decriminalize homosexuality in 1995 (Linda Connelly, 2002: 189). According to Galligan (1998), the feminist movement has been characterized by diversity, but there has been consensus and a dialogue across institutional and autonomous feminism.

But clearly the tendency is towards mainstreamed institutional feminism. The inclusion of the Council on the Status of Women as an official body in the government has meant formal recognition, that women are a social category with specific interests (Galligan, 1998: 60–63). The growing importance of the Council as the body representing women's interests has, in effect, vested the discursive power and policy-making influence of grassroots organizations into an institutional forum. Created as a co-ordinating organization for women's groups in 1980 seeking to redress gender discrimination, the Council's executive board has accumulated more power as the number of organizations has grown (there are eighty-two organizations that send delegates to open meetings).

Has the increased authority of institutionalized feminism meant less diversity? Though a privileged set of actors, the executive board of the Council must still answer to affiliate organizations (Fitzsimmons, 1991). Thus there has been more political space for diverse positions and issues than in Swedish feminism. Groups representing Traveler women's rights, such as Pavee Point, lesbian feminist groups, and organizations advocating disability rights are included in the Council's member organizations. Still, the process of boundary-making around feminist claims operates by the very fact that those who join the Council tend to be in more structured organized associations. Alternatively, the need to appeal to a broad-based coalition of feminists, progressives, and trade-union groups has meant that the Council tends to develop agendas that seek to achieve maximum consensus.

The election of Mary Robinson as President gave new legitimacy to feminism in Irish politics. Though it is a post without power – the President is a figurehead – her position was infused with symbolic power, as she embraced a politics of womanhood in opposition to the conservative vision of an Irish woman (Evelyn Mahon, 1995). Most importantly, she played the critical role in ordering a second Commission on the Status of Women, twenty years after the first. The report covered a range of policy arenas: politics, sport, education, and the labor market, as well policy categories: women in the home, women at work, women in situations of disadvantage. Beyond the actual recommendations, what is significant about the report is its establishment of principles which reveal the diversity of claims in recognition struggles. In the key objectives section of the report, it is clearly stated that women "should be facilitated to develop economic independence based on equal opportunity, mutual support, and equal partnership of men and women" (Second Commission on the Status of Women, 1993: 7). Throughout the document there is an implicit critique of the male-breadwinner norm. Nevertheless, carework is recognized as part of the emancipatory project, as can be seen in the framing of distinctive gendered claims. In the section on women and the home, the experts note that while motherhood receives a great deal of lip service from society, there is little recognition for women's work in the home. As a homemaker, she has no income and the value of her worth is "contingent on her partner's goodwill." The solution proposed that all income in a family be jointly owned as well as property be divided equally appears utopian given the status and privilege of men's property rights (1993: 72).

The problems of Irish Traveler women were considered in the Second Commission report: their poverty, bad housing, and violence towards them. There was even a special report by a national committee studying violence against women, which highlighted the needs of Traveler women. But what has not been considered are the ways in which race and ethnicity are deeply interwoven in the Constitutional constructions of gender distinctiveness (familialism) and Irishness as a national identity (Lentin, 1998).

Boundary-making through the EU policy mirror

Has the EU affected the boundary-making of Irish women's recognition struggles? The EU as a crucial actor and broker in Irish feminist politics has altered the politics of recognition in Ireland, contributing to the privileging of some groups over others. Educated and professional women's groups have been able to use the EU fora for extending rights. The equal treatment principle has increased the resources of women in paid work, particularly those in full-time paid work (as seen in the changes in the laws regarding pensions and unemployment insurance), but provides few protections for women who are unemployed or in temporary or marginal part-time work (Gardiner, 1999: 51). This has not led to a recognition of women's access to paid work, in terms of a lack of daycare services and parental leave with pay, both of which adversely affect working-class women's access to paid work. Moreover, some of the changes in social security and pension benefits have resulted in a weaker economic position for poor and working-class women. Geoffrey Cook and Anthony McCashin (1997) maintain that the women's movement and other pressure groups did not address the problems surrounding these redistributive issues that arose in the 1980s with the EU directives on equal treatment in wages, promotion, training, and pensions. One did not hear any debate on gender equity in the system or the effects on different groups of women. Working-class women fared the worst in the new system, particularly dependent wives upon divorce or the death of the breadwinner (Cook and McCashin, 1997). Finally, the economic miracle of the Celtic Tiger has meant a dramatic increase in Irish women's labor market participation, but many working-class women are in part-time, insecure jobs.

Conclusion

There is a vast body of comparative welfare state research on redistribution, analyzing different institutional contexts and policy regimes. Variations in wages, occupational structures, pensions, unemployment insurance, and education form the basis of typologies, reflected in the degree of stratification in society and the full-time worker's dependence on the market (Korpi and Palme, 1998; Esping-Andersen, 1990). Scholars have gendered these analyses by including other redistributive types of provisions, such as services for the elderly and daycare services, as well as formulated other dimensions that capture women's social citizenship, such as the rights to form an independent household without poverty (Hobson, 1994; Lewis, 1992; Orloff, 1993; Sainsbury, 1996). To be a full member of the community in Marshall's (1950) formula of social citizenship does not necessarily lead to being a peer in social life (Fraser in this volume).

As these two cases illustrate, there is a need for a broader framework for recognition struggles to cover the many dimensions of exclusion that accrue from socially entrenched patterns of disrespect and devaluation in societies. To remedy misrecognition involves strategies for inclusion that enable groups to gain voice and influence in public arenas to recode devalued statutes in law, policy, and practice.

These cases express two different frames for non- and misrecognition; in Sweden, false universalism made invisible gendered devaluation and discrimination; and in Ireland, gender distinctiveness celebrated women's contribution as mothers and wives, while denying them basic, civil, economic, and social rights, which in effect have made them lesser citizens. They also represent two ends of a gender-policy logic in welfare states of individualism and familialism. They are not comparable cases as they have different starting and ending points along the dimensions of recognition and redistribution. My purpose was not to compare them. Rather I want to reveal how institutional contexts shaped gendered claims-making, strategies for inclusion, and political identities.

Swedish feminists in their brokerage with Social Democratic men in their party and unions were able to push through redistributive policies that have increased women's participation parity in education, paid work, and in political representation, as well as increased their agency in family decision-making. In the 1990s, recognition politics became more explicit and feminist actors made the discursive connections between recognition and redistribution in their slogan, "half the power, all the pay": linking power to articulate women's interests and economic justice. Looking at the last election in 2002, we can see that gender equality is recognized in the universe of political discourse, visible in the constellations of power vying for women voters. Not only did every party certify themselves as gender friendly, but each was given a gender equality rating in the newspapers and other publications. In surveys of voters ranking the most important issues, gender equality was placed sixth, ahead of taxes and defense. In the 2002 election, the proportion of women holding parliamentary seats reached 45.3 percent.

The Swedish case exemplifies the best scenario for state feminism. Nevertheless, participation parity does not in itself translate into parity in voice, in decision-making over how a society's resources are distributed, or in influence in different policy spheres. Swedish femocrats have had the most input in constructing family policy and the parent-worker model. However, they lack representation in economic arenas, either in the business sector or in government finance policy sphere. This can be seen in the weak sex-discrimination law in Sweden (Eklund, 1996) and the un-willingness of the state to implement wage equity for women employed in the highly segregated public service sector. The equality ombudsman has lost nearly every case brought before the Labor Court in the last several years, one of which was sent back twice from the European Court for review.[16]

In Ireland, feminist mobilizations and brokerage with EU bureaucrats challenged the familialist gender distinctive frame of Irish law and social policy. EU law has provided a crucial legal and discursive framework to confront the institutionalized male-breadwinner norm in society. How-ever, the EU, even with the carrot of structural funding for Irish economic development, is still a weak brokering partner. Despite the Irish govern-ment's commitment to equality for women in the use of structural funds, only 30 percent of the funds were used for women, minority groups, and the disabled. Lacking a strong base in political parties and unions, Irish feminists are dependent upon mobilized constituencies and transnational lobbies to pressure for change. Brokerage with supranational actors in recognition struggles is still leverage politics, not power resource politics in which women can threaten parties with their votes. Nor does it guar-antee discursive power in the media and other public fora to make visible gender inequalities.

Irish women continue to have one of the lowest proportions of women in paid work in Europe, though over the last decade there has been a dra-matic increase in participatory rates from 42.6 to 53.4 percent. This in-dicates a changing trend, particularly among younger women. Not much headway has been made in increasing the proportions of women in par-liament and municipal governments (currently slightly over 7 percent in parliament). To some extent, Irish women have achieved "a politics of presence" (Phillips, 1995). Most political parties now have established women's units, and women's groups have formed in unions. One could see the inclusion of the National Council of Women in the National Eco-nomic Forum along with the other social partners, as a form of represen-tational parity (Galligan, 1998: 161). Still, the Council of Women does not have the clout or standing that the other social partners do in the corporatist structure of unions, employers, and government in economic policy (O'Connor, 2002).

These two cases are interesting for understanding brokerage and boundary-making processes in shaping power and agency within the politics of recognition, the privileging of some actors, and their claims over others. Although recognition struggles evolved into institutionalized forms of feminism in both these countries, in Ireland there is a broader representation of different groups and a greater diversity in feminist claims (Connolly, 2002). This reflects path dependencies in recognition struggles as well as the brokerage politics among feminists within the National Council of Women in national and supranational terrains.

The fitting of gender equality into the Swedish universalistic frame has meant less diversity in the types of claims that get recognized. The boundary-making in feminism has accorded certain actors policy-making roles to speak for women and certified the hegemonic gender equality ideology, in which paid work is the axis upon which emancipation revolves. The Swedish case brings into focus how the universalistic frame has shaped identities and interests in gendered recognition struggles. It also reveals the exclusionary processes in brokerage and boundary-making; every alliance can be an exclusion.

4   Movements of feminism: the circulation of discourses about women

Susan Gal

Introduction

Social movements regularly demand "recognition" for categories of personhood just as much as they demand "redistribution" of material resources. Despite the current emphasis on respect for identities, economic grievances have continued to be an important element in the claims movements make. Indeed, it is not the broad substance of demands that has changed in contemporary social movements. Rather, there has been a transformation in the social theories and categories through which movements justify themselves. Taken-for-granted terms such as "class," "economics," and "exploitation" have largely given way to a vocabulary of "identity," "culture," and "discrimination." This discursive change in how social movements frame their grievances, understand their goals, and explain their claims deserves attention in its own right.[1]

To understand shifts in forms of justification, one must study the rhetoric and discursive practices of social movements: how they create persuasive arguments and remake political subjectivities. Importantly, the way a movement justifies itself is not the product of local conditions alone. It depends, in part, on the cross-national distribution of discourses in texts. Such texts are disseminated by mass media, by the spread of political practices, and through the travels of activists who might also be labor migrants, scholars, journalists, or tourists. The circulation of texts is not a straightforward matter of production, transmission, and reception. Nor does it follow the systematic patterns of more familiar "flows" such as those that have been suggested for the movements of capital, commodities, and people in transnational circuits. Rather, I argue that the process of extricating texts from one set of sociohistorical contexts and presenting them for interpretation elsewhere occurs through a complex of institutional and organizational practices hinging on *translation*. Translation itself is a multilayered phenomenon, consisting of specific social relations and multiple semiotic processes that mediate the movement of "ideas," creating the conditions of possibility for political action. It constrains the likelihood of success in cross-linguistic and transnational political alliances.

By focusing on translation, my aim in this chapter is to propose a different approach to recognition struggles and social movements than is currently common in the social sciences. Neither a case study nor a comparative analysis, my proposal relies on tracing the movement of texts across regions and linguistic boundaries. To provide an example of how and why one should study the circulation of texts in this way, I focus here on debates about women and "feminism" in East Central Europe. This will illustrate how categories of political subjectivity that enable action – here, specifically, the nature, rights, and place of men and women – circulate around the globe in textual form. I start with a brief outline of the theoretical inspirations for this project and a short discussion of the region itself. Three central sections follow. Their aim is to provide a framework for analyzing "translation," "recontextualization," and "further circulation" in such a way as to grasp their political effects.

Because translation is an academic and business enterprise with its own social relations and political economy, my analysis starts with the organizations and institutions in which translations occur. In this region, as elsewhere, a large labor force is involved, including journalists, state-employed watchdogs, censors, reviewers, publishers, editors, monolingual academics, reading publics, and accountants estimating likely sales. Non-governmental organizations (NGOs) constitute another venue for translation that contrasts with the business model.

In addition to social relations, I suggest that it is equally important to specify the textual practices of translation. These include the means by which writers and translators make a history for the moving texts, creating for them a sense of "foreignness" or "localness" in their new contexts, and placing them within other politically relevant categories. The sections of this chapter devoted to "recontextualization" and "further circulation" examine the ways in which texts are often paired with political practices, and how they are made to "fit" into new contexts that differ from their earlier ones not only in the political institutions and categories in play, but also in their literary and rhetorical traditions, and their reigning assumptions about the role of language in politics. When texts move, both text and context are transformed. The movement of texts frequently precipitates heated debate. The circulation of texts can contribute to establishing the authority of novel arguments and to legitimating the political subjectivities associated with them.

The current debates about feminism in East Central Europe (many of my examples will be drawn from Hungary) provide intriguing instances of these phenomena because this is a historical case of political categories in

the making. Texts associated with these debates – as well as people interested in re-establishing woman-centered social movements – have been
making their way into and out of the region with renewed energy since the
official end of communism in 1989. Although there are numerous small
women's groups with a variety of aims, the label "feminist" is often publicly ridiculed and widely rejected; there is little popular support for the
idea of "women" (*qua* women, rather than, say, as mothers) as legitimate
political actors. My goal is not to join those lamenting the supposed lack
of feminism in East Central Europe.[2] Rather, it seems to me that these
lively debates, accompanied by the presence of cross-regional networks of
activists, present a valuable opportunity to theorize the discursive aspects
of transnational politics.

Conceptual starting points

In order to examine feminism as a traveling discourse, I draw on two
kinds of research: sociopolitical writings about social movements and
the study of the texts-in-context characteristic of linguistic anthropology.
Their integration is necessary for the form of investigation I propose.

Despite important contributions that analyze resource mobilization,
framing, and opportunity structures, most studies of social movements
have not addressed cross-national interactions. For instance, histories of
women's movements have usually studied a single country or have compared the contrasting circumstances of movements in a small group of
countries; they have not focused on links between movements. Another
body of research has tracked the relationship between the activities of
women's movements and the formation of welfare states. Here, family re-
semblances between feminist movements in different nation states have
been noted, but only rarely – mostly in the Scandinavian literature –
has there been attention to alliances and exchanges among them. Post-
colonial critics, by contrast, have been attuned to the relationship between
women's organizations in different parts of the world, and to describing
the obstacles faced by any attempt to create international feminist movements. But they mostly focus on reciprocal imaginings by and about
women across colonial boundaries and between metropole and post-
colony. They rarely analyze organizational links and the movement of
texts.[3]

Those studying NGOs and transnational advocacy networks have been
more directly concerned with the spread or "flow" of what they term
"ideas." Political activism across the borders of nation states has gained
scholarly attention in part because it has increased in volume in recent
decades, but it is not a new phenomenon. The international movement

for woman suffrage in the nineteenth century operated across the European continent, the USA, and other regions. It followed the organizational model of abolitionism, and with some of the same religious inspiration, recruitment strategies, and personnel. Today's networks for women's rights, for environment protection, and against domestic violence operate in similar ways but with considerably faster communication technology. In outlining how such international networks succeed (or fail) to change the internal policies of nation states, Keck and Sikkink rightly emphasize the importance of "... the relationship between the ideas advocacy networks help to diffuse and the domestic contexts in which these ideas do or do not take hold" (1998: 72).[4] Yet terms like "diffusion" or "flow," which are widely used to characterize the globalization of ideas and of political activity, wrongly presuppose the easy intertranslatability of political categories. They give no empirical purchase on the notion of "idea" – how we might recognize or precisely track one. They gloss over the changes that such "ideas" often undergo as a result of travel, and have not tackled the social and semiotic processes that are necessary for circulation to happen.

To conceptualize these processes more precisely I take inspiration from the Bakhtinian insight that we cannot speak except with words already inhabited by others and later taken up by others. A central property of language is its ability to be chunked, disengaged from its current environment only to be quoted, parodied, alluded to, cited, ventriloquized, or in other ways reinserted elsewhere. It is here that the notions of discourse and text – as used within current research in linguistic anthropology – can be fruitfully employed. "Texts" are defined here as segments of discourse that are potentially detachable from their co-occurring social and cultural surround. As such, texts can be embedded in other contexts – "recontextualized" – and hence they can circulate spatially, temporally, and across social, political, and linguistic boundaries. Conceptualizing circulation in this way allows us to investigate with more precision what, in less linguistically-oriented research, is loosely called the movement of "ideas." Texts, defined in this way, need not be written, but when they are turned into writing and disseminated by mass media, they become "text-artifacts" – books, articles, advertisements – that provide good examples and convenient points of departure for analysis.[5]

A chunk of discourse (a text), when quoted, paraphrased, summarized – in short, recontextualized – is thereby put into conversation and competition with other voices or drowned out by other voices that were not earlier relevant to it. Yet speakers can make sure that the earlier context leaves its mark, a trace of where the text has been. The gap between the earlier context and the newer – the earlier form of the text and a later (always partial) repetition or imitation of it – can be highlighted or denied, can be valorized or denigrated. These are ways of handling "inter-textuality," that is, the relationship between texts. By different interpreta-tions of such intertextual links, texts can be made to seem unprecedented and "new," or as continuations and "revivals" of other texts and tra-ditions. Similarly, but this time in the dimension of space rather than time, they can be considered familiarly domestic and "ours," or imports and therefore alien. Clearly, each of these designations carries specific valuations and political meanings in particular sociohistorical circum-stances. The construction of the effect of newness or oldness, of familiar-ity or foreignness always depends on existing presuppositions (what have been called "language ideologies") that connect political categories with assumptions about the nature of language.

The context into which a text is introduced consists in part of insti-tutions and organizations, as social movement research has shown. Any text-artifact requires a large cast of characters for its dissemination, in-cluding publishing houses, broadcast institutions, academic networks, language teaching, and state subventions. When texts are made relevant to politics, all these social actors and the institutions in which they work create the conditions of possibility for social movements. But context is also, in large part, made of other texts and sign phenomena. Reviews, syn-opses, allusions, citations are often as influential in making a text widely known as the availability of the full work itself. Furthermore, text and context are relative terms. Which set of signs is taken to be the "text" for purposes of analysis depends at least in part on which signs are cur-rently the focus of analysts' and actors' attention. As implied by this brief outline, both texts and contexts change in the course of movement.

Intertextuality is constructed even within named languages and within single political fields. But when texts are transferred across languages and fields there are extra steps involved. Translation is a particular form of circulation that is usually accompanied by culturally specific assump-tions defining what constitutes translation, what it is for, and when it is necessary. In analyzing the practice and ideology of translation, it is useful to start with the transfer of denotation from one named language to another. But for my purposes here, the more interesting aspects of translation involve the transfer – and sometimes the creation in the new language – of stylistic effects, textual allusions, and genre conventions. These pragmatic transfers are the means by which the intertextual effects of continuity and rupture, discussed above, are created in translations. Indeed, through such pragmatic transfers translators evoke and can in part create within the target language the rhetorical, literary, or philo-sophical traditions to which a text aspires to belong. As Pannwitz noted long ago, the receiving language is itself changed by translation, indeed any translator should allow "his language to be powerfully affected by the foreign tongue" (Pannwitz, 1917, cited in Benjamin, 1968: 80). In translation, as in intertextual links generally, transfers can be interpreted as overcoming the difference between texts, linking them and thus making parallel versions. Alternatively, under other circumstances – and in the context of other ideologies of language – translation can be understood as highlighting the difference between source and target. Paradoxically, translation allows a language to include foreign materials "within" itself, thereby domesticating them. But this can involve the implicit signaling of the material's foreignness, and thus of its cultural distance.[6]

Intertextuality gains particular significance when the texts concern social movements that define their struggles in terms of their histories. In such cases, proposing an "origin" for a text – either temporally or spatially – is already a political act. Claims to illustrious ancestors can accrue prestige and power, but legitimacy is undermined if the ancestors are impugned. As Tsing (1997) has reminded us, feminism is a case in point: it can be weakened when its predecessors are discredited. This has happened in some parts of the world by claims that feminism is of "Western" origin and thus supposedly speaks only to white, Western, middle-class women. Rather than searching for the ultimate origins of feminism, Tsing suggests, we should ask how the debates of feminism – a movement whose multiple origins in anti-imperial, anti-colonial, and nationalist movements are easily demonstrated – have so often come to be seen as (only and mainly) "Western." She joins others in arguing that social movements need not rely on the ontological sameness of participants, nor on recognition of existential sameness in their experiences. Rather, recruitment, mobilization, and organization depend in part on the creation and circulation of politically usable categories and locally persuasive arguments for alliance. By studying such circulation we gain the advantage of being deliberately agnostic about origin, and writing, instead, a self-conscious genealogy of feminisms in motion – understanding such a history to be itself a discursive act with political consequences.[7]

Background: contacts between "East" and "West"[8]

Since the fall of communism in 1989 there have been numerous articles in social science journals and presentations at international conferences in which East Central European scholars who are women explain to American audiences why they are not feminists (see Havelková, 1997; Marody, 1993; Šiklová, 1997). Simultaneously, other East Central European scholars have insisted that despite the ridicule and misunderstanding they are subjected to on this account, they really are feminists (Neményi, 1994). Women scholars from East Central Europe invited to visit American universities in the 1980s and early 1990s were often surprised at the women's studies and gender studies centers they found. After a seminar at one such center, a visiting Hungarian sociologist (woman) said to me in amazement: "How tiresome. Why would anyone want to be in a roomful of hens?" Or, as a Czech scholar put it wearily: "With Coca Cola, Schwarzenegger, Terminator, and McDonald's [feminism is] yet another thing imported to us from the West." Despite her implied criticism, most of these items, along with marketization, democratization, civil society, and crash economic programs have often been eagerly sought by East Central Europeans. Feminism much less so.

There is little doubt in anyone's mind, least of all the women of East Central Europe, that their wage scales are considerably below those of men, that women operate with serious glass ceilings on promotions, and that they are segregated in low-paying portions of the labor force (for documentation and discussion of these trends see Einhorn, 1992; Ferge, 1997; Gal and Kligman, 2000b). Furthermore, although the early state socialist systems attempted to socialize housework and childcare, this was largely a disaster and soon abandoned. During the communist period and since, women have continued to be the main household workers, while also responsible for childbearing, childrearing, and waged work outside the household. Since 1989, childcare and maternal benefits have been reduced everywhere, and reproductive rights have been partially curtailed in several countries of the region (and liberalized only in Romania). Yet these negative developments have not led to the formation of women's groups, nor the initiation of protest or reform, despite the much touted and newly won right to organize independent political groups.[9] On the contrary, these issues, along with the rise in prostitution, pornography, and AIDS, are rarely seen as women's problems at all or as potential issues for feminism. Rather, they are most often discussed as problems of transition, or of incomplete development, of political immaturity, or of pernicious foreign influence.

In an earlier essay (Gal, 1997) based on my continuing fieldwork in Hungary, I argued that despite the notable presence of gender inequality, there are very few discursive means for women to make identities for themselves as political actors fighting for their own interests. The reigning discourses of the region are neoliberalism, which constructs genderless civic/public individuals, and neoconservative nationalism, whose imagery for women is primarily the self-sacrificing mother. Furthermore, communist regimes constituted women as a corporate entity (very much like workers and peasants), treating them as objects of policy often with separate ministries charged with women's and children's welfare. As a result, and as many have noted, the notion of women's emancipation was already occupied discursively by the communist state, and therefore forcefully rejected by many of communism's opponents after 1989.

But it would be inaccurate to say that "feminism" has no presence in East Central Europe. On the contrary, there are in fact quite a few women's studies and gender studies centers, for instance in Prague, Kiev, Budapest, and Belgrade, among others. There is a growing literature on the subject of men/women/gender and inequality, some of it inspired by feminist scholarship from other world regions. And there are innumerable NGOs – some emerging from grassroots organizing, but many more initiated and supported by Western or international organizations – whose goal it is to deal with the problems of women since the transition from socialism (see Scott et al., 1997; Keck and Sikkink, 1998).

The contradiction was nicely illustrated in the joint comparative research project that Gail Kligman and I organized in the early 1990s on gender relations in East Central Europe. We asked twenty scholars from the region to write about various aspects of the relations between men and women in their countries. Although we never mentioned feminism in our invitation, many of the contributors took the opportunity to describe, in detail, the rejection of the term "feminism" by men and women in their countries, and the negative, even derisive connotations of the term in public discourses (Gal and Kligman, 2000a). Thus, a palpable, active interest in something called "feminism" was combined with a widespread suspicion and dismissal of it. Both stances were common among educated women themselves. The irony of the situation has not been lost on scholars in the region, and on Western observers, many of whom have written sensitively on this subject and on the resulting conflicts in encounters between women in Eastern Europe and Western feminists (see Funk and Mueller, 1993; Snitow, 1995).

In retrospect it is clear that the dilemmas of these encounters are partially explained by the deep structural differences between gender relations in the state-socialist countries and those common in Western parliamentary states. These differences resulted in quite different ideals for relations between men and women, different understandings of what the problems of women were, and what could be done about them. Briefly and schematically put, state-socialist societies practiced a form of paternalism ("public patriarchy") in which all individuals, including individual women, were directly dependent on the state, which intruded quite openly into all aspects of life. This contrasted with what was often called "private patriarchy," more common in the West. In this regime, authority

over women is held by individual men in families. As a result of these differences, Western women's movements aspired to financial independence
from men through access to paid labor and legalized autonomy from men
in decisions about bodily and reproductive matters. For women in East
Central Europe, by contrast, far from being an aspiration, paid labor has
been a state-mandated requirement, experienced as a burden added to
housework. Independence from men was not a high priority. On the contrary, women actively sought the participation of men in families. It was
the state's intrusion into the household that was resented by women as
well as men (see Ferree, 1995; Kligman, 1998; Szalai, 2000). Contrasting
structural arrangements produced different perspectives and positions.
These were further exacerbated by the stark differences in power and
wealth between Western women who traveled to the East and the East
Central European women they encountered there. For example, in any
collaborative research it was most often American criteria that were the
standard of measurement for what would count as acceptable scholarly
work. Funding for research, along with its management and direction,
invariably came from the West. Similarly, Western foundations and the
NGOs they funded were willing to support activities that matched their
own priorities and often served their own interests, rarely consulting East
Central European constituencies.

In countries like Hungary, a dual market for scholarly and media products developed so that those who could establish networks of relationships
with Western scholars and sell their expertise or their writings to foreign
buyers garnered prestige and money. They were able to make a living
from scholarly or journalistic work. Those who had to remain within domestic markets and domestic pay scales often scrambled unsuccessfully
to make ends meet. The willingness to enter the international market
depended as much on political sympathy with Western colleagues as on
the all-important knowledge of foreign languages. These conditions produced animosity and strain between East Central European scholars and
Western scholars, but also contributed to jealousies and enmity among
East Central Europeans with larger and smaller networks, with differentially marketable skills, and with differential access to Western foundations, businesses, and non-governmental agencies.

Such interactions among women from different regions clearly form
a part of the cross-national contacts I am trying to track, and they are
crucial sites at which texts and their contexts get discussed, exchanged,
and transformed. Nevertheless, for purposes of exposition, I treat these
informal and face-to-face interactions as background to the issue that is
my focus here: the choice, translation, and movement of text artifacts
themselves.

Translation: feminisms as traveling discourses

American feminist writings appearing in Hungary will serve as an illustration of how one might investigate the circulation of texts and the consequent political effects. A full analysis would have to map the field of debate in both venues, also attending to differences in the relationship of writers to their audiences, differences in the structure of media markets, and differences in the language ideologies with which people interpret the process of translation. Starting with such comparisons, the ultimate goal would be to trace the full process of transplanting a text. Here, I offer a brief outline, starting with social relations of translation and moving to textual practices, while contrasting socialist and postsocialist circumstances.

Because foreign travel and the teaching of Western European languages were severely limited in the 1970s and 1980s, translations of Western writings occupied a particularly important place in any contact between East and West in the Cold War intellectual life of East Central Europe. Yet, before the 1980s, very little of Western European or American feminist writing of any kind was translated into Eastern European languages. Mass media reported with only slightly veiled contempt and amusement on bra-burning, American concerns with the sexual lives of political leaders, and sexual harassment suits. For Hungarian readers, what emerged was much more American Puritanism concerning sex than any consequential political program. Since 1989, by contrast, there has been much more Western writing of every kind available in translation. A first important question for analyzing social relations of translation is what articles and books are chosen for translation under the rubric of "feminism" or women's issues. In the USA, there are numerous diverse lines of writing on sex, gender, women, and men – arguments among self-styled feminists and between feminists and non-feminists of different political and epistemological persuasions, and among American, French, Australian, and Scandinavian feminists (to name only the bigger debates). Who chooses from this mass of materials, under what circumstances, and how is it published?

The social relations of translation

Before 1989, Hungary's publishing and media industries were entirely owned and controlled by the state. As one commentator has said about the late communist era of the 1980s: the press was not "democratic, nor free, nor independent," but by that period it had become competitive and multicentered rather than strictly censored.[10] Self-censorship

was as common as the more official kind, with reformers and opposition voices palpable next to the state organs (Lengyel, 1998: 35; see also
Haraszti, 1987). After 1989, Hungary moved to a double system, one
which included some state ownership of publishing, TV stations, and
radio frequencies, and primarily private ownership of magazines, newspapers, and print media generally. By 1998, over 55 percent of Hungary's publishing industry was not only private but owned by foreign
conglomerates of which the German Axel Springer and Bertelsmann
were the largest. American participation in publishing occurred mainly
through American-funded foundations (see below). However, Hungarian
editors, managers, writers, and reporters continued to be the major actors. Many smaller, domestically owned, and for-profit publishing houses
also emerged, although they found survival difficult, and much of their
production has consisted of translations of crime novels, romantic novels,
self-help books, and astrology books from German and American presses.
According to recent polls, editors and journalists – and especially journalists in newspapers owned by foreign corporations – now experience
the profit-oriented and often politically partisan demands of owners to
be intrusive on their professional autonomy. Indeed, they compare their
current lack of independence at work unfavorably to the final days of
communist rule (Vásárhelyi, 1998).

It was with this changing environment in mind that I designed a survey of the full range of Hungarian periodicals published between 1985
and 1998, searching for evidence about what has been translated and
published, and by whom, under the explicit rubric of feminist scholarship, feminist issues, and women's problems.[11] From this survey, some
general trends emerged. The most frequent form of attention to feminist research from Western countries was the publication of summaries
and overviews of various kinds. Especially in the communist period, and
in scholarly journals, publication of critical reviews of books and often
even reviews of key articles was the commonest way in which Western
European and American scholarship on women made an appearance in
Hungarian venues. Nevertheless, such reviews were extremely rare in the
pre-1989 period, and even since 1989 one such review a year out of 120
reviews of other topics has been a typical ratio in the well-established
sociological and historical journals.

In these efforts, a close cooperation was required between the editor
who commissioned the review and the multilingual scholar who took on
the job not only of reporting the contents of the books and articles discussed but of putting them into some sort of historical and academic context. The task was enormous, implying a much broader knowledge of the
foreign "scene" than merely the articles under review. It often constituted

an important way of introducing not only the foreign works but also the entire subject matter to Hungarian scholarly attention, and making a judgment about its significance. In the past, such reviews could make scholars' reputations by identifying them with an entire line of foreign research. Such reviews also set scholarly fashion, becoming the articles to cite when alluding to foreign work and guideposts for scholarly reading. This was particularly true in the pre-1989 period when multilingualism among scholars was not as widespread as it is today.

Since 1989, foreign feminist work (or work about male–female relations) has been most saliently present in Hungarian intellectual mass media through thematic "special issues" of interdisciplinary intellectual magazines. This would seem, at first, to segregate questions about women and feminism from other issues on which such journals report. But in fact, the special issues have had far-reaching and significantly integrative potential. This was because, in each of the journals that ran such a special issue on women/men in the 1990s (*Replika*, *Cafe Babel*, *Infotársadalomtudomány*), a noteworthy editorial strategy was followed: without any explicit comment, feminist work from the USA and Western Europe was presented side-by-side with research and opinion by Hungarian scholars on Hungarian male/female occupational statistics, Hungarian women's history, social problems of Hungarian men, Hungarian gay politics, and related issues of current concern within Hungary.

Thus, quite familiar genres, such as reports on Hungarian women's labor force participation and pay scales, were given a new cast. They could escape charges of being hack work about women's communist "emancipation" and could be read instead as a contribution to a topic of current international interest. Hungarian research and reviews of Hungarian books were thus presented as implicit equals of foreign work, occupying the same typographical, editorial, and journalistic world. These special issues have also sometimes published work by Hungarian scholars on gender subjects dealing with other parts of the world: the paintings of Frida Kahlo, for instance, or opinions on American "political correctness." Thus, Hungarian commentary was presented as having a similar breadth to American feminist scholarship. The Hungarian work was shown to be parallel to – implicitly claiming equivalence with – prominent and sometimes classic works in American and Western European feminist traditions. These editorial practices, I suggest, have started to create a respectable space for writing about gender by Hungarians within the Hungarian context.

The choice of foreign works to translate is a further issue. Not surprisingly, patronage and clientage are crucial factors. Choices depend, in part, on who controlled and controls intellectual and more popular journals, on whom these individuals read, and whom they befriended, usually during study trips abroad. Thus, for instance, in Hungary, the first special issue of an interdisciplinary journal of social science devoted to feminist writings appeared in 1994 and was entitled "Male Dominance." Its lead article and apparent *raison d'être* was a translation of a piece by Pierre Bourdieu, who after twenty-five years of feminist scholarship had finally recognized the importance of gender, and whose former student was the editor.

A special issue of another respected journal was devoted to articles about local gender relations and reports of international scholarly disputes. It included the work of Hungarian scholars who had been working on men and women's employment rates and other traditional concerns, as well as discussions about women's social movements, and the relative importance of biology and society in creating role differences between men and women. The volume was co-edited by a very senior scholar, formerly a member of the Communist Party, whose earlier high position had allowed him extensive travel in the West. The topic of gender had caught his eye, not least because of his own tempestuous private life. The journal issue was respected and read. But because the identity and personal arrangements of the editor were known in some intellectual circles, the special issue was also treated with some irony, not least by the editor himself.

Translators and their conditions of work constitute another component of the social relations of translation. And here, changing ideologies of translation become important. Much more so than in the USA, the vocation of translator has for centuries been understood in Hungary as an artistically important and intellectually demanding form of creativity. The greatest poets of the nation have translated Goethe, Shakespeare, and other classical literature of the Western tradition. During the communist period, translating became an even more honorable profession because freelance translation was often the recourse of intellectuals who were dissidents and therefore deprived of other livelihoods. The events of 1989 brought fundamental transformations in this arrangement and these ideologies. Those with knowledge of foreign languages could find more lucrative positions; the wages of translators became relatively low, leading to an abandonment of this kind of work and thus to a precipitous drop in the quality of translations. Meanwhile, the number of multilingual young people increased enormously, and some have argued that with the broad knowledge of foreign languages now emerging in Hungary, translation should not even be a priority for publishers. Anyone with serious intent to study any technical field will have to read the foreign works in their original languages. Others defend the centrality of translation not only because of the ideological insistence on its creative and artistic importance, but as a benefit to beginners in all fields, those who are not going to be experts, and for the general reading audience. Even for experts, it is argued, only through the translation of foreign texts will terminology and forms of argument enter into domestic discussions and the casual conversations of scholars.

In a different vein, many argue that just as translation was a form of censorship in the communist period, so in the postcommunist period translation and the forms of exclusion it allows remain ways of screening potential reading/viewing matter for all domestic audiences. Significantly, however, the process of selection and the institutions that constrain choices have changed fundamentally. For example, most publishing houses in Hungary have been able to survive only with the help of foundations (foreign and domestic) that subsidize publications and translations. In contrast to the late communist period when the choice of translations was in the hands of state officials (tempered by the experts in each field who quite often were the translators themselves), in the postsocialist period the market and foundations have come to play crucial roles. I have already mentioned the choices made on grounds of profit-making. By contrast, foundations support books that correspond in some way with their political, ethical or social "mission" (see Bárány, 1998). Thus the choices of books to translate are directly driven by frankly political considerations and often mediated by organizational personnel far from the translators themselves.

The textual strategies of translation

From social relations, we turn to some of the semiotic aspects of translation. These can be divided into those that concern the transfer of sense relations from one language to another and those that are concerned with features having to do with language use (pragmatics). As an obvious example of the first, translations must sometimes create or borrow new terms or calque entire phrases (i.e., a word-for-word translation) from foreign sources, introducing them into the target language. Neither "women's studies" nor "gender" has an easy-to-hand Hungarian form. This requires a careful mapping of the existing semantic/formal terrain in both languages.[12] Such terminological choices, however, are less interesting for my purposes than the more intertextual aspects of the translation project. A volume appeared in Hungary in 1997 that contained a collection of American and British psychoanalytical work by feminists. Entitled *Freud titokzatos tárgya* [Freud's secret object], it presented what

American audiences would consider some of the most difficult, esoteric, but also influential feminist psychoanalytic work of recent years (e.g. Kristeva, Irigaray). Yet in Hungary the genre of the book was much better understood than some of the more popular American texts because the editors explicitly made the link with a tradition of Hungarian psychoanalytic scholarship that had been neglected in the communist period. The links with this scholarship were made in part within the text itself. Technical terms in psychoanalysis already had a history of Hungarian translation and usage; footnotes and the introduction provided further parallels. Outside the book, the editors, a pair of psychoanalysts, declared in public discussions that they were neither feminists nor interested in feminism at all, but had produced the book to reactivate the formerly much-respected school of Hungarian psychoanalysis.

Similarly, a journal issue devoted to feminist critiques of rational choice in economic theory created few problems. These feminist writings built on liberal, leftist, and conservative economic theories that have been circulating in East Central Europe for at least two decades. Although they were not prominent in the communist period, many have their roots in pre-war writings within the region. Patterns of citation, the list of authors taken to be the classics, and the terminology were all already available in Hungarian and for contemporary Hungarian audiences. Because the feminist works were chosen and translated by graduate students and recent PhDs whose university training had started in Hungary but who had gained their doctoral degrees in the USA, there was an awareness of how the American debates had been represented in earlier Hungarian writings, as well as the more submerged borrowing by Americans of earlier Central European theory. Here there was no denial of feminist goals. On the contrary, the students self-consciously and strategically planned their contributions as political moves, so that these arguments could enter Hungarian university teaching as the negative side of Hungarian discussions, which had enthusiastically embraced theories of rational choice.

In contrast, other works were at first neglected because translating them was considered "too hard" by professional translators who were not themselves familiar with the traditions out of which the feminist material emerged in the source country. For example, students at the Central European University in Budapest had requested that some of the works of Judith Butler be translated into Hungarian, but early attempts proved futile. Neither analytical philosophy nor cultural studies nor queer theory has obvious roots or parallels in Hungarian intellectual life – although some of Austin's work had been translated. Further, there was not, at that time, a political movement around sexualities that could provide a context, and which would itself be buttressed by such a translation. Apparently, the combination on which Butler drew in the works considered for translation was, at that time, difficult to link intertextually to other and more familiar materials; it was harder to create an implied history – and therefore intelligibility – for this work than for psychoanalytic feminism or for liberal and leftist feminist critiques of rational choice.

Another aspect of intertextuality concerns not the history to which the works are sutured and the tradition on which they rely, but rather the contemporaneous arguments in which any text is embroiled. The ideology of translation on which the editors rely in such instances is an important factor. For if they assume that the translator should be invisible, and the text artifacts can "speak for themselves," they will not problematize the social relations of translation but simply present the texts. For instance, Catherine MacKinnon was the first American widely considered a feminist who was translated into Hungarian. Her article appeared in a special issue of a popular intellectual journal in 1996. The editorial collective wanted to introduce to the Hungarian reading public not simply a single scholar's work, but rather an entire American debate. So they reprinted MacKinnon's exchange on pornography with Ronald Dworkin, first published in the *New York Review of Books*. For those familiar with the American feminist scene, the choice of this debate to represent "American feminism" has the effect of erasing the scores of American feminists who have argued fiercely with MacKinnon's view on censorship and pornography on the grounds that it violates rights of free speech. Pitted against a liberal male defender of free speech, and without any further explanation about the role of cross-linguistic choices, MacKinnon's position produced a selective picture for the attentive Hungarian reader of what counted as "American feminism."[13]

The situation becomes more complicated if we also consider the Hungarian context into which the debate was inserted. How did this exchange "read" in Budapest (in contrast to its diverse readings in the *New York Review*)? Clearly, any text moves into an already constituted set of discourses with which it inevitably interacts, and in relation to which it is interpreted. In the Hungary of the mid-1990s, free speech and lack of censorship were sacrosanct for liberal and left-liberal readers. They were made all the more valuable by the memory of communist repressions. The choice to translate this debate had the effect of casting the feminist writer as the upholder of opinions that seemed repugnant and even perverse to many Hungarian intellectual readers who saw themselves as having finally won legal assurances of free speech. It aligned the male legal theorist with the self-evidently reasonable and progressive position.

Recontextualizations

The example of the MacKinnon–Dworkin debate highlights recontextualization, in addition to translation. In this section, I describe some of the ways in which translated feminist texts do and do not "fit" into Hungarian public debates. Fit and appropriateness do not depend entirely on the substantive content of texts themselves, nor even on the new contexts. On the contrary, I argue that the impression of "foreignness" – and its negative valence – that is often attached to feminism in East Central Europe is socially created, achieved in part through specific textual practices. The broader point is that most discussions of circulation take as self-evident the localities from which the texts supposedly come. Yet, sometimes, these locales are themselves constructed as part of sociopolitical and textual practices.

An example that can be contrasted usefully with the MacKinnon–Dworkin debate comes from a more popular medium, the first Hungarian issue of *Cosmopolitan* magazine. Those inventing the advertising for this textual product were also inventing the market for it. Indeed, they had to imagine the kind of subjectivities that would want the magazine. The advertising campaign included two large posters, one of a woman pictured from the waist up, naked and smiling, her breasts covered by the hands of someone (presumably male) invisibly standing behind her. The caption read: "I do what pleases me." This poster was striking in the early years of postcommunist Hungary for picturing nudity and unusual sexual activity. Informants suggested that the caption implied the woman would buy the magazine, even if it was as outrageous as her pose. Connotations of unconstrained sexuality were mixed with tones of independence and female decisiveness. The other poster showed a woman in a business suit with low cut shirt and cleavage showing. Her caption read: "I look my best for work." Native viewers told me the implication here was that she would sell her body for work, if not literally, then at least in the sense of doing whatever was necessary to make money in business. Both advertisements mixed sexuality, money, and market. But only the first attracted disapproving attention from newspaper editorials. The idea of sexuality in return for business success was apparently acceptable; the idea of independent (nude) women deciding what they want sexually seemed less so.

The newspaper attention was exactly what the advertising agency had hoped for. It emerged from further conversations and subsequent media reports that the advertising agency may have paid for the editorial attacks. They had certainly prepared, well in advance, and in expectation of such an attack, large paper strips to be put over the breasts of the first poster, with the lettering: "We are sorry in case we offended anyone." It is not clear that the advertisement actually offended anyone. But the covering strips allowed the advertisement to suggest that the magazine contained or represented something transgressive, yet remained polite and "civilized." Buying the magazine would allow those who did so to think of themselves as slightly daring in a knowing and restrained manner. Note the attempt by the advertiser to selectively evoke and focus on already existing attitudes towards women, sexuality, business, and civility in order to create a product image and a consumer image for an incoming transnational product. Similar logic could be applied to less commercial examples of moving texts.[14]

If the MacKinnon–Dworkin debate was understood in Hungary through neoliberal assumptions and the *Cosmopolitan* advertising through the danger/allure of marketized sex, it is noteworthy that socialist feminist texts and liberal feminist ones also faced distinctive frames that could be mobilized easily in East Central Europe. As many observers have noted, the terms of socialist feminist writings – "liberation," "emancipation," "revolution," and even "equality" – were systematically used in the communist period as part of state-socialist campaigns to enlist the support of the population for one or another plan. Therefore they have since had a hollow ring, sounding either silly and childish or grotesquely insincere. Worse, the "emancipation" of women in particular was, after all, one of the explicit goals of now discredited, utopian communism.

For liberal feminist writings, by contrast, the problematic context was the ideologically loaded discussion of families. As Kligman and I (Gal and Kligman, 2000a) have argued, although the demographics of families and households – age at marriage, divorce rates, number of children, single-parent families – have arguably changed as much and in the same directions in East Central Europe in the post-war years as they have changed in the USA and Western Europe, public arguments about the family have had very different logics in the two local arenas. In the USA, right-wing critics lament the disintegration of families and family values, often blaming broader societal ills on this supposed disintegration. In East Central Europe, however, "the family" was experienced and discussed as a stable institution, one that has provided a form of continuity in times of drastic change. Thus, any social initiative – such as the individualist demands of liberal feminism – that criticized the family found little support anywhere on the political spectrum. Men and women in East Central Europe have generally idealized the stable family, seeing it as a protection against the demands of the communist state and more recently against the capitalist market.[15]

Relying on these idealizations, nationalist politicians throughout the region have argued, at least since 1989, that motherhood is women's main and natural vocation. They have called for anti-abortion and pro-natalist policies that would produce more children for the nation. By focusing on rightist and nationalist publications included in my survey of periodicals, it was possible to detect the textual practices through which they buttress these positions. The most explicit strategy is to label as communist and therefore "alien" or "foreign" to the nation any mention of women's autonomy. Also labeled as foreign are the translations of feminist writings and the advertising discussed above, women's studies centers at universities, as well as NGOs dealing with women's problems (as opposed to the problems of mothers). In their own journals and magazines, nationalist writers criticize these feminist texts, just as they often criticize consumerism, violence, and sex in the media. All are called alien polluters of native womanhood.[16]

How is the charge of foreignness made persuasive in the texts themselves? Certainly, by drawing attention to the fact that a text has been translated, or that a study center is funded by foreign money, one opens the possibility of labeling it alien. In addition, however, nationalist articles and books engage the very issues brought to public debate by feminist NGOs, but transform them in a rhetorical strategy of reversal: when the issue is abortion, talk about the fetus and the woman deprived of her baby; when the issue is domestic abuse, talk about men being beaten; when the issue is divorce, talk about the hard lot of the man after the break-up. This perspective calls itself the protection of the national; any other, by default, becomes the foreign.

It is therefore all the more noteworthy that a small number of scholars in East Central Europe is currently (re)discovering that feminism is by no means "foreign" to East Central Europe in any literal sense. There were feminist movements in most of the countries of the region at the turn of the twentieth century, and movements for women's education and advancement at the beginning of the nineteenth. These were all in close contact with similar developments in other parts of the world, (Acsády, 1997; Fábri, 1999; Joan Scott et al., 1997). The rediscovery of the feminist past is in keeping with the general recuperation of those historical periods and themes that were censored in the communist period. But for my purposes these new studies and interests have a broader significance. For they show how "foreignness" is an emergent phenomenon. The earlier women's movements incited spirited public debates in newspapers, books, clubs, and sometimes, as in Hungary, even in parliament. These debates concerned the proper education for women, their proper roles in families, and voting.

Important for my purposes is the case of the Hungarian Feminist League, which fought for women's franchise in the early years of the twentieth century. Their struggle became entangled with Hungarian governments' attempts to keep the vote out of the hands of ethnic minorities within the territory of Hungary. A unified bloc of minorities would have constituted a majority against ethnically Hungarian voters, so the question of extending the franchise was cast not mainly as a gender but more as a national and patriotic issue. In part because the Hungarian Feminist League did not entirely reject minority voting rights, Hungarian feminism faced charges from Hungarian nationalists that feminism was hostile to, and thus "foreign" to, the Hungarian nation (Kovács, 1994). Just as there have been several waves of domestic feminist movements in Hungary – varying in their political allegiances – so the charge of alienness itself has local historical precedent. In earlier periods, as now, it was a charge that conflated the historical origins of feminist writings and the alliances made by feminists with various domestic political movements that were/are themselves stigmatized by nationalist writers as foreign. Thus, the foreign did not depend on provenance in any direct way, and was not located elsewhere in any self-evident geographical sense. Rather, it was in part through such arguments about loyalty to the nation that the category of foreign was itself constituted.

Further circulations

In contrast to the translations of feminist writings I discussed earlier (but similar to the case of *Cosmopolitan* magazine), most texts coming into East Central Europe have arrived uninvited, as the accompaniments of firms and organizations that have been entering the region at an increasing pace since 1989. When this happens, translation is not limited to written texts and the selections for translation are not usually made by East Central European social actors. Nor does the movement stop with them. Accordingly, I turn in this section to the influx of institutional practices and highlight the fact that circulation is rarely a matter of a single source and a single destination. Rather, texts and practices move together and travel among the cities, towns, and countries of the region – transformed in distinctive ways – and they continue to change as they move yet again, for instance to Western Europe and the USA.

An institutional form at least as important from my perspective as the media firm and advertising agency is the "non-governmental organization." This is a diverse category including local and regional organizations as well as international ones; tiny self-supporting alliances of activists as well as the fabulously wealthy Soros Foundation; religious groups that missionize with conservative agendas; and many foundations that understand themselves to have some kind of progressive feminist agenda. All of them join international personnel and inspiration with personnel from East Central Europe. The ones I focus on here are programmatically committed to enhancing "women's health," "reproductive health," "environmental safety," or women's role in "local government," "participatory democracy," and "civil society." After 1989, East Central Europeans quickly learned how to set up non-profit "foundations" and how to press for support from such organizations with central offices elsewhere. They became adept at the procedures required for making applications, at preparing budgets, progress reports, and accountability reports, and at holding meetings for foreign review committees. These involved what seemed a whole world of novel practices, written and spoken genres, terminology, interactional conventions, and forms of self-justification. Such interactions in NGOs became another major way in which the forms of feminist debate and interaction appeared in the region in the 1980s and since. Much of the political activism of women in East Central Europe since 1989 has been enhanced by the infusion of funds and organizational help from such American, Western European, and international agencies.[17]

Of particular interest is the role of local NGO officers representing the region to an international foundation, while also representing the foundation to local applicants or constituencies. Though rarely thought of as translators, such social actors found themselves in interstitial and often contradictory positions that in fact required great skills of translation, in several senses. In some cases, these educated, multilingual people have created a delicate, working commensurability between the expectations of distant funders and the assumptions underlying East Central European expectations for the NGO. They faced in multiple directions: helping to shape locally identified "needs" so they would somehow make sense to distant sources of money, and simultaneously trying to change NGO procedures and foundations' priorities to match local conditions. People inhabiting such roles have reported a whiplash effect, as they navigate between plush boardrooms in New York, Brussels, or Budapest (a major seat of the Soros Foundation), where they are asked to speak for "their" people's or region's problems, and the more modest town halls, clinics, and shopfronts of their home towns, where they are sometimes seen – with suspicion and/or appreciation – as the sophisticated tools of international money.

In other cases, there has been little mediation or translation by interstitial personnel. Although the NGOs' workers have learned new genres and conventions for political action, they have failed to effect the substantive changes intended by their funders. Reports from Bulgaria (Daskalová, 2000), Romania (Sampson, 1996; Grunberg, 2000), and elsewhere suggest that NGOs have often operated merely as forms of employment for those who were involved in them and have provided a *raison d'être* for funding agencies. In some cases, the local agencies that gained NGO funding, or that contracted to do the local work of international NGOs, had very little contact with any grassroots constituency. Rather than working with their particular target populations, the organizations replicated the centralization of political activity in the state-socialist period. In such cases, local branches of NGOs were attuned to and turned towards the state, congregating in capital cities, mimicking the organization of the ministries assigned to the "problems" they were supposed to deal with. Although widespread in East Central Europe, this phenomenon is by no means peculiar to the region. Similar problems have been reported as a self-critique by members of the West German feminist movement (Lang, 1997).

But I would like to describe in greater detail a case in which an NGO has had a different trajectory, has accomplished sophisticated translation of practices and issues, and has thereby created a new local context. The SOS Hotline for domestic violence in Belgrade was established in the early 1990s, at the start of the war in Yugoslavia. Mršević (2000) reports that it was organized by women who had seen similar efforts in Croatia; the Croatians, in turn, had been involved in feminist organizations while studying in West Germany, Belgium, and other Western European countries. Women recounted being inspired by these experiences to borrow the practices that targeted domestic violence as a central feminist issue. Note that the circulation of these practices involved not only one step of circulation, but a chain of sites. The idea of a hotline became feasible when Croatian and Belgrade women, upon their return from Western cities, received money in small amounts (often anonymously) from foreign and domestic friends and colleagues. Their ability to change the public definition of wife-beating from a normal if regrettable familial event to a social problem owes as much to their own media efforts in radio, TV, and newspaper interviews, as to the heightened alarm over violence that resulted from the Bosnian War.[18] The example of the Belgrade Hotline also shows in another way the multiple steps in the circulation of a political practice: its story has been partially replicated in Budapest and Prague, each of which has taken inspiration from news about the others.

The new category of domestic violence is also evident in popular general-audience magazines and women's magazines throughout the region. And it has been the occasion for further innovations, this time in practices of writing and publicity. Looking over the survey of

Hungarian publications, it is clear that issues of wife-beating, sexual abuse, abortion, sexual harassment in the workplace, rape, prostitution, and pornography – which were almost entirely absent before 1989 – have since been appearing with increasing frequency in the popular press. The articles surveyed were written from a rather wide range of perspectives. Many were taken and translated – often with only minor changes and without permission – from American and Western European magazines such as *Cosmopolitan, Glamour, Stern,* or *Seventeen.* Even those that were not directly lifted from foreign publications nevertheless followed their genre conventions: lead paragraph with a pseudonymous first-person account of suffering, brief interviews with other "victims," interspersed with commentary from medical, psychological, or sociological experts, with a note of moral uplift throughout.

Some of these articles sympathetically portrayed what were identified as women's troubles, they endorsed women's civil rights and familial rights, implicitly supported women's and men's equality at work and in household matters, and opposed sexual and physical abuse. Others took much more complicated and ambivalent stands. However, the term "feminism" was rarely mentioned. Nevertheless, it has been in these articles that one could watch the construction and reproduction of the irony and sometimes wry disdain with which many of these issues and feminism itself have frequently been handled. A fine example is the titillation, bemusement, and dismissive tone that appeared in an article portraying women who earned money to go to university by engaging in part-time prostitution. At other times, however, the magazines abstained from ridicule of women, sending up male privilege instead by treating it with knowing amusement or biting humor, and sometimes combining the traditional responses to male abuse (irony, resignation) with novel organizational actions. This kind of writing is helping to produce, I suggest, the possibility of political organizing around issues such as domestic violence, reproductive rights, prostitution, or maternal benefits, without a link to the stigmatized term "feminism." These examples – women's NGOs, hotlines for domestic violence, changing media genres – illustrate the circulation of feminist-inspired practices, organizations, and texts.

My final point is the way in which the scholarships and grants of various NGOs and other organizations have made possible the further movements out of the region. These further circulations involve people – scholars, journalists, activists – as well as texts, modified significantly through a version of the translation processes I have already described, and marked as well by the power discrepancies between regions. Western publishers, news services, and activist and research organizations have commissioned writings or chosen texts to be translated, always with an eye on American and Western European markets and the delicate resonance of political arenas far from East Central Europe. Just as the American feminist works translated into Hungarian were chosen and interpreted with Hungarian (indeed Budapest) political relevancies in mind, so the choice, movement, and reception of texts out of East Central Europe have a social organizational and ideological dimension. It is commonplace in the region that the images about the East Central European countries held by policy-makers in Brussels and Washington are based in part on the discursive frames created and reinforced by what bureaucrats and businessmen read in the major newspapers. Thus journalistic writings are understood to have serious consequences, as much for EU expansion, trade agreements, and capital investment as for the tourist industry.

The means by which American and Western European media create powerful images for other geopolitical regions have been closely examined by scholars. Therefore, it will suffice here to provide an example to show how stories coming out of Eastern Europe fit into the broader processes of circulation I have been discussing. The Serbian and Croatian participants of the Gal–Kligman collaborative project mentioned above repeatedly complained about the ways in which the gendered aspects of the Yugoslav wars were presented in the USA. For example, in American media, the reports of rape invariably served as evidence of barbarism in a primitive backwater of Europe (see Todorova [1997] for a review), or as the predictable attacks by the eternal masculine warrior on his natural victim: woman (e.g., Stiglmayer, 1994). The net effect, as noted by the Croatian and Serbian women in the collaborative project, was to standardize the stories and elide the violation of individual women in the Balkans.

Those of the participants who had spent time in the USA suspected that various local American political battles were being fought with the aid of this Balkan imagery. Indeed, American critics were also quick to point out that the stories of rapacious men in the Balkans were told not for their own sakes but used instead to strengthen one side in a long-standing dispute among American feminists arguing whether sexuality for women constitutes "pleasure or danger," and whether male sexuality is necessarily violent, with women as inevitably its victims. These critics were not denying the factuality of the rapes, but rather questioning the way in which the incidents were inserted into American discourses by linking them directly to national and gender essences. In keeping with the theme of this chapter, one would want to investigate closely how the stories told on the scene of such crimes get mediation through multiple tellings and translations into abstracted media reports that are themselves further recontextualized worldwide.

The logic of my argument suggests that scholarly work is an important part of circulation. Thus, this chapter – presenting as it does images of East Central European women, quoting and translating various opinions about feminism and about translated American feminist texts – is itself a text unavoidably involved in a further circulation of such discourses.

Conclusions

As scholars have pointed out, most social movements make claims for both recognition and redistribution; it is the primary terms in which movements justify and explain those claims that have changed. Forms of justification – as evidenced in texts and practices – are prime examples of materials that are translated, moved, and then reinterpreted in new political fields. To be sure, how a particular form of justification fares in any locale is determined by many non-discursive factors, as my examples of the Hungarian case made plain. But we cannot leave out the processes of circulation, if we are to understand how some arguments become persuasive in one location but not another, or how some arguments spread widely, providing novel means for people to conceptualize themselves, construct political goals, and make alliances across regional boundaries. Thus, for example, to explore feminism as a traveling discourse will allow a more subtle analysis of the vexing "misunderstandings" and "prejudices" among women that have been so salient in East Central Europe, but are also often evident in interactions among activists from different countries and regions.

More generally, my aim in this chapter has been to propose and briefly illustrate an approach to social movements that problematizes the notion of globalizing "ideas" by taking a linguistically precise approach to their circulation. It relies on tracing the way that texts – defined as chunks of discourse, often written or mass mediated – get (re)contextualized into varying political and cultural contexts which are themselves changed in the process. Rather than looking for the origins of political ideas, one assumes that origins are multiple and the version activated in any instance is constructed within already existing political debates. Accordingly, one important effect of movement relies on intertextuality to create or support a sense of sociocultural continuity vs. rupture. Another is to introduce categories of politicized subjectivity – in excess of local/foreign – that can then become the focus of further debate and activism. The movement of texts does not necessarily follow the direction and pace of more familiar "flows," for instance, of capital, commodities, and people in transnational circuits; nor does it happen in the way that classic analyses of migration or commodification suggest is true for people and things. Rather, it occurs through institutional and practical activities hinging on translation. Translation itself is a moment in the circulation of texts. It is a complex phenomenon, consisting of specific social relations and ideologies about language, as well as distinct semiotic processes that produce contexts for debate and create the conditions of possibility for political subjectivities and further action.

Part 3

Competing claims: struggles in dialogue

5   Contesting "race" and gender in the European Union: a multilayered recognition struggle for voice and visibility

Fiona Williams

Introduction

This chapter is about the struggle to get the needs and claims of black, minority ethnic, and migrant women in the European Union (EU) member states on the policy agenda of the Commission of the European Communities (CEC). It charts the history of a campaign[1] which began in 1990 as an attempt to press for greater voice and visibility of black, minority ethnic, and migrant women within the European Women's Lobby (EWL), a non-governmental organization (NGO) representing women in the EU.[2] As such, this part of the campaign sought recognition for minority women at several different levels – not simply at the policy-making level of the EU, but also at the level of the then predominately white, middle-class European Women's Lobby. At the same time, those who have been actively campaigning for the recognition of black, minority ethnic, and migrant women's claims have also supported and encouraged the collective struggles by grassroots' organizations in member states to gain greater voice and visibility as women within their own communities, and as minority ethnic or migrant women within the nation states in which they live.

However, not only have the claims for recognition been multileveled, they have also, insofar as they cut across issues of gender, "race," ethnicity, and migration, been generated by actors with multiple identities. The campaign has therefore been forced to be strategic in relation to alliances and sites for action. This need for strategic alliances and sites for action has been sharpened by the process, within the EU, of institutionalizing into largely separate and discrete organizational forms the claims for gender equality and equality in relation to "race," ethnicity, and migration. In attempting to organize at the intersection of "race" and gender for legal, civil, and social rights, the campaign for black, minority ethnic, and migrant women has simultaneously challenged different dimensions of the policy discourses of citizenship which underpin EU law and policy. Furthermore, not only has the campaign sought to transform gendered and radicalized notions of European citizenship, but it also, at various points, attempted to put into practice a form of politics which respects intragroup differences whilst seeking a common ground for claims.

As a contemporary struggle for voice and visibility, the case study highlights, but also questions and develops, the theoretical issues raised in the analyses and debates on "struggles for recognition."

Recognition struggles

The recent body of work on social movements and social conflict centered upon concepts of "recognition" (Charles Taylor, 1994; Honneth, 1995b), "multiculturalism"[3] (Charles Taylor, 1994; Kymlicka, 1995), and "recognition/redistribution" (Fraser, 1995; 1997b; Young, 1997; Phillips, 1997) has been important in several ways. First, it provides a historical explanation for the development of a politics which is about more than the distribution of goods; second, it elaborates the theoretical links between identity and political agency; third, it provides a better understanding (and validity) of contemporary transformatory politics in terms of the tensions between universalism and difference; and, fourth, it enables us to reread so-called "class politics" through a different lens. In addition, Honneth's study provides a theoretical framework which links psychological and emotional development in the private sphere to the striving for self-realization in the public sphere. He also demonstrates the limitations of the concept of "interests" as the motivating force for collective action and proposes that we take into account the "everyday web of moral feelings" (1995b: 161) which are assaulted in the process of misrecognition and disrespect. By contrast, Fraser's arguments plant the concept of recognition firmly back in a justice framework by defining recognition claims as struggles against cultural injustices. This enables her, usefully, to develop an analysis which acknowledges the ways in which recognition claims against cultural injustices are "mutually imbricated" with redistribution claims derived from economic injustices (Fraser, 1995).[4] In developing further a "bivalent" conception of justice attached to these redistribution and recognition claims, she looks for a "normative core," and suggests that this is the principle of "participatory parity." In the process, she disposes of what she sees as Taylor's "culturalism" and Honneth's "psychologization" in favor of a materialist account of cultural and economic injustice.

These theories and debates beg a number of questions which can only be answered by a reference to empirical cases. Here I draw attention to those further questions which my case study signals and/or explores. The first is: What is the nature of the community from which moral respect is sought? Is it singular or multiple? In Taylor, Honneth, and Fraser's work there is an implicit assumption that recognition claims are directed at society and/or the nation state. However, this and other studies reveal multiple "audiences" of recognizers in contemporary societies – one's "own community," locality, workplace, national community/state, and supranational and international bodies.

Second, how far do struggles for recognition/redistribution set in motion their own forms of exclusion and modes of disrespect, and, if they do, how do we explain this? How far is this the consequence of "fixing" identities in singular ways in order to strengthen solidarity (sometimes referred to as "strategic essentialism")? Or, to what extent is it to do with political practices and cultural legacies the members of that struggle bring with them and, if so, what strategies make collectivities more fluid and able to deal with intragroup differences? Is participatory parity a sufficient normative core and what does it mean in practice? Are "voice" and "visibility" in this case study equivalent to Fraser's objective and intersubjective conditions for participatory parity? I refer in the case study to ideas about a politics of *transversalism* which may flesh out more specifically some of the processes and tensions involved in the pursuit of participatory parity.

Third, individuals generally have multiple identities for which more than one may be subject to exclusion from rights and to disrespect – what difficulties does that pose for the mobilization and articulation of claims? Further, while Fraser refutes the attempt by Honneth to bring ontological meaning to the concept of identity and link it to the political, she runs the risk of assuming an unproblematic and possibly congruent relationship between pre-existing categorical identity and collective political identity. And, by deontologizing her account, she cuts off an opportunity to examine the more complex, two-way, reconstituting relationships between ontological, categorical, and political identities. There is some truth in the criticism that Honneth's analysis verges on the psychologically essentialist in parts; nevertheless, his attempt to conjoin theoretically the psychoanalytic, social, and political subject is important. Most social scientists limit themselves only to the social and political subject and implicitly remain within a framework which assumes that we are unfragmented, coherent, rational, unitary subjects (see for contrast Henriques et al., 1998; Hoggett, 2000). My case study poses the question of whether it is possible to understand recognition as *both* a "matter of self-realization" *and* as "an issue of justice"?[5]

Finally, how far are recognition and redistribution claims necessarily intertwined? Is it not the *effects* of cultural and economic injustices which are necessarily imbricated, rather than the *process* of struggling against them? In this case study, as I shall show, women had to struggle to gain recognition as valid political actors from other women before they could put their claims against cultural and economic injustices on the agenda.

The EU and black, minority ethnic, and migrant women

The political context of the EU

The struggles by black, minority ethnic, and migrant women within the EU and its member states represent the claims of a group at the sharp end of a number of political, economic, and social changes. Two of the EU bodies that became both enabling for and constraining upon the black, minority ethnic, and migrant women's claims were the European Women's Lobby and the Migrants' Forum. The following brief account explains the creation of these bodies in the context of EU political developments.

The EU originated in the creation of the European Economic Community (EEC) in 1957 which aimed to provide a structure through which France and Germany could work together and maintain peace in Europe. One part of this involved the revival of economic growth in Europe; over time this became the main objective. During the 1970s and 1980s, there was greater commitment to the development of a social dimension of EEC policy through a form of European corporatism, known as the social dialogue, in which employers and trade unions could hammer out social policy at the supranational level. Since the mid-1980s, however, the EU has witnessed growth in unemployment and restructuring of welfare states along with the increasing power of business interests in promoting deregulation and the casualization of labor, flexible working, and contracting out. Black, minority ethnic, and migrant women have been disproportionately affected by these changes in employment practices, and unemployment is higher among these groups than among white women, as many work in areas of occupational decline (Bhavnani, 1994; Knokke, 1995; Phizacklea and Wolkowitz, 1995).

Policies for gender equality have a long history. From the 1970s, Article 141 [119][6] on equal pay for equal work (originally passed in 1957) both fitted and framed women's claims-making within the EU and focused upon equality between men and women in the context of the labor market. By the 1980s, there was pressure from women to extend the discourse of women's citizenship into women's specific needs created in part by the public–private divide. Thus, issues such as caring, unpaid work, sexual harassment, and violence emerged onto the agenda, challenging the dominant economistic discourse of EU policy-making (see Hoskyns,

1996; Simon Duncan, 1996). In the same period, a number of significant bodies were set up, for example, the European Parliament's Committee on Women's Rights, the Equal Opportunities Unit (formally the Women's Bureau), and the European Women's Lobby.

There have, however, been major constraints on the effectiveness of such developments. First, the concept of equality tends to be restricted to women as paid workers and therefore limits the opportunities which address those specific conditions which restrict women's capacity to act as independent workers, such as caring responsibilities, reproductive rights, unequal divisions of domestic labor, and so on. Second, the diversity of national policies in relation to gender and social policy has always limited the scope and interpretation of EU policy. National implementation of equal opportunity directives tends to be tailored to suit the particular discourses within any given regime. Furthermore, nation states often have considerable leeway in implementation, and those hostile to equality policies are able to "level-down" directives to suit the status quo in their own country. Third, the dominant EU model tended to be derived from what were male-breadwinner regimes and, in these terms, has constituted something of a threat to gender equality by those countries (Sweden, Finland, and Denmark) which have already modified the male-breadwinner model.

A fourth issue centers upon the nature of democracy and representative politics within the EU. In some ways, women's policies are more developed than other strands of social policy in the EU, not only because of the need for women's labor, but also because of the direct and indirect impact of the second wave of feminism in Europe combined with the existence of Article 141 [119] in creating political spaces for women to act (Hoskyns, 1996). For example, in spite of the conceptual inadequacies of notions of gender equality in the Social Security Directives, they began to provide a space for discussion of reproductive, sexual, and caring rights and responsibilities.[7] At the same time, major political constraints on the development of women's policies at the EU surface in the nature of democracy and representative politics. Although the women's movement's capacity for both networking transnationally and acting locally enabled it to seek to influence EU bodies, attempts at intervention have revealed real problems of male-dominated policy-making bodies, lack of sufficiently funded support for transnational political activities, dominance of EU women's organizations by professional women and professional women's interests, as well as an encouragement to participate without any guarantee of power or influence. Problems of representation operate on two levels – the absence of women and women's issues in EU institutions and debates and the extent to which individual spokeswomen and consultative groups and committees are representative of "grassroots" women and women's organizations in Europe.[8] These factors contributed to a bureaucratic and elitist approach to political representation which reinforced a unitary approach to women's interests and constrains the possibilities for acknowledging differences between women. Yet the Commission and Parliament are very aware of their lack of contact with grassroots in their member states and the so-called "democratic deficit." This places the Commission in a contradictory position of welcoming moves to make contact with its grassroots while resisting any claims that may emerge from such contact which threaten its political and economic status quo.

In relation to "race" and migration, member states have fought harder here to retain their sovereignty over policies concerning migrants from outside the EU, and the Commission's competence to, for example, monitor or scrutinize national procedures in this area has been restricted – a position effectively condoned by the European Court of Justice (ECJ) (see EWL, 1995; Hoskyns 1996: 172–73). At the same time, however, the creation of a Single European Market raised the question of who was and who was not to be granted freedom of movement. Member states preferred to leave this issue to intergovernmental negotiation and agreement rather than debate it more openly through the Council or Court. One of the outcomes of this was the Schengen Group, set up in 1985 to deal with the policing of migration and asylum seekers as well as the prevention in arms' trafficking and drugs. Not only did this place the issue of "race" and migration within the sphere of crime and public order (rather than "race" equality and citizenship), it also placed it within highly unaccountable and secretive bodies, away from public scrutiny. In addition, freedom from racial discrimination was not included as part of workers' rights in the Social Chapter.

However, the 1980s also saw an increase in Europe of emancipatory movements based on "race" and ethnicity. As a result of the pressure and concern of the Parliament, Commission, and Council with the rise in neofascism and racism, a number of important declarations were made, but with little policy outcome. In 1991, the Migrants' Forum was set up to represent the interests of migrants and, like the European Women's Lobby, act as a consultative body to the Commission.

By the mid-1990s, the CEC, concerned at increased racism in member states and under pressure from the non-governmental anti-racist organizations and Parliament, set out, in 1995, its communication on *Racism, Xenophobia and Anti-Semitism* (CEC, 1995), which amongst other things launched 1997 as the European Year Against Racism. It was followed, in 1998, by a detailed strategy communication. As a result of growing influence of NGOs upon the EU Intergovernmental Conference, the Amsterdam Treaty of 1997 famously extended, in Article 13 [6a], its anti-discrimination remit beyond gender equality to include discrimination based on sex, racial or ethnic origin, religion or belief, disability, age, or sexual orientation, thus providing an important reference point for NGOs, activists, and those groups in member states whose equality and anti-discrimination laws have not been developed. In terms of the issue of overlapping inequalities and injustices, which concerned the campaign for black, minority ethnic, and migrant women, this was a big step forward, for it has helped frame, for example, calls for research proposals to examine the interlocking of inequalities.[9] It could also be said to be the consequence of pressures for a new, more complex way of thinking about intersecting inequalities of which the campaign was one part. However, by the beginning of the new century, increasing panics about refugees and asylum seekers entering the EU, along with increased Islamophobia following the attack in the USA on September 11, 2001, has legitimized racist discourses within European political debates.

The social and economic context of black, minority ethnic, and migrant women's lives

As noted above, deregulation, casualization, and unemployment have particularly affected black, minority ethnic, and migrant women.[10] These groups of women tend to be more active in the labor market compared with their white/indigenous counterparts (although there are ethnic variations). This is influenced by the fact that either they are sole breadwinners or their partner also earns a low wage. However, many migrant women, because their legal residency status is dependent on a male partner or father, cannot gain work permits and, until they can, are forced, initially, to work in the underground economy. This makes them particularly vulnerable to exploitation within domestic service or as homeworkers within the service sector, catering and clothing industries, and also the sex industry (EWL, 1995; Phizacklea and Wolkowitz, 1995; Bridget Anderson, 2000). There are also a growing number of undocumented women migrants and women from Eastern Europe and Russia. Other factors, such as lack of access to any form of social security benefits, also force women into the homeworking economy. These jobs have little social protection and entail long hours with low wages. Furthermore, a combination of cuts in public expenditure and the increase of white/indigenous women in paid employment has led to an increase in the demand for cheap domestic labor (Knokke, 1995). In fact, growing social polarization is also marked by a polarization between women, where middle-class professional women have benefited more from equality policies and suffered less from economic restructuring. Furthermore, black and migrant women's employment situation is connected to, and exacerbated by, widespread racism in the workplace in EU member states (see Wrench, 1996).

The issue of racism relates to a second set of contextual changes which are significant for black, minority ethnic, and migrant women. Racial violence has increased since the 1980s, as have the ethnicization and racialization of politics, both in terms of the growth of influence of some neofascist parties (in France, for example) and mobilization and resistance to racism from black, minority ethnic, and anti-racist organizations. In addition, ethnic, religious, and nationalist fundamentalism has also increased.

Policies to counter racism vary in member states and are particularly underdeveloped where minority ethnic groups and migrants have historically had less access to political and social citizenship rights (see EWL, 1995). Immigration policies also vary (see Castles and Miller, 1993), but since the 1970s most European countries have restricted immigration controls and access to citizenship rights and to settlement. Against this should be set a growing intensity of international migration from poorer countries to richer countries. This has been marked also by an increasing feminization of migration as the demand for female labor increases and women come to join family members. In addition, with a rise in civil wars and ethnic conflicts there has been an increase in asylum seekers (Castles and Miller, 1993). There has also been a growth in permanent settlement of migrants and their families.

A third area of social and political change concerns the influence of transnationalization in the formation of social identities, in the creation of new levels for political intervention, and in the growing significance of NGOs. For many of those from third-world countries, whether permanently settled or second or third generation, the notion of the diaspora has surfaced in different ways in the formation of identities. Diasporic identities – a sense of belonging located in a country of settlement as well as a country or culture of origin – provide a link between the local and the global. They have also given rise to forms of activism and solidarity within the local as well as across national boundaries. Furthermore, this capacity to link grassroots activism to transnational networking provides an important resource in the attempt to intervene on the international and supranational stage.

Linked to this is the increasing significance of the international and supranational stage as the focus for claims of recognition. This applies not only to the development of EU political and legal institutions, but the increasing importance of international agencies such as the OECD, the World Bank, the World Trade Organization, and the IMF, as well as international conferences such as the 1995 Beijing International Women's Conference, for setting political priorities and policy agendas. Thus, in relation to the rise of racism in Europe it would seem that the role of a supranational body such as the EU would be critical in checking any further racism or diminution of rights of minority ethnic groups. However, as already described, the EU has only recently developed a strategy to counter racism in the member states, whilst its border controls have become stricter. This situation produces a double imperative for black and minority women to have representation at the EU level, for restrictive immigration controls and practices have a knock-on effect on black and minority women's lives within and across member states. Yet the existence of tougher policies around anti-discriminatory policies and the recognition of multiculturalism provide important political hooks for those groups whose member states do not recognize such policies. EU policies on "race" and immigration also carry not only material but symbolic implications for the construction of geographic, ethnic, racial, and cultural borders, for the identities of those within and outside those borders, and for the negotiation of diverse policies and racial politics within and between member states, as well as for the recognition of an economic order which depends upon, yet conceals, its migrant workers. In this way, the EU has the potential to reinforce nationalisms, to conflate citizenship with white Europeanness, or to move towards a multiethnic, post-national citizenship.

Connected to the growing importance of the supranational and international political forum is the increasing significance of NGOs as *mediators* between the state, the suprastate, international agency, or conference, and grassroots activism. Increasingly, as well, the constituencies which NGOs represent are precisely those social movements which originally developed around claims against social, economic, and cultural injustices. Yet, as the case study illustrates, where NGOs are "fixed" as lobbyists for constituents along a single axis (say, women or migrants) then this, along with other factors, circumscribes their capacity to respond to the claims of those whose identities are created at the intersection of different axes (in this case, gender and "race"), for minority ethnic and migrant women have claims both as members of minority ethnic communities and as women. For example, while, as already noted, an increasing number of migrants are women and a high number of migrant and minority women are breadwinners (some countries directly recruit migrant women into particular industries, for example, electronics in Germany and France), immigration legislation in most countries is underpinned by assumptions of a male-breadwinner system (see Lutz, 1996). This means that in many

EU countries migrant women do not enter as independent legal subjects and they only have rights derived from their husband's status. This not only makes them vulnerable to economic exploitation but also to loss of residence rights if a woman divorces or becomes a widow. It can also serve to entrap women who want to escape from domestic violence. Furthermore, the right of spouses to entry has been tightened up in many countries (Lutz, 1996).

In a number of different ways, then, this campaign for black, minority ethnic, and migrant women encapsulates an attempt to resist the intensification of some of the economic, social, cultural, and political injustices that characterize the transformations of Western democratic societies under late capitalism. While the policies of the EU increasingly impact upon the lives of these women, the political practices of different institutions of the EU have, in different ways, provided limited spaces and significant closures on their capacity to intervene.

The campaign: the main elements

In 1992, the European Women's Lobby (EWL), the consultative body established by the European Commission, set up a Black and Migrant Women's Project in response to the concern shown by one of the organizations represented on the Lobby, the European Forum of Left Feminists, that the Lobby had neglected the interests of black and migrant women (Hoskyns, 1991). There were no representatives from this group amongst the founding group, no programs specific to the needs of the group in its policy on human rights, and little contact between grassroots organizations and policy-makers, despite the fact that issues directly affecting black and migrant women were being discussed within the EU. They proposed that the project should "identify contacts and organizations among black and migrant women, and look at the barriers which exist to the greater visibility and representation of black and migrant women at the European level" (EWL, 1995: 5). The Black and Migrant Women's Project, a group made up of black and white women,[11] contacted organizations within member states representing black and migrant women, interviewed activists, experts, and officials, analyzed national and EU documents, and produced a report, *Confronting the Fortress: Black and Migrant Women in the European Union*, a version of which the Lobby was eventually persuaded to publish (EWL, 1995).[12] Its main aim, as discussed later, was to give a voice to black, minority ethnic, and migrant women in the member states, but it also produced important recommendations. These focused on immigration policy; action against racism and xenophobia; health, housing, and reproductive rights; education and training needs; protection from violence and sexual exploitation; basic employment rights – especially where their dependent status as women and migrants or their racialized status makes women vulnerable to a single employer in domestic service or in the sex industry; a recognition of skills and qualifications (many domestic workers have other skills and educational qualifications); and political and representational rights – for example, the right to vote or stand for election at local, national, and supranational levels. The Report also called for more data on the specific experiences of black and migrant women, for these are generally hidden in overall categories. In relation to immigration policy, the demands were fourfold: independent legal status for black and migrant women, distinct from their partners and fathers; emergency provisions for women who are subject to domestic and other violence; special monitoring of the status and conditions of black and migrant domestic workers; and a recognition of the specific discriminations and abuses experienced by women applying for asylum (EWL, 1995: 8 and 255–57).

The production of the Report, its initial reception by the EWL, the eventual publication of the Report by the EWL, and maintaining pressure to ensure there was action and follow-up, all constituted struggles in themselves. A measure of some success was that in 1997 the Commission, through one of its "arms" (DGV, which deals with social affairs, amongst other things) provided funds for a project to investigate good practice in member states in combating racism and sexism. Subsequently, too, the EWL included a recognition of the intersectionality of inequalities as part of its commitments.

Meanwhile, pressure from the European Parliament's Women's Rights Committee led the Migrants' Forum – one of the main anti-racist consultative bodies – to set up a Women's Committee. It also elected its first woman executive member. Between 1995 and 1998, seminars were held on migrant women in the media and on ethnic minority women's health needs. By 1998, its vice-president was a black woman (Martha Osamor, who had been on the Black and Migrant Women's Project Group). At the same time, within the EWL, representation of minority ethnic women in the General Assembly rose slightly – from 2 percent in 1992 to 5 percent by 1997, and a black vice-president was elected. This raising of the anti-racist profile in the EU provided new opportunities (as well as difficulties) for minority ethnic women to get their voices heard as women within an anti-racist strategy and not only as ethnic minorities within a gender equality strategy. Before looking in greater detail at the different strategies deployed to get voice and visibility for black women, the chapter examines how a collective identity of black, minority ethnic, and migrant women was constituted.

Cross-cutting and fluid identity formation

When the Black and Migrant Women's Project started it used the term "black and migrant women" to signify the collective identity of the grass-roots organizations whose claims it was articulating. In the 1980s, the term "black" was understood in some European countries as a political term covering racialized groups. The term "migrant" was used by other European countries to describe those who had migrated, usually from third-world countries, and was a term assumed by those migrants themselves.[13] However, the collective term "black and migrant" proved problematic because some grassroots organizations identified neither term, "black" or "migrant." By 1997, the collective term had become "black, ethnic minority, and migrant women." This covers women in member states whose origins lie in third-world countries – Africa, Asia, the Middle East, the Caribbean, and South America – or in Southern European migration countries such as Turkey. Diversity marks more than their countries of origin for they may have different legal status: some are citizens of an EU member state, some have rights of residence, some are refugees or asylum seekers, and some are undocumented. Some are indigenous in that they have been born in a member state and identify their nationality as, say, British, or in a diasporic sense as Black British or British Asian. Furthermore, the Report found that the interests and experiences of black, minority ethnic, and migrant women may, in some respects, coincide with other women outside this category – internal migrants (from Southern Europe and Ireland – see Ackers, 1999),[14] women gypsies and travelers, and the increasing number of women migrants from Central and Eastern Europe (part of which may soon be integrated into the EU) (EWL, 1995: 10).

The experiences that the group holds in common derive from three interlocking areas of struggle for recognition and rights: first, as women vis-à-vis men within their own communities; second, at the local and national levels as minority ethnic women; and third, as minority ethnic women within Europe. As described earlier, these areas may feed back on themselves – lack of independent legal status sustains economic dependency in the home and both these conditions contribute to vulnerability and invisibility. The supranational level of the EU constitutes a further tier where symbolically and materially minority ethnic women find themselves marginalized and denigrated. The contradiction for Europe and the irony of "free movement" of the Single Market is that in constructing a new supranational European identity, it is doing so by defining Europeanism in relation to the otherness of people whose origins lie in the third world or poorer migrant countries. In the case of the EU, many members of racialized groups do not have freedom of movement, and are denied full voting rights and rights to social benefits. In some cases, they are denizens – with entitlement to civil and social rights but not voting rights (see Yuval-Davis, 1997). The intervention on behalf of black, minority ethnic, and migrant women challenges the construction of a European supranational identity which symbolizes Europe as white, Christian, enlightened, and modern, and in which European womanhood serves as a standard for measuring women elsewhere (Lutz et al., 1995: 11). What underpins these interlocking areas is also a diasporic identity (British Asian, African-Caribbean German, and so on).

This diasporic identity gives women both a sense of history in personal and cultural terms, but it is also what links together, in historical and political terms, women from different minority ethnic groups. One of the women involved in the Black and Migrant Women's Project as researcher, Emma Franks, used the term "global identity."[15] She said that the women she spoke with often did not feel European, but that their identities and networks went beyond Europe. The report the Project produced, *Confronting the Fortress* (EWL, 1995), attempted to use the commonalities shared by black, minority ethnic, and migrant women as a starting point for exploring different experiences and claims. She emphasized the importance within the Project of respecting differences by acknowledging them in the Report. At the same time, she stressed that the black women involved in the Project knew they could not act as *representatives* of all these different groups of women in the EU, but as mediators of their voices. A common political identity of this group was therefore constituted at different levels, through diverse ethnicities, member states, and across race and gender (not to mention class, sexual orientation, disability, and age). Even though the Project could be said to have helped construct this common identity, this is not to say it was simply a political construction. It was the common claim for "voice and visibility" which constructed a political identity, as the following quotation from the Report illustrates:

Black and migrant women cannot be "represented" at a European level by even the most sympathetic of voices; they must be there to represent themselves. (EWL, 1995: 267)

There is a further twist in this story of the relationship between constructed national, European and diasporic identities. While the political institutions of the EU create the possibility for a forging of European identity, they also create, at the same time, the conditions in which the *national* identities of individuals, and particularly representatives of the different member states, are sharpened. There is thus a tension between whether, in this case of the EWL, the representatives are primarily representing, say, *Belgian* or *German* women, or Belgian or German *women*. One of the negative responses in the EWL to the publication of the Report was from those representatives who felt that the accounts from minority women in their own countries had let down their country, had been disloyal, or had failed to show gratitude for being allowed to live there. National position became more important than solidarity with other women, and the assertion of a diasporic identity challenged this form of nationalism.[16]

The number of women in these groups in the EU, based on 1993/94 statistics, is around 3.5 million, that is 43 percent of all black, ethnic minority, and migrant people (EWL, 1995). However, these are approximate figures as definitions of ethnicity and migration status vary and they do not include undocumented women.[17] In terms of transnational activism, the Report (see also Stolz, 1994) describes a number of important Europe-wide black and migrant women's organizations/groups, including the Black Women in Europe Network, *Babylan* Philippine Women's Network, Aqui NASOTROS (Latin American women in Europe), African Women in Europe Network, and the European Women's Network for International Action and Exchange. These networks organize and operate in very different ways and with different emphases (from a very loose network for information exchange purposes to those with more formal structures and an active membership, such as *Babylan*). In addition, within nation states there are large numbers of black and migrant women's groups organizing for different purposes (see EWL, 1995). The extent to which they are engaged with the EU and EU policy-making processes varies significantly but, in common with majority ethnic women's groups, the "opportunity that . . . [they] have to exploit the EU policy process . . . is dependent on the remit of the EU itself, as well as the organizational hierarchy and politics within which they operate" (Sperling and Bretherton, 1996: 309).

The next section examines the problems that the Project had in securing its own voice and visibility within these two dynamics: the remit of the EU, and the organizational hierarchy and politics of the European Women's Lobby and the Migrants' Forum.

Racing gender and gendering "race" in the politics of the EU

The intervention by representatives of black and migrant women, supported by white women, to challenge the lack of voice and visibility represented a challenge to the assumption that social policies are constructed on the basis of a single logic of gender equality or a single logic of "race" equality. Black, ethnic minority, and migrant women's claims stand at the *intersection* of "race" and gender issues. Within the EU, their interests fell between two stools – the European Women's Lobby, which represents women, and the Migrants' Forum, set up in 1991 to consult and lobby on issues affecting black and migrant workers. Whilst the EWL did little, to begin with, to represent the interests of black, ethnic minority, and migrant women, the Migrants' Forum, likewise, marginalized women's interests. Furthermore, as described earlier, policies for women and policies around "race" and migration have developed in quite different ways, with the latter having, until recently, far less legitimacy as an area for action within the EU.

The initial raising of claims around "race" and gender originally within the EWL rather than the Migrants' Forum reflected to some extent the greater political opportunities generated by the higher profile of gender equality. In addition, opportunities to prioritize the claims of those experiencing greater marginalization were made possible by the original terms of reference of the lobby: "To act on behalf of its mandatory organizations to promote the interests of women living in the European Union Member States, including immigrants, ethnic minorities, vulnerable and marginalized social groups, within the framework of a united and democratic Europe" (quoted in EWL, 1995). It was possible to get the EWL to agree to this reference to marginalized and vulnerable groups partly because of the growing concern within the EU of the effects of economic recession, increasing social exclusion, racism, and the feminization of poverty. This meant it was possible to argue for issues such as disadvantage and migration to be put on the women's equality agenda and, through those concerns, to raise the issue of differences between women. However, as is explained later, this entailed a clash of political practices, priorities, and cultures.

"Race" and migration policies also reflected institutional separation of the "race" and gender issues. The CEC's Third Action Programme on Equal Opportunities for Women and Men for 1991–95 did not refer to black or migrant women. Similarly the European Parliament's Committee of Inquiry into Racism and Xenophobia in 1990 made little reference to women's experiences of racism and only two out of seventy-seven recommendations specifically affected women (EWL, 1995). The CEC's (1998) Action Plan Against Racism similarly has few specific references to the needs of minority ethnic women. This lack of discursive or organizational framework means that when research or activities *are* organized around "race" and gender issues they are often not able to be followed up.[18]

However, the significant shift in CEC commitment to fighting racism from 1995 seemed to offer political opportunities to raise claims for "race" and gender recognition from within the Migrants' Forum. In addition, the Migrants' Forum had created its own Women's Committee. However, unlike the creation of the Black, Minority Ethnic, and Migrant Women Project Group which had emerged from grassroots organizations within the EWL, the pressure to form a Women's Committee in the Migrants' Forum came from outside the Forum – from the Parliamentary Women's Committee. This meant that from the start it could not be assumed that the Migrants' Forum Women's Committee would have a gender equality agenda. Nor, to begin with, did the issue have much legitimacy, indeed the former male president of the Migrants' Forum insisted on being present at the women's early meetings. In the experience of Martha Osamor, who later became vice-president of the Migrants' Forum, it had often been necessary to argue for women's issues under a more generic heading in order to get funding allocated within the Migrants' Forum. Thus, money for developing a project concerned with migrant women's political involvement had been argued for as a "support project" rather than a women's training project.[19] By the late 1990s stronger links existed between black women in the EWL and the Migrants' Forum; however, internal difficulties led to the demise of the Migrants' Forum.

Doing politics, respecting differences

The Black and Migrant Women's Project saw its role as both intervening in the policy-making process and actively networking with grassroots organizations. Indeed, this capacity of women's organizations to make contact with their own grassroots *and* to network transnationally has provided women lobbying in the EU with one of their strongest organizational resources and forms of credibility. The form of politics based upon semi-informal networks of issue-based support or self-help groups has been a feature of women's politics since the 1970s. The European Forum of Left Feminists, an organization set up in the 1980s, had developed from a politics that was "committed to the representation of all groups of women" (EWL, 1995).

The Report (EWL, 1995) illustrates the practice of the politics of grassroots transnational networking in that it managed to bring the experiences together of some thirty groups of black, ethnic minority, or migrant women in the EU member states. One of its priorities was that "the Report should give space for black and migrant women to speak for themselves, and should aim to provide information and contacts to allow dialogue, researching and networking to develop. No attempt has been made to impose an artificial coherence on the Report: It speaks with many voices" (EWL, 1995: 11).[20] This notion of "speaking with many voices" reflects an attempt to find ways in which groups can actively pursue their specific *and* common claims to entitlements and recognition, and how issues of difference within social movements should be voiced, discussed, and prioritized. It also reflects an attempt to surmount some of the difficulties experienced in equal opportunities politics in member states where the specific claims from specific groups (black, disabled, women, etc.) ossified the differences between the groups, inhibited the acknowledgment of either cross-cutting or common interests, and fell too easily into competing claims, especially within the context of scarce resources. It was trying, too, to avoid a politics based on universal citizenship where a consensus may merely hide the specific needs of the most marginalized groups.

The Project members were therefore attempting to put into practice a form of politics, both within their own constituency and within the EWL, where differences could be respected but common values could emerge to frame the ways in which agreement is sought for claims – the pursuit of unity in dialogues of difference. Some have used the concept of "transversal politics" to signify a politics which is neither only universalist nor only based upon diversity, recognizing different perspectives but sharing a common vocabulary of values (see, for example, Yuval-Davis, 1997). The dialogues upon which such a politics is based involve the principles of "rooting" and "shifting," that is, where the partners in the dialogue are centered upon their own experiences yet are empathetic to the different ways in which other partners are positioned.[21] The Project was also raising the question of how a multiply positioned polity could be represented within the multilayered politics of the EU. In raising these questions, it clashed with the political practices and priorities of the European Women's Lobby. To begin with, women's issues had been framed from the start in terms of the restricted notion of women as paid workers (see earlier) and women still tended to be viewed as a unitary category – white/European and in paid work. However, even though the notion of women as a unitary category had, by the 1980s, been challenged by black feminists in a number of EU member states (the UK and the Netherlands, for example), this took time to filter through to the NGOs in the EU.

Although the EWL had supported the funding of the Project, the experience of the Project researcher, Emma Franks, in trying to get the EWL to accept and act upon the recommendations of the Report was one of profound personal disrespect, a disrespect which was racialized.[22] Originally, the Project had had few black women on it and Emma brought in black women who were active in their own communities, a move welcomed by other Project members. However, in Emma's experience, the EWL showed continual suspicion and distrust of these women. When the the Project women asked to view the committee processes of the EWL as part of the research, they were refused access. And when, eventually, after a great deal of effort and hard work, the Report was ready to be presented to the General Assembly meeting, Emma and Marika, another black woman, traveled from England to Brussels to attend the meeting. (It should be noted that, by any standard, the information gathered and presented in the Report is unique and remarkable. It contains 250 pages of detailed information and analysis of the organizations, politics, and conditions of black and migrant women in nine EU countries).[23] The women were asked to wait outside the meeting until it was their turn to speak. When they were asked in, Emma went to the podium and, as she began, was interrupted by the Treasurer who remembered she had an announcement for delegates: there was a Turkish market taking place outside the conference building and they needed to watch their purses. During her presentation she was "harangued" by (almost entirely white) Assembly delegates and, at the end, only one person clapped. This was one of the interpreters. Emma's view was that it was a combination of suspicion of bottom-up political ways of working, along with no experience of prioritizing differences as part of gender equality, especially racialized differences, that created difficulties. The top-down, bureaucratic EWL form of politics stood in direct contrast to the Project where "the group had great respect for each other." Her sense of personal invalidity was, she feels, exacerbated by the fact that she did not, herself, have a constituency of grassroots people to report to or call upon. This, she felt, is a necessary prerequisite for anyone who wants to challenge issues at the EU.

From the perspective of Jyostna Patel, a black woman who was working within the EWL at this time, the clash was partly to do with the political and practical constraints placed on NGOs.[24] To seize political opportunities they have to be mindful of the Commission's agenda and work to that rather than against it. In the case of the EWL and the Migrants' Forum, they were set up by the CEC and they are responsible to the CEC and are not therefore politically well placed to fundamentally challenge policy. Nevertheless, they are also accountable to, indeed, as far as the CEC is concerned, constitute a key link with, grassroots organizations. This relationship varies amongst NGOs. The EWL elects representatives from countries and from women's organizations (not necessarily feminist ones and often almost entirely white European in leadership). The ways in which member states elected their representatives to the EWL also varied. For example, national representatives from Britain were elected to represent Wales, England, Scotland, and Northern Ireland, thus limiting the opportunity for minority group representation. However, some transnational organizations which are members of the EWL, such as the

European Forum of Left Feminists, made the election of black women a priority. Similarly, the Dutch national system favored minority representation. By contrast, national representatives from Germany tend to come from white professional women's organizations. These variations reflect differences in the political and cultural histories of both gender and "race" politics in these countries.

Grassroots issues

Eventually the Report was published and the struggle moved to putting the recommendations into practice. An example of this is research into grassroots activism by Jyostna Patel and the documentation of models of good practice for black, minority ethnic, and migrant women in combating racism and sexism.[25] These activities reflect another important level, or set of audiences, against whom claims are made. One aspect of "good practice" to emerge is where projects aim to empower women on a personal level by increasing self-confidence and self-worth and encouraging their participation in the public sphere in their local communities, in employment, and/or in political organizations and public bodies (such as local or regional education boards).[26] Most of the projects researched combined improving access to resources, such as education, training, and employment (for example, in new information technologies), or legal rights, such as independent legal status, with building confidence and identity. Not only do the projects demonstrate women as political actors and not simply victims, but they also show the strategies minority ethnic women use to resist what Kymlicka calls "internal restrictions" (Kymlicka, 1995: 7). For example, one grassroots organization of minority ethnic women in Paris organizes against the practice of genital mutilation of women. In doing so, they stipulate that the only people to speak out against it in the communities who practice it should be women who themselves have experienced genital mutilation. This emphasizes the need for strategies against patriarchal practices within minority ethnic communities to be organized *from within* those communities. In this situation, white feminists' action is seen to be best placed in supporting these women (in the French case, white French women provide support through training and work with the medical profession) rather than in articulating opposition to those communities and their claims for cultural respect. The research also suggests that the experience of denigration most alarming in the lives of many minority ethnic women in Europe was violence at one or more levels of their lives – domestic violence, racial and sexual harassment on the street or in the workplace, and the state violence of police, immigration officers, and other officials.[27]

Challenging discourses of citizenship

The intervention on behalf of black and migrant women in the European Women's Lobby challenges almost every dimension and meaning of citizenship within EU political and policy discourses. As the Report itself acknowledges:

> The starting point of the Project contrasts with that which is usual in EU discourse: it breaks with the view that defines black and migrant communities as "problems" to be dealt with by tightening immigration controls and holding closed meetings outside normal EU procedures. It challenges the orthodoxy which sees black and migrant women as being without a separate existence, as passive adjuncts to predominantly male migration flows.
> The implications of European unity for black and migrant communities are overwhelming, as shown by the 1989 European elections, in which the extreme right polled more than seven million votes, but there has been no attempt to pick up and emphasize, at the EU level, anti-racist policy, action and research. [This subsequently changed as this chapter has shown.] This Project is part of an attempt to redress the balance and to present a truer picture of the complex reality of the lives of black and migrant women in Europe. (EWL, 1995: 9)

The campaign pushed at the discursive boundaries of citizenship in two ways: as a widening of feminist politics around citizenship and as a challenge to EU policies and politics. In terms of the former, the engendering of citizenship involved demonstrating how the private and the public are intertwined. Feminist politics and scholarship has been further refined by a recognition of the multifaceted nature of citizenship, in other words an understanding that women are positioned differently in relation to citizenship and structures of social rights according to class, "race," ethnicity, nationality, disability, marital and maternal status, sexual orientation, and age (Lister, 1997). In these terms, the intervention to articulate the interests of black, ethnic minority, and migrant women challenges the close connection between nationality and access to the social rights of citizenship. And in doing this, it challenges the ways in which nationality is constructed in both material and symbolic ways – territorially, but also linguistically, culturally, ethnically, and racially. Again, a further concern of feminist scholarship has been with how a feminist politics based upon a recognition of differences between women could be effective in securing political gains. In relation to this, the campaign raised the issue of how a group based upon a single identity (as women) can develop strategies which address differentiated interests. For not only did the Report *Confronting the Fortress* (EWL, 1995) challenge the separation of "race" from gender issues and the implied homogeneity of women, its commitment to continual dialogue with its grassroots, to respecting differences whilst seeking common policy recommendations, can be seen as an example of negotiating consensus around difference.

The second set of discursive boundaries that were contested were those of EU policies and politics. Ostner and Lewis (1995: 182) identify "the assumption of the readiness and capacity of women to take part in paid work on equal terms with men" as one of the central discourses which constrain the development of women's policies in the EU. The campaign highlighted the complexities of factors affecting minority ethnic women's opportunities for paid work, including not only the lack of attention to the conditions within the private sphere, but also racism, immigration policies, flexibilization, and casualization, some of which are the consequence of EU policies. The second dominant discourse contested the nature of pan-Europeanness being generated by the development of the EU. The fixing of supranational identity within a culturally and geographically bounded Europe makes difficult the acceptance of the diasporic identities to which first, second, and third generation Asian, African-Caribbean, North African, or Turkish citizens of Europe might lay claim. The experiences documented by the campaign demonstrated how black, minority ethnic, and migrant women shared a position of otherness in relation to a notion of white Europeanness which contributed to shared experiences of economic, social, and political marginalization.

The third area that the demands of the Black and Migrant Women's Project came face to face with was the elitist nature of politics and lack of accountability at the political, policy-making, and consultative level. By demanding that those who *experience* racism or immigration policies should have a voice in the process of policy-making, the Report challenged what in many ways is the Achilles' heel of the EU. Indeed, that there are possibilities for these issues to be raised reflects the Commission's need to create spaces in response to its own feelings of remoteness and concern with its legitimacy. In addition, one of the resources that ethnic minority women's groups as well as other women's groups have been able to exploit well is their own traditions of grassroots organizing and cross-country alliances (see Hoskyns, 1996: 15–17).

Along with pressures from other quarters, the Black and Migrant Women's Project has had some success in shifting the framing of some areas of policy. An example is the recognition of multiple inequalities in the Amsterdam Treaty mentioned earlier. However, in view of the restraints on the implementation of women's policies, opportunities for the realization of the social policy demands of black, minority ethnic, and migrant women seem less likely than for those which demand improved forms of representation. Progress on representation can of course contribute to progress in policy. However, what the past history of women's involvement in pushing for change in the EU shows is that women wield more discursive power than they do direct political power. That is to say, their mobilization in the EU has had the effect of shifting forward the terms on which social policy debates are constructed and conducted.

Conclusion

The claims by black, ethnic minority, and migrant women within the EU reflect their positioning within current social, economic, and political changes. These changes, on the one hand, reinforce their social, economic, and political marginalization within the EU, whilst, at the same time, creating solidarities and opening spaces for the articulation of challenges to the dominant meanings of citizenship which inscribe their marginalization. In the process, this group contributed to the reformulating of feminist politics in ways that can account and organize for difference and diversity between women. It also represents an example of an attempt to redefine the gendered and racialized contours of European citizenship, emphasizing the importance of a citizenship in which people have a voice which is both participative and representative, connecting the local to the international, combining a multipositioned constituency within a multileveled polity.

How, then, can this illuminate theories of recognition struggles? I return to the questions I raised at the beginning of the chapter. First, it confirms the ways in which cultural and economic injustices are intertwined, but it cannot be drawn from this that the process of struggle against them is similarly interlaced. The women in this case study had to fight within the EU for voice and visibility in order to place their economic and cultural injustices on the table. Furthermore, this process was crucial in order for them to take control of their own definitions of cultural and economic injustices. Theoretically, it could have been possible for the Parliament to have raised the issue of economic injustices on their behalf through the discourse of "exclusion." However, the casting of black, minority ethnic, and migrant women within this discourse would have limited the policy outcomes to integration through job opportunities rather than combating racism and sexism, or the democratic deficit.

Second, the study marks the importance in contemporary politics of the transnational sphere, as well as the need to continually work across and within the political spaces opened up at local, national, and transnational levels. Recognition and recognizers operate at multiple levels.

Third, in relation to identity, there appeared to be no simple congruence between social identities and the political identities forged in this campaign. The political identity of black, minority ethnic, and migrant women held as many overtly recognized differences as it did the common diasporic identity and position of otherness within Europe. The commonality was formed *out of* and *across* difference and *within* struggle. This presupposes the possibility of a politics that can, at one and the same time, respect those differences and work in common cause – very different from older notions of "a united front" where differences were dropped. This appears to mirror other identity politics developments which have moved away from essentialist notions of identity to more consciously constructed ones, as, for example, in the queering of sexuality politics.

The practices of a politics of difference in this study suggest that, for "participatory parity," as Nancy Fraser terms it, to operate for black, minority ethnic, and migrant women at the EU, it would require proper funding for local and national groups, networking in order to disseminate information, and a form of politics in which the principle of the mutual respect for difference is established, accepted, and operationalized. It would also require more activities of the sort in which many grassroots activists are currently engaged – in the reclaiming of self-esteem by those for whom it has been shredded by the combined effects of racism and sexism. Talking to the women involved in these politics suggested to me that we should not be too hasty in foreclosing the possibilities opened up by Honneth's analysis for exploring the links between political agency and the denial of, and need for, self-esteem. The importance of developing and sustaining self-esteem emerged not only in accounts of personal psychological damage inflicted in the process of demanding recognition, but also as the basis for developing the capacity to intervene politically – to engage in participatory parity.

Any attempt to develop further an understanding of the imbrication of redistribution and recognition struggles, and the forms of resistance to cultural and economic injustices, needs to be able to account for the horizontal and vertical complexity of claims-making. By that I mean, with reference to this case study, the complex intersectionality of identities and claims formed in the crucible of racialized, gendered, and other marginalized categories is important, as are the different levels – local, national, and supranational – at which claims are voiced. Second, we need to separate out three elements of recognition/redistribution struggles: the nature of the injustices fought; the nature of the claims articulated; and the process of the struggle to voice these claims, each of which may refer to the redistribution/recognition bivalence in different ways. The struggle to establish voice and visibility was, in this case study, about the redistribution of power and legitimacy organized through the discourses of institutionalized politics. Third, and finally, no simple congruence can be assumed between ontological, categorical, and political identities (that is, the identities through which we (a) experience ourselves; (b) are positioned; and (c) make claims. Instead, the dynamic relationship between the three needs further exploration. In my study the political identities which emerged required the careful negotiation of differences between the women along with a reconfiguring and restaking of the boundaries of categorical identities. Furthermore, the denial of claims for dignity and respect rebounded back onto ontological identities, making the demands for the rebuilding of self-esteem and self-confidence an integral part of claims-making.

6   Woman, black, indigenous: recognition struggles in dialogue

Marilyn Lake

> Black women look at white women and see the enemy for they know that racism is not confined to white men and there are more white women than men in this country.
>
>   Toni Morrison (quoted in Larissa Behrendt, 1993: 31).

> Within the feminist movement, non-Indigenous women have marginalised minority women, through lack of recognition and the presumption that they can speak on behalf of all women.
>
>   Lynette Morris (1996: 203).

Identity and recognition

In his influential essay on "The Politics of Recognition," Charles Taylor (1994) has explored the emergence in recent times of political movements animated by the need, indeed the demand, for recognition – recognition of people's identity, of who they are, of their defining characteristics as human beings. Recognition struggles arise in response to an absence of recognition or misrecognition, or both. Nonrecognition and misrecognition have been identified as grave harms constituting distinctive new forms of political oppression.

Taylor explains that recognition struggles have become definitive of modern times, because in earlier ages "recognition was built into the socially derived identity by virtue of the very fact that it was based on social categories that everyone took for granted" (1994: 34). Only with the simultaneous rise of the idea of individual identity and the advent of democracy's promise of human rights – the move from honor to dignity – could the failure of recognition become a cause of grievance and the withholding of recognition a political offense. The emphasis on equality gave rise to the idea of universal human rights; the importance attached to identity has given rise to the politics of difference and the concomitant refusal of assimilationism, of being forced to fit into someone else's mold. A paradoxical shift was made possible:

The politics of difference is full of denunciations of discrimination and refusals of second-class citizenship. This gives the principle of universal equality a point of entry within the politics of dignity . . . The universal demand powers an acknowledgment of specificity. (Taylor, 1994: 39)

Thus, perversely to some, the *refusal* to discriminate, to recognize that the self is constituted in difference, comes to be seen as itself highly discriminatory.

Taylor (1994: 32) explains the connection between identity and recognition in terms of "a crucial feature of human life" which is its "fundamentally dialogical character." Identity is affirmed through others signifying recognition: thus recognition struggles are characteristically discursive in nature, conducted in the domain of culture and civil society, in the media, in schools and universities. In this chapter, I shall explore the "dialogical character" of recognition struggles themselves, the interaction and interdependence of seemingly independent movements. The literature on the variety of recognition struggles usually treats feminist and anti-racist or nationalist movements as if they were independent, if parallel, phenomena. I want to highlight their "dialogic character" as being fundamental to the way in which identities are made and remade in the process of the recognition struggles being waged.

My subject is the dynamic interrelationship of the white women's movement in Australia and Aboriginal women's struggles for recognition and self-representation. The dialogue between the white women's movement and Black women shaped a new sense of racialized identity on both sides but, in a further development, Aboriginal women came to assert the distinctiveness of their claims as Indigenous Australians, as the colonized and dispossessed. And they claimed their right to political voice through self-representation.

Women's demand for recognition

The 1970s Women's Liberation movement in Australia was itself a demand for acknowledgment of women's exclusion from the national culture, polity, and history. In the name of "women," its spokespeople demanded equal rights and opportunities in the present and, crucially, appropriate representation in the national histories of the past. Women's Liberation in Australia was informed, as elsewhere, by the new international discourse on "sexism" and "sex roles," but it addressed, not patriarchy, but the nation. It was the condition of women in Australia, not women in general, that was the object of their inquiry and, from the outset, feminist historians spoke on behalf of the women's movement in addressing their demands for recognition to the national community and to their fellow historians.

Significantly, the first four monographs produced by the Women's Liberation movement in Australia, in 1975 and 1976, were all national histories, the protests against misrecognition *and* lack of recognition evident in the titles: Beverley Kingston's *My Wife, My Daughter and Poor Mary Ann, Gentle Invaders: Australian Women at Work* by Edna Ryan and Anne Conlon, Anne Summers' *Damned Whores and God's Police: The Colonization of Women in Australia*, and Miriam Dixson's *The Real Matilda: Women and Identity in Australia 1788 to 1975*. The link between the lack of national recognition and the experience of disrespect was made explicit by Dixson in her now famous opening line: "I propose that Australian women, women in the land of mateship, 'the Ocker', keg-culture, come pretty close to top-rating as the 'Doormats of the Western World'." (Dixson, 1976: 11)

On the face of it, this was a bold assertion about the standing of the first women in the world to win the right to both vote and stand for election to the national parliament, women whose enfranchisement in 1902 followed almost immediately upon the creation of the Commonwealth of Australia as a nation state in 1901. Dixson's point, however, was that women had been victims of systematic cultural denigration and disavowal, not least by the practitioners of her own craft. In defining what it was to be Australian, historians had valorized the deeds of men: bushrangers, shearers, nationalist writers, trade unionists, men at war. Writing in 1976, Dixson was perceptive in the connection she drew between history, identity, and recognition, which she had signaled in her subtitle:

Australians are now increasingly discovering their past. But the explorers are mainly males and what they are uncovering tends to concern the lives and achievements of males. Their work is thus a kind of unacknowledged affirmation of their present identity through a celebration of their past selves. They believe, however, that they are uncovering "the past", and fail to notice that they deny that same affirmation to women through school, university, the novel and the mass media. Thus in this proud democracy, women figure as pygmies in the culture of the present and are almost obliterated from the annals of the past. (Dixson, 1976: 12)

Anne Summers also described her influential work, *Damned Whores and God's Police*, as "a book about Australia" and she provided an extended account of the particular ways in which the "sexism" of Australian culture rested on the operation of the two historical stereotypes of women, those of "damned whores" and "God's police."

The book carried what would come to be seen as a highly problematic subtitle: *The Colonization of Women in Australia*. Women had been colonized by men.

Within a supposedly free and independent Australia women are a colonized sex. They are denied freedom of movement, control of their bodies, economic independence and cultural potency. (Summers, 1975: 4)

Summers elaborated this argument at length, in a separate chapter, making the point that it was "no metaphor," but rather a "salient political description" of the condition of women. She continued:

Colonization is accomplished by the brute force of invasion and by the partial or complete destruction of the native people's culture... The native people is persuaded, or forced, to concede that its own culture is inferior and that it should strive to emulate and adopt that of the colonizing power. (Summers 1975: 198)

The native people here, of course, were not Indigenous Australians but women; the colonizers were all men. The disputed territory was woman's body.

Will the real colonizers please stand up?

Black women reacted with rising anger to these political and historical representations made on behalf of and about "women." What was in dispute were the assumptions of common experience and common interests. In her 1975 essay, "Black Women in Australia – A History," Black activist Bobbi (Roberta) Sykes sketched a history of Aboriginal Australia following the "invasion" by the British, in which Blacks lost their land, were poisoned and shot, deprived of food, and infected with introduced disease. The British also "took [the Black man's] women" (Sykes, 1975: 313–21). Sykes stressed the prevalence and invisibility of the rape of Black women and girls, in the past and present, an emphasis that her autobiography would later make clear was informed by personal trauma. Black women, Sykes insisted, were subjected to a particular form of contempt in Australia. On the other hand, Aboriginal people had survived largely through the work of women in raising families and sustaining communities. But the Black woman remained oppressed:

Burdened down with the complexities of bringing up children in this sophisticated and complicated society, she remains an object of sexual fulfilment for the white man, and an "invisible" woman to her white female contemporaries, especially the "establishment" of Women's Liberationists who chatter on about sexual oppression and the competitive orgasm, and who spare not a thought for the true object of sexual oppression in this country today. (Sykes, 1975: 318)

The most important obstacle faced by Black women, Sykes (1975: 319) concluded, was "the barrier of racist attitudes."

The following year, in an extended critique of the politics of Women's Liberation, Aboriginal activist and lawyer Pat O'Shane asked "Is There Any Relevance in the Women's Movement for Aboriginal Women?" She advanced several related arguments as to why the white women's movement failed to attract Black women: first, like Sykes, she insisted on the

importance of history – Aboriginal society had been destroyed by ruth-
less and greedy "white invaders"; second, racism was a more significant
problem for contemporary Aboriginal women than sexism ("Sexist attitudes did not wipe out whole tribes of our people today – racism did,
and continues to do so!"); third, the women's movement should "examine carefully whether or not their aims as white women are necessarily
those of black women"; and finally, O'Shane argued that the most important political goal for Aboriginal Australians was land rights (O'Shane,
1976: 32).

The women's movement, in short, was asked to recognize itself as
"white" with "white" interests, preoccupations, and power.

So far as the women's movement is concerned it is necessary for women involved
to examine carefully whether or not their aims as white women are necessarily
those of black women. Necessary because there appears to me at times, to be an
attitude amongst some of the "activists" that black women ought to be involved in
the women's liberation movement at the same level and in the same organizations
as are the white women. (O'Shane, 1976: 34)

By the 1980s, the idea of "difference" elaborated in the theoretical
framework of post-coloniality gave strength to Aboriginal critiques of
white feminist presumption. In "A Contemporary View of Aboriginal
Women's Relationship to the White Women's Movement," published
in the early 1990s, Aboriginal historian Jackie Huggins (1994: 70) was
moved to decry "the lack of recognition and real understanding of...
difference": "Aboriginal women insisted that the Women's Liberation
Movement recognise that the conditions they faced were different."
Above all, white women were taken to task for their failure to acknowledge their own privileged position as the descendants of colonizers. White
women were being challenged to interrogate their history anew.

In a 1993 article entitled "Aboriginal Women and the White Lies of the
Feminist Movement," published in the *Australian Feminist Law Journal*,
Larissa Behrendt reminded her (mostly) white readers, "White women
lived and profited on the land stolen violently from Aboriginal women."
She demanded acknowledgment of the real relations of oppression in
Australia:

Aboriginal women have been oppressed by white women. White women were
missionaries that attempted to destroy Aboriginal culture. They used the slave
labour of Aboriginal women in their homes. White women were the wives, mothers and sisters of those who violently raped Aboriginal women and children and
brutally murdered Aboriginal people. White women can be as racist as white men.
White women have benefitted economically from the dispossession of Aboriginal
people. (Behrendt, 1993: 31)

White women, including feminists, had to recognize that Aboriginal women had a different history and, thus, a different political agenda. High on their agenda was the demand for recognition of land rights and the need to protect women's sacred sites. Aboriginal women were also necessarily pro-family: there was a need to rebuild families which had been systematically smashed by the state through the removal of children. They emphasized the preservation of language and culture and improved access to health, education, and legal services. Aboriginal people's (especially men's) high rates of imprisonment were also a major issue.

Writing "as an indigenous woman" in a collection of "young feminist" writings, called *DIY Feminism*, Lynette Morris confirmed, Aboriginal women had different priorities compared to most feminists. She specified that Aboriginal women's main concern was racism, rather than "gender inequalities".

We must consider the violent oppression that indigenous women suffered at the hands of both non-indigenous men and women. This oppression has happened in many ways: for example, stealing indigenous children away from their families and institutionalising them, exploiting young black women as domestic slaves, and the overall genocide of indigenous cultures and peoples. (Morris, 1996: 202)

"I don't identify myself as feminist," concluded Morris. "I am a Murrie woman" (Morris, 1996: 203).

Aboriginal women were intent on debunking the cherished feminist myth of "sisterhood" and refusing the political identity "woman." "I am no more woman than I am Aboriginal," insisted Morris (1996: 203). "What white women do not realise is that, despite the general diversity of opinions in Aboriginal society, the strong stance that Aboriginal women take against the white women's movement remains universal," said Jackie Huggins. "In evidence for this there has not been in australia [sic] to date, one published document by an Aboriginal or Torres Strait Islander woman who avidly supports the women's liberation movement" (Huggins, 1994: 76). Huggins, like O'Shane, Behrendt, and Morris, pointed to Aboriginal women's different needs and priorities, and reiterated the refusal of Indigenous people to assimilate themselves to the white mold, the white feminist mold. Huggins drew attention to the "politics of representation." The struggle for identity, for recognition, was taking place on the terrain of culture and in opposition to "white feminism and women's studies":

Aboriginal women fight not only the material, but also the cultural pressures which have sought to construct them according to someone else's mould. Western theory, language, academia – to name a few – are foreign constructs in which Aboriginal women do not fit. Therefore an oppressive society controls and manipulates Aboriginal women and in turn dictates how they should behave, think, learn, speak, write, etc. White feminism and women's studies are white cultural products which have been guilty of all the above. (Huggins, 1994: 70)

No longer could white feminists cast themselves as the marginalized and oppressed in the context of the Australian nation. Aboriginal women's demand for recognition cut two ways: there was the demand that feminists acknowledge Indigenous women's different experiences and interests, but at the same time feminists were called upon to see themselves as "white women" complicit in the historical dispossession of Aboriginal women; they were to accept a new identity as imperial oppressors, indeed as the agents of "cultural genocide":

Aside from the domestic servant sphere, the oppression of Aboriginal women and children by white women was also extreme in the fields of welfare and education, and this situation continues today. Many Aboriginal children have suffered brutally at the hands of white women who have always known what "is best" for these children. White women were and still are a major force in the implementation of government policies of assimilation and cultural genocide. (Huggins, 1994: 73)

Recognition struggles are waged in the cultural domain and Aboriginal women stressed the importance of self-representation. Speaking for themselves, they would stress their important ties with communities, with children, with women, with men. The use of alienating and culturally insensitive theoretical discourses perpetuated oppression: "Without recognition of the above, there is no point in Black and white women entering into or continuing discussions together" (Huggins, 1994: 78).

Aboriginal women also demanded that white women recognize them as powerful, autonomous, and independent within their traditional culture. There they were respected, spiritually empowered, and self-sufficient. Unlike white women, they did not suffer cultural denial and disavowal. It was feminists who failed to show due respect, not Aboriginal men:

Women's position in Aboriginal culture, both traditional and contemporary, situates them within a powerful network of female support. This means that Aboriginal women put into practice the ideal which white feminists refer to as "sisterhood" ...

This powerful relationship between Aboriginal women has been practised since the Dreaming. It has been absolutely vital to the Aboriginal struggle to survive the attempted genocide since the invasion, and certainly will not be done away with for the sake of protecting white feminism! Some white women display a complete lack of respect for Aboriginal women's cultural values and political structures in their attempts to create divisions between Black women to serve the purpose of their tokenism. (Huggins 1994: 76)

"Lack of recognition and real understanding of this political difference," concluded Huggins, "is a major issue still to be resolved by the white women's movement" (Huggins, 1994: 70).

Recognition struggles demand not just recognition and respect from those who would deny these things, but also that the oppressors own (up to) their "real" identities, to their own investments and power. Recognition struggles are fundamentally dialogical in character: they presuppose an audience and seek a response; the protagonists hold up mirrors to their oppressors, so that they might see themselves anew. It was crucial to this process of mutual recognition that the Aboriginal women's critique of white feminism was published in feminist anthologies and journals. Invited to participate in the feminist project, Aboriginal women denounced it for its irrelevance. Invited to join a movement, Aboriginal women replied that they had a movement of their own. Invited to identify as women, Aboriginal women have responded by emphasizing their identity as Aboriginal, as the Indigenous people of Australia, whose dispossession was produced, in part, by white women. Recognition struggles are provoked by domination and the perceived nature of the domination shapes and sharpens the resultant assertion of identity.

The destabilization of the category "Black"

When Aboriginal women mobilized in the 1970s and 1980s against the claims of the white women's movement to represent women's interests, they initially identified as "Black" and defined the nature of their oppression as a generalized racism. They were influenced in this direction by the writings of African-Americans such as bell hooks and Toni Morrison (as is evident in the opening quotation), but increasingly their struggle for recognition led them to emphasize their distinctive identity as Indigenous. As Aboriginal women confronted white women with their identity as "colonizers," so they positioned themselves as the "colonized" and "dispossessed." Theirs was a politics of grief, a response to cumulative loss: Aboriginal people had lost their lands, their languages, their communities, their identity. By the 1980s, the issue had become country and culture, not color.

The broader history of campaigns for Aboriginal rights encouraged this demand for recognition as a people, as the government-based goal of assimilation gave way to demands for self-determination. In 1967, Australians had voted in an historic constitutional referendum pertaining to Aboriginal citizenship, when over 90 percent of the predominantly white electorate voted "Yes" to constitutional reform. The aim was to delete the "discriminatory clauses" from the Australian constitution, in order to, first, enable the federal government to acquire concurrent powers with the states and thus take responsibility for Aboriginal welfare and, second, enable Aboriginal people to be counted in the national census. The referendum did not extend new civil or legal rights to Aboriginal people (they already had the vote and entitlement to social security benefits), but it assumed enormous symbolic significance, signifying the inclusion of Aboriginal people in the nation. It was especially important to non-Indigenous Blacks, such as Faith Bandler, the daughter of a Pacific Islander, who was appointed Director of the New South Wales "Vote Yes" campaign (Lake, 2001). Bandler's father, Peter Mussing, had been brought to Australia from the Pacific island of Ambrym, in the then New Hebrides, in the late nineteenth century, to labor on the sugar cane plantations in north Queensland. One of the first laws passed by the new Commonwealth of Australia was the Pacific Islands Labourers Act aimed to deport these Black laborers. Like Aborigines, they were deemed to have no place in a future "White Australia" – but a large number escaped the authorities' net and remained to marry and form families and communities.

Peter Mussing raised his family in northern New South Wales, and Faith and her brothers and sisters grew up in the segregated towns of northern New South Wales, where they experienced racist abuse and exclusion from the local hospitals, swimming pools, and picture theatres. For Faith, this memory of racial exclusion bred a yearning and a demand for acceptance, which fueled her ten-year political campaign for the referendum. "I wanted to understand," she told a journalist, "I wanted to know why a man should be an outcast in his own country just because his skin is black." Her thinking on race had been influenced by the work of Paul Robeson and the American writer, Howard Fast, who had promoted the ideal of blacks and whites living together, and working together, in his novel *Freedom Road*. This was also Faith's ideal. "Tell the world there's only one Australian," she declared to a meeting to support the "Yes" vote in May 1967, "and his colour doesn't matter at all" (Attwood and Markus, 1997: 107).

The passage of the referendum signified that Blacks would be part of the Australian nation, but many Aboriginal people felt deeply ambivalent about this new status, fearing that it also signified their final extinguishment as a people. As Aboriginal leader Bert Groves cautioned: "We want to be part and parcel of the community, but we want to do this without losing our identity as Australian Aborigines." Assimilation was "a modified method of extermination over a long time. Once assimilation was complete the Aboriginal race would cease to exist, and the Aboriginal problem would cease with it" (Attwood and Markus, 1997: 108).

One important consequence of the referendum was the creation of a national Aboriginal constituency. Once the federal government had the power to legislate with regard to Indigenous people, who would say what legislation should be passed? Who would represent the Aboriginal view? The passage of the referendum drew Aboriginal people, from across the country, into a national politics of representation, which in turn sharpened the distinction between Indigenous and non-Indigenous Australians, a conceptual distinction that cut across distinctions based on "color." Another result of the referendum was that Aboriginal activists regrouped, with many leaving the coalitional organizations, such as the Federal Council for the Advancement of Aborigines and Torres Strait Islanders, with which they had worked from the late 1950s, in favor of all-Aboriginal bodies such as the National Tribal Council. Political campaigns increasingly focused on achieving land rights, the establishment of Aboriginal legal, medical, and housing services and self-government.

In a study of "Feminism and Institutionalized Racism" in an Australian feminist refuge, the author Tikka Jan Wilson, an African-American immigrant to Australia, refers to her shock at being described by an Aboriginal man as a "whitefella." She explains:

In this naming of the world, all people who are not Indigenous Australians are whitefellas, whatever their skin colour or background. Positioning us as whites highlights the substantial economic and social benefits all migrants reap from the colonial appropriation of Aboriginal people's land and resources. While many immigrants, both in Australia and elsewhere, analyse and struggle against racial/ethnic subordination in the "host" country, it is equally important for us to acknowledge and respond to any new positions of structural privilege we assume as a result of migration. (Wilson, 1996: 5)

In the struggle against racist discrimination within the women's movement, "white women" were initially castigated by "Blacks," but in the course of their recognition struggle, Aboriginal women began to insist on and privilege their identity as Indigenous Australians, and in one well-publicized case, denounced a leading Black woman activist for being an impersonator.

Roberta Sykes, who had written "Black Women in Australia: A History," in 1975, to point out the particular oppressions suffered by Aboriginal women in Australia had, in the 1990s, attracted considerable media attention with the publication of her three-part autobiography, called *Snake Dreaming: Autobiography of a Black Woman*. In her account of growing up in the north Australian city of Townsville, Sykes discussed her uncertainty about her father's identity – her mother was white – but she suggested she had reason to believe she was of Aboriginal descent and her totem was the snake. Following the publication of the second volume, *Snake Dancing* (Sykes, 1998), Aboriginal women from the Birrigubba clan in the Townsville area publicly cast doubt on her claim to be Indigenous, stating that Sykes grew up in the white community and had given everyone to understand that her mother had told her that her father was a black US serviceman stationed in Townsville during World War II.

Associate Professor Gracelyn Smallwood, a member of the Birrigubba nation and director of Aboriginal Studies at the University of Southern Queensland, who wrote a report on the matter, commented: "She has constructed an identity closely aligned to the snake as a totem in a desperate search for Aboriginality. There is no evidence to show she understands the seriousness of such an action" (*Sydney Morning Herald*, 1998). Then in a full-page article in the national newspaper, the *Weekend Australian*, leading Aboriginal activist and Chancellor of the University of New England, Pat O'Shane (who had in the 1970s joined Sykes in challenging the white women's movement's relevance to Aboriginal women) accused Sykes of fraudulently misrepresenting herself as Aboriginal to reap material rewards, such as a scholarship to Harvard University, where Sykes had graduated in 1984, with a PhD. Sykes, claimed O'Shane, had claimed an identity to which she was not entitled (*Weekend Australian*, 1998).

Writing their own story

Central to Aboriginal women's struggle for recognition has been the production of life stories or autobiographical narratives, a genre which, as Anne Brewster (1996) has noted in her study *Reading Aboriginal Women's Autobiography*, women have come to dominate. In her recent book on Indigenous women and feminism in Australia, *Talkin' Up to the White Woman*, Aileen Moreton-Robinson (2000), a Koenpul woman from Quandamooka, has pointed to the crucial importance of these "self-presentations," noting, however, that in their writings "self" is constituted in fundamentally different ways from those in white women's writing:

In these life writings experience is fundamentally social and relational, not something ascribed separately within the individual. Indigenous women's life writings are based on the collective memories of inter-generational relationships between predominantly Indigenous women, extended families and communities . . . These relationships are underpinned by connections with one's country and the spirit world. In all these life writings, Indigenous people are related either by descent, country or place or shared experiences. In this sense the life writings of Indigenous women are an extension of Indigenous relationality in that they express the self as part of others and others as part of the self within and across generations. (Moreton-Robinson, 2000: 1–2)

The proliferation of Indigenous women's life writings has been a publishing phenomenon. Margaret Tucker's *If Everyone Cared* was published in 1977, quickly followed by Monica Clare's *Karobran: The Story of an Aboriginal Girl* (1978), Ella Simon's *Through My Eyes* (1978), Shirley Smith and Bobbi Sykes's *Mum Shirl* (1981), Elsie Roughsey's *An Aboriginal Mother Tells of the Old and the New* (1984), Marnie Kennedy's *Born a Half-Caste* (1985), and Ida West's *Pride Against Prejudice* (1987).

The most successful of the genre was Sally Morgan's *My Place*, which became a national and international bestseller. Published in 1987, it had sold over 400,000 copies within ten years. *My Place* is a quest narrative, telling the story of Morgan's search for and discovery of her Aboriginal heritage and the history of her mother's and grandmother's removal from their families and communities and consequent shame about, and denial of, their Aboriginality. Following the publication of Morgan's book, another ten Aboriginal women's life stories appeared within six years: Glenyse Ward's *Wandering Girl* (1987) and *Unna You Fullas* (1991), Ruby Langford's *Don't Take Your Love to Town* (1988), Della Walker and Tina Coutts's *Me and You* (1989), Ellie Gaffney's *Somebody Now* (1989), Patsy Cohen and Margaret Somerville's *Ingelba and the Five Black Matriarchs* (1990), Doris Pilkington's *Caprice: A Stockman's Daughter* (1991), Mabel Edmund's *No Regrets* (1992), Alice Nannup's *When the Pelican Laughed* (1992), and Evelyn Crawford's *Over My Tracks* (1993).

As collective life stories these narratives told of their people's history of dispossession and colonization. As Ruby Langford wrote:

We are invaded people, and have been since 1788...We have always had to conform to the laws and standards of the invaders. Our tribal laws mean nothing to the white man, our traditional people were classified as heathens and vermin to be cleared off the face of the earth. Assimilate us or wipe us out was the order of the day. (cited in Brewster, 1996: 2)

Many of the life stories tell of the removal of children and whole families from traditional country, their incarceration in white homes and institutions, under government laws allegedly passed in the interests of Aboriginal "protection."

While white women were urged to bear large families in the interests of the nation and the race, Aboriginal women were deemed ineligible for motherhood and constantly faced the possibility of having their children taken from them. Doris Pilkington tells of the effect of the removal of her mother and aunty from their families and community in Western Australia:

Molly and Gracie sat silently on the horse, tears streaming down their cheeks as Constable Riggs turned the big bay stallion and led the way back to the depot.

A high pitched wail broke out. The cries of agonised mothers and the women, and the deep sobs of grandfathers, uncles and cousins filled the air. Molly and Gracie looked back just once before they disappeared through the river gums. Behind them, those remaining in the camp found strong sharp objects and gashed themselves and inflicted wounds to their heads and bodies as an expression of their sorrow. (cited in Moreton-Robinson, 2000: 8–9)

Indigenous women's narratives also tell of their coercion into various forms of unpaid or low-paid labor and the experience of working in domestic service for white women and, as Moreton-Robinson notes, "acts of humiliation and cruelty by white women pervade Indigenous women's life writings" (Moreton-Robinson, 2000: 28).

Together these self-presentations offered a new and dramatically different account of national history. As Langford has observed: "My story is about twentieth century Aboriginal life . . . About the way we live today. And it's probably the only information that a lot of students get that puts the Aboriginal point of view. Because Koori history and culture is almost never taught in schools, and if it is, it is seen by whites, and not from an Aboriginal perspective" (Brewster, 1996: 44). In this new history, Indigenous people became the agents of their own stories, while white women were positioned on the side of the colonizers.

Crises in identity: feminism and/as the nation

In this dialogical relationship, the relations of dependence and the need for recognition were mutual. White feminists needed Aboriginal women to teach them about the centrality of "race" to identity, their own as well as that of others. As a politics of morality, feminism needed Aboriginal women to reaffirm the legitimacy of the feminist project itself. As a result, Aboriginal and other non-white women have more invitations to speak and write than they can possibly accept. Australian post-colonial theorist Ien Ang has commented on this need:

For some time now, the problematic of race and ethnicity has thrown feminism into crisis. I am implicated in this crisis. As a woman of Chinese descent, I suddenly find myself in a position in which I can turn my "difference" into intellectual and political capital, where "white" feminists invite me to raise my "voice", *qua* a non-white woman, and make myself heard . . . In this sense, feminism acts like a nation; just like Australia, it no longer subscribes to a policy of assimilation, but wants to be multi-cultural. (Ang, 1995: 73)

But for Ang, this desire to include, to absorb difference, remains problematic, replicating the original injury. The only satisfactory outcome of the politics of recognition is, she argues, a politics of partiality. Feminists must recognize their Western whiteness and accept that feminism is "a *limited* political home."

A politics of partiality implies that feminism must emphasise and consciously construct the limits of its own field of political intervention. While a politics of inclusion is driven by an ambition for universal representation (of all women's interests), a politics of partiality does away with that ambition and accepts the principle that feminism can never ever be an encompassing political home for all women, not just because different groups of women have different and sometimes conflicting interests, but, more radically, because for many groups of "other" women other interests, other identifications are sometimes more important and politically pressing than, or even incompatible with, those related to their being women. (Ang, 1995: 75)

But Australian feminists had been challenged by Indigenous women not just to recognize their "whiteness," but their colonial presence. It was not just feminism that had been thrown into crisis, but their national identity.

In their struggle for recognition, Aboriginal women had caused white women to rethink the relationship between feminism and nationalism, and to ponder on the implications of their status as "colonized" subjects, as Summers had cast white women in 1975. New historical research began to acknowledge and interrogate the ambiguities of white women's historical agency. As was noted in the introduction to a new feminist history of Australia, *Creating a Nation*, published in 1994:

In agency there is also responsibility. As beneficiaries of the dispossession of Aboriginal peoples, European women, along with men, were complicit in an imperialist, civilising project that saw the near destruction of Australia's indigenous peoples and their languages and culture. Aboriginal women's memories of white brutality focus on domestic violence and confinement perpetrated by the white mistress in the home, as well as the exploitation and sexual violence that so often characterised their encounters with white men on the frontier. (Grimshaw et al., 1994: 1)

Indigenous women's struggles for recognition have led white feminists and especially feminist historians to think more deeply about the political ambiguities of national belonging (Curthoys, 1993; Lake, 1994a; 2000; Sheridan, 1995). Feminist historians have been central to the reconceptualization of nation-building as a profoundly racialized endeavor – naming it the "blatant racism that underlay Federation" – which led to the creation of the Commonwealth of Australia in 1901 (Grimshaw 2002: 29).

Recognition struggles and the making and dissolution of identities

In Australia, during the last thirty years, the women's movement and Aboriginal rights movements have been engaged in a dynamic and interdependent relationship, with the different struggles influencing and shaping each other. In the process of waging recognition struggles, Aboriginal and non-Aboriginal women had made their relationships to country and nation definitive for their assertion of identity – white women had raged against their national subordination by men, while Aboriginal women had identified white colonization as central to their oppression – and thus the writing of national history became a contested field and key site of struggle.

In the process, feminists came to see themselves as colonizers as well as the colonized, as benefiting from, as well as subordinated by, nation-building. Non-Indigenous Black women were repositioned in terms of the dichotomy of Indigenous and non-Indigenous as "whitefellas." The proliferation of Aboriginal women's life stories – their coming to political voice – changed understandings of national history, challenged white women to acknowledge their privilege as the descendants of colonizers, and contributed importantly to the popular movement towards "reconciliation," that remains one of the most important political challenges for Australians at the beginning of the twenty-first century.

In an influential argument that frames the essays in this volume, Nancy Fraser posited a distinction between political movements geared towards recognition, on the one hand, and redistribution, on the other. It seems clear that Aboriginal peoples' struggle for recognition as the first owners and custodians of the country now called Australia has far-reaching economic implications, as their call for the redistribution of national resources, not least, land, is central to their political claim. They have achieved some success in this regard with the High Court's recognition of the continuing existence of Native Title in the Mabo judgment in 1992 and the Wik judgment in 1996. Recognition of Indigenous claims to land rights has seen the return of country to Aboriginal peoples, especially in Western Australia, Queensland, and the Northern Territory, but there have also been setbacks as the process is always contested. As a step towards meeting their goal of self-determination, the Aboriginal and Torres Strait Islander Commission (ATSIC) was established in 1990, an elected "Aboriginal parliament," with responsibility for the distribution of its own budget to support Aboriginal educational, health, employment, and cultural programs in regional communities. Calls for reparation for the harm done to the "Stolen Generations" – children removed from their families – are ongoing.

For Indigenous Australians, recognition and redistribution struggles have necessarily been intertwined, and central to those struggles has been the discursive power of Aboriginal women's critique of feminism and Aboriginal women's life stories. As Moreton-Robinson (2000) has argued, their "self-presentation" has been "a political act" – an enactment of their relationship to the country and the past, inspired in part, as was Moreton-Robinson's book, by the provocations of the women's movement. They have played a crucial discursive role in educating the women's movement and the broader community about Indigenous Australians' relationship to the country, their historical oppression, and the justice of their current claims. The dialogue first sparked between Aboriginal and non-Aboriginal women in the 1970s has been a key aspect and dynamic in this broader movement towards the recognition of historical injustice that underpins the yearning for reconciliation.

7 US women's suffrage through a multicultural lens: intersecting struggles of recognition

Diane Sainsbury

Introduction

With the emergence of multiculturalism, many observers have heralded a major turn in contemporary politics. They claim that a "politics of difference" has displaced a "politics of universalism." The ideal of equal rights and entitlements has given way to the aspiration of differentiated rights and citizenship; recognition has supplanted redistribution; and claims and solidarity are no longer primarily based on class and interests but on culture and identities.

Several theorists also suggest the newness of recognition struggles. One of the clearest statements about the newness of the politics of recognition has been formulated by Charles Taylor. He argues that identities were unproblematic in the past, because "general recognition was built into the socially derived identity by virtue of the very fact that it was based on social categories that everyone took for granted" (1994: 34). According to him, what is new is that the demand for recognition is now explicit and recognition can be withheld. The making and sustaining of identities involves the recognition of others, and recognition must be won through struggles within and among groups. This, in turn, has created an awareness that misrecognition and lack of recognition are forms of oppression. In effect, misrecognition has been elevated to a harm of the same rank as inequality, exploitation, and injustice.

The claims of newness are further reinforced by assumptions about time and the sequential nature of the politics of recognition. Taylor assumes that a politics of equal respect, grounded in universalism, precedes a politics of difference. Axel Honneth sees recognition struggles as a historical process of moral progress evolving towards successive levels of recognition where the ultimate outcome will be that all human beings are recognized as "both autonomous and individuated, equal and particular persons" (1995b: 175).

As distinct from the other chapters of this book, my focus is on a historical case: US women's efforts to win the right to vote. I propose to

161

examine women's struggle for political rights using the lens of multiculturalism and recognition as a framework. Through a historical case we
can interrogate if and how current recognition struggles are new.

How does a multicultural lens increase our understanding of women's
struggle for political rights? By focusing on cultural identities and multiple identities, the notion of multiculturalism underscores the complexity
of the US experience. The Native American–settler cleavage was compounded by the ethnic and racial diversity of the settler population. The
settlers included Hispanics, Africans, Asians, and virtually every European nationality. Diversity also characterized Native American cultures,
making political unity or even cooperation among tribes difficult. Furthermore, this lens raises the issue of the interrelatedness of recognition
struggles, that is, the extent to which they either overlap reinforcing group
claims or set in motion an exclusionary dynamic.

Several chroniclers of the suffrage movement have emphasized that
extending the franchise to African-American males and women was fa-
tally intertwined in the USA.[1] Much less attention has focused on Native
Americans or Hispanics. The official history of the suffrage movement,
however, portrays Indians and Mexicans as the opponents of women's
rights or unwitting pawns in campaigns to block the introduction of
suffrage. More generally, the official chroniclers argued that the racial
and ethnic diversity of the USA delayed the advent of womanhood
suffrage.

Despite the centrality of race in many accounts of women's fight for
the vote, the subtext of these narratives is white female citizenship. As
black feminist historians have pointed out, African-American female citizenship has a different chronology from white rights (Ann Gordon et al.,
1997; Terborg-Penn, 1998). This is also true for Native Americans whose
routes to citizenship differed from the majority population. For them and
African-Americans, the landmark years for formal and de facto inclusion
are not the same as those celebrated in history books. The subtext of white
female citizenship also manifests itself in the suffrage movement's official
histories (HWS, vols. 1–6, 1881–1922; Catt and Shuler, 1969 [1926])
and studies concentrating on movement leaders and the national suffrage association (Kraditor, 1981 [1965]; O'Neill, 1969; Graham, 1996;
Marilley, 1996) in that they ignore the contributions of African-American
women, Hispanic women, and Native American women. Instead the accounts that deal with race and ethnicity underline the racism and nativism
of suffrage leaders and the national suffrage organization.

To overcome these shortcomings, it is necessary to shift attention from
national leaders and the national organization – the National American
Woman Suffrage Association (NAWSA) – to the state campaigns and

grassroots activists. Many state campaigns have the potential to shed light on how the recognition struggles of African-Americans, Native Americans, and Hispanics impinged upon and shaped women's struggle. Rather than using representativeness as the criterion for selection, I have chosen a heuristic case – one that reveals the fruitfulness of applying a multicultural lens to the women's suffrage struggle.

In selecting a state campaign that can provide insights into the importance of intersecting recognition struggles, Oklahoma is an immediate candidate. At the turn of the century, statehood was the pressing issue and the period constituted a formative "moment." During these years, Indians, African-Americans, an alliance of labor and farmers, and the women of Oklahoma were locked in struggles for recognition of their rights and social worth. The Indians fought against dissolution of their tribal governments and dispossession of their lands, setting their hopes on the creation of an Indian state. Oklahoma blacks struggled against segregation and disenfranchisement. A labor–farm alliance battled corporate and banking interests; under the banner of social justice, they advocated reforms to strengthen the rights of the toiling classes. Women, confronted by unprincipled opposition and ridicule, sought to alter their status as "political nonentities" through the right to vote.

Oklahoma also presents us with an intriguing puzzle. It was the only state with a slave and confederate legacy that granted full suffrage to women prior to the federal amendment enfranchising women. The Oklahoma victory was all the more remarkable because of the stiff requirements for approval of a state constitutional amendment. Like several other states, the Oklahoma constitution required a majority of the highest number of votes cast in the election – not merely a simple majority for the amendment. The *only* successful campaign for a suffrage amendment waged under these conditions occurred in Oklahoma (Catt and Shuler, 1969).

In order to understand the outcome of the Oklahoma campaign we need to examine multiple struggles of recognition instead of focusing exclusively on women's struggle. An examination of multiple recognition struggles requires a broad conceptual framework. For my purposes, I combine the theoretical insights of Axel Honneth and Nancy Fraser. Unlike most theorists of recognition, Honneth (1995b) offers an *encompassing* framework. He envisions a permanent struggle among social groups where they attempt to elevate or valorize their distinct traits and abilities, and through recognition they gain social esteem. The breadth of his theoretical scheme contrasts with that of Will Kymlicka (1995), which is limited to a politics of cultural difference. Kymlicka's theorizing underlines the distinction between national minorities (distinct and potentially self-governing societies incorporated into a larger state) and ethnic groups (immigrants who have [voluntarily] left their national communities to enter another society). This is problematic for two reasons. As he acknowledges, African-Americans do not fit neatly into his categorizations, yet their struggle for recognition cannot be left out of the US context. Nor does Kymlicka's framework accommodate women's struggle for recognition.

Nancy Fraser (2003, see also her chapter in this volume) criticizes Honneth because he views recognition as a matter of self-realization rather than justice, and further because the locus of recognition is individual psychology rather than social relations. She argues that existing theories of recognition cannot adequately accommodate problems of redistribution, insisting that recognition and redistribution are dimensions of justice that cut across all social movements. Despite her insistence that recognition and redistribution are in practice intertwined, she analytically links recognition to the cultural sphere and redistribution to the economic realm. To illuminate their intertwinement, Fraser provides us with the conceptual tool of dual perspectives. Application of the recognition perspective enables us to identify the cultural dimensions of what are usually regarded as redistributive economic policies; conversely the redistributive perspective aids in understanding the economic dimensions of recognition issues. Similarly, she emphasizes dual obstacles to parity of participation – defined as social arrangements that permit all adult members of society to interact with one another as peers. The dualism consists of *cultural* obstacles, involving misrecognition, and *economic* obstacles, such as maldistribution. Fraser acknowledges political obstacles but does not develop this idea. My analysis stresses both recognition and redistribution as dimensions of social conflict and puts added weight on a third dimension that is explicitly political, which I term "empowerment." All three dimensions are integral to the struggles examined here. The struggles involved cultural, economic, and political impediments to participatory parity.

With respect to empowerment it is appropriate to return to Honneth because of the significance he attaches to the interrelationships between rights, self-respect, and collective agency. He stresses that rights and self-respect are inseparable. To live without rights forecloses the possibility of developing self-respect. The public character of rights empowers the bearer to engage in action and discourse which demonstrate that he or she is recognized as a morally responsible person. Through recognition of rights, one can view oneself as a person who shares with other members of the community the capacity to participate in discourses shaping interpretations of societal goals and social worth.

The hegemonic discourse of the Oklahoma struggles revolved around civilization, which formed a master frame in making claims of social worth. Couching claims in terms of civilization was central for Native Americans, but such claims figured prominently in all four struggles. Each argued that recognition of their worth would enhance US civilization or, contrariwise, that the acts of their opponents were unworthy of civilized nations, that they contradicted the very notion of civilization.

I argue that these three other simultaneous but often separate struggles formed a crucial part of the context of the women's suffrage campaign, and how they intersect provides a key to understanding the unusual victory of female suffrage prior to the federal amendment. Initially, the struggles merged to produce an inclusive stance on suffrage – a position which was far more radical than that of NAWSA at the time. Eventually, however, the success of African-Americans' struggle and the unprecedented strength of the socialists in the mid-1910s produced countermobilizations whose adherents were convinced that women's suffrage would weaken their opponents. This combination of radical and conservative support, comprising long-standing activists and newer recruits, sealed the success of the suffrage amendment in 1918.

The following pages present a broad brush picture of the four struggles, women's position in each struggle, and the repercussions of the struggles on one another. Subsequently, I discuss in more detail how the struggles intersected and produced conditions in Oklahoma that differed from those in the southern states. The concluding discussion returns to the question of the newness of recognition struggles.

Tribal citizenship versus US citizenship: inclusion or exclusion?

The Native Americans of Oklahoma held a unique position of strength because of the treaty rights of five Indian nations. Prior to statehood, the nations were the legal owners of Indian Territory – roughly half of the state – and Oklahoma was the first state to grant all Native American males citizenship rights. This inclusion, however, masked a process of exclusion – a process of increasing misrecognition, maldistribution, and disempowerment. Both the inclusion and exclusion of Native Americans impacted on women's struggle for political rights. Native Americans were part of the suffrage coalition, and the plight of disinherited Indians spurred women's mobilization and their engagement in the public sphere.

The unusual position of Native Americans in Oklahoma can be traced back to the forced removal of the Cherokees, the Choctaws, the Chickasaws, the Creeks, and the Seminoles. With much suffering and loss of human life, the tribes were forced to leave their homelands in the southeastern USA and settle west of the Mississippi during the 1830s. In exchange, the tribes received new lands originally encompassing nearly all the territory of the present state of Oklahoma. The removal treaties promised the five nations ownership of these lands in perpetuity, and that no territorial or state government could be set up without their consent.

The Indians' strategy for survival as nations, before and after removal, was to gain recognition of their sovereignty through treaties, and their claims to rights and social worth turned upon demonstrating that they were "civilized." Eventually, they became known as the five "civilized" tribes.[2] As testimony of their civilized accomplishments, the tribes could point to high literacy rates and an informed citizenry, the formation of constitutional governments, and the establishment of their own public school systems.

Becoming civilized, however, was a double-edged strategy. Native Americans were disadvantaged in the discursive struggle over the meaning of civilization. Moreover, the strategy was divisive. Their identity as "civilized" tribes set them apart from other Indians who were "savage," largely excluding the original inhabitants as well as relocated tribes of Oklahoma. Even more detrimental, acculturation produced cultural, political, and economic differences within the five nations. The divisions led to contestation in defining Indian identity and weakened the social fabric of the Indian nations, making them more vulnerable to external pressures (McLoughlin, 1993).

The process of acculturation also changed the gender order and women's position in tribal society. Originally, the five tribes depended on both hunting and agriculture for their livelihood. In the division of labor, men hunted and women were responsible for farming. Clans owned the land, and rights to the land passed through the mother – not the father. Matrilineal kinship systems and women's control over crops positioned them favorably. Before the establishment of the Indian nations as republics, the local councils had a stronger say, and women participated in the local councils.[3]

This gender order clashed with that of the first colonizers of the continent, and it created sharp tensions concerning citizenship and the proper role of women. It ran counter to the settlers' notions of yeoman citizenship where men were rights-bearing individuals by virtue of the ownership of property and as tillers of the land. The increasing importance of agriculture, formal government, and the coming of Christianity weakened the position of women. Men became the farmers, the constitutions granted political rights to men, and Christianity brought new sexual norms. Even so, Native American women had stronger ownership rights than the women settlers. Communal ownership did not vest property rights in the head of the household. All tribal members – men, women, and children – had a right to common domains.

Education was also integral to the civilizing strategy, and it opened up opportunities for women. The tribes established elementary and secondary schools for girls and boys. The most famous school for young Indian women was the Cherokee Female Seminary. It, and others, were modeled after Mount Holyoke, noted for its rigorous curriculum and emphasis on religion and teacher training, preparing students for mission work throughout the world. During its years of operation from 1851 to 1909, the Seminary educated Indian women as teachers and missionaries who would bring civilization to their own people (Mihesuah, 1993). Many graduates embarked on a career in education, and a surprising number of Native American women entered the mission field, most of them from the five civilized tribes (Myres, 1982). At the turn of the century, the alumni of the Indian schools were community activists. Together with other women, they organized local branches of the Woman's Christian Temperance Union, the YWCA, and Indian women's clubs (Reese, 1997).

The ultimate flaw of "civilization" was the tribes' adoption of slavery, which had disastrous consequences. The civil war ravaged the Indians' land, and it divided the tribes internally and against one another. Many fought on the losing side for the confederacy. After the war, the tribes were forced to cede nearly half of Indian Territory to the USA. The US government used the land to resettle pacified Indians but also created Oklahoma Territory and opened it to homesteaders.

Settlers eventually engulfed the Indians, making them a minority in their own land. The growing imbalance intensified clashes over principles of land ownership, tribal government, and the appropriateness of a separate nationality in the heart of the American nation. The struggle of Native Americans underscores the interconnections between disrespect, maldistribution, and disempowerment as Indian lands were reallocated and tribal governments dissolved.

The Indians' principle of communal ownership was a major target of criticism; opponents maintained that this form of ownership put a brake on progress and civilization. H. L. Dawes, who eventually administered the allotment of Indian lands, argued:

There is no selfishness, which is at the bottom of civilization. Till this people will consent to give up their lands, and divide them among their citizens so that each can own the land he cultivates, they will not make much more progress. (cited in Debo, 1972 [1940]: 22)

In arguing against the end of tribal ownership, Native Americans invoked their treaty rights, stressing that the USA as a civilized nation was obligated to honor its word. They also pointed out that common ownership was intrinsic to the Indians: "It is based upon peculiarities and necessities of the race" (McLoughlin, 1993: 370). Finally, the Indians warned of the consequences of allotting land on an individual basis:

What about our people, who are, now, the legal owners and the sovereigns of these lands?... Crushed to earth under the hoofs of business greed, they would soon become a homeless throng... (cited in Debo 1972 [1940]: 30)

The issue of statehood came to a head with the passage of legislation to terminate all tribal government by early 1906. This meant that the Indian Territory had either to be reorganized along the lines of a regular territory or become a state. Many Indians, fearing a loss of influence in a single state that combined the two territories, preferred separate statehood. In an effort to create a separate state (to be called Sequoyah), a council of the chiefs called a constitutional convention in 1905. Over three hundred delegates, predominantly of Indian stock or intermarried citizens, assembled and drafted a constitution (Maxwell, 1950). Congress chose to ignore the Sequoyah constitution. Instead, it passed the enabling act for a single state comprised of the two territories, and Oklahoma became a state in 1907.

Statehood and US citizenship irreparably widened the distance between the civilizers and the traditional Indians. For many prominent tribal members, US citizenship brought possibilities for participation and political office, especially in the first years of state politics. Candidates of Indian lineage and intermarried tribal members were elected to the US Senate and House of Representatives, major state offices, and local posts (Debo, 1972 [1940]). For less prominent Indians and the so-called fullbloods, the exchange of Indian citizenship for US citizenship marked the end of communal property rights and self-government. Twenty years after the introduction of individual property rights, two-thirds of the Cherokees had lost their allotments through inability to pay taxes, selling their land, or outright fraud (McLoughlin, 1993). Traditional Indians had had a voice in tribal government as jurors, voters, and office-holders, but now many of them grew apathetic. US citizenship completely marginalized them, and disempowerment was a fact.

A final paradox was that recognition of the Indians as civilized tribes legitimized their early acquisition of US citizenship. However, US citizenship robbed the Indians of their status of civilized tribes. Their claims to this status rested on the accomplishments of the Indian nations, but US citizenship dissolved the institutions they had created or transferred them to the larger society.

The Indians' struggle for self-government and tribal citizenship had repercussions for the struggles of women and African-Americans. On two issues – prohibition and child welfare – Native Americans and women reformers forged alliances. To combat the evils of drink, temperance societies were among the earliest associations organized by the Indians, and in 1884 Cherokee women established a branch of the Woman's Christian Temperance Union (WCTU) (Perdue, 1980). In the 1890s, two Cherokee women served as president of the WCTU of Indian Territory and were listed on the honor roll of the national organization. One of them was a close friend of Frances Willard, the national president of the association and an avid advocate of female suffrage (Bordin, 1981).

The issue of separate statehood, however, drove a temporary wedge between women's organizations. After the tribes recommended separate statehood, several Indian women's clubs withdrew from the twin territory federation. Their stated reason for withdrawal was that they wanted their own organizations where they, as Indian women, would be recognized as the equals of other club women. After statehood, the clubs joined the state federation (Allen, 1988). They also formed their own suffrage association, the Indian Women's Suffrage League of Indian Territory, and made a bid for voting rights at the Sequoyah convention. Native American women later served as officers of the state suffrage association and delegates to national conventions.

Not only did the issue of separate statehood temporarily fragment women's organizational efforts to win the vote, it indirectly strengthened forces opposing woman suffrage and black rights. The Sequoyah convention aided opponents in gaining positions of influence at the state constitutional convention and later high offices in the state government. In these positions, they were well placed to block women's suffrage and divest African-Americans of their political and civil rights.

Perhaps most damaging to the blacks' struggle was the state constitution's definition of "colored." Although the Indians lost the battle for separate statehood, their prominent position and widespread intermarriage between whites and Indians made it politically impossible to define whiteness without taking Native Americans into account. The state constitution delimited the term "colored" to persons of African descent, while the "white race" included all other persons (Debo, 1972 [1940]: 292). This definition isolated African-Americans, depriving them of potential allies.

The African-Americans' struggle for recognition as the "joint heirs to US citizenship"

The African-Americans of Oklahoma straddled the divide between the Indians and non-Indians, coming to the territory either as Indian slaves or settlers. Irrespective of their Indian or non-Indian backgrounds, the blacks were eventually the victims of segregation and disenfranchisement.

As in the case of Native Americans, the struggle of the Oklahoma blacks involved their disempowerment. It also impinged upon women's fight for the vote in contradictory ways. Positively, in response to African-Americans' demands to safeguard their rights, the Oklahoma suffrage association adopted an inclusive stance on suffrage, repudiating restrictions based on sex and race. Negatively, the threat of disenfranchisement concentrated the energies of the black community on protecting the rights of men, and white supremacists pointed to the political activism of African-American women as a reason not to endorse female suffrage.

The African-Americans who came to Oklahoma as Indian slaves were freed and, in most cases, granted tribal citizenship as result of the civil war. As Indian citizens, the freedmen voted and held office as tribal legislators (Quintard Taylor, 1998), and at least five blacks from the Creek nation were delegates or alternates to the Sequoyah convention (Maxwell, 1950). They were also entitled to individual allotments during the division of tribal lands. However, restrictions protecting the freedmen's land from sale were quickly removed, and poorly educated black tribal members were among the first to be swindled out of their newly acquired property.

Black settlers moved to territorial Oklahoma in the hope of finding new opportunities. Developers and promoters founded all-black towns and gave glowing accounts to attract newcomers. Publicity campaigns claimed that Oklahoma was a land where African-Americans would be free and have their rights respected. Changing race relations in the south also prompted blacks to move to the twin territories.

Although black immigration did not always end in success, many black towns and African-Americans prospered. In their new communities, African-Americans built schools, which nearly all children attended, and an institution of higher learning was established in 1897. They started newspapers, business associations, lodges, ladies' auxiliaries and women's clubs, and local branches of the Republican Party. A businessman from Langston, one of the all-black towns, was elected to the territorial legislature in 1890 and he was later followed by another African-American (Quintard Taylor, 1998). In Guthrie, which was not an all-black town, they were elected aldermen and members of the school board. In many respects the new black communities exemplified Booker T. Washington's philosophy of racial uplift through self-help, community betterment, hard work, and economic success.

In speaking of one of the Oklahoma towns as an example of all-black towns, Washington declared:

Boley, represents a dawning of race consciousness, a wholesome desire to do something to make the race respected; something which shall demonstrate the right of the Negro, not merely as an individual but as a race, to have a worthy and permanent place in the civilization that the American people are creating. (cited in Tolson, 1972: 101–02)

Women's activities were vital to the new communities. In addition to their economic contributions as entrepreneurs and employees, women organized service clubs. The original impetus came from the founding convention of the National Association of Colored Women (NACW) in 1896, which Oklahoma women attended. As distinct from the white club movement, the NACW was formed to defend the honor of black woman-hood against slanderous accusations and to gain recognition and respect for African-American women. Feminists in the club movement empha-sized that a race could rise no higher than its women, echoing the words of Monroe Majors's book, *Noted Negro Women* (1893): "The criterion for Negro civilization is the intelligence, purity and high motives of its women" (cited in White, 1999: 43). The local newspapers published articles by national leaders who urged women to organize for reform. According to one national leader, women should work through social, economic, and moral reform for "enlightened motherhood, intellectual development, individuality and with all a steady growth of the develop-ment of noble womanhood" (Reese, 1997: 174).

Statehood was an issue of deep concern to the territorial blacks. Most important to them were the conditions of franchise in the new state and the framing of the constitution so that it contained no provisions legal-izing racial discrimination. The African-Americans called their own in-terterritorial conventions on statehood, and they lobbied in Washington for a single statehood bill that ensured black rights. The enabling act for Oklahoma statehood emphasized that the state constitution could not de-prive citizens of equal rights because of race, color, or previous servitude (Tolson, 1972).

As statehood approached, the Republican Party, fearing that it could not win a majority of the votes, distanced itself from the blacks who com-prised a small portion of the population. This tactic proved disastrous. The Republicans failed to convert Democrats, and in anger the blacks stayed away from the polls. The Democrats swept the convention elec-tion, and an overwhelming majority of the delegates were born in states or Indian Territory where slavery had existed (Clark, 1970–71). The white supremacist tone of the convention was set by its president, William H. (Alfalfa Bill) Murray, in his opening speech. He declared:

We should adopt a provision prohibiting the mixed marriages of Negroes with other races in this State, and provide for separate schools and give the Legislature power to separate them in waiting rooms and on passenger coaches, and all other institutions in the State . . . it is an entirely false notion that the Negro can rise to the equal of a white man in the professions or become an equal citizen. (cited in Tolson, 1972: 137–38)

Many delegates favored the measures advocated by Murray as well as complete disenfranchisement. The fear that the president, Theodore Roosevelt, would not approve the constitution, thus denying Oklahoma statehood, restrained the Democrats from crafting a Jim Crow constitution. After statehood, segregation was introduced, and the Democrats moved to disenfranchise African-Americans in 1910 through a constitutional amendment introducing a grandfather clause.[4] By underhand methods, the Democrats secured passage of the grandfather clause amendment. It would have been defeated, if it had not been for the mysterious appearance of 20,000 blank ballots (Scales and Goble, 1982; Tolson, 1972).

Contrary to Booker T. Washington's stance of race accommodation, the Oklahoma blacks fought vigorously to retain their rights. Their most successful efforts focused on litigation, and in 1915 they scored a major victory. The US Supreme Court ruled that the Oklahoma grandfather clause was unconstitutional and violated the rights of African-Americans. No sooner had the grandfather clause been stuck down than the Democrats attempted to place new restrictions on black voting rights, but they were not completely successful (Franklin, 1982; Scales and Goble, 1982).

Just as the Indians' struggle for self-government and recognition of their rights impinged upon the struggles of African-Americans and women, so the black men's fight for the vote affected women's quest for suffrage. The territorial blacks' concern that the enabling act safeguard their rights brought them into a head-on collision with the national women's suffrage movement – but not the territorial organization. The Oklahoma blacks strongly endorsed the 1904 statehood bill that guaranteed their rights, but it also stated "the right of suffrage should never be abridged except on account of illiteracy, minority, *sex*, conviction of felony or mental condition." This clause caused a storm of protest as women railed against being bracketed with criminals, lunatics, the feeble minded, and incompetents. Enlisting the support of over twenty-five national women's organizations, the NAWSA started a campaign that deleted the word "sex" from the bill (HWS, vol. 5: 129). The response of the Oklahoma suffrage association was quite different, however. Rather than concentrating on eliminating sex as a legitimate basis for exclusion from citizenship rights, the territorial association rejected restricting suffrage on the basis of sex, race, color, or previous servitude (HWS, vol. 6).

The black Oklahomans' fight to preserve their rights was all important, and there was little mention of woman suffrage. In struggling to maintain the status quo, they couched their language in that of their foes. Their discourse on black political rights pertains solely to men (Tolson, 1972). After disenfranchisement, however, a black convention declared its support of woman suffrage (James R. Green, 1978). African-American women in Oklahoma had long before formed a suffrage association (Terborg-Penn, 1998). They also appeared to have voted in school elections more than white women, primarily to ensure black representation on school boards in mixed communities. African-American women's political activism was repeatedly used by white supremacists as an argument against enfranchising all women.

Before examining women's struggle, it is necessary to put another piece of the puzzle in place – the importance of the labor–farm alliance to Oklahoma politics and the unusual strength of the socialists. They were crucial in shaping the opportunity structure of the suffrage movement, and the populists' espousal of female suffrage and the socialists' demands for equal and unrestricted voting rights aided women in their cause.

The labor–agrarian alliance and the rights of the toiling classes

The mobilization of the working class and the poor is seen as a struggle of redistribution par excellence. Applying Nancy Fraser's dual perspectives allows us to identify the recognition dimension in this struggle. For the populists and socialists, human dignity and social worth were inextricably bound up with the eradication of poverty, but they also sought a valuation of toil. Their reform agenda additionally called for the removal of political obstacles to participatory parity through equal voting rights and direct democracy. Not only did organized labor, the socialists, and, earlier, the populists champion women's political rights, thus serving as much needed allies of the suffrage movement, they also provided more space for women than the two major parties.

Organized labor and farmers saw statehood and the framing of the state constitution as a chance to secure the demands of their reform agenda. It included more direct democracy – the initiative, referendum, and recall; a blanket primary; making all state offices subject to election and creating publicly elected commissioners of labor and agriculture; regulation of railroads, insurance, telephone, and telegraph companies, and other corporations, along with broad rights of the state to engage in industry and enterprise; a radical bill of rights for labor; progressive taxation; and a liberal homestead and exemption law (Goble, 1980). Nearly all of their demands, along with other reforms, were adopted, making the Oklahoma constitution one of the most progressive in the nation.

The labor federation also provided a political platform for Kate Barnard, Oklahoma's most renowned progressive reformer. Although Barnard opposed women's suffrage, her actions challenged the conventional views of women's role in politics. She was a delegate to the joint labor–farmer convention that drew up the reform demands for the state constitution. Barnard was also instrumental in the establishment of the state commissioner of charities and corrections and the decision that either sex was eligible to hold this office. In 1907, she ran for commissioner and won the election. However, her office's involvement in the protection of Native American children whose guardians cheated them out of their land and property income led to her political demise in 1915 (Reese, 1997; Debo, 1972).

The progressive coalition behind the state constitution soon fell apart, and in its wake the socialist party gained unprecedented strength.[5] The Oklahoma party embraced a brand of agrarian socialism, which emphasized the rights of the toiling classes. The socialists maintained that "the small farmer as well as the tenant and farm laborer had a 'natural right' to the use and occupancy of the land as long as it was utilized for productive not exploitative purposes" (Green, 1978: 82). Their demands for rights rested not only on claims of human dignity but also on the special contributions of their labor. They argued that since the toiling classes bore the burdens of civilization on their shoulders, they were entitled to share in the blessings of the civilization that they had made possible (O'Hare, 1914, cited in Foner and Miller, 1982). Party speakers were also quick to point out the contradictions between the evils of capitalism and a civilized state, claiming "socialism was the next step in civilization after capitalism" (Green, 1978: 164).

The party's notions of equality extended rights to women and African-Americans of the toiling classes. As expressed by Kate Richards O'Hare, a national party leader and organizer in Oklahoma from 1904 to 1909:

I, as a Socialist, most emphatically state that I demand Equal Suffrage not merely as a sex right, but also as a class right . . . I do know that any sex, class or race that has been denied the right to vote has always worn the chains of servitude . . . I, as a Socialist and a Suffragist, want to give each of them [the Negro, the working-class woman, and the working-class man] a ballot and protect them in the use of it. (O'Hare, 1914, in Foner and Miller, 1982: 99)

In the rough and tumble of Oklahoma politics, it proved impossible for the socialists to limit their discourse on the rights of women and African-Americans only to those who were laborers and farmers.

Socialist and populist utopias assigned women a new place in the future social order. The practices and political demands of populist and socialist women transcended and challenged the existing gendered boundaries of political activities. Forceful women orators crisscrossed the country, recruiting and educating the party faithful; and women ran for office (Buhle, 1981). Both parties also espoused woman suffrage, and the socialists made it a plank in their national platform in 1904, and subsequently called for "unrestricted and equal suffrage for men and women" (CQ, 1975: 62). Socialist women, like Kate Richards O'Hare and Winnie Branstetter, were active in Oklahoma suffrage campaigns, using them to attract women to the party. Especially pivotal was Winnie Branstetter, who sat on the state executive committee of the socialist party at the same time as she was an activist in the suffrage association.

The labor–agrarian alliance's fight for political and social rights was interwoven with the struggles of Native Americans, the blacks and women. Initially, the demands of the labor–agrarian coalition often conflicted with the interests and political aspirations of the Indians. Members of the farmers' alliance urged settlers to move into "vacant" Indian lands. Organized labor and farmers had also demanded immediate and joint statehood for the two territories, undermining the Indians' goal of a state of their own. The dispossession of the Indians, however, fueled agrarian radicalism because it benefited wealthy speculators and large landowners, while small farmers were forced to become tenants or sharecroppers. Farmers and workers also shared the Indians' indictment of business greed and the lack of moral consciousness of capitalists and moneyed men. As victims of capitalism, the Indians were eventually among Oklahoma's dispossessed whom the socialists tried to mobilize, and Kate O'Hare (1906) claims that the socialists won adherents among Native Americans. Disinherited Indians, however, were difficult to recruit because they despaired at the loss of their tribal rights and often spoke only their native languages.

The socialists supported the blacks in their struggle to preserve their rights, and they were a stauncher ally than the Republicans. However, support of black rights converted few voters, and it created dissension within party ranks. Most black voters remained loyal to the Republicans, perhaps because the socialist philosophy was alien to many leaders of the black community who were self-made men. Disenfranchisement of the blacks came precisely when the socialists were making gains, precluding the multiracial class party that several socialist leaders hoped to build (Burbank, 1976).

Labor–agrarian politics were important to the women's struggle, shaping opportunities in three respects. First, the populists, the labor federation, and the socialists were crucial allies of the suffragists. Second, their reform agenda led women to mobilize across class and party lines, initially around issues of child welfare. Women's reform activities eventually made many of them realize the importance of the vote. Third, the reform demands of the labor–agrarian alliance shaped the state constitution, and its progressive features were part of the suffrage movement's opportunity structure. The initiative furnished women with the means to circumvent a hostile legislature.

Women: from "political nonentities" to citizens with equal rights

The struggle for women's political rights and recognition as equal citizens dates from the establishment of territorial government in the Oklahoma district in 1890. Women, primarily organized in the Woman's Christian Temperance Union (WCTU), petitioned the first territorial legislature to alter the franchise bill to read: "Every citizen of the age of 21 shall have the right to vote" from "every male citizen." This proposal failed to pass, but the legislature gave women the right to vote in school elections (HWS, vol. 4: 887).

In the mid-1890s, organizers from the NAWSA came to Oklahoma, and a women's suffrage association was formed. The national organization gave priority to Oklahoma because it was a territory. The introduction of woman suffrage required only a majority decision of the territorial legislature, and three territories had already granted women the right to vote. The Oklahoma association, with the aid of the NAWSA, mounted two campaigns – the first in 1897 and the second in 1899. Both bills passed the lower house but were killed in the upper chamber. The defeat of the 1899 campaign, headed by Carrie Chapman Catt who later became president of the NAWSA, was especially bitter. A majority in the upper chamber had pledged to support the bill, and it was killed by a minority who prevented a vote on the bill through delaying tactics (HWS, vol. 4). After this defeat, the Oklahoma suffrage organization lapsed into inactivity (NAWSA Proceedings, 1900–06).

The prospects of statehood, however, revitalized women's efforts to gain the vote. At the Sequoyah convention, women presented their case to the committee on suffrage, elections, and purity of government. The newspapers reported that the issue of woman suffrage had consumed much of the committee's time, although the committee did not recommend female suffrage. An amendment to grant women voting rights was introduced during the consideration of the final draft of the constitution, but it was defeated (Maxwell, 1950).[6]

The Oklahoma constitutional convention produced a more concerted campaign because of the high stakes. As spelled out in a message from Susan B. Anthony to the territorial association in 1904, "No stone should be left unturned to secure suffrage for women while Oklahoma is yet a Territory, for if it comes into the Union without this in its constitution it will take a long time and great deal of hard work to convert over one-half of the men to vote for it" (HWS, vol. 6: 520). In response, the Twin Territorial Suffrage Association was founded, with Mrs Kate Biggers from Indian Territory as president. In a resolution calling for statehood, the association condemned any enactment of voting restrictions based on sex, race, or color.

Supporters of woman suffrage included the Indian Women's Suffrage League, individual officers of women's clubs, the WCTU, teachers' associations, the Labor Federation of the Twin Territories, and the Farmers' Union. Of these organizations, the Labor Federation was especially important because many convention delegates had pledged to support the constitutional demands of labor. The president of the Labor Federation, Peter Hanraty, also led the fight at the convention. The leading opponents were well positioned: the president of the convention, the majority floor leader, and the chairman of the convention committee on suffrage.

The racial issue had been brought up before the floor debate on woman suffrage. Laura Clay of Kentucky, one of the NAWSA's organizers, had addressed the entire convention earlier. Seeking to allay fears that woman suffrage would give African-Americans the balance of power in elections, she argued, "By enfranchising the white women of the south, the white race will be put in such numerical majority as to do away with the necessity of any doubtful expediency." Contrary to Laura Clay's intentions, the race issue seems to have worked against female suffrage. In his memoirs, Murray, the convention president, claims that he submitted the proposition to a vote, saying, "If the Northern woman won't vote what do you expect of the Southern woman and particularly an Indian woman? If you adopt this provision, it will mean giving balance of power over to the Negro vote" (Wright, 1973–74: 441–2).

The speech by Charles Haskell seems more likely to have swayed delegates pledged to labor. He declared: "Katie Bernard's [sic] life is a lesson that every suffragist should study and profit by, and let me appeal to every mother that is in this audience to go back home to your boys, and continue to rock the cradle, and through that well-known medium continue to rule the world" (James, 1978–79: 389). These words would have carried more weight with the labor delegates who viewed Kate Barnard as the angel of reform, and her position on suffrage was known to them. Judging from the vote, abstentions were crucial in defeating womanhood suffrage, and Haskell's speech planted doubts.

The convention voted fifty to thirty-seven against female suffrage, with twenty-one abstentions. In addition, women nearly lost the right to vote in school elections; the continuation of school suffrage passed by only one vote (James, 1978–79). An editorial in the Republican *Oklahoma State Capital* claimed that the southern Democrats turned down equal suffrage "just because colored women in Guthrie registered and the white women did not" (Wright, 1973–74: 442). Racial considerations of another sort probably loomed larger. A constitution providing universal suffrage might have made disenfranchisement of the blacks at a later date more difficult.

Despite this setback, women refused to give up. They started lobbying the legislature to submit a suffrage amendment to the voters. When it became clear that these attempts were futile, they bypassed the legislature, using the initiative to put a woman suffrage amendment on the ballot in 1910. After gathering the necessary number of signatures, the suffragists filed the petition with the secretary of state. He complimented them for their good work, but the members of the delegation were humiliated when they as women were denied a receipt for the petition because they were "political nonentities." Instead the receipt was made out in the name of the man who offered to stand as their guardian. The campaign for the referendum ran into stiff opposition. Immediately, opponents tried to torpedo the initiative, charging that 5,000 signatures were fraudulent but without producing any evidence. When the charges were dismissed, the complainant appealed to the state supreme court, prolonging uncertainty about the initiative's validity for nearly six months (NAWSA Proceedings 1910: 136).

More damaging, the referendum on the amendment to disenfranchise African-Americans occurred in the same year but in different elections. Judging from the votes cast in each referendum, the disenfranchisement amendment overshadowed the woman suffrage amendment. Even worse, the disenfranchisement amendment divided those supporting female suffrage. The socialists campaigned vigorously against disenfranchisement and for universal suffrage. Simultaneously, the southern suffragist, Kate Gordon, well known for her outspoken views on the inferiority of the blacks, and that woman suffrage would uphold white political supremacy, stomped the state as the NAWSA's representative. The referendum was further disadvantaged by interjecting partisan sentiments when Kate Biggers, president of the state suffrage association, also ran for a state office as a Republican in the election. She challenged Kate Barnard, the commissioner of charities and corrections (Reese, 1997), and lost.

Although there were isolated attempts to put a suffrage amendment to the voters during the 1910s, it was not until 1917 that the second amendment campaign got underway. The legislative committee of the Oklahoma federation of women's clubs and individual officers of the suffrage association secured a resolution in the state legislature to submit the amendment to voters in 1918.

This fight for a woman suffrage amendment was plagued by several difficulties. First, the state suffrage association was in disarray, and without funds; it therefore appealed to the NAWSA for assistance. Moreover, tensions existed between the NAWSA and the state association. In 1913, the Oklahomans had joined the Southern States Woman Suffrage Conference which favored state action as the route to suffrage – not a federal amendment which was the *raison d'être* of the NAWSA. Furthermore, Oklahoma suffragists had deviated from Carrie Chapman Catt's "winning plan." The plan called for four different strategies: getting state legislatures to pass resolutions for woman suffrage, working for presidential suffrage, seeking primary suffrage, or mounting a campaign for a state constitutional amendment. States were assigned a specific strategy according to the likelihood of their achieving the goal. Oklahoma was not one of the states designated to work for a suffrage amendment, but the women had done so anyway. Now that the amendment was to be voted on, the NAWSA had little choice but to throw all its resources behind the campaign because a defeat might endanger passage of the federal amendment (HWS, vol. 6).

As in 1910, opponents held key political posts. The governor, the lieutenant-governor, the attorney general, and the chairman of the state election board – all democrats – openly opposed woman suffrage. In fighting the amendment, they used unscrupulous methods, reminiscent of the amendment disenfranchising the blacks, such as initially refusing to put the amendment on the ballot, then printing separate ballots but not supplying them to all the voters, breaking sealed returns to include invalid votes in the count, and delaying returns in an attempt to achieve adverse majorities. Despite all these subterfuges, the amendment carried (106,909 to 81,481) (Catt and Shuler, 1969).

Unraveling the Oklahoma puzzle: the importance of intersecting struggles

Oklahoma – the only state with a slave and confederacy legacy to grant women full suffrage – is a source of puzzlement, which cannot be fully understood by looking only at the record of the Oklahoma suffragists. Insight is instead gained by considering the role of interlocking but separate struggles of recognition – and how these struggles produced conditions that were different from the southern states.

The "civilizing" strategy of the five tribes in Oklahoma had two major repercussions on the coalition of women reformers. It affected both the composition and agenda of the coalition. Quite uniquely, Native Americans were part of the women's movement in Oklahoma. They were temperance leaders, teachers, reformers, club women, and suffragists, and their presence was crucial to the initial inclusive stance of the suffrage association. The Indians' civilizing strategy also had an impact on women settlers. In contrast to areas occupied by warlike tribes, the letters and diaries of Oklahoma frontierswomen chronicled relatively peaceable relations, characterized by intermarriage, fast friendships, and positive attitudes (Riley, 1984). This positive outlook was transformed into concern for the plight of the Indians as revealed by Kate Barnard's activities or the commentary of Kate Richards O'Hare, who condemned the grafters who preyed on the Indians (1906). The concern cut across women's class and partisan persuasions. Barnard's efforts to aid Indian children led to her political downfall; her fate further alerted many women to the necessity of the vote.

At first glance, the African-Americans' struggle seems to represent a similarity between Oklahoma and the southern states. It also appears to substantiate the interpretation of the official history of woman suffrage that the fight for black political rights delayed the introduction of the franchise for women. As distinct from the southern states, however, the Oklahoma blacks had political rights as settlers and Indian citizens in the 1890s and the subsequent decade. African-Americans also influenced the early inclusive position of the Oklahoma suffrage association. Bills for statehood sponsored by Republican members of Congress safeguarded the rights of blacks, and Republican women who were officers of the Oklahoma (twin territorial) suffrage organization chose to oppose voting restrictions based on sex, color, and race. This stance also corresponded with the socialists' position of unrestricted and equal suffrage, and socialist women were members of the suffrage association. The existence of Indian and African-American suffrage activists and organizations reinforced the position. In effect, several struggles came together at this point, producing an inclusive stance – a stance that was much more radical than that of the NAWSA, which at the time advocated restrictions on voting.

The impact of the Oklahoma blacks' struggle in the 1910s is more difficult to gauge. It appears to have influenced the introduction of woman suffrage in contradictory ways. On the one hand, the blacks succeeded in getting the grandfather clause invalidated. The socialists, in their campaign for unrestricted suffrage, together with the Republicans, thwarted the renewed efforts of the Democrats to disenfranchise African-Americans through a poll tax and later a literacy test in 1916. The black community – both men and women locally and nationally – came out more strongly in support of female suffrage during the 1910s. The protection of black voting rights ensured a wider constituency of voters in favor of women's enfranchisement, and the Republicans started to register the blacks to vote (Schrems, 2001). On the other hand, when the Supreme Court overturned the grandfather clause, Kate Gordon argued that woman suffrage could counter the effects of the court's decision (Kraditor, 1981). Contacts with the southern women's conference may have inspired Oklahoma suffragists to seek a constitutional amendment; it was in full accord with the conference's emphasis on states' rights and the belief that only the states should determine the franchise. It was also congruent with Gordon's argument that women's votes could weaken the influence of African-American votes.

The struggle of the toiling classes – whether organized as populists, reform democrats, or socialists backed by the labor–farm alliance – was critical in shaping the opportunities of the Oklahoma suffragists. One of the most significant contrasts between Oklahoma and the southern states was the suffragists' differing legacies of activism. Dissimilar historic precedents and institutional differences configured their opportunity structures. Territorial government, late statehood, and the framing of a "progressive" state constitution providing for a larger measure of direct democracy offered a distinctive set of opportunities shaping Oklahoma suffragists' activism. Upon formation of the territorial government, women immediately asked for the vote, and they gained school suffrage. By the close of the 1890s, they had petitioned the territorial legislature three times, and on each occasion the margins of defeat of the franchise bill had diminished. Statehood and the framing of the constitution afforded new opportunities. Prospects of victory loomed larger at the state constitutional convention than at the Sequoyah convention, as the coalition for woman suffrage widened. The broadening coalition, labor's petitions with thousands of male signatures, and the enactment of other reforms led the suffrage organization to believe that it could succeed in getting a constitutional amendment passed. As distinct from the southern states, and indeed a majority of the states, Oklahoma's constitution provided for initiatives for amendments, and the Oklahoma suffragists were among the first to seize this opportunity.[7] While the 1910 amendment failed to pass, its impact should not be underestimated. Of the votes cast, slightly over 40 percent were for the suffrage amendment. In conclusion, there was a strong legacy of past attempts. With each campaign, circles of support incrementally widened. In 1918, both the Republican and Democratic Parties pledged to work for the amendment. There was also broader community support in 1918; the campaign committee consisted of seventeen organizations of men and women representing different groups with widely diverse interests (HWS, vol. 6). In most states where victory was won before the federal suffrage amendment, it was achieved through repeated efforts and successive campaigns[8] – and a broad winning coalition.

The reformism and policy agenda of the labor–farmer alliance was important in two additional ways. First, reformism brought women into public office, undermining the logic of excluding them from the vote. The reform spirit during the early days of the territory aided women in securing them the right to vote in school elections, legitimizing women's role as office-holders in educational affairs. At the turn of the century, several women were county superintendents (HWS, vol. 4). The constitutional convention further exacerbated the contradiction. It established the office of the state commissioner of charities and corrections, which could be held by either sex but was only elected through the votes of men. Second, reforms mobilized club women. This assumed special significance because of the disarray of the suffrage organization. It was club women who took the lead in the final campaign; they were responsible for getting the suffrage amendment on the ballot and were often the grassroots organizers. The key role of grassroots organizations was revealed in the pattern of voting. The amendment carried in those precincts where a suffrage committee had been working since the early part of the year (HWS, vol. 6). The suffrage committees were often located in communities with a local women's club or temperance union.

Finally, the unusual strength of the socialist party put pressure on the Republicans and Democrats to write woman suffrage into their platforms. The Republicans were first to do so in 1913, and by 1918 the Democrats officially declared their support. This contrasts with the one-party southern states. In Oklahoma state politics, the Democrats were often the majority party (after statehood all the governors were Democrats, and the state legislature had a Democratic majority). However, in the 1910s the Socialists and Republicans challenged the majority position of the Democrats. The combined vote of the two parties was larger than that of the Democrats in the 1914 and 1916 elections. In 1917, many former foes of suffrage changed sides (HWS, vol. 6). Ironically, the strength of the Socialists, their growing militancy, and their armed resistance to the draft may have spurred the conversion of opponents to female suffrage, viewing women's votes as a means to weaken the Socialists.

In conclusion, a multicultural lens directs attention to the interrelatedness of recognition struggles – and the extent to which they are overlapping or exclusionary. It also demands that we examine the racial and ethnic diversity of the suffragists, which appears critical to the original inclusive stance adopted by the Oklahoma suffrage association. Through this lens, we can challenge the official homogenized narratives of the suffrage movement and recover the contributions of ethnic and racial minority women and men. The official history holds that the multiethnic and racial composition of American society delayed the introduction of women's voting rights (Catt and Shuler, 1969). The success of the Oklahoma campaign and those of other states in securing female suffrage through a state constitutional amendment suggest that the tardiness stemmed from the nativism and prejudices of several suffrage leaders. Their prejudices often prevented an inclusive strategy necessary for victory, and only belatedly did they overcome their misgivings as in the case of the New York campaign. A flaw of a strictly multicultural lens is its concentration on race and ethnicity; it fails to bring class into focus. Just as the race and ethnicity of suffrage activists are often excluded from the official history of the movement, many activists with working-class backgrounds and socialist affiliations are eclipsed in these annals. In the Oklahoma case, however, class cannot be omitted from the story. Without a consideration of the struggle of the toiling classes, the Oklahoma puzzle remains an enigma. The Oklahoma experience cautions against replacing the privileged position of class in Marxist analysis with a privileged position of the nation in multicultural analysis.

Multiculturalism: old struggles in new guises?

The literature on multiculturalism, the politics of difference, and identity politics stresses the newness and contemporary nature of recognition struggles. In many ways, however, these past struggles resemble contemporary struggles. To assess this issue, let us compare the struggles in Oklahoma with several criteria of newness found in the literature: the mounting importance of national and cultural identities as sources of political mobilization; the awareness that the dominant culture is a site of oppression; distinctive identities rather than the shared attribute of human dignity increasingly forming the basis of claims for justice; and claims for differentiated rights instead of universal rights.

In the USA, mobilization based on national identities is a long-standing and recurrent feature of politics; and Oklahoma is a paradigm case of recognition struggles that existed in the early twentieth century. It reveals that the awareness of misrecognition as a form of oppression is not a new phenomenon. Already in the 1870s, a letter home asked how the Cherokees could sustain their independence and dignity. "What sort of people will we be? We are already regarded as inferior . . . I never see anything in the papers about Indians but something that is low and mean, and I have almost concluded that there is no good in us" (Ann Bell Shelton to Sarah Watie in 1873, quoted in McLoughlin, 1993: 379). Similarly, W. E. B. du Bois in *Souls of Black Folk* (1907) insisted that black self-doubt and self-hatred stemmed from "ridicule and systematic humiliation, the distortion of fact and wanton license of fancy, the cynical ignoring of the better and the boisterous welcoming of the worse, the all-pervading desire to inculcate disdain for everything black" (du Bois, quoted in Higginbotham, 1993: 188).

Furthermore, the protagonists of each struggle did not restrict their claims for justice to the shared attribute of human dignity. Their claims for justice were made on the basis of distinctive identities and contributions of the group. At the core of the Indians' discourse were their collective achievements, as witnessed in a final plea for respect by Pleasant Potter, principal chief of the Creeks:

We are the original discoverers of this continent . . . and first planted institutions of virtue, truth and liberty . . . We have given to the European people on this continent our thought forces – the best blood of our ancestors having intermingled with [that of] their best statesmen and leading citizens . . . We have led the vanguard of civilization in our conflicts with them for tribal existence from ocean to ocean. The race that has rendered this service to the other nations of mankind cannot utterly perish. (Debo 1941: 377)

African-Americans voiced their claims as a race and for the race, stressing their specific contributions to the nation. Suffragists called for woman suffrage, using "woman" in the generic sense of embracing all women and emphasizing the distinctive attributes of the female sex as reasons for the vote. They invoked womanliness, motherhood, their nurturing capacities, and special concerns for the home and children as arguments for enfranchisement. The socialists sought improvements for the toiling classes because it was their due. Like national minorities today, the socialists argued for differential rights – and obligations. By demanding rights based on need and obligations through graduated taxes, the populists, reform Democrats, and socialists call for differentiated rights and obligations, which are now commonplace.

Equally important, the Oklahoma case clearly demonstrates that recognition struggles are entwined with conflicts over economic resources and political power. The Indians of Oklahoma illustrate the inappropriateness of separating struggles of recognition from struggles of redistribution and empowerment. Misrecognition was pervasive, injuring self-esteem, as Ann Bell Shelton's letter patently reveals. However, misrecognition not only demeaned the group; it also paved the way for despoiling and disempowering the Indians. As they were stripped of their recognition, they were robbed of their land and their institutions.

For the blacks, the introduction of segregated institutions entailed both insults and a redistribution of resources, and through disenfranchisement they were disempowered. In relating his initial encounter with the Jim Crow laws, S. R. Cassius wrote:

Sitting in the waiting room at Ardmore . . . I drew my first impression of the Jim Crow Law. The room set apart for Negroes joins the men's closet. This closet is the most filthy place I ever saw . . . I entered the Jim Crow car . . . It was just half of an ordinary smoking car; in one end there was a toilet for both men and women. (cited in Tolson 1972: 150)

African-American women were particularly outraged by the lack of separate toilets as a sign of disrespect (Higginbotham, 1993). Simultaneously, separate institutions barred the black community from better funded facilities, such as schools, universities, and libraries. Justifications for disenfranchisement maligned African-Americans, underlining their inferiority in political affairs. Limited voting rights, especially through biased apportionment of election districts, kept Oklahoma blacks out of state office from 1910 until the mid-1960s.

For socialists, human dignity and social worth were inextricably bound up with redistribution and the eradication of poverty. All too often, the struggle of the toiling classes is seen as solely one of redistribution and not one of recognition and respect. However, socialists demanded recognition of their honest toil – for the "full social value for the workers" (Burbank, 1975: 108). The socialists also faced disempowerment. The swift decline of the socialist party in Oklahoma coincided with increasing political harassment, as national leaders were jailed. In fear of trial and imprisonment, the Oklahoma party dissolved itself.

As women suffragists sought recognition of their political rights and capacities, they faced ridicule and humiliation by their male opponents. Through demeaning tactics, women were dismissed as politically incompetent. At the state constitutional convention, women's voting was treated as a joke and greeted with laughter (James, 1978–79), and members of the state legislature tore up the suffragists' appeal for an amendment, jestingly referring to them as the committee on geological survey (HWS, vol. 6). This lack of respect veiled the fact that this struggle for recognition involved a power struggle.

In one crucial respect, the struggles of the past were different from those of today in that the hegemonic discourse centered on civilization – not multiculturalism. For the five tribes, recognition turned upon civilization, and the other was the "uncivilized" or the savage. The Indians also played upon the Americans' pride in their civilization, inquiring how they as a civilized nation could break the treaties. They pointed to other contradictions between civilization and the white man's actions. As early as 1873, the Cherokees questioned the whites' claims to be civilized because of their treatment of the blacks. An editorial in the *Cherokee Advocate* remarked that "if the Cherokees were to be as civilized as the whites, they must learn to abuse the blacks, legislate against them, and administer the law unequally. But alas, the Cherokees were 'greatly behind' the whites in advancement" (Littlefield, 1978: 70).

A discourse based on civilization had fatal limitations, especially for the Indians and African-Americans. While useful for making specific claims, it was detrimental as a foundation to claim respect since, as the hegemonic discourse, dominant norms and images were embedded in definitions of civilization. This discourse, drawing on social Darwinism and notions of evolutionary progress, emphasized higher stages of development and racial hierarchies, and made it difficult for Native Americans and African-Americans to counter with representations of their social worth based on cultural distinctiveness.

The Indians faced an additional disadvantage, as claims for Indian land were framed as a requirement of civilization. "However the Indians may regard this quest [for land], we, as American citizens cannot turn our backs upon our own civilization. We can neither deny its superior excellence, nor refuse to follow the dictates of its necessities" (Miner, 1976: 80–81). In a more threatening tone, the *Emporia News*, a friend of the corporations, editorialized in 1870: "Extermination is a terrible word; but finally, we fear, they will come to know fully its bitter meaning unless they subdue their wild restless natures and consent to engage in the peaceful pursuits of civilization" (Miner, 1976: 31).

African-Americans experienced similar pitfalls in making their claims as the joint heirs of American citizenship. Positively, the strategy of clarifying the contributions of blacks to American civilization and democracy served to undercut the very formulation of the "Negro problem." Negatively, the aspiration of sharing American civilization entailed assimilation, compelling African-Americans to deny or play down their distinctiveness; it impinged upon their struggle for a changed self-image. Claims to citizenship were based on recognition and respect, but Eurocentric images and ideals of respectability prevailed, such as social purity, thrift, and industriousness, and the patriarchal family based on male protection (cf. Gaines, 1996). Leaders of the black community often voiced an assimilationist message implicit in respectability, and sought to bring African-Americans in line with the values of the dominant society.

In sum, examining the past through a multicultural lens brings new understandings of both distant and contemporary social conflicts. A lesson of these past struggles is that they should instill in us a wariness about framing a struggle solely in terms of culture. As Kevin Gaines (1996) argues, in the African-American struggle at the turn of century up to the outbreak of World War I, cultural aspirations intrinsic to racial uplift supplanted a broader vision of emancipation and equality. A parallel can also be drawn with the women's movement, whose emphasis on motherhood eventually displaced an equal rights discourse. Although motherhood and women's caring capacities provided a powerful argument in winning the vote, it created an impediment to parity between women and men in gaining elected office. In short, the analysis of this chapter points to the need for social movements to advocate recognition, redistribution, and empowerment simultaneously.

8 Conflicting struggles for recognition: clashing interests of gender and ethnicity in contemporary Hungary

Júlia Szalai

Introduction

As the growing literature on the politics of recognition richly demonstrates, the ongoing struggles of socially/politically disadvantaged groups are important for understanding the contests over the reshaping of established welfare states (Mishra, 1984; Williams, 1989; Charles Taylor, 1994; Habermas, 1994; Fraser, 1995; Kymlicka, 1995; Honneth, 1995b; Fraser and Honneth, 2003). Among the highly diverse groups who have mobilized, it has been women and ethnic/racial minorities that have played the key roles in these struggles. As it has been pointed out time and again, their struggles have not been restricted to the values and formation of intergroup relations, but have also encompassed the spheres of power, redistribution, labor market participation, and welfare provision.

Acknowledging the importance of struggles for recognition in recent Western history, it is logical to raise questions about the respective processes in the new democracies in Eastern Europe. It took a surprisingly short time after the collapse of Soviet rule to (re)establish democratic governance in the region, but can we also assume a similar swift change in the role of civil society? More concretely, do we find formation of social movements and militant groups making claims for altering the prevailing distribution of power, social esteem, and material wealth? Which groups engage in such struggles, and what is at stake in their challenges? How do these struggles relate to the ongoing massive restructuring of the once state-controlled labor market and welfare redistribution, and how does the communist legacy influence their outcomes amid the arising peculiar conditions of the transition from a command economy to a market-regulated one?

It is perhaps needless to say that an exhaustive answer to these questions goes beyond the scope of one single chapter. By restricting myself to one case, Hungary, I will attempt to illustrate the specific features of recognition struggles in a postcommunist regime. I am analyzing two different

188

groups whose struggles for recognition, at first glance, seem to have little in common, but turn out to be deeply interrelated. First, I will focus on the attempts by Hungarian women to gain recognition and respect in work that had been forcibly locked into informal work within the household and the immediate community, and was thus non-recognized and unpaid under the old regime. This example highlights the "trade-off" that has emerged between decreasing gender inequalities and increasing class inequalities in the process of marketization in contemporary Hungary. The latter issue will lead me to the presentation of a totally different example of recognition struggles: the mobilization among the Roma, who experienced discrimination and poverty under communism as well as postcommunism, although the causes and legitimizing ideologies have gone through substantial changes.

The choice of the two types of struggles are not arbitrary: both highlight the dialogical character of recognition struggles. Both are responses to the way in which the once omnipotent socialist state has been decomposed and reshaped, creating the sociopolitical space for their conflicts. Hungary's major drive for marketization and the simultaneous sharp curbing of the state's roles and responsibilities in matters of social protection have clearly brought negative changes for the Roma, in terms of chronic poverty and accompanying social and political deprivation (Standing, 1997; Kochanowicz, 2000). But for women, the immediate consequences of these processes are opportunities for entering new occupations and the betterment of their economic and social position.

The discussion below will start with the presentation of two concurrent histories of the recent past: tracing the Hungarian women's successes in the post-1989 labor market and the Roma's dramatic losses in the same sphere during the past decade. This will be followed by an analysis of the grave consequences of the commingling of the "social" and "minority" aspects of poverty, and its impact on the running of daily minority politics. In the final section, I place the recurrent conflicts between women's interests in the new social occupations and Roma minority politics in the context of democratic politics amid the rather instable sociopolitical conditions of postcommunist transformation.

Women's silent movement for making private production public

I refer to the struggle of Hungarian women in the current transition period of "systemic changes" as a *silent* mass movement for improving their economic and social positions, because it has not developed into a mobilized movement with a visible political discourse. Although the lack of mobilization, ideological backing, and clearly voiced claims would make a strong argument for omitting the case from what is usually called a *recognition struggle*, I would suggest otherwise. True, there has not been an organized movement with leaders who articulated women's grievances and their mis- and nonrecognition rooted in histories of disrespect and constructed around a feminist identity. Nor has their struggle been made visible in political arenas. However, in post-Soviet societies, with the retreat of the state, many power struggles have occurred in economic spheres (Manchin and Szelényi, 1986; Szelényi, 1992; Kuczi and Vajda, 1992; Róna-Tas, 1997; Standing, 1997; Greskovits, 1998; Gal and Kligman, 2000b). Groups of women lobbying in unions, at their workplaces, and in their communities reflect this – their mobilization has been on the local front. Though rarely framed in terms of gender inequalities, their struggles for recognition involve claims of respect for the non-recognized work that they had been doing in the domestic informal economy during the decades of late-socialism; implicit in this claim is a realization that, by now, much of men's earlier work in the informal economy has become well paid and has grown to be a recognized constituent of the market economy, with the accompanying status and respect that such a change implies. Hence, one can say that the Hungarian women's struggle in the marketplace has had a great deal of politics in it which has "aimed at overcoming subordination, making them into full members of society, capable of participating on a par with other members" (Fraser in this volume).

Although it is a surprise to sociologists, political scientists, and economists studying the features of postcommunist transition (Einhorn, 1992; Lessenich, 2000; Szalai, 2000), for large groups of Hungarian women the transition has meant opportunities for upward occupational mobility and the improvement of their economic and social positions. Clear signs of general advancement can be seen in various aspects of daily life; labor-market surveys and sociological studies unanimously register incremental female gains in comparison both to men's situation, and to women's pre-1989 conditions (CSO, 1993; Timár, 1994; Laky, 1995).

Let me mention a few examples. First, the annual national educational reports clearly indicate women's rapidly rising participation in higher education. The yearly rate of enrolled female students has regularly exceeded those of male students during the past decade. As a consequence, women took the lead in the gender composition among full-time students by the late 1990s (CSO, 2001). Further, statistics signal relative gains for women in the labor market, although there remains a gendered earnings differential. As the regular surveys on employment show, women have been less affected by the negative side effects of economic restructuring – unemployment and poverty – than men (Janky, 1999). Data from the regular household-budget surveys show that women face a smaller risk of falling into deep poverty and, at the same time, are slightly over-represented in households with higher-than-average per-capita income (Janky, 1999).

When searching for an explanation for these undeniably "women-friendly" outcomes, it is important to emphasize that they cannot be attributed to either any deliberate government policies aimed at closing the gender gap or affirmative action policies to improve women's socio-economic advancement. In fact, the subsequent postcommunist governments in Hungary have, at best, been insensitive to the issues of gender or, worse, taken a clear conservative stand on women's participation in paid work, often making political statements about the expected return of women to the classical roles of mother and homemaker.

However, such conservative attempts proved to be ineffective. Instead of a massive withdrawal to the household, women took exactly the opposite route. They responded to the experience of earlier forced "emancipation" through compulsory employment in the command-economy by freely choosing to enter and play a visible role in the now marketized world of organized labor (Gal and Kligman, 2000; Szalai, 2000). In this sense one can say that the remarkably extensive and effective struggle for recognition on the battlefields of labor and employment over the past decade has occurred *despite* some loudly propagated political wills from above, but still in harmony with the nationwide political consensus to rapidly establish a well-functioning and modernized market-regulated economy. The issue at stake in this struggle has been due acknowledgment of women's earlier accumulated knowledge of providing services through home-based work. Although, as mentioned above, the campaign has not taken the form of an organized movement with a clear ideology and identifiable leaders, women have made their struggle mainly within the framework of residential communities and local lobbying, alongside the silent but visible actions of hundreds of thousands of individual women making claims in their homes, workplaces, and immediate neighborhoods.

The "tactics" applied in this movement originate from and clearly build upon the decades-long practices of massive social opposition to totalitarian rule after the defeat of the 1956 Revolution. Although the Revolution failed, its lessons could not be forgotten by either the ruling government or the vast majority of the Hungarian population. During those thirty years, what emerged was a strange and fragile compromise between the ruling Communist Party and the society, which then remained in force until the actual collapse of the regime. The essence of this compromise was voiceless toleration by the population of the totalitarian forms of ruling without limitations and a tacit acceptance by the ruling regime of a gradual expansion of the space for individual autonomy, within the one and only institution which was legitimately independent of direct political control under communism, namely the family.

Nobody could foresee the extent of change that the apparently "minor" political concessions to the restricted private autonomy induced in the daily life of the country. Significant numbers of families were able to combine their mandatory participation in formal institutions of the regime with freely chosen forms of participation outside the socialist arena that allowed them to develop alternative cultural patterns, values, skills, and routes for social mobility in the freely chosen forms of participation. The spreading of these new norms and patterns was based on and inspired by people's restricted independence to follow self-set rules in the *informal economy*.

Participation in informal productive activities to realize individually chosen ends slowly developed into a vast social movement (Kuczi and Vajda, 1992; Szelényi, 1992; Róna-Tas, 1997). Given the traditional key functions in the family in which women played a crucial role, they not only shared the massive workload of combining gainful activities in the two spheres of the economy, but also became the organizers and managers of the complex and difficult tasks which families had to face in the schizophrenic combination of diverse and contradictory rules, principles, goals, and duties. Given the liberating functions of the family under the prevailing totalitarian rule, the otherwise patriarchal gender division of roles turned out to be a source of relative freedom. On the basis of their multiple roles in production and reproduction, women were able to withdraw from time to time from the formal segments of production, since they had an acceptable "excuse" in their responsibility for the home. In time, these "excuses" for temporary exit from compulsory employment became semi-legalized through a series of new employment regulations. At the same time, the recurrent short-term exits made it possible for women to renegotiate the proportions of their participation in the two economies with an ever more pronounced turn towards the informal one. The gradual extension and intensification of their informal contribution developed, in turn, into a major source of self-esteem and prestige. Thus, besides its face value of material rewards, the increase of production within the private units of the informal economy had further significance. It expressed alternative notions about modernization and it led to alternative tastes (opposing the cultural patterns dictated by the authorities in control over the public realm). Finally, it created scope for alternative socialization of children, and helped them to acquire alternative knowledge, which they could never get in institutions in the officially run system of formal education (Szalai, 1991).

The post-1989 years have brought dramatic and complex changes in the position of such informal work within the economy. First, there was the abolition of rules for compulsory full employment and labor-force participation, which has now become a matter of free choice. Second, much of women's earlier informal work rapidly became liberated, publicly acknowledged, and regularly paid for.

This development has followed from a rapid reordering of the different segments of work, and people's attempts to unite all of their activities under the regulatory power of the market. Household properties which earlier could be utilized exclusively for purposes of private consumption have become productive capital for providing for sale a wide range of services that are in great demand (Farkas and Vajda, 1990; Vajda, 1997; Szalai, 2000). Likewise, skills and labor once frozen into the households also have now become marketable.

As a result of these processes, the Hungarian economy proved to be one of the fastest to convert to a service-sector economy in the region. This is evident through statistics that reveal a remarkable shift in the sectoral composition of the labor market. Taking industry, construction, and agriculture together, their share in employment dropped from its 60 percent level in 1980 to 40 percent by 1999 (CSO, 2001). At the same time, the service sector has been expanding dynamically. Data show that this growth was due to the rapid expansion in service work which – during the socialist period – had been either non-existent or seriously underdeveloped and understaffed within the formal segment of the economy. For example, banking, public administration, social security, personal social services, preventive medicine, welfare assistance, adult education, etc. are all fields that have provided employment to a steadily increasing number of people – mostly women – in recent years (Laky, 1999; Timár, 1994; Ványai and Viszt, 1995).

It has to be seen that women's current move on the labor market transcends the passive, adaptive attitude of the "classical" worker amid the conditions of a market economy, and also contributes to the alteration of fundamental social relations. By mobilizing their knowledge, diverse expertise, and readiness to accept a wide range of job arrangements, women cross an important borderline: that between the *private* and *public* spheres of social life (Hobson, 2000b; Gal and Kligman, 2000b). As mentioned above, during the late decades of socialism it was more and more their achievements in the private, informal domain that gave self-esteem, pride, and respect to those women who were otherwise confined to fulfill the dimmest, least paid, and least acknowledged positions of production. Still, their recognition remained locked into the informal networks of family, kinship, neighbors, and friends, and rarely did they receive payment.

With the 1989–90 regime change, the irons of forced "privateness" have been removed, and the very same sources of self-esteem, pride, and respect have become grounds for publicly acknowledged *social* positions, together with the accompanying material rewards (Vajda, 1997; Gal and Kligman, 2000b; Szalai, 2000).

However, such an important reinterpretation did not come automatically. While suitable conditions were provided by the nationwide commitment to marketization, women had to act as active agents to achieve the necessary institutional and legal guarantees. Without the strong backing of an organized women's movement, the new institutional arrangements frequently proved fragile, poorly protected, and uncertain. Despite such weaknesses, the break-up of the strict border between women's public and private economic contributions is still an irreversible fact of history, which has utterly changed women's opportunities on a mass scale and which has created the base for future claims for attaining the as-yet missing firmer legal and institutional guarantees. In this sense, women's massive move in the labor market has not only brought about better economic rewards and improved social positions, but it also has led to the recognition of their rightful participation in the public arena and the issues and matters that are discussed there.

The irreversible shift between the public–private divide is perhaps the most remarkable outcome of the processes discussed so far (Gal and Kligman, 2000). This unquestionable achievement of women's "silent movement for recognition" has been paired, however, with a serious conflict: the simultaneous *individualization* of poverty. The two processes are not independent from each other. First, the recent rapid growth of inequalities of income and wealth between women in the higher and lower ranks of the social hierarchy provides fertile soil for ideologies that view mobility and advancement as only a matter of personal effort. Perhaps an organized feminist movement with established social critique and articulated political claims might challenge this, but there are no alternative discourses for understanding these inequalities other than one of "discipline" and "merit." Success in this discourse depends only on individual exertions, while falling behind is viewed in terms of lack of internal drive.

In addition, sheer self-interest and the demands of making a living drive a large group of women towards becoming involved in defining poverty as a matter of personal fate and behavior. After all, it has been the dramatic individualization of poverty which has opened up certain opportunities for female employees, who have been moving from the lower positions of the social hierarchies of labor to the new jobs in personal and welfare services. These new posts have been set up to ease poverty, but are built on the personified new perception of it and the concomitant exclusive use of the case method approach in deciding individual needs. The booming of individual guardianship as the sole response to poverty is an immediate consequence, a "precondition" of women's employment in the welfare sphere, and also a source of status and valuation for them. Hence, whether known to them or not, women in the welfare profession have a great deal of vested interest in the maintenance of poverty strictly separated from the market, strictly driven and regulated by other rules, and strictly remaining under "their" control. In short, their risk of falling back into poverty is dependent on their clients' failure to get out of it.

It is not the task of the present paper to explore all the varied causes and aspects of the drama of the clashing interests between women in welfare and women (and men) on welfare. Nevertheless, there is a distinctive group among the present-day poor, in whose case the above-discussed individualization of poverty has led to dramatic conflicts on ethnic grounds: the Roma. Their recognition struggle for getting due acknowledgment for minority rights distinct from their social rights has led to serious, face-to-face clashes with women's claims for self-esteem and recognition in the service sectors, who have been the providers of welfare for them. Before discussing these conflicts, I will give some historical background, including the intermingling of the "social" and "minority" aspects of poverty and its consequences for Hungary's Roma minority.

The ethnically reshaped welfare question

In recent years, widely reported clashes around the "Roma question" have exploded in Hungary. In the overwhelming majority of the cases, the issue at stake was the enforced segregation – not infrequently the outright "ghettoization" – of the Roma within a given local community. Such attempts at segregation were imposed upon the Roma not primarily because of their material or cultural status, but rather because of their *ethnic difference* (Kis, 1997). Tensions now are not social – as was the case in communist times – but rather take the form of open struggles around diverse interpretations of minority rights. Of course, this is not to say that the economic and social situation of the Roma has improved recently, and that the social dimension has thereby been driven into the background. In fact, the available research data show the opposite: whether one considers their employment opportunities, schooling, incomes, or housing conditions, the gap between the majority and the Roma communities has widened dramatically in the course of the last decade (Glatz and Kemény, 1999; Horváth, Landau, and Szalai, 2000). One might see this gap and the social conflicts accompanying it in terms of the reshaping of prevailing ethnic relations in Hungarian society, but it is more complex than that. Closer examination of the historically informed process of "reshaping" is important for understanding the current recognition struggles of the Roma, and the more immediate political consequences of their battles concerning different aspects of daily life. The ongoing dissolution of the "social" element in the "minority" dimension has a considerable influence on the physiognomy and everyday utilization of the minority institutions now beginning to take shape in Hungary. Furthermore, it is of decisive importance for the delivery of different social services, thus affecting the entire welfare system of contemporary Hungary, together with women's recently established positions in it.

The social–historical antecedents of the intermingling of the "social" and the "minority" dimensions of poverty can be found in the earlier period of state socialism, and the process by which the once ruling party-state sought to forcibly assimilate the Roma during the late decades of the regime. It was by no means accidental that the program of forced assimilation was connected to two developments of late socialism: on the one hand, the level of employment of Roma in industry, which was growing by leaps and bounds, and on the other hand, the changes in their traditional settlement and living conditions accomplished within the framework of a national campaign. The first development was closely connected to the socialist large-scale industry's unlimited appetite for cheap labor, of which the Roma represented the last available source. The second development was partly a consequence of the first, and resulted from political considerations about the existence of poverty in a communist society. Those in power could not remain blind to the fact that the living conditions common in the Roma wretched settlements constituted a "political time bomb" for the system. In their very existence, they represented a refutation of both the post-Stalinist consolidation policy of the 1960s and the program of "improving living standards for all" which formed its foundation. Hence, it was in the basic interests of the then prevailing Kádár regime – which was doing its best to restore an international reputation that had taken a beating as a result of the suppression of the 1956 Revolution – that it adopt measures to ameliorate the scandalous conditions of the Roma communities. But it had further reasons for doing so. It was also unacceptable to the regime for the Roma to live in separate communities because, paradoxically, that kept them outside the various domains of totalitarian control, among which, under the above-outlined post-1956 "soft dictatorship," it was no longer the police station and the prison, but more the schools and the workplace which were the most important. However, by getting "inside" the socialist workplace in the space of a decade – the 1970s – the Roma became socialist employees just like any other group. They became subject not only to the comprehensive control exercised through the workplace but to the same kind of remuneration to which any other socialist worker was entitled – in other words, they attained that kind of "social membership" which the system unequivocally bound together with compulsory employment. As socialist employees, central policy had to take the same kind of measures in relation to the Roma as it did with other groups; socialist "Gypsy policy" therefore became just like – and for the same reason – socialist "women's policy," "youth policy," or "worker policy."

This represented a real change, and signified the transformation of the relations both between the Roma and the non-Roma populations and between the Roma and the state. Up until then, relations between the Roma and non-Roma communities had been governed by rules and traditions which had been in place for decades, if not centuries. In this sense, every village, every town, every district had its own "Gypsy policy." Nevertheless, one element was common to all: *the fact that the Roma were outside society.* All of this, however, suddenly changed. On entering the same building company, mine, or textile factory as the majority population, the Roma became part of the same workplace, canteen, street, washroom, doctor's waiting room, and council anteroom. Furthermore, the Roma came into contact with the same foreman, party secretary, and, similarly, work discipline and working time of the factory. The "supreme will" (that is, of the "omnipotent" Party) and the system's totalitarian logic created this commonality – and what is more, it did so in a very short time, in the course of one or two decades.

Now that the Roma were *inside* the system, the same expectations and rules came to apply to them as to everyone else. In order that these rules could be implemented, it was necessary to configure ideologies: *race-based social exclusion* became, without any particular warning, classified as a *disadvantageous social situation*, and "Gypsy policy" became "social policy." Bearing in mind that socialism did not recognize communal rights – and particularly the most important ones, namely, minority rights – this could not have happened otherwise. The system's own logic necessitated a procedure for molding socialist citizenship that rested upon political subjugation, and the only possible route to this was the forced assimilation of the Roma, framed in terms of social policy. To surmount their "disadvantages," it was necessary to integrate them into those institutions in which everyone else was integrated: that is, in compulsory education, council-estate living, the socialist health care system, and the state-run administration of child protection. Naturally, the services intended for "them" were a little "different," generally lower in quality, but nevertheless they were part of the same institutional system – and this was what mattered.

True, the Roma's acceptance of subordination and "obedience" to their assimilation demanded by the regime bore real fruit over time, in terms of improved living conditions and a certain material security that resulted from stable incomes and social security payments, which they now also received as "socialist" workers. However, their compliance was different in two important ways from that which had been required from all the other groups in Hungary before them.

First, the Roma were forced to renounce not only a particular social situation, a community characterized by extended family and neighborly relations, customs, and norms, but also their *ethnic affiliation*. Under socialism, the mere existence of communities, indeed any kind of collective expression of mutual belonging, was viewed as organizing against the system and thus deemed a "crime." Second, compliance by the Roma to the socialist rules markedly differed also in its "rewards and opportunities." As discussed above, the working compromise between the majority and the state opened the doors to participating in the informal economy and to share all of the material, cultural, and social rewards that this participation brought about. However, Roma employees were sharply excluded from this restricted autonomy.

There were manifold interests in maintaining such a demarcation line between the two groups. It was the "disciplining" principle guiding the "education" of the freshly socialized Roma workers with extreme rigor that did not allow for the maintenance of old ties to the Roma community that were considered – as mentioned above – anti-socialist. Moreover, the desire to maintain popular support for the regime led the state authorities to leave some room for forbidden racial discrimination where it was least visible and least seemed to cause harm: in the informal relations regulating access to the social networks around the informal economy.

Also to be considered is the fact that the Roma themselves lacked a number of conditions necessary for successful participation in the informal economy. Due to their earlier outcast position, they had neither the land nor any other resources to take advantage of the largest segment of informal production: agriculture outside the domain of the socialist farms and cooperatives. Similarly, they lacked the cultural capital, the necessary infrastructure, and the skills to develop modern, household-based services. Furthermore, they were outside those webs of community relations which provided the basis for the complex exchange relations for the majority, which allowed families to reduce their spending on labor, material, and services (Kuczi and Vajda, 1992). In sum, a deficiency of all kinds of capital alongside the prejudices of the majority effectively obstructed the integration of the Roma into the informal economy. Thus, they remained totally excluded from what later turned out to provide the basis for successful participation in the market-regulated arrangements of production and the learning processes that led to material advancement. In addition, they were deprived of the alternative paths of self-protection that those who participated in the two-pillar way of existence had, which allowed them to weather the crisis of the post-1989 transition.

Briefly summarizing the attempts at attaining social membership, one can say that ultimately the cause of mass failure can clearly be identified in the "socialist" way of carrying out the assimilation of the Roma. Given that the program was built on the full denial of ethnicity, the failure of "socialist assimilation" was to be expected from the outset: it promised social progress, but only for those who – whether by compliance, "wise" consideration, or choice – were ready to "forget" (in certain cases, even to deny) their ethnicity. If they did not chose to do so or they were unable to integrate into the majority community, the system defined their ethnic difference as a disadvantageous social situation or a "defect," which often resulted in penal sanctions (Horváth, Landau, and Szalai, 2000). The transformation of ethnic otherness into a matter of social policy prevented, however, the "Gypsy question" from being referred to by name, and forced majority–minority conflicts into the enclosed spaces of the workplaces, local councils, residential communities, schools, orphanages, and doctor's offices.

The transmutation of the ethnic question into a social policy matter backfired, however, after the collapse of communism. The rejection of the old system was not followed by the creation of a protective, democratic, modern welfare state. The rapid falling apart of the old "hoops" of softened totalitarianism suddenly released all of the earlier suppressed and diffused ethnic conflicts. In such an atmosphere, with the sharp drop in demand for unskilled labor, it was the Roma workers who were first ejected *en masse*. However, massive and terminal unemployment soon became but one link in a chain of other negative effects of marketization, in the spheres of housing, schooling, health care, and child protection. In short, while the withdrawal of the state allowed the majority of Hungarian society to unite the earlier formal and informal pillars of their lives, the same process resulted in the Roma's fall into extreme poverty *en masse*. In fact, they are the *only* social grouping in contemporary Hungary whose poverty can be visibly linked to membership in a pre-existing *community* (Glatz and Kemény, 1999; Havasi, 2002). In the eyes of the public, being Roma is identical with being poor, and more and more there is an assumption that Roma are *born* to be poor. In this way, the old equation between social deprivation and ethnicity still prevails, but the reasoning behind it has changed. While it was earlier the "ethnic" dimension which was dissolved in the "social" issue, now it is the matter of "social status" which is tied to "ethnicity" (Horváth, Landau, and Szalai, 2000). This should be seen in the broader context of "state desertion" (Standing, 1997) from the sphere of social protection, which created such a twist in the logic. In contrast to the former state of affairs under state socialism, the "social" element has now been merged into the "minority" one in both policy and discourse. However, this is not simply a matter of wording, but can have dangerous consequences in respect to a group's social status. The latest version of the commingling of poverty and ethnicity "ghettoizes" the minority question while it "ethnicizes," to an extreme degree, the social question. This confused "equation" has been raised to the level of policy-making. Hence, the case of the poor who have been left behind is defined rather as a "racial" issue. Building upon this shift, the political discourse represents a whole minority group as the "social burden" for the majority (Kis, 1997).

In these circumstances, it is probably needless to argue at length that the sorting out of the hopelessly intermingled "social" and "minority" aspects of poverty is the key to any further development of democratic conditions in Hungary. Yet surprisingly little has been done in these directions so far. The recent construction of a new institution – the minority self-governments – to exercise minority rights can perhaps be considered, however, as a promising step to start the lengthy and – most probably – contradictory sorting-out process.

Attempts at practicing minority rights: the built-in dilemmas of Roma local self-governance

After several years of heated debates behind the doors of government of-fices, in the Constitutional Court, and in other national decision-making bodies, it was in late 1993 that the Parliament enacted the much awaited Act on "The Rights of National and Ethnic Minorities of Hungary" (Act LXXVII, 1993). This was the first attempt in the history of post-war legislation at defining minority rights as distinct from all other rights and entitlements, and to specify the institutional framework for practic-ing them in newly installed minority self-governments. Details of the Act also prescribed the methods for setting up the new institutions at the local level, and circumscribed their authority. Following the year-long negoti-ations with the representative cultural bodies and influential associations of the respective communities, the 1993 Act formally acknowledged the existence of thirteen "national and ethnic" minorities, and – together with their registration – granted them the right to select nominees for the upcoming minority elections.[1] As a result of the first held minority elections in 1994, 679 minority governments came into being, out of which 416 were Roma. Despite all of the controversy surrounding them in the beginning, self-government institutions are on the increase. Thus, in 1998, four years after the first minority governments were elected, the new elections resulted in twice as many institutions as before: their number suddenly jumped to 1,363, with 771 Roma governments among them.

Considering these spectacular figures on Roma governments, it is important to note that at the time of the codification into law of minority-based self-governance, the Hungarian minorities were not center stage. Instead, two important foreign-policy issues lay behind the motivation for the enactment: (a) Hungary's relatively recent accession to the European Council, and, most importantly, (b) the problem of ethnic Hungarians living beyond the borders of the nation (Molnár and Schafft, 2002). These conditions underlying the birth of the law continue to shape the limitations of the institutions that it sought to establish.

This is especially true for the country's largest minority. What is at issue here is the fact that, however important their case is in deciding the contours of ethic/minority relations in Hungarian society, the law was not made primarily for the Roma. This is evident in the comprehensive introductory chapter of the Act, entitled "Basic Provisions." When this was drafted, the legislators did not have the needs of the Roma in mind. Consider the following sections of the law.

1.§ (2) Within the meaning of the act a national or ethnic minority (hereafter: minority) shall be any ethnic group whose members are citizens of Hungary which, domiciled on the territory of the Republic of Hungary for at least one century, constitutes a numerical minority in the population of the state, is distinguished from the rest of the population by its own language, culture, and traditions, and at the same time exhibits a consciousness of homogeneity, such that all of these things tend towards the preservation of their historically formed communities, and the expression and protection of their interests.

3.§ (4) Every minority community and every person belonging to a minority shall have the right to live in his homeland, and to maintain contacts with his homeland undisturbed. The right to a homeland shall mean the freedom and safeguarding of contact not only with a person's place of birth, but also with the place of birth or residence of their parents, foster-parents, or forebears, as well as with the old country and its culture and traditions. (Act LXXVII, 1993)

The second passage begs many questions, among them is: *Where* might the "old country" be and whose culture and traditions should be strengthened in order to create their sense of belonging? Which culture were the Roma supposed to cultivate? Likewise, is the Roma community recognized in the law if it constructs its definition of "minority" *from the outset* as a historically settled consciousness of homogeneity? In this respect, the law does not even gesture in the direction of acknowledging a minority which has been historically denied its minority-group consciousness through forced assimilation.

Similarly, all of the entitlements in the Act that provide education for the minorities in their native language, preservation of architectural and cultural heritage, observation of traditional celebrations, and establishment of their own network of academic institutions render the content of minority rights empty for the Roma. For them, the entitlements listed above are of little use. In fact, the provision of "separate" minority education, which is intended to increase self-esteem and community cohesion, could have perverse effects for the Roma, since it does not protect a group who could be marginalized through the majority population's clamor for their out-and-out segregation.

While the entitlements enumerated in the Act are, by and large, of value to the other twelve small and well-assimilated minorities, who wish to safeguard their cultural identity, the phrase "*and* ethnic" attached to the word "national" does not offer a solution as to how the law might also guarantee the rights of the Roma community. What the law does not consider is perhaps the most important for the Roma: the statutory protection of their *human dignity* and *self-esteem*. True, the aforementioned "Basic Provisions" prohibit discrimination to the detriment of minorities. But in the construction of the law, it is clear that in the eyes of the legislators the national minorities' historical injuries were of primary importance. Above all, they wanted to bring the force of the law to bear against possible repetitions of discrimination against Hungarian minorities in other countries. A logical consequence of this was, however, that the Minority Act provided a single sphere of action for the prohibition of discrimination: international law. That there might be any discrimination *within* the borders of Hungary was simply not acknowledged. It is therefore logical that it did not consider as its task the establishment of domestic institutions responsible for guarding against such actions.

If one considers the scope of the law in terms of regulatory spheres and authority to implement rights, the minority institutions are empowered with but narrowly limited agency. Minority self-governments are able to:

a) seek information;
b) make a recommendation;
c) initiate measures;
d) raise objections to practices and individual decisions related to the functioning of institutions which contravene minority rights, and initiate the modification or repeal of a decision.

The person in charge of the responsible and authoritative body . . . shall be obliged to *give a detailed reply* to the request within 30 days. (Act LXXVII, 1993: 26 §§ [1–2], italics added)

Regardless of the stated principle laid down in the preamble of the Act concerning self-governance as the foundation of the democratic system, "externally" – that is, in respect of the representation of interests, injuries, and their own needs – the minorities' new constitutional-law institutions when translated into everyday practices do not provide minorities any more influence than *any ordinary Hungarian citizen* who turns to the authorities with a request. Their proposals and requests are at most worthy of an "answer on the merits," although the competent authorities have no obligation in respect of either reporting or enforcement.

It is not necessary to go into further details to deduce that the regulations concerning spheres of authority and material resources can only amount to a very limited expression of minority rights: taken from the regulations, the minorities' local self-governments are not really more than *tradition-maintaining associations*. The question naturally arises: What was the point of all the legislative fuss, given that several associations of this kind had been already in existence?

The purpose of the Act can be seen as symbolic, aimed at ethnic Hungarians living beyond the borders who should be able to have some ground for participating in the politics of their homeland. For the minorities living within Hungarian borders, it provides, as discussed earlier, rights to organize native-language education, publishing, and culture. These are areas in which the law has created something new. In the latter case of cultural rights, the law gave the tradition-maintaining associations a *constitutional-law status* and the statutory possibility of *institution founding*. But these cultural rights are disconnected from material rights, even from guarantees for their public financing.

If a local minority is to found its "own" kindergarten, school, theater, or museum, it must be extremely rich. If not, such an institution will simply *not* be established. In this way, the minority's right to recognition is linked to the possession of assets: without the necessary resources, poor communities remain excluded from exercising them. The law *in principle* gives this right to everyone, but to practice these rights reveals the linkages between claims for recognition and claims for redistribution.

That the Roma cannot do much with these possibilities is partly because their communities are not rich. But also to be taken into consideration is the fact that the Roma cultural associations, which were considered forerunners of the self-government institutions, were not concerned with the preservation of traditions, but rather with obtaining education, employment, and material support for Roma citizens. From the Roma standpoint, entitlements in the law have little meaning because they assume a legally comprehensible framework, but in fact this is what the law lacks. The Act fails to specify basic issues of governance, the frame of authority of self-governments in local affairs, which affect minorities. Hence, it remains unclear whether the elected local minority self-governments can ensure organized legal protection to mistreated members of the community; and whether they can have an influence in the shaping of local welfare regulations and in weeding out their hidden discriminatory contents. Can they have a say in the local redistribution regime and its prejudicial practices? Do they have the right to demand training programs for unemployed members of the community? Do they have the right to revise the kindergarten admissions system or the composition of school classes? Do they have the right to a say in the appointment of school principals or the directors of local healthcare institutions? And so on.

From the legal aspect, no one, least of all the disadvantaged groups within the majority, can answer these and similar questions with a definite "yes" or "no," because of murkiness in the Minority Act itself. For example, should complaints about discrimination be treated as "citizens issues" handled in the administrative and legal channels built up on the grounds of citizen's rights? Or, in the case of the Roma, now that they have their "own" minority institution, should their claims be channeled into the – still painfully imperfect – legal procedures of protecting *minority rights*? As can be expected, attempts at shifting matters from one "box" to the other are made on a wide range of issues of daily life. Thus, as it seems, the conflicts arising from the earlier intermingling of the "social" and "minority" aspects of rights have hardly been settled by the new legislation – at best, it has changed the appearance of the controversies, but certainly not the substance of them.

By emphasizing the shortcomings and uncertainties in the Minority Act, I do not want to suggest that there are only negative aspects to the law. The creation of officially acknowledged, elected institutions has been significant for the Roma community as a form of recognition, since for the first time in history, it granted Roma in Hungary a *framework* to articulate collective needs in an organized form. In fact, many of the local communities have interpreted the new law as an opportunity to do this, which explains the remarkable growth of minority self-governments among the Roma.

The new self-governments have also offered opportunities for minority communities for institution building. First, they could provide a path for political education. Given the fact that the Act entrusts the elected representatives with no more (but also with no less) than opinion-forming and lobbying functions, the new self-governments help to select the actual opinion leaders of the community, and delegate to them the role of formally representing all those cases and issues where the local administration cannot make decisions without the consent of the minority. Though the influence of the minority representatives remains limited in most of the claims, their participation in the political discourse assists the coupling of majority and minority argumentations, and helps to put together the first building blocks of a meaningful local policy on majority–minority coexistence.

Second, the new institutions could be used as a channel for promoting social mobility within the Roma community. Representation of the community has become an "occupation," or a "profession," resulting in material rewards in most cases, and in increased respect in all of them. Further, the simple fact of electing several thousand representatives has also meant a rise in civil organizations on the part of the majority to assist the minority's local activities, courses, training programs, and professional activities that have been set up. The mere existence of local minority governments has made thicker the tiny layer of a capable, informed, talented elite of the Roma community.

Nevertheless, despite these positive sides of local minority governments, they have not generated a fundamental turn in the administration of the "Roma question" in contemporary Hungary. On the one hand, by creating a weak institution in defense of the rights of the individual and collective identity, the Minority Act has opened the door for "lawful" attempts at turning citizens' issues into distinct "minority cases." In this respect, the law has contributed to segregation and the impoverishment of the contents of citizenship. On the other hand, the very same legislation has created instruments to promote struggles for recognition, and has set in motion the evolution of a militant, knowledgeable leadership within the Roma community.

It is still an open question which of the two trends will predominate. Much of the outcome depends on the public acknowledgment of the fact that the local struggles of the Roma do not take place in a social vacuum, but are embedded in the terrain of other conflicts surrounding the ongoing postcommunist systemic transformation. In the following section, I focus on one set of these conflicts between women social workers and Roma minority representatives, which questions who the recognized authority to distribute welfare resources is.

Clashing claims for recognition: women and Roma on the battlefield of welfare assistance

As mentioned earlier, despite the advantages that followed from the framework-making character the Minority Act failed to resolve the key problem of the "Roma question": it did not address the dangerous commingling of the "social" and "minority" aspects of rights for the Roma. This failure was a consequence of the interplay of the earlier discussed motives to draft a law that was primarily targeted at the well-assimilated, well-to-do minorities, which were small in number. For them, the content of the now legal status of minority rights is merely a cultural and emotional matter, an additional entitlement above all other social and citizen's rights that they had access to within the "ordinary" institutions of Hungarian society. However, the case is – as we have seen – utterly different with the largest minority actually using the law in its day-to-day struggles; the Roma community is neither well assimilated, nor well-to-do, and, at the same time, it is substantial in numbers. In addition, the post-1989 economic and political processes have led to the actual *impoverishment* of the Roma social and citizen's rights, and have done so on the grounds of ethnicity.

In these circumstances, the granting of minority self-governance forced the local Roma communities to face a devilish dilemma that could not be resolved without further conflicts. Either they take the new organizations as the institutional framework for struggling against social deprivation, or stick to the narrow confines of the formal parameters of the Minority Act, which would mean concerning themselves with misdeeds. A sequence of dramatic local conflicts between the Roma and non-Roma parts of the communities clearly demonstrates this. Entitlements provided by the wording of the law to the minority self-governments as to how to act in cases of conflict are unclear; they are therefore made the object of daily bargaining. As a result, although in recent years majority–minority clashes in the towns of Székesfehérvár, Tiszavasvári, and Sátoraljaújhely have received great publicity, the intervention of leaders of the local Roma self-governments has had no influence on the outcome. It did not matter whether they were courageous or submissive: no matter who they sided with, their decisions were no more significant than those of any other "private person." Their mandate as representatives entitled them to do *only so much*, and no more (Kis, 1997; Horváth, Landau, and Szalai, 2000). Clearly, these experiences taught serious lessons to the local Roma leaders: in their maneuvering to enlarge the scope of the law they might risk undermining the newly gained minority-driven legitimacy of their local government institutions. Furthermore, their actions put them into conflict with all the officials and institutions of the local majority that regard these attempts at extended minority protection as an offense and a hostile border-crossing activity.

However, the other route also leads to an impasse. If the new Roma minority self-governments stick to the strictly written ordinances of the law, they define their role as "smoothing" agents between the majority institutions and the local minority. What they risk is the dilution of any purpose for the institutions. From the perspective of the deprived minority community, they jeopardize not only the legitimacy and use-fulness of the minority self-governments, but also they risk undermining *all* rights-based protecting institutions. In addition, by refraining from the necessary interventions, the self-governments give "official" consent and tacit approval to the continuing process of withdrawing social and citizen's rights from those whom they should protect.

In the course of the past eight years, the Roma local self-governments have experimented with both of these problematic choices, as well as with various fine-tuned combinations of them. Although the second, "con-formist" path seemed less hazardous for many of them at the outset, the quickly withering local support led to the dying out of these organiza-tions. As a consequence, the termination of the representation of mi-nority interests has intensified the defenselessness of the local minority. This resulted in campaigns by the Roma community to elect replace-ments at the next election. Since it was not only their decision, but also the entire electorate of the locality, the selection of local Roma candi-dates became a conflictual issue. Hence, the preparation for the second round of the minority elections in 1998 was accompanied by corrup-tion, blackmailing, and attempts at breaking down the unity of the Roma community.

In those cases where the first path was followed from the beginning, the conflicts took different forms. Though the militancy of the elected representatives had the effect of strengthening the cohesion of the local minority community and protected it, with somewhat greater efficiency, from discrimination and against poverty, these committed local politi-cians did not win either. Their attempts at extending the framework of minority governance into the spheres of welfare, health care, and ed-ucation led to heated local conflicts with the clientele of the majority competing with the Roma for social benefits and services. The major-ity began to mobilize government authorities and the court against the "unlawful" actions of the minority representatives. Ultimately, these in-tensified conflicts convinced the majority groups of the locality that they had to rid themselves of the trouble-making minority leaders during the second round of the minority elections and they found strategies to do this in an "orderly" fashion. Nevertheless, the lessons from these first endeavors of local recognition struggles have not been lost by the Roma communities, and today they guide their tactics.

A closer look at the conflicts that arose when the minority governments began to act as interest-protecting institutions making attempts to extend the social aspects of the rights of the Roma highlights the collision between the struggles for recognition of the Roma and those of the women in social welfare occupations.

Claims for recognition and redistribution are interwoven in the contests surrounding welfare assistance. Following the earlier outlined economic and social processes, some 50 to 70 percent of the Roma can now
be regarded poor even according to the most rigorous assessment (Sik
and Tóth, 1997; Havasi, 2002). However, agreed and legally prescribed,
official indicators of poverty simply do not exist in current Hungarian
welfare policy. Apart from a few loosely defined centralized measures,
the acknowledged criteria are matters for local decision-making, depending on the capacity, political structure, and sensitivity of the community
(Horváth, 1995). Local regulations therefore further determine the list
of concrete entitlements for assistance, and – as mentioned above – leave
the actual distribution to extremely discretionary means-tested schemes,
run by the local welfare administration and social workers. Amid these
conditions, the available resources are few *by definition*, and the tough
competition between various groups in need is an in-built constituent
and also a major self-regulatory instrument of the system. It is justifiable
to say that, instead of welfare, this arrangement is a form of *warfare* of
the poor against each other, of the providers against the poor, and of the
poor fighting back against them.

In these local welfare wars, the Roma easily and often get blamed for
the "overuse" of resources. When looking at the composition of the queue
in the anteroom of the welfare office, it appears that the Roma are heavily
over-represented among the needy. Within the system, the task of those
running the scheme is to tighten up the conditions, and not to provide
assistance to "everybody." Thus, welfare officers, social workers, teachers, health care workers, etc. are called upon to unite against the "unjust"
exploitation of scarce resources; in other words, to find ways of reducing
the number of Roma eligible for public provisions. Given the feminized
nature of these professions, ultimately it is mostly women who are supposed to carry out these tasks on a day-to-day basis. What this implies
for those who took these jobs to protect the poor is that now their job
consists of *policing* the poor.

Many of these women welfare administrators and social workers are
reluctant to make such a turn. "Policing" is alien to them as a "masculine" activity with the (un)necessary use of power and force – thus,
it is too close to "politics" that they learned to avoid during the former
regime. They chose a caring profession exactly because of its "safe" distance from authority, and for its supportive role. As testified by a number
of interviews with newly minted social workers, a frequent motive behind opting for employment in the welfare services had been the wish to
"guard," to "help," and to "provide caring" for those in great need of that
support. As the interviews reveal, these strong motivations for exercising

goodwill usually followed directly from the women's earlier experiences of defenselessness and abuse. Now that they are supposed to turn against their clients to carry out the rules from higher authorities, this represents a betrayal of their motives in choosing the profession.

In these circumstances, the minority self-governments seem to come as "saviors" for the troubled women of the welfare agencies. Instead of second-best ways out of the traps of the "protective–policing" trade-off, the new institutions with their drives to extend the Roma's social rights are at hand to take over the task. This is why in an increasing number of local communities, the elected leaders of the minority have "unexpectedly" been invited to "make just decisions" among "their" people. These invitations seem at first sight to be the acknowledgment of certain Roma claims: after all, their long-standing struggle for recognition implicitly sought increased autonomy in decision-making, and they strove for the recognition of their community-specific features of poverty and for the application of purposeful methods to combat them. Hence, the shifting of certain responsibilities in welfare assistance appears to meet some of the claims on both sides.

However, this shift in moving the burden of who decides the welfare provisions for the Roma has had consequences for both the women in social work and welfare administration, on the one hand, and the Roma welfare seekers on the other. On the one side, women in the respective welfare occupations left "only" with the task of assisting the non-Roma poor soon became redundant, and, besides going on the dole, their institutions (local family centers, services for children, the elderly, the sick, etc.) shortly became "superfluous" in the eyes of the local decision-makers. On the other side, the creation of a "distinct" scheme for the Roma poor has sped up and pushed forward the processes of segregation. After all, the call to assist in creating a "distinct" system of welfare distribution with "specific" regulations outside the framework of the general law has further weakened the otherwise loose system of welfare protection and has dramatically increased the costs associated with maintaining separate schools, health care units, family centers, etc. for both the majority and the Roma ethnic minority. It is also important to remember that control over resources has still remained with the majority, so there has not been any increase in the decision-making autonomy of the minority. Thus, instead of enlarging social rights, the takeover of welfare assistance by local minority governments has ultimately led to further reductions in such assistance and further marginalization of the entire Roma community.

In light of these outcomes, it is no surprise that the practice of mutual blaming has been visibly on the increase between women in welfare services and the Roma claiming welfare. These conflicts are interpreted as local affairs that could have been avoided with some "goodwill" on either side. However, the deeper causes of the conflicts lie outside the local framework, and can hardly be attributed to the conflicting, though powerless, parties. First and foremost among these causes is the extreme decentralization of redistribution, which aimed to enable the state's quick desertion in matters of social protection (Standing, 1997; Lessenich, 2000; Kochanowicz, 2000; Szalai, 2000). This left a vacuum in settling the disputes around the differing interpretations of rights and entitlements to welfare. The lack of regulations, weak protection, and publicity of the conflicts has meant a weakening in the power of both groups, particularly the Roma.

Conclusions

The struggles for recognition among the Roma and the women's movement in the new caring professions are a provocative example of the complex and dialogical character of these struggles. First, groups striving for recognition can easily work against each other, if often unwillingly. In the case of the social work providers, their movement into social work offered recognition of women's distinctive capacities as caretakers. But the newly formed Roma local governments challenged the authority and capacities of these women to decide on day-to-day issues involving the well-being of an ethnic minority. The struggles of the Roma, in turn, were driven by attempts at clearing up the continuous commingling of the "social" and "ethnic" dimensions of their status. However, these attempts have been recurrently failing under the pressure of neediness, which make them strongly dependent on the "goodwill" of the local welfare administration, which is mainly run by women. Hence, these cases illustrate that contesting recognition struggles are often the result of broader political and economic processes.

The continual clashes of interests between women entering the enlarged job market of social services and the Roma fighting back against their social deprivation through the arena of minority politics follow from the process of postcommunist transformation. It is in this complex process of the withdrawal of the once omnipotent state and its simultaneous turn into desertion from its traditional responsibilities in matters of welfare, that there has been a recasting of social policy that affects poverty and the status of minorities. Their redefinition has been left to the internal fights of local communities, but reflects deeper power struggles in the society over recognition and redistribution. It is not women flowing into the social services nor the Roma struggling for the acknowledgment of minority rights who create these dilemmas. Rather, both of them seem to be responding to circumstances beyond their control: the desertion of the state from matters of redistribution and welfare policy.

As I have highlighted in this chapter, the decomposition of the institutional pillars of the old state has been an unquestioned precondition for the transition from a command-economy to a market-regulated one. It was also seen as a prerequisite for the establishment of new democratic political institutions. Although the first years of the transformation brought about serious economic difficulties and uncertainties for a large number of social groups, these crises have been overcome by the majority of Hungarian society, which has adapted to the changes and benefited from the new institutions. This has been the case for women, a vulnerable group in the transitions from state socialism. In Hungary, women without formal voice in the political arena (and whose numerical representation in formal politics has precipitously declined in all post-Soviet societies) nevertheless have benefited from the opportunities in the transformation, and gained recognition of their earlier unpaid work, which had been consigned to the private households of the informal economy under the old regime.

Nevertheless, I would argue that that the Hungarian majority population has paid a price for their success, in the withdrawal of the state from supporting the poor and in its management of the most visible group of the poor, the Roma. Most of the difficulties follow from the fact that the legal, regulatory, and practical changes implemented in the name of curtailing the state's influence in matters of welfare policy have hindered rather than helped the separation of the "social" and "minority" elements of the "Roma question." This has led to an increase in majority–minority tensions. Welfare redistribution, with its sharp bifurcation into systems for "citizens" and systems for "the poor," alongside the decentralization of the provisioning for the poor, has intensified the competition among the poor for meager local resources, which have been diminishing year by year. Nevertheless, while ethnic clashes have become more frequent and more intense over the last few years, they have not escalated into a nationwide "civil war." The reason for this is that conflicts are cast as "quarrels" between the poor in local communities and thus as a local concern.

Ultimately, society's better positioned strata can thank the welfare reform for this: in the course of the transformation of the system, both the issues of poverty and that of the defenseless ethnic minority were pushed into the background, within the administrative borders of villages and towns and far from "big politics." In this way, the blame for conflicts can be attributed to individual local abuses. Such occurrences are not considered the responsibility of the "rest" – who live outside the settlement – nor is it seen as appropriate to interfere in the internal affairs of local communities.

The commingling, both in principle and in practice, of the "social" and "minority" elements of the "Roma question" is for this reason still – just as it was before the transition – the principal safeguard of the daily maintenance of social peace. At the same time, there is an implicit danger here: if a legal system based on democratic principles fails to recognize the rights of the minority, it cannot guarantee the rights of the majority either.

It is women working in the welfare service system who are among the first to learn these lessons. Their success enhanced self-esteem, which followed from their entry into new welfare service jobs, has started to wither away as a consequence of the sharpening local wars around welfare distribution. On the one hand, the short-sighted attempts to place the burdens of administering an unworkable system without clear regulations onto the shoulders of the service providers has resulted in high proportions of them leaving their jobs, a higher proportion than in any other profession in contemporary welfare occupations (CSO, 2001). On the other hand, those who do not leave on their own accord can be forced to do so as a result of the local wars between the poor. These conflicts speed up the ghettoization of distinct services for the Roma part of the community, which, in turn, leads to the closing down of the "superfluous" provisions, including women's jobs.

These competing struggles for recognition have not only weakened the influence of both but have consequences for the governing elite. The segmented local wars undermine the legitimacy of politics and democratic institutions, and increase distrust. These tendencies favor illegal and arbitrary actions at "making justice" outside the law, and thus threaten general security (Kis, 1997; Glatz and Kemény, 1999). Further, the recurrent attempts of ghettoization lead to the evolution of two societies within the same national borders.

It is easy to conclude that such a development might result in a foreseeable war of the deprived against the privileged, but, even if this does not occur, it is obvious that legitimacy for democratic institutions is difficult to maintain with differing rights for different parts of the citizenry. This brings us back to where this paper started: the guaranteeing of fundamental social rights in recognition struggles. The prerequisite public discourse about the content of these rights has to start, however, with a sorting out of the "social" and "minority" elements of poverty, and with the state taking responsibility for properly protecting these rights.

Part 4

Authenticity: who speaks for whom?

9   Scandalous acts: the politics of shame among Brazilian travesti prostitutes

Don Kulick and Charles H. Klein

In a small, dimly-lit hotel room, a man and a transgendered prostitute have just had sex. The price of this transaction had been agreed on before the couple entered the room, and the man, now dressed and anxious to leave, removes his wallet from his back pocket.

The travesti straightens her bra-straps and eyes the man. "No," she murmurs, as she sees him open the wallet and take out a few notes. "More. I want more."

The man is startled. "What do you mean, you want more?" he asks warily. "We agreed on thirty *reais*, and here's thirty *reais*. Take it."

The travesti slips towards the door, in a swift, resolute gesture. "Listen, love," she says calmly, blocking the man's exit. "The price went up. You wanted me to fuck you. You sucked my dick. That's more expensive. That's not thirty *reais*. It's sixty."

The man growls that the travesti can go fuck *herself* if she thinks she can rob him like that. He flings the notes in his hand at her and moves towards the door. But the travesti moves too. Practiced. Fast. She slams her purse on the floor and plants her feet firmly apart, in a stance that makes her seem thicker, stronger, more expansive. A pair of tiny nail scissors flash in her hand. Suddenly afraid, the man stops in his tracks. He stands in front of the travesti, staring at her and wondering what to do next. Suddenly, he sees her coral-red mouth open and he hears her begin to shout; to utter loud, harsh, venomous screams that fill the room, the hotel, and, horrifyingly, it seems to the man, the whole neighborhood:

Have shame you pig! You disgraceful faggot! You act like a man but you come in here and want to be fucked more than a whore! You sucked my dick and begged me to fuck you! Disgusting faggot! *Maricona* without shame! You're more of a woman than I am! Your asshole is wider than mine is! You're more of a *puta* than me!

In travesti parlance, what is occurring here is *um escândalo*, a commotion, a scandal. A scandal is an example of what ethnographers of communication call a performative genre: it is a named act that has its own structure, dynamics, and intended consequences. Like all performatives, scandals have illocutionary force; that is, they announce a specific intention on the part of the speaker – in this case, the intention is the conferral of shame. Scandals also ideally produce a set of perlocutionary effects, namely the surrender by the client of more money than he had agreed to pay in the first place.

Scandals as performatives can only operate and make sense within structures of shame. They work to the extent that they elicit shame and channel it into service that benefits travestis. What is the specific configuration of this shame? In this case, it hinges on widespread and violently upheld sanctions against male homosexual relations. For the flame being fanned here is the fact that travestis are males. They are males who habitually consume estrogen-based hormones and who often have impressively feminine figures, due to those hormones and to the numerous liters of industrial silicone that they pay their colleagues to inject into their bodies. But they are males nonetheless. They have penises. These penises are usually kept tightly pressed against a travesti's perineum and well out of anyone's view. But in their professional lives as prostitutes, travestis remove their penis from concealment and frequently put it to use. And during a scandal, a travesti's penis is rhetorically unfurled and resoundingly brandished at anyone within hearing distance of her shouts.

The point of drawing dramatic attention to that part of the travesti's anatomy that she normally keeps concealed is to publicly reconfigure the social status of her client. The overwhelming majority of men who pay travestis for sex are married or have girlfriends, and they identify themselves as heterosexual. Even if these men are publicly revealed to have been in the company of a travesti (for example, on the relatively rare occasions when they go to the police to report that a travesti robbed them, or on the relatively more frequent occasions when police arrest them for having shot a travesti), the majority will steadfastly maintain that they were unaware that the prostitute they picked up was a travesti. Travestis, however, know better. They know that the men who pay them for sex come to the specific streets on which they work looking for a travesti, not a woman. They know that the sexual service requested by many of the men (travestis say 'most of the men') is anal penetration, with the travesti assuming the role of penetrator. Finally, travestis also know that the last thing one of these men ever wants revealed in public is the fact that he has paid money to have a transgendered prostitute insert her penis in his ostensibly heterosexual ass.

So in order to blackmail her client and scare him into parting with more money than he would ever agree to, a travesti will "give a scandal" (*dar um escândalo*). Scandals constitute one of the everyday, mundane means by which individual travestis see to it that they earn enough money to support themselves. They are not collective actions. Although scandals can turn into brawls, in which other travestis within hearing distance will come to the aid of their colleague and help attack a particularly violent or recalcitrant client, for the most part they are singular actions taken by individual travestis. Indeed, travestis actually prefer not to involve other travestis in scandals, since they know that they will have to split their takings with any travesti who helps them extract money from a client.

Despite their individualistic nature, scandals can be analyzed as a kind of politics – a micropolitics certainly, and one that produces only small-scale and temporary crinkles in the overall social fabric. But these little crinkles are not altogether without interest. Or irony. For note: in excoriating their allegedly heterosexual clients for being effeminate homosexuals, *travestis are drawing on the exact same language that is habitually invoked by others to condemn travestis and to justify violence against them.* What is perhaps most striking about scandals is that they do not in any way correspond to the noble "hidden transcripts" of resistance that liberal scholars like James Scott expect to find among oppressed groups (Scott, 1990). Scandals do nothing to contest or refute the sociocultural basis of travestis' abject status in contemporary Brazilian society. Quite the opposite – instead of challenging abjection, scandals cultivate it. And with a skill that is nothing short of dazzling, travestis use scandals as a way of extending the space of their own abjection. A scandal casts that abjection outward like a sticky web, one that ensnares a petrified client, completely against his will.

But not only do scandals compel their recipient to explicitly acknowledge his relationship to a travesti (and listen as his own ontological distance from travestis is challenged and mocked); scandals also force the client to part with more of his money than he had intended. In this way, scandals can be seen as resolutely political actions that result in both recognition *and* redistribution – to use the two terms continually bandied about and debated in philosophical and political science debates about recognition struggles. Furthermore, despite their locally managed nature, scandals draw on large-scale structures for their intelligibility and their efficacy. The existence and salience of these large-scale structures suggest the possibility that scandals could be tapped and extended into larger, more organized, and more collectivized spheres.

Our contribution to this volume on recognition struggles concerns the relationship between scandals and the emerging political activism of Brazilian travestis. Since the early 1990s, Brazilian travestis have been forming activist groups and making demands for recognition and rights. These demands – which include protection from brutal police violence, the possibility of using their female names on certain official documents, and the right to appear in public space unharassed – seem modest and even self-evident in our eyes. However, we want to argue that there is something fundamentally *scandalous* about travesti demands. In emerging as a public voice and asserting entitlement to equal citizenship rights with others, we see travesti activism as building on the same kinds of principles as those which structure scandals. In both cases, travesti politics is a politics anchored in shame. It is a politics that invokes and activates specific structures of shame, not in order to contest them, but, rather, in order to extend their scope, to imbricate others. In both scandals and their more recognizably activist modalities of political action, travestis transgress public decorum and civil society not by rejecting shame (and championing something like "Travesti Pride"), but by inhabiting shame as a place from which to interpellate others and thereby incriminate those others. In doing this, we want to argue that travestis are deploying what Eve Kosofsky Sedgwick has called a "shame-conscious" and "shame-creative" vernacular; one that inflects the "social metamorphic" possibilities of shame (Sedgwick, 1993: 13, 14). This means, in turn, that travesti demands for more money from clients or for uninhibited access to public space are not what Nancy Fraser (1997a: 23) has dubbed "affirmative" demands for redress. They are not demands that build upon and enhance existing group differentiation in order to claim additional recognition. Instead, travesti demands are *transformative*, in Fraser's terms – they work to undermine group differentiation (between normal, upstanding citizens and low-life, perverse travestis) by foregrounding and challenging the generative structures that permit that differentiation to exist in the first place.

Travestis in Brazil

As already mentioned, travestis are males who refashion their appearance, their self-presentational styles, and their physical bodies in a markedly feminine direction. The word *travesti* derives from *transvestir*, or cross-dress. But travestis do not only cross-dress. Sometimes beginning at ages as young as eight or ten, males who self-identify as travestis begin growing their hair long, plucking their eyebrows, experimenting with cosmetics, and wearing, whenever they can, feminine or androgynous clothing such as tiny shorts exposing the bottom of their buttocks or T-shirts tied in a knot in above their navel. It is not unusual for boys of this age to also begin engaging in sexual relations with their peers and older males, always in the role of the one who is anally penetrated. By the time these boys are in their early teens, many of them have already either left home, or

been expelled from their homes, because their sexual and gender trans-
gressions are usually not tolerated, especially by the boys' fathers. Once
they leave home, the overwhelming majority of travestis migrate to cities
(if they do not already live in one), where they meet and form friendships with other travestis and where they begin working as prostitutes.
In the company of their travesti friends and colleagues, young travestis
learn about estrogen-based hormones, which are available for inexpen-
sive over-the-counter purchase at any of the numerous pharmacies that
line the streets in Brazilian cities. At this point, young travestis often begin ingesting large quantities of these hormones. By the time they reach
their late teens, many travestis have also begun paying their colleagues to
inject numerous liters of industrial silicone into their bodies, in order to
round out their knees, thighs, and calves, and in order to augment their
breasts, hips, and, most importantly (since this is Brazil), their buttocks.

Despite irrevocable physiological modifications such as these, the overwhelming majority of travestis do not self-identify as women. That is, despite the fact that they live their lives in female clothing, call one another
'she,' and by female names, and endure tremendous pain to acquire female bodily forms, travestis do not wish to remove their penis, and they
do not consider themselves to *be* women. They are not transsexuals. They
are, they say, homosexuals – males who feel "like women" and who ardently desire "men" (i.e., masculine, non-homosexual males). Much of
a travesti's time, thought, and effort is spent fashioning and perfecting
herself as an object of desire for those men.

Travestis occupy an unusually visible place in both Brazilian social
space and the national cultural imaginary. They exist in all Brazilian cities
of any size, and in the large southeastern cities of São Paulo and Rio de
Janeiro, they number in the thousands. They are most exuberantly visible during Brazil's famous annual Carnival, but even in more mundane
contexts and discourses, travestis figure prominently. A popular Saturday
afternoon television show, for example, includes a spot in which female
impersonators, some of whom are clearly travestis, get judged by a panel
of celebrities on how beautiful they are and on how well they mime the
lyrics to songs sung by female vocalists. Another weekly television show
regularly featured Valéria, a well-known travesti. *Tieta*, one of the most
popular television *novelas* in recent years, featured a special guest appearance by Rogéria, another famous travesti. Another widely watched
novela featured a saucy female lead whose speech was peppered with
words from travesti argot, and who sounded, everybody agreed, just like
a travesti (Browning, 1996). But most telling of all of the special place
reserved for travestis in the Brazilian popular imagination is the fact that
the individual widely acclaimed to be most beautiful woman in Brazil in

the mid-1980s was . . . a travesti. That travesti, Roberta Close, became a household name throughout the country. She regularly appeared on national television, starred in a play in Rio, posed nude (with strategically crossed legs) in an issue of *Playboy* magazine that sold out its entire press run of 200,000 copies almost immediately, was continually interviewed and portrayed in virtually every magazine in the country, and had at least three songs written about her by well-known composers. Although her popularity declined when, at the end of the 1980s, she left Brazil to have a sex-change operation and live in Europe, Roberta Close remains extremely well known. A book about her life appeared a few years ago (Rito, 1998), and in 1995 she was featured in a nationwide advertisement for Duloren lingerie, in which a photograph of her passport, bearing her male name, was transposed with a photograph of her looking sexy and chic in a black lace undergarment. The caption read "*Você não imagina do que uma Duloren é capaz*" – "You can't imagine what a Duloren can do."

As it happens, famous individuals like Roberta Close, Valéria, and Rogéria are not representative of Brazil's travestis. Instead, they are more like exceptions that prove the rule. And the rule is harsh discrimination and vituperative public prejudice. The overwhelming majority of travestis live far from the protective glow of celebrity, and they constitute one of the most marginalized and despised groups in Brazilian society. Most travestis (like most Brazilians) come from working-class or poor backgrounds, and many remain poor throughout their lives – even though many, these days, also travel to Europe and earn enough money working there as prostitutes to return to Brazil and secure their own futures, and those of their mothers. In most Brazilian cities, travestis are harassed so routinely that many of them avoid venturing out onto the street during the day. And at night while at work, they are regularly the victims of violent police brutality and random assassinations by individuals or gangs of men who take it upon themselves to "clean up the streets," just like local governments periodically order their police forces to do – despite the fact that neither cross-dressing nor prostitution is criminal under the Brazilian legal code.

So the nature of the relationship between the Brazilian populace at large and travestis is hot–cold and love–hate: hot and loving enough to propel a handful of travestis to national celebrity, and also to sustain a thriving market in which tens of thousands of travestis are able to support themselves through prostitution. But cold and hateful enough to ensure that the majority of those travestis live in continual anxiety that their right to occupy urban space will be publicly challenged and perhaps violently denied. Jovana Baby, founder and president of Brazil's first travesti activist organization *Grupo Astral* (*Associação de Travestis e Liberados de Rio de Janeiro*), provided a pithy summary of popular Brazilian sentiments towards travestis when she remarked in an interview with Kulick that "Brazilians love travestis, as long as they stay on television or on the covers of magazines. A travesti on the street or, God forbid, in the family – that is another story altogether."

Deferred signifiers

Ambivalent public sentiments towards travestis are mirrored in ambivalent public perceptions about the precise composition of travesti identity. One of the most striking dimensions of the Brazilian preoccupation with travestis is that, despite the habitual presence of travestis in both what we might see as the "high" contexts of popular culture and the "low" contexts of seeing them on city streets and in the crime pages of the local newspaper (frequently in lurid close-ups as murdered corpses), there appears to be no clear consensus about what exactly travestis are. In the press, travestis are sometimes referred to as "he," and sometimes as "she." Some commentators insist that travestis want to be women; others insist that they self-identify as men. Still others, especially those commentators influenced by postmodernist ideas, claim that travestis reject identity altogether. They are usually depicted as homosexuals, but occasionally this identity is elided, and they are identified, instead, as transsexuals. Expressed in structuralist terms, the result of these various depictions of travesti identity is that the signifier "travesti" is continually deferred and never finally coalesces with a specific signified. This means that the Brazilian public can never be certain that it knows what "travesti" means from one context to the next.

All of this is evident from the language used to discuss travestis, and we want to examine one example in detail to illustrate the kind of indeterminacy to which we are drawing attention here. On January 7, 1996, the São Paulo-state-based newspaper *A Tribuna* ran a full-page story about an individual named Márcia Muller, who was identified as a travesti in the headline, in a head-shot photo captioned "The travesti Márcia Muller," and throughout the text. The story appeared under the headline "Travesti spends 45 days detained in Women's Jail" (*Travesti passa 45 dias preso na Cadeia Feminina*). In bold print and large lettering directly under the rubric, the following text appears:

What can have caused the police of [the city of] Dise to imagine that the travesti Márcia Muller was really a woman and put her (*a prendessem*) in the Women's Jail of Santos? Did the pseudo-hermaphrodite really look like a woman or was there just a tiny resemblance? The terrible mistake committed by the police has already been cleared up, but there could be lasting disagreeable developments. The female prisoners, naturally, protested against the intimacy of having to use the same bathroom as Márcia, her being a man (*sendo era homem*). For the first time in this region, the Courts face such a problem.

The article reports that thirty-eight-year-old Márcia Muller was arrested with eighty grams of cocaine and taken to the local police station. According to the newspaper, "In the police station, during a body search conducted by a policeman, the male sexual organ of the accused was perceived (*foi percibido o orgão sexual masculino do acusado*), but because he was convicted (*porém como ele foi convicto*) claiming to be a hermaphrodite, and presenting documents plus check stubs with the name Márcia Muller on them, the end result was the Women's Jail."

"In the jail," the article continues, "there was a climate of speculation. The topic was discussed in all the jail cells. Some women believed that she was a hermaphrodite, but the majority doubted this and thought that their new colleague (*a nova colega*) was really a travesti."

One of the inmates who did not want Márcia in the jail contacted a criminal lawyer. This lawyer could do nothing, the newspaper explains, because "the girl (*a moça*; i.e., Márcia) was detained in the custody of Justice." In order to move Márcia out of the Women's Jail, a court order was needed. The lawyer brought the case to the attention of a judge, who had Márcia examined by a medical doctor.

"The doctor confirmed, after various examinations, including touching (*inclusive de tocque*)," that *Márcia era homem mesmo* – Márcia was really a man. But at this point, Márcia's lawyer intervened and argued that if his client was transferred to a male jail, her life would be in danger. In the end, Márcia was moved to the Men's Jail, but placed in a cell in the male jail that contained "two more travestis."

The final paragraph of the article contains the following coda, which, given the outcome of the doctor's examination, does more to add to the mystery of Márcia's identity than it does to resolve it:

Márcia Muller has all the features of a woman [?!], but has big feet and coarse hands. If it weren't for a low voice and a light sashay when walking (*sua voz desafinada ę um ligeiro requebro no andar*), her conduct could easily be confused with that of a woman.

So even by the end of this 1,400-word report, Márcia Muller's sexed and gendered identity remains unresolved. Despite the fact that the article makes an explicit reference to Márcia's "male sexual organ," and to the medical examination that concluded that Márcia was "really a man," she is referred to with a masculine pronoun only once throughout the entire text (in the context of having had her male sexual organ "perceived"). In all other cases where gendered grammatical pronouns, articles, and adjectives are used, Márcia is consistently referred to with female forms. At one point she is even called "the girl." In the series of questions prefacing the article, Márcia is called a "pseudo-hermaphrodite," even though it is later determined that she is, in fact, not one. And even though it would seem that the issue of Márcia's sex/gender is finally resolved with the Court order to transfer her to the Men's Jail, the closing coda of the article reopens the issue, ending on a note of provocative indeterminacy.

The public uncertainty about what travestis are and who qualifies as a travesti that newspaper articles like this promote lays the foundation for what scholars like Charles Taylor (1994) and Axel Honneth (1995a, 1995b) would identify as the "misrecognition" of travestis. In other words, by keeping the referent of "travesti" vague, articles like the one about Márcia Muller encourage people to not recognize their particular identity. And such a lack of recognition is not trivial or merely insulting – both Taylor and Honneth argue at length that it is pernicious and profoundly harmful.

When it comes to travestis, these scholars are, of course, in a sense, right. Uncertainty about Márcia Muller's identity led to her being subjected to invasive physical examinations, and had her lawyer not succeeded in getting her placed in a cell with two other travestis, she would have been in real physical danger by being transferred to a men's prison. A more politically significant example of the harmful nature of travesti misrecognition occurred not long ago in an interview with the then-mayor of Rio de Janeiro, Luis Paulo Conde, in the monthly gay magazine *Sui Generis*. In an otherwise generally affirmative and sympathetic interview about homosexuality, the mayor suddenly announces that he finds travestis "offensive" (*O que agride é o travesti*). The reason? "A travesti doesn't admit to being gay. He dresses in women's clothes to be accepted by society. When he puts on the clothes, it's to be accepted by society. Since society doesn't accept homosexuality, he creates a woman so that he will be accepted." Now, leaving aside the mayor's intriguing suggestion that Brazilians might be more tolerant of men in dresses than they are of homosexuals, here we have a case of misrecognition in which mayor Conde denies the homosexual component of travesti identity, thereby necessarily disqualifying them from any of the rights or protections that he might eventually be willing to grant homosexuals.

But while public ambivalence about travesti identity is indeed harmful in many of the ways discussed by Taylor and Honneth, it not *only* harmful; and this is a point that seems likely to be missed by the analytical frameworks elaborated by those scholars. For besides constituting damage, public uncertainty about the precise nature (and hence, the precise boundaries) of travesti identity *also* generates a space of ambiguity that travestis can use to their advantage. If travesti identity remains fuzzy, it becomes possible to suggest that the identity, or at least key dimensions of the identity, are not specific to travestis, but are, instead, shared by others who do not self-identify as travestis. Hence, ambivalence provides travestis with a wedge that they can use to insert themselves into the identificatory constellations of others, and, in doing so, compel a reconsideration and perhaps even a reconfiguration of those constellations.[1]

A forced realignment of identity is what we believe travesti scandals accomplish. Scandals publicly accuse a travesti's client of being a depraved effeminate homosexual, one who is so pathetically abject that he actually pays money to be abased at the hands of a person who herself is at the very nadir of sociocultural hierarchy.

The reason why scandals work (that is, the reason why they nine times out of ten produce the desired result of more money) is because travestis are right. Or, rather, scandals work because travestis *might be right*. The great majority of a travesti's clients would certainly hotly disagree with travesti assertions that they are depraved effeminate perverts. However, because the boundaries of travesti identity are not neatly demarcated or entirely clear-cut for most people, the possibility remains open that travesti ontology does not occupy the place of the absolute Other, in relation to the public at large. On the contrary, because the contours of travesti identity are ambiguously outlined in relation to others, there is a distinct possibility that travestis might be right when they point a finger and assert affinity with a particular individual. Especially if that individual did what the travesti says he did (and he may or may not have – who can know for sure?), public perception of the man will change, and he will be resignified by anyone who hears (or hears about) the scandal as someone who does indeed share an (until that moment) secret affiliation with his travesti accuser.

So travesti scandals raise a specter of ontological similarity between the travesti and her client. But they depend for their effectiveness on the simultaneous assertion of the shameful nature of that ontology ("Have shame you pig! You disgraceful faggot!"). Shame here becomes the channel through which identification flows, the contours within which it takes form. Eve Sedgwick (1993) has addressed this identity-delineating power of shame in her essay on the politics of performativity. Sedgwick argues that whereas guilt is an affect that focuses on the suffering of another (and the self's blame for that suffering), shame concerns the suffering of the self at the hands of another.[2]

Furthermore, while guilt is a bad feeling attached to what one does, shame is a bad feeling attaching to what one is. "[O]ne therefore is *something*, in experiencing shame," Sedgwick explains (1993: 12). But that is not all. For, conferred by another, shame always responds. It *performs*, as Sedgwick phrases it. Often, embarrassment, a blush, an aversion of eyes, a turning away – these are the responses, the performances, of shame. In the case of scandals, shame performs by compelling acquiescence to the travesti's demands for more money.

Sedgwick suggests that this performative dimension of shame has overtly political consequences. In order to better understand the importance of this suggestion, let us first contrast it with the way in which shame has figured in the work of another scholar who has recently discussed shame and politics. In his writings on recognition struggles, philosopher Axel Honneth (1995a: 256–60; 1995b: 131–39) identifies shame as the "missing psychological link" (1995b: 135) that allows us to understand how economic privation or social repression can motivate people to engage in political struggle. Shame, in other words, explains how a subject can be moved from suffering to action. Honneth argues that shame is raised when one's interactional partners refuse to grant one the respect to which one believes oneself entitled. When this occurs, the disrespected subject is brutally brought up against the normally unreflected-upon fact that it is dependent on the recognition of others for its own sense of self. The affronted realization that the other's view of the self is, in Honneth's terms, "distorted," constitutes the motivational impetus to identify specific others as the source of oppression, and, hence, as the target of political struggle. In Honneth's framework, shame is thus the psychological bedrock of political action. And the psychological goal of political struggle is the elimination of shame.

Sedgwick's view is different. Like Honneth, Sedgwick argues that shame in the self is conferred by others, and that the experience of shame is a constitutive dimension of the identities of oppressed people. Unlike Honneth, however, Sedgwick stresses that shame is a crucial component in *all* identity formation. "[O]ne of the things that anyone's character or personality is," she insists, "is a record of the highly individual histories by which the fleeting emotion of shame has instituted far more durable, structural changes in one's relational and interpretive strategies toward both self and others" (1993: 12–13). In other words, all of our socializing experiences in which our behavior and expression are controlled with sharp reprimands like "People are looking at you!" are important nexuses in the construction of our identities. This implies that forms of shame cannot be considered as "distinct 'toxic' parts of groups or individual identity

that can be excised" through consciousness raising or recognition struggles (1993: 13). Instead, shame is integral to the very processes by which
identity itself is formed. This which means that the extinction of shame
would be, in effect, the extinction of identity itself. Therefore, instead
of fantasizing about the end of shame, Sedgwick proposes that shame
be acknowledged, embraced, and put to transformative political use. In
this framework, the goal is not the end of shame. The goal is the refigura-
tion of shame as "a near inexhaustible source of transformational energy"
(1993: 4), and its creative deployment in political struggles.

This creative deployment can occur in a variety of registers, many of
them, Sedgwick speculates, as yet unimagined. But travestis certainly hit
on one of them when they began to claim shame as a place from which they
might speak and hail others, asserting power to resignify those others, and
compelling them to respond in wished-for ways. In scandals, what gets
redesignated are the public (and sometimes perhaps also the privately felt)
identities of a number of individual men. It seems that, for a long time, this
was enough for travestis. Nowadays, though, some travestis have decided
that they have bigger fish to fry. Instead of contenting themselves with
redefining the public perceptions of a few men who pay them for sex, these
travestis are turning their attention to redefining the public perceptions of
more consequential entities, such as the concept of Brazilian citizenship
and the nature of human rights. These are the targets that get focalized
in travestis' more recognizably activist modes of political activism, and it
is to these forms of political struggle that we now turn.

Travesti political activism

The emergence of travesti political struggles in Brazil can only be understood in the context of the rise of Brazilian gay and AIDS activism during
the past two decades, since these movements, although not always welcoming travestis or responding to their concerns, have heavily influenced
the content and organizational structures of travesti activism (Daniel,
1989; Daniel and Parker, 1990; James N. Green, 1999; Klein, 1999;
MacRae, 1990; 1992; Parker, 1994; 1999; Terto, 2000; Trevisan, 1986).
Brazilian gay and AIDS organizing has in turn been strongly shaped by
two larger political processes, namely, the redemocratization of Brazilian
society during the late 1970s and 1980s (Alvarez, 1990; Skidmore, 1988)
and the rapid expansion of non-governmental organizations (NGOs) during the 1980s and 1990s (Fernandes, 1994; Landim, 1988; 1993). The
following discussion traces the development of Brazilian gay and AIDS
activism and highlights the various interconnections between the two
movements. We then turn our attention to contemporary travesti political

struggles and their complex blend of AIDS, gay, and specifically travesti-related issues.

In 1964, the Brazilian military staged a coup d'état and forced João Goulart, a leftist president, to flee the country. Over the next few years, an authoritarian regime was gradually institutionalized (Skidmore, 1988; Burns, 1993). Repression was particularly strong from 1968 to 1973, and many who actively opposed the dictatorship were imprisoned or forced into political exile. In the mid-1970s, a more "moderate" wing of the military assumed power and instituted the *abertura* – or political opening – thereby beginning Brazil's lengthy redemocratization, which was only completed in 1989 with the first direct presidential elections in more than twenty-five years.

The *abertura* generated an intense surge of political and social mobilization. In the late 1970s, movements such as workers' organizations, neighborhood associations, ecclesial base communities, women's organizations, environmental groups, and Afro-Brazilian groups sprang up throughout Brazil. Building on democratic principles and grassroots mobilization, this "revolution in everyday life" (Scherer-Warren and Krischke, 1987) represented a break from traditional Brazilian politics and its history of clientelism, hierarchy, and populism (see Burns [1993] for excellent summaries of these dimensions of Brazilian political history, and Scheper-Hughes [1992] for a vivid account of their continued existence in contemporary Brazilian life). Given the continued dangers of directly confronting the legitimacy of an "opening" but still authoritarian regime, the new social movements served as an important organizing arena for social and political sectors that opposed the dictatorship.

It is within this context of widespread political and social mobilization that the Brazilian homosexual movement arose (Green, 1999; MacRae, 1990; 1992; Trevisan, 1986).[3] In 1979, Brazil's first homosexual newspaper, *Lampião*, was launched in Rio de Janeiro. That same year, *SOMOS – Grupo de Afirmicão Homosexual* (We Are – Homosexual Affirmation Group) was established in São Paulo. During the same period, homosexual liberation groups were established in several other Brazilian states and, in April 1980, representatives from these organizations met in São Paulo at the first Brazilian Congress of Organized Homosexual Groups. The movement achieved particular public notoriety several months later through a historic protest march against police violence in São Paulo that brought together nearly one thousand people, including many travestis (MacRae, 1990).

In terms of its sexual politics, the early Brazilian homosexual movement stressed the subversive dimensions of sexuality, including sexual freedom, androgyny, and what today is often referred to as "gender fucking."

Rather than decry the social marginality of homosexuals, movement leaders argued that outrageous and "shameful" dimensions of homosexuality, such as camp, gender-bending, and promiscuity, should not only be celebrated at the personal level; those phenomena also constituted a creative, anti-authoritarian force that could work against the dictatorship and transform society. Although they focused on gender and sexual politics, the homosexual liberation activists also worked with the opposition movement more generally, and with movements such as those developed by feminists, Afro-Brazilians, and indigenous peoples. In these political alliances, homosexual leaders adopted a discourse that emphasized citizenship and democracy (MacRae, 1990; Trevisan, 1986).

It did not take long, however, for the marked gender, class, racial, and political differences among group participants to threaten the cohesion of the still-young gay liberation movement. For example, internal tensions within the São-Paulo-based SOMOS (We Are) group, which had become the most influential Brazilian homosexual liberation organization, reached crisis proportions in May 1980, when nearly all of its female members left en masse to form the Lesbian-Feminist Action Group. The remaining men then largely divided into anarchist and Trotskyite factions. Similar schisms occurred at the *Lampião* newspaper. By the end of 1981, with SOMOS in tatters and *Lampião* having closed its doors, the first wave of Brazilian homosexual mobilization had more or less ended. As Edward MacRae (1990; 1992) argues, this decline resulted from a combination of the internal conflicts noted above and a more general shift in political energy from social movements to party-oriented electoral politics in the multiple-party, democratic electoral system that was implemented in the early 1980s. These conflicts and the changing political landscape were compounded by significant transformations in the organization of Brazilian homosexuality during this period, including the rapid growth of gay identity politics and gay consumer culture, neither of which was easily reconcilable with the movement's anarchism and anti-consumerism (Green, 1999; MacRae, 1990; 1992; Parker, 1999).

The beginning of the AIDS epidemic in Brazil in the early to mid-1980s raised new challenges for an already fragile and fragmented movement. Was AIDS a gay issue? If gay groups worked on AIDS, would they be reinforcing the public perception that AIDS was (only) a gay disease, thereby potentially reinforcing the shame and stigma associated with AIDS and increasing discrimination against gay Brazilians?[4] Given governmental apathy in response to an increasingly out-of-control epidemic, would taking on AIDS issues overwhelm gay groups and prevent them from working on specifically gay issues (e.g., fighting anti-gay discrimination and violence, supporting gay rights legislation, building a gay community)?

Facing these dilemmas, Brazilian gay groups in the 1980s made different choices – some, such as the *Grupo Gay da Bahia* (Gay Group of Bahia) in Salvador and the *Grupo Atobá de Emancipação Homosexual* (Atobá Group for Homosexual Emancipation) in Rio de Janeiro, were among the first groups, gay or otherwise, to develop AIDS prevention and education activities in Brazil (see Daniel and Parker, 1993; Galvão, 1997; Parker, 1994; Terto et al., 1995). Others, such as *Triângulo Rosa* (Pink Triangle) in Rio de Janeiro, initially declined to work extensively on AIDS-related issues (Câmara da Silva, 1993).

With the founding of Brazil's first AIDS service organization – the Support Group for AIDS Prevention/GAPA – in 1985 in São Paulo, a new type of organization entered the Brazilian political stage and greatly influenced the shape of AIDS and gay activism in Brazil. Like many political groups formed in Brazil in the 1980s and 1990s, GAPA-São Paulo structured itself as an NGO. It sought and received considerable financial support from North American and European philanthropic organizations to work on AIDS-related issues (on the dramatic growth of NGOs and the "third sector" in Brazil during the past two decades, see Fernandes, 1994; Landim, 1988; 1993). With these resources, GAPA-São Paulo implemented a comprehensive array of AIDS-related programs and activities, including providing social services for people with AIDS, conducting AIDS education and prevention campaigns, countering media misinformation, criticizing governmental apathy, and attempting to mobilize civil society in response to the epidemic. This model of responding to the AIDS epidemic through semi-professionalized, internationally funded AIDS-specific NGOs (AIDS-NGOs) became the dominant paradigm for AIDS activism in Brazil (Galvão, 1997; Klein, 1994; 1996). Beginning in 1989, a national AIDS political movement began to articulate itself through a series of semi-annual and then annual National Meetings of AIDS-NGOs. By 1992, there were nearly one hundred AIDS-NGOs in Brazil (Galvão, 1997). Today, there are more than 400.

Not surprisingly, given the significant impact of the Brazilian AIDS epidemic on men who have sex with men, throughout the 1980s and well into the 1990s many of the leaders and active participants at these AIDS-NGOs were gay-identified men, including some who had participated in the first wave of the Brazilian homosexual movement. Yet despite the involvement of many gay-identified men, these organizations did not consider themselves to be gay groups, and until the mid-1990s most AIDS-NGOs primarily directed their prevention activities towards the "general population." This is not to say that gay-related issues were of no interest to AIDS-NGOs, as can be seen in the work of Herbert Daniel, a noted writer and leftist and gay political activist.[5] In 1987, Daniel began working at Brazil's second oldest AIDS-NGO, the Brazilian Interdisciplinary AIDS Association (ABIA) in Rio de Janeiro. At ABIA, Daniel played a leading role in developing some of the first sexually explicit and culturally sensitive AIDS prevention materials directed towards men who have sex with men. In early 1989, Daniel discovered that he was HIV+ (Daniel, 1989). Recognizing the need for an organization focused primarily on the political dimensions of living with HIV/AIDS, Daniel formed *Grupo Pela VIDDA* (Group for the Affirmation, Integration, and Dignity for People with AIDS) in Rio de Janeiro later that year.[6]

Grupo Pela VIDDA represented an epistemological and practical break in Brazilian AIDS activism and served as a critical reference for AIDS-related programs and politics throughout the 1990s.[7] Unlike its counterpart AIDS-NGOs in the late 1980s and early 1990s, *Pela VIDDA* did not provide direct services to people with HIV/AIDS or focus on developing educational materials and activities. Instead, under the leadership of Daniel, *Pela VIDDA* articulated a political project that emphasized citizenship and solidarity in the face of the "civil death" (*morte civil*) experienced by people living with HIV/AIDS in Brazil. By civil death, Daniel referred to the then prevalent practice in Brazil – and indeed throughout the world – of treating people with HIV/AIDS as already dead even though they were still alive. This civil death was often internalized by people with HIV/AIDS. Facing the various shames associated with AIDS (i.e., its rhetorical links to promiscuity, contagion, and homosexuality), many individuals became either socially invisible or the passive subjects of sensationalistic media coverage (see Daniel, 1989; Daniel and Parker, 1990; Galvão, 1992; Klein, 1996; Terto, 2000).

A significant dimension of Daniel's political project was to openly assume the "shame" of AIDS, and to use it to formulate political goals. From the position of a person living with the stigma of HIV, Daniel asserted that *everyone* in Brazil was living with AIDS. This argument is not a new one – it had been powerfully formulated by gay groups in the USA and the UK as soon as the magnitude of the epidemic – and also the magnitude of government inaction – became evident. What is important about the argument, however, is that it reterritorializes shame, relocating it not so much in individual bodies, as in the political structure of society. It also importantly refigures people associated with AIDS as active articulators, rather than passive recipients, of shame. In other words, arguments like those deployed by Daniel and *Pela VIDDA* fashioned shame as a powerful position from which individuals could speak and demand hearing.

Despite the vitality and political possibilities of Daniel and *Pela VIDDA*'s vision of "living with HIV/AIDS" and its explicit incorporation of both (homo)sexuality and AIDS within a broader political discourse, throughout the 1980s and into the early 1990s the relationship between AIDS-NGOs and gay groups – and gay and AIDS activists – remained complex and often antagonistic (Câmara da Silva, 1993; Vallinoto, 1991). Part of this antagonism resulted from different approaches to sexual politics, since during this period most of the more visible Brazilian gay groups, such as the Gay Group of Bahia, adopted a vision of sexual politics that focused on promoting gay identities and eliminating – rather than reterritorializing – the shame associated with homosexuality. But equally important were questions of money, expertise, and representivity, particularly as AIDS-related organizations came to outnumber and, in many respects, eclipse gay groups in the late 1980s and early 1990s. This ascendancy of AIDS-NGOs resulted in competition and at times antagonism between AIDS and gay groups. On the one hand, AIDS organizations, positioning themselves as the "AIDS experts," questioned the quality of gay-group-based AIDS prevention activities. On the other hand, prominent gay leaders criticized AIDS organizations for not developing more activities directed specifically towards male homosexuals. They further resented that AIDS groups were receiving considerable funding from agencies of international cooperation which was largely unavailable to groups who focused exclusively on gay issues.

These tensions between AIDS and gay organizations diminished throughout the 1990s. One critical factor in this rapprochement was Brazil receiving a loan of more than $150 million from the World Bank in 1992 to develop and implement a comprehensive National AIDS Program (Galvão, 1997).[8] As part of this so-called "World Bank Project," over the period 1993 to 1998 more than $9 million dollars was distributed to nearly 200 community-based organizations who worked on AIDS-related issues – not only AIDS-NGOs, but also gay, travesti, sex worker, and women's organizations who had previously been largely outside AIDS-related funding circles.[9] This expansion in the types of organizations receiving federal AIDS funding was complemented by the creation of projects and subcommittees within the National AIDS Program that focused on specific "higher risk" populations, such as men who have sex with men and sex professionals (both categories explicitly referencing travestis) as well as injecting drug users and incarcerated populations. The availability of these funds and the opportunities for constructive dialogue offered through the National AIDS Program helped to decrease competition between AIDS-NGOs and gay groups and stimulated a significant growth in the 1990s of AIDS-NGO and gay-group-based HIV prevention activities directed towards men who have sex with men. These programs in turn have played important roles in the emergence of more visible gay communities in Brazil.[10] Cooperation between AIDS and gay groups has been further reinforced with the re-establishment of the *Commissão Nacional de AIDS* (CNAIDS/National AIDS Commission), which includes various gay and AIDS activists.[11]

These shifts in the content of AIDS prevention programs and the patterns of AIDS industry funding must be situated alongside the changes in the landscape of same-sex sexuality that have been occurring in Brazil over the course of the AIDS epidemic (Klein, 1999; Parker, 1996; 1999; Parker and Terto, 1998; Terto, 2000). For despite much hyperbole predicting the demise of homosexuals and their supposedly "contaminated" ghettos in the early years of the epidemic, Brazilian gay-oriented commercial establishments expanded in both number and type during the 1980s and especially the 1990s, and male homosexuality – including travestis – became everyday topics within the mainstream media. This increase in gay visibility has been complemented by gay-oriented national magazines (e.g. *Sui Generis, G*), which have been critical nodes in the emergence of a vital and media-oriented national gay culture (Parker, 1999). At the same time, gay political activism grew dramatically in Brazil during the mid- to late 1990s. From a handful of groups at the end of the 1980s and sixty groups in 1995, there are now nearly a hundred gay groups in the *Associação Brasileira de Gays, Lésbicas and Travestis* (ABGLT, Brazilian Association of Gays, Lesbians, and Travestis). In addition, gay rights issues are being seriously considered in the national political arena. For example, a domestic partnership proposal was introduced in the National Legislature in 1998, where it initially faced little organized opposition. More recently, opposition to the measure from conservative and religious sectors (e.g., Protestant fundamentalist groups and certain sectors of the Catholic Church) has intensified, and gay rights activists have been working with legislators to mobilize political and popular support around these and other gay rights issues.

How do travestis fit within these emerging gay communities and the resurgence of the Brazilian gay movement? As discussed above, travestis occupy a complicated and shifting position within Brazilian (homo)sexual worlds. If travestis are sometimes admired and desired for their beauty and sensuality, many Brazilians – including a significant number of gays and gay leaders – consider travestis to be a shameful group whose ostentatious presence and frequently scandalous behavior discredit gay Brazilians and the gay political movement. This marginalization of travestis within gay worlds is further demonstrated by the relatively low levels of travesti involvement in non-travesti-specific gay activism. For example, despite the existence of a travesti-led "department of travestis" at the Brazilian Association of Gays, Lesbians, and Travestis (ABGLT), the overall presence and influence of travestis within the ABGLT is quite limited. This lack of presence of travestis within the organized Brazilian gay movement also occurs at regional levels – at the 1994 Southern Regional Meeting of Lesbian and Gay Groups in Porto Alegre, only one of the more than thirty participants who attended was a travesti. Nor are travestis generally active participants in the growing Brazilian "pink market" (Klein, 1999; Parker, 1999), since its costs, middle-class cultural values (e.g., respectability), and emphasis on masculine gay male aesthetics present an inaccessible and often hostile environment for most travestis.

Facing these barriers to participation in Brazil's emerging gay culture and gay political movement, over the past decade and a half, travestis have grounded their political organizing around AIDS-related issues. Jovana Baby of *Grupo Astral* observed pithily in an interview with Kulick that travesti activism has "ridden on the back of the AIDS." In other words, to the extent that travestis have established formal organizations, programs, and venues, it has been entirely through AIDS-related funding, usually from the Ministry of Health. This kind of funding has placed specific limits on how travesti activism is articulated and how it is perceived. However, travestis like Jovana Baby have made sure that those limits have been enabling limits.

Scandalous citizenship

As sex workers, travestis were particularly hard hit by the AIDS epidemic. It is difficult to estimate the number of travestis who have died of HIV-related illness since statistics on AIDS in Brazil do not report on travestis – travestis are subsumed under the category "men" and "homosexual transmission." Travestis are agreed, however, that they have lost innumerable friends and colleagues to AIDS, and they are emphatic that the transmission of HIV continues to constitute a profound threat.[12]

Travesti involvement in the Brazilian response to AIDS dates to the mid-1980s, when the travesti Brenda Lee founded a support house/hospice for travestis living with HIV and AIDS in São Paulo. In most cases, travesti-focused AIDS-related projects and the travesti organizations they support have been established by charismatic leaders like Brenda Lee and Jovana Baby, although several important travesti groups are ongoing programs within AIDS-NGOs and gay organizations (e.g. GAPA/Belo Horizonte, GAPA/Rio Grande do Sul, Gay Group of Bahia). With the expansion of the National AIDS Program in the early 1990s, and its commitment to the distribution of condoms and safer-sex education within "special populations" such as men who have sex with men and sex professionals,[13] the number of travesti-led and travesti-related programs in Brazil has grown from a handful in the early 1990s to approximately twenty today.

Since 1993, the Ministry of Health, at times in collaboration with international philanthropic agencies that fund AIDS-related programs, has underwritten an annual national conference called the "National Meeting of Travestis and Open-Minded People who Work with AIDS" (*Encontro Nacional de Travestis e Liberados que Trabalham com AIDS*). These meetings usually gather together about 200 participants, and they have developed into crucial arenas where politically conscious travestis meet one another and discuss strategies and demands. However, even though travestis are thematically foregrounded at these conferences, they are numerically far outnumbered (by three to one) by the "open-minded people" who work with AIDS.[14] Many of these "open-minded people" have little contact with travestis in their day-to-day work and seem to attend the conference because it is one of the more colorful of the AIDS-circuit conferences that occur throughout Brazil every year.

The focus on AIDS, in addition to resulting in travestis being outnumbered at these conferences, has also had a constraining effect on which topics can be discussed. A recurring complaint from travestis is that too much time is spent discussing condom use and safer-sex programs, and too little time is devoted to other issues that are of great importance to travestis, such as police violence or the construction and maintenance of travesti in-group solidarity. Nonetheless, despite having AIDS as their principal focus, travestis have been able to expand the agendas of these national conferences to include issues such as social exclusion, gender and sexual identity, violence, sex work, and citizenship.[15]

One of the effects of conferences like the "National Meeting of Travestis and Open-Minded People who Work with AIDS" is that they cement an association in the public mind between travestis and AIDS which dates to the beginnings of the Brazilian AIDS epidemic. One of the first published reports about AIDS in Brazil, for example, reported the research of a Brazilian clinician who claimed that the recently discovered epidemic could be traced to the injection of female hormones and "infected" silicone by travestis (Daniel, 1993: 33). As a result of this history, an already well-established connection between travestis and AIDS is reinforced every time a travesti group receives government funding, since these resources are inevitably tied to HIV prevention work. In political activist contexts, this continually foregrounded link between travestis and AIDS is restricting in some ways, as the travestis who want to talk about issues like police violence at the annual conference regularly point out. However, the fact that travesti claims are channeled and heard through an

AIDS discourse gives travesti political actions a particular character and potential in which shame emerges as a key position from which travestis speak and demand hearing.

Much like Daniel and *Pela VIDDA*'s politics of "living with AIDS" discussed above, travesti political strategies have been centered upon highlighting and reterritorializing shame. Whenever travestis organize a protest march, which they do at the conclusion of every "National Meeting of Travestis and Open-Minded People who Work with AIDS," and which local groups occasionally do in their home cities to protest police brutality,[16] many of the protestors take care to wear their most outrageous attire – revealing lingerie-style clothing that they would normally only display while working the street late at night. In other words, in these contexts travestis play up, rather than down, their difference from others, and they fill public space with their most scandalous avatars. Just like a scandal turns space inside out by making the most intimate interactions public, travestis walking down a city's main street in broad daylight in tight bodices and miniscule shorts resignify that space and saturate it with an intimacy that refuses to be contained by normative notions of privacy. This kind of public manifestation of normally concealed persons and intimacies is a striking example of what sociologist Steven Seidman (1997) calls queer politics. "Queer politics is scandalous politics," Seidman argues, writing generally, but in language that is highly felicitous to the point we are making here: "Queers materialize as the dreaded homosexual other imagined by straight society that had invisibly and silently shaped straight life but now do so openly, loudly, and unapologetically."[17]

In travesti protest marches, this loud unapologetic body of the homosexual other is significantly juxtaposed with a particular kind of linguistic form. What is interestingly absent from travesti street demonstrations is language and placards asserting things like "Travesti Pride" or "Proud To Be A Travesti." On the contrary, on the surface of things, the language of travesti public protests is not particularly outrageous: "Travestis Are Human Beings," a placard might propose, modestly. "Travestis Are Citizens," a chant might proclaim. Nothing seriously scandalous here, one might think. However, the scandal in this case lies precisely in the very straightforwardness and simplicity of the message. For if travestis are human beings, they deserve to be accorded respect and human rights, like other human beings. And if they are citizens, then the very concept of citizenship has been revised. Linguistically, what gets foregrounded in these activist manifestations is sameness with non-travestis. Non-linguistically, however, stark difference from non-travestis is conveyed through dress, demeanor, and the sheer fact that so many travestis gather together in one place at one time. So what is happening here is that at their most different, their most shameless, travestis assert that they are most *like* everyone else.[18]

Once again, this brings us back to scandals. In the same way they do when they challenge the ontological difference between their clients and themselves by shouting that the client is just as abject as they are, travesti political activism refuses what Nancy Fraser calls "affirmative" demands for redress. That is, travesti activism refuses to build upon and enhance group differentiation in order to claim additional recognition without disturbing the underlying framework that generates them. Instead, travesti demands work to destabilize group differentiation (between normal, upstanding citizens and low-life, perverse travestis) by declaring sameness from a position of difference, thereby challenging the generative structures that produce particular configurations of hierarchically ranked differentiation in the first place. In Slavoj Žižek's (1999) terminology, this is a "political act proper."[19]

Conclusion

The question that remains to be asked is whether the scandalous acts of travesti activists constitute a politically effective strategy. Are travesti assertions of shared ontology politically transformative? Do they produce desirable results? Do they work?

That, alas, is difficult to say. Travesti political activism is still nascent in Brazil, and it is still far too bound up with the initiatives and actions of charismatic individuals like Jovana Baby to constitute anything even approaching a coherent political movement. The overwhelming majority of travestis have little political consciousness, and they are much more concerned with being beautiful, earning money, and traveling to Italy to become what they call *européias* (that is, rich and sophisticated "European" travestis) than they are in participating in activist protest marches or travesti political organizations. Furthermore, despite the enormous visibility accorded them in the Brazilian press[20] (which is sometimes positive, even though it remains heavily slanted towards images of travestis as vaguely comic, but hard-nosed and dangerous criminals), travestis continue to face grave discrimination from politicians like the mayor of Rio de Janeiro, who, it will be recalled, is of the opinion that travestis are confused cowards who dress in women's clothes only to be accepted by society. Travestis are also openly disparaged and discriminated against by Christian churches of all denominations, and by large segments of the Brazilian population who find them scary and shameless.

Equally problematic for travesti political organizing is the grave discrimination travestis experience from one of their seemingly most likely political allies, gay men and lesbians. Not only are travestis at the margins of Brazil's emerging gay culture, pink economy, and gay political movement, but, as we have mentioned previously, many Brazilian gay men and lesbians are hostile towards travestis because they think travestis give homosexuals a bad name. In their formal political statements, however, travestis disregard this, and they typically position themselves alongside – if not within – gay rights discourses. For example, the 1995 Constitution of the National Network of Travestis, Transsexuals and Open-Minded People defines itself as a "non-profit, civil organization fighting for the full citizenship of female and male homosexuals in Brazil, giving priority to travestis and transsexuals, encompassing as well sympathizers and friends who we call open-minded people."

This 1995 Constitution also identifies at least one political strategy through which to work towards this objective, namely, the promotion of:

actions [undertaken] together with groups that suffer discrimination and social prejudice, with the intention of guaranteeing Travestis, Gays and Transsexuals the right to exercise their full citizenship, always respecting the autonomy of their organizations.

Given the often antagonistic nature of travesti/gay interactions described above, it remains to be seen whether the realities of travesti difference and the goal of political sameness (i.e., full citizenship) can be reconciled. If travestis face major challenges in working with gay groups with whom they share certain affinities and previous collaborations, what is the likelihood that they will be able to reach out and form new partnerships with other socially oppressed groups, many of whom hold travestis in even more disdain? And even if these political alliances could be formed in ways which respect the autonomy of travestis and travesti activist organizations, might they not require travestis to renounce – or at a minimum downplay – the very qualities (i.e. gender/sexual ambivalence, scandalous acts) that are central to travesti social identities and scandals?

Despite all these challenges, there is some indication that travesti political activism might be making some headway, at least in some contexts and in some circles. For example, at a July 2000 meeting in Brasília (the country's capital) between travesti representatives and officials from the Ministry of Health, it was decided that all future material pertaining to travestis published by the Ministry would be examined by a travesti before it went to press.[21] It was also decided that in future the Ministry would break with Portuguese grammatical convention and employ feminine grammatical articles, pronouns, and adjectives when referring to travestis – so instead of writing *o travesti* (singular) or *os travestis* (plural), using the grammatically prescribed masculine articles, future texts will write *a travesti* and *as travestis*, using the feminine forms. These may seem like purely symbolic concessions, but the travestis present at the meeting regarded them as significant victories.

And then there is Lair Guerra de Macedo Rodrigues, former Director of Brazil's National Program on Sexually Transmissible Diseases and AIDS. Guerra de Macedo Rodrigues is one influential individual who seems to have understood and appreciated the message that travesti political actions strive to convey. In a speech delivered in 1996, the Director referred to travestis as model citizens. "Our society is one that can no longer live with fears and taboos that certainly only impede our objectives," she asserted,

[We must] involve ourselves in this ceaseless battle against discrimination and violence. Even if it means that we must fight against the intolerance of more conservative juridical and religious postures. *The organization of travesti groups, especially following the advent of AIDS, is evidence of the beginning of the arduous task of defending citizenship.* (quoted in Larvie, 1999: 539, emphasis added)

Just as Brazil is one of the few countries in the world where a travesti could be declared the country's most beautiful woman, so it is perhaps the only one where travestis could be held forth as beacons of civil responsibility that other citizens ought to follow. In the eyes of those who do not like travestis and wish they would just shut up and disappear, this, perhaps, is the biggest scandal of all.

10 Mobilizing for recognition and redistribution on behalf of others? The case of mothers against drugs in Spain

Celia Valiente

Disadvantaged groups in the very process of mobilization against their marginalization and devaluation can achieve respect and self-esteem. According to Axel Honneth (1992), this is the essence of the politics of recognition, in which individuals realize that their injury and degradation are shared by others. Paralleling this assumption is its corollary, that being able to speak on one's own behalf as a member of a mis-recognized group in political arenas is crucial for overcoming marginalization and exclusion of the group (Phillips in this volume; Young, 1990). In this essay, I am presenting a case in which groups speak on behalf of others: motherist movements on behalf of their drug addict children. This is a very complex example since mothers are seeking to remove the stigma and disrespect from their children as well as seeking to gain validation of themselves as those best able to represent their children. One can see the struggle of mothers against drugs as a response to the blame and shame that they experience as mothers of "failed children."

Perhaps, the greatest problems about a case in which groups speak for others are the issues of authenticity and efficacy (who are best able to speak for the group and get the best results). For example, many of the claims against the medical profession in the AIDS movement were made by their relatives and friends. I would argue that, in the case of mothers against drugs in Spain, we have a case in which people who suffer maldistribution and disrespect are not in a position to speak for themselves. Those who mobilize on their behalf, mothers, have access to discursive resources to plead their case in the political arena, to remove the stigma against drug addicts, and to obtain state resources for their rehabilitation. Taking Fraser's status model of recognition justice (Fraser, 1995), one could make a case that in order to become a full member of society, these groups need to be represented by others.

The case of mothers against drugs poses interesting questions not only regarding the issues around authenticity, who represents whom and on what basis, but it also provides a case in which recognition struggles are

239

mutlilayered. These groups are mothers struggling for the dignity of their children, as well as for the validation of themselves: both as caretakers of social needs in society and as mothers who have suffered and have gained knowledge from their contact with drug addicts.

Within the framework of this book, mothers against drugs represent a paradigm case of the interconnectedness of claims against misrecognition and claims for redistribution of resources. Without support and resources, these drug addicts are forced to go out on the street and rob others and thus become stigmatized and marginalized. Yet unless the extreme prejudice and disrespect against them is challenged, there is no possibility of gaining resources for rehabilitation and for their re-entering society.

In this chapter, I examine a movement of mothers against drugs in Spain which began in the 1980s. This chapter is mainly based on semi-structured personal interviews with members from various mothers-against-drugs groups and with two social workers in the city of Madrid and in a working-class suburb near Madrid, Fuenlabrada. In their neighborhoods, the mass media, and society in general, members of the groups and/or the groups under study here are usually called "mothers against drugs" (*madres contra la droga*), which is the term I use. However, the formal names of the particular groups often do not use the word "mother(s)."

The chapter is separated into five parts. First, I discuss research on motherist and maternalist movements. Second, I examine the basis of mobilization of mothers' associations against drugs. I look at them within the context of the politicization of motherhood and reveal that motherhood is not synonymous with parenthood; and motherhood is not merely a biological condition. Moreover, in this case of mothers against drugs, mother identity is linked to issues of economic inequality – these mothers cannot support their children because they are working-class mothers. Third, I focus on the construction of motherhood as frame of claims-making on behalf of others (drug addicts), paying particular attention to mothers' agency in affecting claims made upon the state and society. Fourth, following this discussion, I turn to mothers' claims for recognition and respect for themselves as mothers. In the last section, I take up the sensitive question of their speaking for others, and the infantilization of their sons and daughters that may be implicit in the process.

Motherist movements

Mothers' movements often take part in collective action not on behalf of themselves but on behalf of others, usually their relatives. Social science researchers have recently turned their attention to motherist groups in Latin America (Alvarez, 1990; Jaquette, 1994; Jaquette and Wolchik, 1998; Molyneaux, 1985; Schirmer, 1993). There, groups of mothers and female relatives of victims of human rights violations have existed since the 1970s. The best-known group of this type is the *Mothers of the Plaza de Mayo* in Argentina, although similar groups have also been established in other countries. Another strand of motherist movements in Latin America comprises women who have mobilized in poor neighborhoods and shantytowns in order to improve the conditions in which they and their families and communities live. Motherist movements have also developed in contemporary societies in other places (Miles, 1996) as far apart as North America and South Africa (Christiansen-Ruffman, 1995; Temma Kaplan, 1997; Pardo, 1995). Historians have also researched movements of women who have used their position as mothers to advance demands in historical periods in different geographical locations including Spain (Temma Kaplan, 1982; 1999). In other Western countries in the formative period of their welfare states, historians have also studied groups of women who have demanded the formulation of social policies for mothers and children using the maternalist argument that women take care of children and have special needs in order to fulfill their duties as mothers (Linda Gordon, 1994; Koven and Michel, 1990; 1993; Muncy, 1991; Pedersen, 1993; Skocpol, 1992; Skocpol et al., 1993).

Motherist movements can be analyzed within the conceptual landscape of "practical gender interests" and "strategic gender interests" developed in the 1980s. While analyzing women's mobilization in Sandinista, Nicaragua, Maxine Molyneaux (1985) argued that since women are usually in charge of looking after the home and feeding and caring for their families, some women mobilize if social, economic, and political conditions do not allow them to perform their maternal responsibilities according to the standards existing in a given society. Therefore, women may demand, for instance, that prices of foodstuffs be affordable, that health services be provided to the community, or that schooling be available for children. According to Molyneaux, all these needs constitute "practical gender interests" and are defined as such by the women who mobilize. In contrast, other women mobilize for "strategic gender interests." These are demands directed towards the improvement of women as a whole and the weakening of women's subordination. Similarly, Temma Kaplan (1982), while studying episodes of women's mobilization in Barcelona, Spain, in the 1920s, coined the term "feminine consciousness" to describe the set of ideas, beliefs, and perceptions that propel women to engage in social movements demanding the satisfaction of the needs that Molyneaux called "practical gender interests."

Scholars' assessments of motherist groups are mixed. On the one side, these groups are viewed as providing an opportunity for many women to demand things that are important to them, instead of letting men mobilize on their behalf. Women who are active in motherist groups usually (but not always) find the experience rewarding and empowering. Mobilization often helps mothers to develop an awareness of their capacities and creates a bond of solidarity among group members. Some members of mothers' associations go on to participate in other civil society groups. Women in motherist movements may also take part in joint action with other groups mobilized around other issues. Some women active in motherist circles pursuing "practical gender interests" may develop a "feminist consciousness," which leads them to question the unequal position of women in society, and mobilize seeking "strategic gender interests." Moreover, it has been argued that concerns around motherhood may potentially attract the interest and attention of many women, and are therefore the true basis for an encompassing feminism (Miles, 1996).

On the other side, there are negative assessments of motherist groups. According to their critics, mothers' mobilization movements are limited from a feminist perspective since members of this type of movement do not usually question the unequal gender order and sometimes they take stands against gender equality measures.[1] In some cases, the activities of these women look similar to "Not in My Backyard" campaigns. Such motherist groups often do not demand broad solutions to general problems, such as an unfair criminal system or environmental pollution, which could be viewed as concerns of "mothers" as protectors of family. Rather, they tend to take part in collective action when problems affect their families directly, for instance when a prison, a parole office, or a toxic waste incinerator is established in their neighborhoods. To some extent, this is the case with mothers' movements to support drug addicts, but there is a range of motives and different goals for different groups.

Motherist movements often highlight the interplay between recognition and redistribution. However, it is important to note that not all motherist movements are struggles for recognition. For instance, the mobilization of the *Mothers of the Plaza de Mayo* in Argentina and their demands for the return of their disappeared children and relatives and for the prosecution of perpetrators of human rights can be seen as movements for human rights in which mother identities provide protection against authoritarian regimes. They could also be analyzed as movements in which motherhood gives legitimacy to their claims, as they are assumed to experience the loss and suffering of their children. Much of the literature on motherist organizations tends to portray them as groups of women making claims for redistribution, involving economic justice.[2] Some examples include the ability to keep their homes, feed their children and care for their relatives (Temma Kaplan, 1982; 1997; 1999). But in the case of motherist movements in Spain, recognition and redistribution are interlocking dimensions: their claims for redistribution, resources from the state, and respect for their children are linked to the claims for recognition and respect for themselves as mothers of drug addicts. Here, authority (who speaks for whom) is bound up with authenticity (who has suffered injury and devaluation).

Bases of mobilization: mothers, motherhood, and social class

Groups of mothers against drugs began to mobilize in the 1980s. Members of these groups are mainly, although not exclusively, mothers of drug addicts. In general, these members come from one of the sectors of the population least likely to form voluntary associations in Spain: women with low levels of income and education. In Spain, people tend to join voluntary associations to a much lower extent than in other Western countries (Subirats, 1999). Women become members of associations in civil society even less frequently than men. The likelihood of belonging to voluntary associations increases as people's income and level of education rise, and decreases as age increases. For all of these reasons, the emergence of groups of mothers against drugs is far from inevitable or likely, but is thus significant. Moreover, unlike in the USA, in Spain drug addicts themselves (or former addicts) have rarely formed associations or mobilized in search of recognition and redistribution. Therefore, mothers' groups are also significant as they are still some of the only spokespeople for drug addicts.

Motherhood as a social condition

Motherhood is the principal basis of mobilization of members of groups of mothers against drugs. Mothers of drug addicts who participate in mothers' groups usually view motherhood as a moral condition that enables them to claim recognition and redistribution on behalf of their children and all drug addicts. They believe that they are legitimized to make claims, since they have already suffered.

It is important to understand that, comparatively speaking, being a mother is more permanent a status in Spain than in many other Western countries. Young adults in Spain (whether drug addicts or otherwise) tend to live in their parents' home much more and longer than in other Western countries. One study in 1998 found that more than nine out of ten

(92 percent) of people aged fifteen to twenty-four lived with their parents (or with one of them) (Elzo et al., 1999: 486). Another survey, carried out in 1995, showed that even among those aged twenty-five to twenty-nine, 52 percent were still living with their parents (Martín, 1996: 5).

As Spaniards start living on their own later, teenagers or young adults who become drug addicts are usually still living in their parents' home, where they are likely to remain over the next few years. Only in the case of one mother interviewed for this paper had her daughter started consuming drugs while living independently from her family (interview #2).

Though most mothers in these groups were organizing to protect their children, some of the mothers continued to be active in the associations even after their children had been rehabilitated or died. Seven children of the sixteen (biological) mothers interviewed for this paper had already died. The fact that some of the mothers that I interviewed no longer have drug addict children but remain active (and even very active) in groups of mothers can be explained by the fact that they want to help solve the problem of drug abuse in general. In this sense, the bond that links mothers to their biological children is extended to cover all other children dependent on drugs.

A minority of the members of mothers' groups are women whose children are not dependent on drugs. This reflects the broader basis of mobilization of motherist movements, which is reminiscent of the social motherhood movements in the early twentieth century (Koven and Michel, 1990; 1993). Two leaders of the group Mothers United (Sara Nieto and Carmen Díaz) were not mothers of drug addicts. These women called themselves and are called by others in the neighborhood "the mothers" (meaning the social mothers of drug addicts). These women argue that drug addiction is not a personal problem but a social problem, which can affect the children of any mother. Therefore, any woman can collaborate in the fight against drug addiction and can be called a mother against drugs. Moreover, members of the group "Mothers United Against Drugs" (*Madres Unidas Contra la Droga*, hereafter "Mothers United") argue that at least in theory this definition of motherhood can be extended to men. Members of this group declared (with irony) that the group is open to men, and that men are welcome by the group "to be mothers" (Sara Nieto, personal communication with the author, June 14, 1999).

Motherhood colors part of what most groups of mothers offer directly to others. When the first motherist groups were formed in the early 1980s, mothers themselves provided services to other mothers and to drug addicts (not only to their children). These services can be characterized as "maternal" in the sense that these were an extension of what mothers do in Spanish society: speak to their children, feed, accompany, and protect them, and interact with other mothers. Later they expanded their claims to include claims upon the state for services.

Mothers and not fathers

It should be noted that motherhood in this context is not synonymous with parenthood. There are very few fathers or men in these mothers' groups. The absence of fathers in associations of parents or relatives of drug addicts is not due to the absence of fathers in drug addicts' homes. In comparison with most Western countries, levels of divorce in Spain are relatively low. The Spanish divorce rate (0.8 per 1,000 population) is the second lowest in the European Union after Italy (0.5), and is less than half the European Union average (1.8) (European Commission, 1998: 63).[3] Therefore, fathers of drug addicts usually live in the same home as the children concerned.

In the interviews, mothers explained that fathers see their children's drug addiction as a problem that their mothers should deal with (interview #3). In general, given the gendered division of labor within most Spanish families, mothers are the family members who are largely responsible for their children's education and upbringing (although fathers may collaborate in these tasks). Despite the fact that more mothers are entering paid work, fathers are still seen as the breadwinners, the family member who is mainly responsible for the economic maintenance of the household.

As research has documented (Finkel, 1997), the gender division of labor is especially marked in working-class families. Among the majority of those interviewed in this study, this gendered division was pronounced in terms of responsibility for the problems of the children. Mothers claimed that the authority over drug-addicted children seems to lie with mothers, not the fathers. The best that can be expected is that fathers respect the authority exercised by mothers (interview #2).

Some mothers reported that their husbands are ashamed of their children's dependence on drugs. This feeling of shame paralyzes fathers, preventing them from taking action on behalf of their children (interview #4). Similarly, other fathers interpret their children's drug addiction as a dishonor to them and their families (interview #5).

Multiple identities: motherhood and social class

As gendered identities are multilayered, this case is no exception; class inflects gender identities and interests. The majority of mothers in this movement come from the working or lower-middle class; they were brought together by what they wanted for their children: respect, services, and treatment for their children, the latter that they could not afford.[4] Generally speaking, upper-class drug addicts can buy and consume drugs in discreet places and ways. Their families can afford to buy drugs, and to pay for visits to private doctors and private treatment, in which children live in centers far away from their homes. Hence, upper-class families can to a certain extent hide the drug addiction of their children from neighbors, friends, relatives, and acquaintances. In contrast, working-class families cannot afford to buy all the drugs that drug addicts use. Working-class drug addicts spend a lot of time in their neighborhoods. They buy and use drugs in the streets of their neighborhood, where they frequently rob in order to obtain money to buy drugs. As one of the mothers stated: "Posh youngsters do not have to rob to get heroin or cocaine; the poor wretches like our children have to rob" (interview #3). They visit doctors in the local clinics within the public health system which are full of neighbors. Hence, it is more difficult to hide the drug addiction of somebody in a working-class neighborhood than in an upper-class area. Since members of mothers' groups and their children are openly exposed to the censure of the community in which they live, they and their children are misrecognized. Upper-class families may look respectable by hiding the drug addiction of their family members.

Claims of behalf on drug addicts

As is obvious from the above discussion about economic inequalities, mothers are making claims upon the state for free services. In the early 1980s, very few state services were provided for drug addicts. The main service was emergency treatment in public hospitals for those drug dependents who had critical health problems, while some drug addicts also visited family doctors working in the public health system in search of a solution to their health problems derived from drug abuse.[5] Some public hospitals and health centers were receptive towards drug addicts, although most sought to deal with drug addicts as quickly as possible without offering them much in the way of treatment. Most interviewees in this research claimed that the majority of health professionals at that time knew virtually nothing about drug addiction. Some private organizations began to develop detoxication programs designed to enable drug addicts to abandon drug consumption altogether. As these were experimental, pilot programs, they were followed by very few drug users. In short, the state and private organizations provided very little for drug addicts.

Mothers' claims on behalf of drug addicts to the state required a redistribution of resources, since these demands involved the transfer of income from tax payers. At different points in time, mothers demanded the following services: detoxication and rehabilitation programs; policies to facilitate the incorporation of former drug addicts into the labor market (such as job-training courses); health services to meet the special needs of some users (for instance, those suffering from AIDS and tuberculosis); prevention programs (for example, in schools, which would help stop teenagers and young adults from becoming dependent on drugs); and measures to improve the living conditions of drug dependants who do not (or do not want to) undergo detoxication, such as methadone delivery.

Mothers also addressed the issue of drug addiction in the broader context of maldistribution in society, which resulted from high unemployment in the Spanish economy. They argued that paid employment was one of the main mechanisms favoring the social reintegration of former drug addicts (interview #2). Yet a paid job has been an impossible goal for many people who take or have taken drugs, given that Spain has the highest unemployment rate in the European Union.[6] Since 1982, unemployment has never fallen below 11 percent. It is extremely difficult, therefore, for many people (and not only for those dependent on drugs) to find a job. Therefore it is not surprising that employers with a large pool of unemployed can justify discrimination against former drug addicts.

Mothers also sought to make visible the mis-*recognition* of their children and drug addicts by both state authorities and society in general. Their demands embraced "upwardly revaluing disrespected identities" (Fraser, 1995: 73), who have been totally marginalized by the authorities. When dealing with state officials, mothers argued that drug addicts are people of equal worth as other citizens, and hence that they are entitled to rights that have to be respected (interview #4).

Time and time again, mothers challenged the assumption hidden in the discourses and behavior of state workers (police, health professionals, and personnel in the judiciary) that drug dependents are undeserving criminals. Mothers did not deny that their children had committed criminal acts, but they maintained that they did so because of their drug dependency. In the interviews conducted for this paper, mothers recalled that drug addicts usually start asking for and/or robbing money from their relatives in order to buy drugs. If their families refuse to give them money, drug addicts rob their families, neighbors, acquaintances, or strangers. Nevertheless, mothers emphasized that drug addicts should not be treated abusively, that they also have rights. Mothers United constantly denounced the innumerable abuses that drug addicts allegedly experience when they are arrested or imprisoned. These include harassment, threats, intimidation, and physical and psychological violence (interview #8). Because of their involvement with the criminal justice system's treatment of their drug addict children, many became engaged in the broader struggles for prisoners' rights.

A complete assessment of what mothers have gained from the state as a result of their campaigns on behalf of their adult children and other drug addicts is beyond the scope of this chapter. Nevertheless, it can be noted that the state now provides many more services and resources to drug addicts than in the past. These include state provision for detoxication programs, health services, psychological support, job-training courses, methadone delivery, and some non-contributory pensions for drug addicts or former addicts who are severely handicapped and whose family income is below the level established through means-testing. There may be many reasons for the increased state provision, but mothers' demands, mobilization, and publicizing of the problems of people dependent on drugs were one significant factor. Of course, it is also true that drug addicts themselves also presented a threat, with their problem visibly fueling crime rates. The police still mistreat drug addicts and their relatives, but probably less so than in the past. Some state officials now see drug addiction not exclusively in terms of a law and order problem, or a public health problem, or a problem caused by criminals, but also as a social problem. Arguably, this broader perspective among some state officials has been achieved in part because respectable mothers mobilized on behalf of their children and other addicts.

In their claims for respect for their children, mothers' groups were responding to a deep-seated contempt for drug addicts, an image of drug addicts as a criminal element who could not be rehabilitated. In the interviews, mothers gave examples of the contempt towards their children or drug addicts in general. For instance, a neighbor of one of the interviewees suggested that he would give drug addicts a basin full of drugs so that they would die of an overdose (interview #4). Other mothers reported people saying that drug addicts are animals who deserve hanging. In fact, *Should they be hanged*? (*¿Hay que colgarlos?*) is the controversial title of a book written by the priest who helped to set up the group called Mothers United (de Castro, 1985). In this book, the author provocatively reacted against the proposal that the solution to the problems of urban insecurity created by drug addicts and other criminals was to murder them.[7]

At the day-to-day level, misrecognition of drug addicts involved stigma and marginalization that prevented the reintegration of drug addicts into society. One mother interviewed told about her son's attempt to return to society. After undergoing detoxication and taking up a job as sales clerk in a shop, the son was identified by a neighbor who spoke to his employer, asking why he had hired a former drug addict. This was a rare enlightened shopkeeper who responded that any problem of drug dependency formed part of his employee's past personal life, and therefore was none of his business (interview #4). Had the employer held the widespread prejudiced view of drug addition her son, a rehabilitated drug addict, would probably have lost his job.

To ask for respect is not an easy task when many people have such negative views of drug addicts. For instance, in 1998 almost half (46 percent) of Spaniards aged fifteen to twenty-four declared that they would not like to have drug dependents as neighbors (Elzo et al., 1999: 478). In order to gain recognition for their children and other drug users, mothers used various discursive frames. Some mothers claimed that drug addiction is not a problem linked to the personal characteristics of drug addicts, but rather a social problem caused by many factors including the availability of drugs and the profitability of drug trafficking (interview #10). Other mothers argued that drug addiction could strike any family, not just those with special problems, such as divorce, alcoholism, or poverty. According to Sara Nieto from Mothers United, her association was formed to show society that "our children are not sons of a bitch but ordinary youngsters. They had also had measles. They also feel and suffer. They are not mere criminals" (*El Mundo*, 1999). Other mothers argued that drug addicts are sick people. These mothers countered the notion that drug dependents were lazy and "degenerates" who could give up their "vice" (drug consumption) if they wished (interview #6).

It is difficult to gauge how much of a change has occurred in the discursive landscape around drug addiction as a result of mothers' mobilization. It is easier to evaluate change in terms of state policies and programs. Since the 1990s, services for drug addicts have been mainly offered directly by the state or provided by private organizations which receive state subsidies

Although in many circles it is not politically incorrect to speak of drug addicts in very negative terms, we see that in the media and public discourse on drug addition, pejorative statements are openly made, for example identifying drug addicts with criminals or degenerated people. As two of my interviewees concluded, in Spain it is still common to hear very derogatory comments about drug addicts (interviews #5 and 6).

Recognition of motherist movements

One can also see these mothers' movements in support of drug addicts as movements for recognition of themselves on two levels: (a) as a response to misrecognition of mothers of "failed children," a reaction to society's blaming of the mother for all problems with children; and (b) as a claim for their capacities as mothers to speak for the needs their children, in contrast to experts who have marginalized them from therapies and expert discourses.

Organizing mothers of drug addict groups can be seen as a way of coping with both the shame and isolation of being a mother of a drug addict. Here, we find an example of Axel Honneth's (1992) analysis of the importance of sharing one's sense of injury with others. According to many interviews conducted for this chapter, when mothers realized that their children were dependent on drugs, they felt that they could not tell anybody, neither their relatives, friends, nor neighbors. As one mother explained: "At that time, you could not talk about it [children's drug addiction] with anybody... if you talked about it, people stopped speaking to you, and when you walked down the street, people crossed to the opposite pavement to avoid you" (interview #6).

A very common reaction of many mothers of drug addicts is to feel responsible and guilty for their children's drug addiction. Mothers usually think that they have miseducated their children, and that this miseducation is the cause of their drug addiction. A mother interviewed for this paper initially thought that she was in part responsible for her son's drug dependency because she had not left her alcoholic husband. This mother thought that her son's cohabitation with his alcoholic father, and the continuous family conflicts caused by the alcoholism of one of its members, might have irreversibly affected her son in a detrimental way (interview #6). In contrast, a tiny minority of mothers did not experience this feeling of guilt. A mother thought that her daughter had consumed drugs because she wanted to do so. This mother did not feel at all responsible for what she thought was the result of her daughter exercising her own free will (interview #2). In motherist groups, many mothers learn to stop blaming themselves for their children's drug addiction. They come to realize that their children are dependent on drugs not because of mistakes in their upbringing, but for many reasons, including lack of information about drug addiction and the easy availability of drugs – some even admit this is a "personal choice" (interview #10).[8]

Recognition by the state

The politics of recognition for these groups involved claims for subsidies from the state for their movements' activities. To receive funds for an organization is to be accorded legitimacy. When mothers started to form their groups in the 1980s, they had few supports or resources. The first groups were normally formed around Catholic parish churches. It is important to keep in mind that the overwhelming majority of Spaniards consider themselves Catholic (85 percent in March 2000). Although the number of practicing Catholics is much lower than the number of self-declared Catholics, it is still significant.[9] Six out of the eight mothers' groups where interviews were conducted for this paper were originally established in Catholic parishes (the two exceptions are the Adelfa and ALAD-Latina associations).

Social movements researchers have often stressed the centrality of pre-existing associations when explaining the appearance of collective action. This connection has been found in many instances, including the importance of churches in the origins of the civil rights movement in the USA (McAdam, 1982). Similarly, for Spanish mothers' movements the church was an ally. Parish churches offered mothers a place to meet. Very often, Catholic priests encouraged and helped mothers to form motherist groups, as was the case, for instance, of Father Enrique de Castro in a parish in the working-class neighborhood of Entrevías in Madrid. He was a part of the worker priest movement in which priests participated in social movements and organizations related to the working class, such as trade unions or the neighbors' movement.[10] Worker priests maintain that Christian teaching implies an obligation to denounce socio-economic inequalities. In their parishes, these priests attempted to encourage their parishioners to mobilize in search of solutions for social problems, including the problem of drug abuse. Some of the women active in mothers' groups had also been previously active in a church, where they were schooled in the belief that some problems are more effectively faced by people working together rather than by individuals acting alone.

The first mothers' groups generally had two aims: to help drug addicts and to support one another. The following dialogue between two mothers summed up this dual goal:

MOTHER 1: [The association] was formed for this, to support mothers, but we are helping the kids.
MOTHER 2: Well, this has grown. But before, we were only mothers. Now, kids come, kids from all places, kids of all sorts.

(interview #4)

Groups provided mothers with a space where mothers could talk about what they called "the problem": their drug-dependent children.

Only one of the groups studied in this paper (Mothers United) does not accept state funding (albeit with some exceptions). Consequently, professionals are not hired in this association (see below). Mothers United rejects state money not just to avoid having to use their resources to hire experts, but more generally to avoid being coopted by state authorities. This group wants to remain free to continue advancing demands to the authorities, denouncing police abuses and violations of prisoners' rights, and criticizing policy-makers when they incompletely implement (or do not implement at all) the programs that they devise (interview #8). Mothers of other associations who receive state subsidies acknowledged that they had to tone down or stop their criticism of state policies if they wanted to receive subsidies in the future (interview #14).

Misrecognition by experts

As the above discussion suggests, state subsidies imply conditions; the recognition of experts as authorities in drug addiction came to be one of them. The first groups were almost all self-help groups, and during consciousness-raising sessions mothers became empowered by talking about "the problem," advancing demands on behalf of their children (and drug addicts in general), and helping people dependent on drugs (see below), which laid the groundwork for their demands for recognition of their movement.

The nature of mothers' groups changed quickly in the 1990s with the arrival of state subsidies. Associations in civil society became suppliers of internships and temporary jobs to be taken by university graduates with degrees mainly in psychology and social work. This development is not surprising, given the very high rate of unemployment in Spain. Rapidly, most self-help mothers' groups became groups of mothers helped and led by "experts," who organized the meetings and activities of these associations.

The relationship between mothers' groups and professionals is an ambivalent one. Some mothers learned (mainly from professionals) how to encourage and help their children to undergo detoxication and rehabilitation. These mothers followed professional advice by offering their children unconditional support only if they were willing to attempt to stop using drugs, but would not support them if they continued to use drugs and damage family life. But others refused to accept the conditions set by professionals, which involved expelling their children from the family home if they refused to obey rules such as maintaining regular schedules (interviews #2–5, 7, 9, 11–14).

Mothers' groups challenged the professionals, asking if they, not professionals, were the true "experts" on drug dependency, because they had learnt from "real" cases: their children and other drug addicts whom mothers' groups tried to help. As one mother assessed the situation: "At a certain point, many years ago, I told a psychologist the following: 'You cannot teach me anything, it is me who can teach you' . . . because it is not the same to be in the problem as to see the problem from the outside" (interview #6). Some mothers went so far as to argue that people recently graduated from the university had absolutely no idea about how to deal with drug addicts and in fact that the university graduates should come to mothers' groups to learn this (interview #10).

Although many professionals applaud the involvement of motherist movements in the fight against drug addiction, others do not value the support given by mothers. These professionals argue that drug addicts and their families need services, programs, and advice provided by "experts" who can treat drug addiction professionally, rather than services and empathy given by amateur mothers. Some of these experts disdainfully refer to the support that mothers offer as "the soup and the hug."[11] Through derogatory expressions such as these, some professionals judge mothers' services as clearly insufficient (or even detrimental) when the problem is dependency on drugs.

Interestingly, this process of taking on the experts has been documented by international scholarship on other social movements, for instance the AIDS movement in the USA (Epstein, 1998). The AIDS movement has been able to exercise a profound influence on medical research and practices in the USA. But in most cases, these were AIDS patients themselves, not their families. These mothers' movements have not had the same type of influence on the professional establishment in drug treatment.

A by-product of state subsidies was the appearance of experts in most mothers' groups. As noted above, one of the demands of the first mothers' associations was that the state (alone or with private organizations) develop programs for drug dependents. With the passage of time, this is what happened. Now one finds an increasing number of state and private associations providing the majority of services for people dependent on drugs, which are complemented by programs and support groups for their relatives. In fact many of these new support groups are managed by professionals, who lead the meetings and provide counseling to parents (mainly to mothers, because far fewer fathers attend the meetings).[12]

Shifting goals

The first groups of mothers found it very important to have a regular place where they could meet. This had to be a known location in the neighborhood, so other mothers and drug addicts could show up at any time. Administering a phone line was also rapidly seen as a very important task. The premises and the phone line would be the points of contact for any drug addict and their relatives with a group of people (the mothers) who shared their concerns, could understand them, and were willing to help. Mothers rapidly organized shifts to open the meeting place, make coffee for anybody who turned up, and answer the phone as many hours a day as possible. However, mothers knew that it was unlikely that many drug addicts would visit the premises of their association, so they patrolled the neighborhood in order to contact drug-dependent youngsters hanging out on the street and offer them support (interview #14). Some mothers continue to patrol their local areas today (interview #4).

Accompanying drug addicts to many places was another task per-formed by the first mothers' groups. For instance, they accompanied drug addicts to centers to undergo detoxication, to the hospital when they were ill, and to the police station when they needed to get a dupli-cate of their National Identity Card, which they often lost (interview #4). Some mothers even spent days and nights in the premises of the associa-tion or in their own homes accompanying youngsters going through "cold turkey" (the abstinence syndrome) immediately after stopping drug con-sumption. Some mothers became so familiar with the pain and suffering involved in this process that some drug addicts thought that these moth-ers had previously been drug users (interview #14). Mothers also tried to find detoxication programs for drug addicts who wanted to stop taking drugs. In addition, mothers provided some material things to drug ad-dicts, for instance buying clothes for drug addicts who moved into centers (interview #2) or paying for the photographs for their National Identity Card.

Members of the first groups frequently went to police stations and pris-ons to visit drug addicts (their children and others). All mothers describe visits to prisons as particularly difficult experiences. They also interceded on behalf of drug addicts in police stations and before the prison author-ities regarding visits, the release of prisoners or arrested drug addicts, or the improvement of conditions for people under arrest or in prison. Members of the first groups of mothers even took drug addicts who did not live with their families into their own home for short periods (interview #6).

These "maternal" services provided by mothers are less important to-day than they were two decades ago. Now, professionals (mainly psycholo-gists, social workers, doctors, nurses, and lawyers) are responsible for pro-viding some of these services. Nevertheless, mothers still continue to offer some of these services in the premises of their associations. Some moth-ers' groups also manage a new service: the so-called "flats." These are flats where people who have undergone detoxication live to complete the process of rehabilitation. Professionals live in these flats and supervise the former drug addicts day and night. Mothers do not live in these flats, but visit them frequently to make sure that former drug addicts maintain regular schedules, clean the flat, and eat a balanced diet (these drug addicts are not the mothers' own children). Mothers teach former drug addicts how to cook and clean. Overall, they provide a lot of affection to these people, and speak to them very frequently. Mothers also think that it is very positive for these children to have maternal figures around them and believe that people need a lot of attention, intimacy, warmth, and friendliness once they stop taking drugs. One of the associations under study here (ASPAD) manages a flat of this type with support from state subsidies.

The definition of motherhood forged in these motherist groups in this study has expanded to include caring for small children of their drug addict children. Several of the drug addict children themselves have children, and these babies live with and are cared for by their grandmothers. Some of the interviews for this paper were carried out in the presence of very small children.[13]

Since the motherist identities in this movement encompassed the caretaking roles of mothers in society, it has allowed the objectives of some associations to evolve over time. This is particularly so in the case of Mothers United. This group has increasingly specialized in denouncing mistreatment of arrested or imprisoned people and publicly criticizing the slow and poor functioning of the justice system. In the 1980s, Mothers United believed that drug consumption could be eliminated. Therefore, they combated drug trafficking and made public denunciations to the low chamber of the Spanish Parliament (*Congreso de los Diputados*) of the places were drugs were sold. Since then, realizing that drug addiction would not disappear, Mothers United has become a supporter of the legalization of drugs (*El Mundo*, 1999).

The broad definition of motherist politics enabled a minority of mothers' associations to collaborate with other social movements around issues other than drug addiction (as has also been the case of other motherist movements in other countries: see Pardo, 1995). Mothers United is the best example. It is a group sensitive to social class inequalities, and campaigns against socioeconomic inequalities have become another objective of this group. Since 1998, Mothers United has participated in an annual joint action with other groups called "the seven days of social struggle" (*siete días de lucha social*). This consists of seven days of mobilizations undertaken in the city of Madrid by groups from many different social movements, including environmentalist and squatters' movements, and left-wing Catholic associations and voluntary organizations which work in favor of underprivileged groups such as prisoners, poor people, and drug addicts. They have copied the civil disobedience non-violent strategies used in the mobilization of unemployed people in Paris in 1998, such as entering restaurants and eating meals without paying the bill, occupying the stock market, banks, and employment offices, buying in supermarkets without paying, and occupying empty private apartments and empty public premises.

Through these and other actions, Mothers United and other social movements seek to make visible the fact that many Spaniards live on the breadline, housing prices are prohibitive, there are very few public spaces where citizens can develop common activities, and grave abuses are committed against prisoners. Their claims-making has had an emphasis on both redistribution as well as recognition to gain respect for their drug addict children.

Infantilizing drug addicts?

Even a provisional assessment of the achievements of mothers' claims towards the state and society on behalf of their children and drug addicts in general would be incomplete without asking if mothers (whether consciously or otherwise) have taken away the agency of their children, by mobilizing on their behalf rather than encouraging them to mobilize themselves. This question of agency is crucial in recognition struggles, since recognition politics assumes that subjects are able to speak on their own behalf (Phillips in this volume).

There are many instances of former drug addicts becoming actively involved in rehabilitation programs in other countries. Why is it that drug addicts or former drug addicts in Spain do not form associations, while their mothers do? The majority of drug addicts were already adults (aged eighteen or over) when their mothers started to mobilize. This means that people dependent on drugs had the legal capacity to make claims for themselves. Nevertheless, drug addicts did not mobilize, but it was their mothers who acted as their voice in the public arena. One important factor may account for the failure of drug addicts to mobilize themselves. Generally speaking, in Spain when drug addicts are detoxicated and rehabilitated, they are strongly advised to stay as far away as possible from the world of drugs and the people who deal in and take them. Therefore, the majority of former drug addicts tend to try to find jobs and social relations that have nothing to do with drug dependency. Although some former drug addicts, after rehabilitation, use their knowledge of drug addiction and find jobs related to the problem of drug abuse, this is rare in Spain.[14] Therefore, only a very few former drug addicts have an institutional base from which to mobilize.

One cannot rule out the fact that some drug addicts are overprotected by their mobilized mothers. These overprotected drug addicts do not feel the need to mobilize themselves, since their mothers do so for them. One daughter actually blamed her mother for her dependency because she had overprotected her. This daughter lived on her own when she started taking drugs and, despite living independently, still demanded that her mother go to her apartment to help her with domestic work and childcare (interview #2).

Social workers have made the claim that some mothers enjoy keeping their children dependent. They have in some cases profited from it, as seen in the mothers' mobilization. One social worker interviewed gave the example of an infantalized adult male drug addict who was living in his parents' home when he discovered that his partner was pregnant. He continued to play the role of child in his parents' home, refusing to find a job to support his family, move to a different flat with his partner and the baby, and assume the role of father (interview #9).

Given that this paper is based on interviews with mothers and social workers, it inevitably reflects their points of views. A deeper analysis of how the drug addicts themselves perceive the situation is a matter for future research. This paper can merely point to the existence of evidence partially supporting the infantilization thesis, but also some evidence which challenges it. It is true that many mothers describe their drug-dependent children in disempowering ways. For instance, children dependent on drugs are described by some mothers as very nice and charming people but with absolutely no willpower or initiative, as youngsters who would stop using drugs only if their mothers would make Herculean efforts to encourage them to do so (interviews #2, 5, and 6), as sick people who irremediably need a special "medicine" (drugs) (interview #6), or as people who consume drugs in order to calm hidden and profound unavoidable personal dissatisfactions. However, other mothers also portray their children from a more empowering perspective. For example, a mother described her (dead) daughter as a very politically conscious person, even when under the effects of drugs. The daughter was very critical of socioeconomic inequalities, and never robbed working-class people in order to obtain money to buy drugs; rather, she would steal from department stores or banks (interview #10).

In other families, mothers set limits on what they would do for their children. For instance, a mother with an imprisoned child went to the prison to leave clean clothes and food for him, but did not visit him for a short period as a punishment for his extremely rude and demanding behavior towards her during previous visits (interview #3). In some families, children do not require their mothers to mobilize alone. While a mother was out of prison protesting and demonstrating with relatives of prisoners against abuses committed by prison personnel, her daughter mobilized inside the prison with other prisoners (interview #10).

Because most of the "children" in this group are adults, speaking on behalf of others raises ethical issues about infantilization. Many of the drug-dependent "children" in these sudy are now in their thirties, and some of them even in their early forties. Concerns of this type have already been raised in the international literature on other cases, including the disability movement. In both movement and scholarly literature, it is been argued that a core component in the recognition of disability groups has been that disabled people's needs are presented differently when they are defined by themselves or by their carers (often parents) (Jenny Morris, 1999).

Conclusion

This paper has shown that agency in recognition struggles is a complex and multilayered phenomenon. Spanish mothers mobilized on behalf of their drug addict children and drug addicts in general as well as on behalf of themselves. The idea of a recognition struggle on behalf of others may in itself appear to be a contradiction in terms, but it may also be a way of gaining recognition of specific groups with special capacities to speak for others, as was true of the motherist movements in Spain.

Mothers' movements are very special movements because in this type of mobilization mothers use the rhetoric of selflessness instead of the rhetoric of self-interest. The rhetoric of selflessness allowed Spanish mothers to make claims to increase the services for drug addicts. But in doing so, they may have hindered their adult children from speaking for themselves and gaining self-respect, weakening the misrecognition of drug addicts by wider society.

Scholars may feel uncomfortable with the rhetoric of self-abnegation of mothers' movements, be skeptical, and suspect that mothers do not represent the "true" interests of drug addicts. Nevertheless, these movements have been able to make claims that could not have been made in terms of self-interest. Regardless of whether false representation takes place or not, the point to underscore here is that there is a gender-specific acceptability of discourses based on self-denial. The use of arguments based on motherhood and selflessness is a discursive opportunity structure available to mothers, less so to women who are not mothers, and much less so to men (whether fathers or childless), because many people believe that mothers are the epitome of abnegation. The case of mothers against drugs reveals a cultural context in which mothers were able to speak with legitimacy for their drug addict children. This may be less true in societies with more egalitarian ideologies in the family, such as in Scandinavia (see Hobson in this volume).

Finally, this paper has shown that redistribution and recognition struggles usually go hand in hand in the real world. Fraser (1995) affirms many times that this is the case, although she distinguishes recognition and distribution for analytical purposes. In this case, the solution to recognition implied socioeconomic change as well as cultural transformations. Spanish mothers against drugs seemed to have understood this point since the very beginning of their mobilization.

Research on motherist movements (Schirmer, 1993) has found that while members of these groups mobilize to achieve practical gender interests, in the struggle some of these mothers may develop a feminist consciousness that leads them to question the subordination of women as a whole. Apparently, this has not been the case for most of the mothers interviewed here. In the interviews, some women drew a connection between their mobilization and the increasing participation of women in all arenas of life (interview #14). Nevertheless, this is the only verbal reference to the potential emergence of a feminist perspective. This question requires further research.

Perhaps the women analyzed in this paper are not verbally questioning the gender order but questioning it in subtle ways, and are doing so not with words but through behavior. It may be the case that "feminism" is reflected in the fact that these women are playing very independent and public roles, for instance representing their families, speaking with state authorities in their neighborhoods, and engaging in collective action in the streets. Further analysis should investigate not only what these mothers say about gender inequality but also what they do, in order to draw more definitive conclusions about the potential development of feminism among members of motherist groups.

Part 5

Epilogues

Recognition and the struggle for political voice

Anne Phillips

When Nancy Fraser identified the movement from redistribution to recognition as one of the characteristics of the postsocialist age, she named a problem that had been troubling many of us. The struggle for recognition, she argued, was "fast becoming the paradigmatic form of political conflict," group identity was supplanting class interest as the chief medium of political mobilization, and a new language of identity, difference, and recognition was replacing an earlier vocabulary of interest, exploitation, and redistribution (Fraser, 1997a: 11). Others had noted these shifts – there have been plenty of "left" critics of identity politics bemoaning the retreat from class – but Fraser has been unusual in insisting that "justice today requires *both* redistribution *and* recognition" (1997a: 12). Challenging the notion that one matters more than the other, she delineated a particular kind of injustice she saw as the focus of struggles for recognition: the institutionalized patterns of cultural value that constitute certain categories of people as less worthy than others of social respect or esteem, and prevent them from participating as equals in social life. This injustice is related in all kinds of ways, she argues, with injustices in economic distribution, but should be regarded nonetheless as a distinct type. The task Fraser set herself was to think of these as two equally compelling issues of justice, and the difficulty she has focused on is that some ways of pursuing recognition claims lead them to float dangerously free from issues of redistribution. As reformulated in the paper that opens this volume, Fraser seeks a model of recognition that breaks with what she sees as the limits of the identity model: "a *non-identitarian* politics that can remedy misrecognition without encouraging displacement and reification" (Fraser in this volume).

As the essays in this volume demonstrate, the naming of two distinct but potentially connected spheres of political mobilization has proved enormously illuminating, casting new light on campaigns that were previously conceived in more exclusively distributive mode, and focusing attention on the historical and contemporary relationship between recognition and redistribution. What they also demonstrate, however, is that

the distinction can be misleading, and one of the key questions the collection suggests to me is whether the recognition/redistribution binary
has outlived its useful life. The overall message of the essays is in many
ways more sanguine than that delivered by Fraser, for while Fraser has
become increasingly concerned with the risks of displacement and reification, many of the contributors stress a more healthy interplay between
achieving recognition as a distinct and legitimate social group and building on this to redress inequalities in resources and power. While most
share Fraser's perception that there *are* two different kinds of issue at
stake, they also note that no phenomenon falls neatly into one or other
of the ideal types. Most of what goes on in the messy world of real politics turns out to be a combination of the two. The general thrust, if any,
is that the dichotomy has been overplayed (it seems to be part of our cycle
that as soon as one person comes up with a dichotomy, the rest of us set
to work to dissolve it); and that the two elements of struggle are already
in reasonably satisfactory condition.

This more sanguine tone arises from a redefinition of recognition struggles as struggles for citizen inclusion and political voice. When recognition
is theorized primarily in terms of respect or validation, this does make it a
more self-standing issue, for while it may (contingently) be the case that
the disrespect meted out to any particular group is sustained by structures
of economic disadvantage, the righting of their economic wrongs will not
be regarded as a sufficient solution. Demeaning stereotypes may long
outlast demeaning conditions of employment, and racist abuse does not
stop when people become millionaires. In most of the examples explored
in this book, however, people are not primarily battling against demeaning stereotypes that have denied them their self-respect, or calling for
a public validation of their identities that will restore their self-esteem.
Often enough, they are battling to be recognized as a distinct group with
a right to speak on its own issues and concerns.

When Myra Marx Ferree and William Gamson, for example, argue
that German women have more successfully challenged the "gendering"
of governance than women in the USA, they contrast a German discourse around abortion that recognizes women as the significant political
actors with a US discourse that treats the right to abortion as a general right (to privacy) that just happens to apply to women. When Júlia
Szalai criticizes the treatment of the "Gypsy question" in Hungary as a
primarily social policy issue, she draws attention to the failure to recognize the Roma as political actors: at certain moments, this "silencing"
of difference transmutes their situation into a de-ethnicized question of
social disadvantage; at others, the fusion of minority question with social
problem criminalizes the Roma and refigures them as a social burden on

the rest. "Recognition" in this context becomes a code word for the idea that gender and ethnicity matter, that these are not differences to be subsumed away in a seemingly gender-neutral or race-neutral discourse of social justice. Groups marked out by these characteristics need to be recognized as political actors in their own right – recognized, to that extent, as a distinct and different group – for without this recognition, they will have limited influence on the formation of public policy. As formulated in these essays, this is more often a claim about political voice than the moral worth of the groups in question.

Two questions then arise. First, if "recognition" struggles commonly take this form, does this reduce the anxieties Fraser has voiced about the reification of group identities, and the dangers of decoupling recognition from redistributive claims? In many ways, it seems it does, for what is then being validated is not the collective identity per se, but the political agency of the group. Self-organization emerges as a central theme – people shaking off external perceptions of what they are or ought to be and establishing their right to define themselves – and the major claim throughout is that neither the injustices they experience nor their most likely solutions can be adequately grasped without the group's full involvement. This is partly a practical claim: that those who have not experienced an oppression will misread the problems and come up with inadequate solutions. It is also a statement about what it means to participate as equals. Oppressed or subordinated groups have to be able to find their own voice, to speak for themselves, to be recognized as active participants. They can no longer be treated as a "problem" for some other social group to resolve. This is a profoundly democratic vision, and it is in my view democracy (rather than what Charles Taylor has theorized as the loss of more secure and unquestioned forms of identity) that fuels the struggles for recognition explored in this book. It is not so much that political movements have come to identify a layer of more "cultural" injustices flourishing alongside the economic injustices that were the staple of an earlier socialist politics. Struggles for recognition are and have been very much struggles for political voice.

Understood in this way, they do not necessarily involve assertions about the group's distinctive qualities and values, for while such claims certainly figure in what we have come to term recognition struggles, they usually live alongside more cosmopolitan claims. One recurrent theme through the history of such struggles is that there is no significant difference between peoples that could justify their unequal treatment: thus, that women are no less capable of reasoning than men; that homosexuals are no different from heterosexuals in their desire for loving relationships; or, as in Diane Sainsbury's fascinating account of the Oklahoma suffrage

campaign, that Native Americans are no less "civilized" than their counterparts who are white. This discourse of universality often coexists with
assertions of group difference, but the insistence on difference can be
contingent rather than a claim about the group's distinctive qualities or
concerns.

When feminists, for example, have insisted on the "recognition" of
gender difference, they have sometimes meant no more than that men
and women are differently positioned in contemporary societies, and
that any advance towards gender equality depends on taking this into
account. Thus in the arguments about women's under-representation in
politics, it has been suggested that part of the problem is a gender-neutral
discourse that calls on citizens to ignore the sex of the candidates and
treat men and women equally regardless of their sex. Since women *are*
differently positioned in a sexual division of labor that makes it harder for
them to put themselves forward as candidates for political office, and *are*
discriminated against in a culture that regards them as less authoritative
on political affairs, appealing to people to ignore differences of gender
usually has the effect of reinforcing the status quo. As many campaigners
have come to believe, it is only when gender is explicitly recognized as a
salient characteristic that it becomes possible to devise strategies that will
raise the proportion of women elected. This is a "group-based" strategy,
and clearly takes issue with the silencing of gender difference, but it does
not of itself say anything about the value to be attached to "women"
or "womanly qualities." It sometimes get combined with a thesis about
women bringing to politics a higher set of values (the – possibly dubious –
notion that women are more cooperative, or less prone to warmongering),
but it does not depend on these. Reframing struggles for recognition as
primarily struggles for political agency helps clarify this dynamic, for
recognition then appears as a means to further ends rather than an end
in itself. The object is not so much the recognition of the group as of
equal worth, but the recognition of group specificity *in order*, for example,
to challenge a gender order that has established masculinity as its norm,
challenge a racial hierarchy that has marked out Roma or blacks as deviant
or criminal, or achieve a more just distribution of resources between
privileged and disadvantaged groups.

In feminist politics, the really strong assertions of women's distinctive qualities and values have been relatively few and far between. This
is partly because women have been made painfully aware of the many
differences among them: a point reinforced by Marilyn Lake's essay on
the making and remaking of white and Aboriginal identities in struggles over the meaning of Australian history, or Fiona Williams's analysis of European movements to contest unitary conceptions of women's

interests and address the relationships between gender, ethnicity, and race. The resistance to strong assertions of women as an identity group also reflects a long-standing ambivalence towards the characteristics that have come to define "femininity." Some of the most powerful feminist texts resonate with what by other authors might be read as misogyny: Mary Wollstonecraft's near despair at the narcissistic manipulation practiced by women who have been encouraged to view their beauty as their only significant characteristic; Simone de Beauvoir's treatment of the "bad faith" of women who always blame others for what goes wrong in their lives. In this complex refiguring of femininity and the female, we repeatedly encounter what Joan Scott has termed the "paradox" of feminism:

> Feminism was a protest against women's political exclusion: its goal was to eliminate "sexual difference" in politics, but it had to make its claims on behalf of "women" (who were discursively produced through "sexual difference"). To the extent that it acted for "women," feminism produced the "sexual difference" it sought to eliminate. This paradox – the need to both accept *and* to refuse "sexual difference" – was the constitutive condition of feminism as a political movement through its long history. (Joan Scott, 1996: 3–4)

Claims for inclusion rely on and reproduce collective identities; and, in many cases, they will involve claims for inclusion not just as individuals but as organized members of a group. But even the most group-based arguments for inclusion can remain agnostic on the value to be attached to the group. They will clearly be associated with a claim that members of the group should be recognized as of equal value with the other members of their society; they may or may not be associated with a further argument about needing to be valued precisely for their difference. Most groups, indeed, turn out to be pretty divided on the second issue, often disagreeing over what are supposed to be their quintessential group characteristics, and usually disagreeing about whether these characteristics should be considered as superior to those most valued by the larger society, as different but equally valid, or not really so different after all.

Fraser noted in her original statement of tensions between recognition and redistribution that women have typically argued both that gender should be recognized as a salient and legitimate difference and that it should be put out of business as a way of organizing social and economic affairs. One of the points that emerges forcibly from this collection – incidentally confirming arguments Fraser herself has made – is that this tension cannot be mapped onto a difference between the strategies appropriate to recognition (put more emphasis on gender/racial/ethnic difference) and those appropriate to redistribution (strike difference out). It is not that we face a choice between pursuing the "recognition" objectives that require us to consolidate collective identities or the "redistribution" objectives that depend on reducing the salience of group difference. It seems, rather, that these two elements coexist whatever the political objective.

This account leaves us with continuing and troubling tensions between universalism and assertions of group difference, but in more clearly detaching these from either side of the redistribution/recognition binary, it also allows for greater optimism about whether the two kinds of struggle will collide. Hence, as I have suggested, this collection's more sanguine tone. But on my reading, the resulting analysis is both stronger and weaker than Fraser's current formulation. A number of the essays suggest that the recognition of the group – not just, as Fraser now puts it, the recognition of subordinated *individuals* marked by the group characteristics as full partners in social life – may be a crucial part of citizen inclusion; and that achieving the necessary political voice means not only challenging the gender- or race-blindness that has been the preferred mode of operation in liberal democracies, but also enabling people to speak as *members of a group*. If it is voice that is at issue, there seems no getting away from the group that is struggling to be heard. This seems stronger than the position Fraser now adopts, where parity of participation may sometimes depend on giving more weight to a hitherto unacknowledged group distinctiveness, but sometimes on precisely the opposite.

The account is weaker, meanwhile, in not so obviously delineating a distinct sphere of injustice as the object of recognition struggles. As already noted, Fraser has been at pains to insist that the injustices associated with demeaning stereotypes form an analytically distinct category, and she presents struggles for recognition as essentially struggles against this type of injustice. Shifting the emphasis to a struggle for political voice makes it less obvious that they are *about* a distinct category of injustice. They seem, rather, to be aimed at a wide range of injustices (some of which may be more centrally located in the cultural sphere, others in economic life) that can only begin to be addressed when the right of the group to speak on these issues has first been acknowledged. My comments undoubtedly understate the variety of positions adopted in this collection, but the focus on voice and inclusion seems to me to more radically change what "recognition" is about.

The second question raised by this shift of emphasis – not fully addressed in the collection – is whether the recognition/redistribution dichotomy has outlived its usefulness, either as an analytic distinction or heuristic device. This returns us to questions that were much discussed after the publication of Fraser's initial essay (in 1995), when it was suggested that her categorization wrongly differentiated what could never be pulled apart; bought into an understanding of the "cultural" that over-stated its separation from economic and political relations; and misread "identity struggles" as if they had no purchase on redistribution claims (Young, 1997; Fraser, 1997b; Phillips, 1997; Butler, 1997; Fraser, 1998). Fraser herself has always acknowledged the close interpenetration of culture and economy, stressing the distributive implications of cultural claims and recognition subtexts of economic claims. But she has also in-sisted on these two as analytically distinct, partly so as to pre-empt the standard socialist move that makes one an epiphenomenon of the other, mostly because of her pressing conviction that certain ways of promot-ing recognition claims are "better suited than others to synergizing with claims for socio-economic equality" (Fraser 1997b: 129). The extended understanding of recognition that underpins this collection makes this last ambition more likely to be realized. It also raises questions about whether the original distinction should be maintained.

When I first tried to think about these issues, I argued that whatever the theoretical difficulties in Fraser's distinction (how to decide what fell into which camp), it had the immense value of directing our attention to the possibility of conflict. Fraser was surely right to argue that the pur-suit of one desirable objective can block the pursuit of another equally desirable; that we need to recognize the possibility of conflict and not console ourselves with a rosy vision of our political endeavors in which everything is mutually reinforcing and we never have to make any diffi-cult choice. Since I also shared her perception that urgent questions of economic distribution were receding from the political agenda, I found the distinction she made enormously illuminating. Partly as a result of reading this collection, I am now less sure.

The most obvious aspect of this is simply that the more we examine social and political movements, the more intertwined the recognition and redistribution questions appear: this is one of the central messages of these essays. But it also appears that the distinction can work to validate partic-ular forms of mobilization, in ways that may intensify the very dilemmas Fraser has addressed. One element of this (this is highly paradoxical, con-sidering Fraser's own starting point) is that the dichotomy can lull us into a false optimism about the extent of redistribution claims. In seeking to identify what can be categorized as a movement for recognition and what as a movement for redistribution, it is tempting to employ the metric of money: does the group in question make a bid for social resources, or does it "merely" campaign around some cultural claim? It is hard, of course, to think of any form of political mobilization that does not involve some claim on social resources. Money is clearly at issue when we say that governments should be spending more on helping the long-term unemployed back into employment, modifying public buildings for wheelchair access, or supporting language classes for refugee children; but it is also at issue when we say the school curriculum should be redesigned to incorporate the history of slavery and women's suffrage, that pornography should be banned, or that there should be tighter monitoring of sexist and racist advertisements. Calling for any of these measures is calling for a reallocation of public resources. In most instances, however, groups make such demands without forming any consensual view on where the money should come from. Some may say the government should tax the rich to pay for these crucial services; this would be the most obviously redistributive claim. Others may point to some windfall revenue not yet earmarked for any particular purpose, and still others will feel it is the job of the government to work out the details and not their task to provide a payment strategy before staking their resources claim. We might, at a pinch, say that anything financed out of taxation involves a redistribution of resources – thus turns out to be redistributive, whether this was intended or not – but tax regimes do not always hit the rich so much harder than the poor. (In most countries, indeed, there are repeated scandals about the very richest paying no taxes at all.)

The point here is that claims on social resources are not always envisaged as part of a grand scheme to redistribute from more to less privileged members of society, nor, indeed, do they always have this effect. If we are to describe any movement that makes a bid for social resources as engaged in "a struggle for redistribution," this may lead us to exaggerate the ubiquity of such struggles – and in the process minimize one of the problems to which Fraser has directed us. My own preference would be to reserve the term for movements that seek redistribution rather than addition, and actively take issue with what they see as the injustices of the present distribution. This would indeed be more in tune with Fraser's original terminology, which drew explicitly on a language of socioeconomic injustice, exemplified in "exploitation (having the fruits of one's labor appropriated for the benefit of others); economic marginalization (being confined to undesirable or poorly paid work or being denied access to income-generating labor altogether); and deprivation (being denied an adequate material standard of living)" (Fraser 1997a: 14). A Marxist purist might object that redistribution is also a misleading term for these, for Marx repeatedly queried the socialist emphasis on distribution, arguing that relations of production were prior, but this would be excessively pedantic. It is clear, at any rate, that Fraser understands struggles over redistribution as challenging injustices in the distribution of resources and power. Not all claims on social resources fall into this mould.

The point on the other side of the binary is that describing mobilizations as struggles for recognition can encourage precisely that validation of identities Fraser warns us against. This is something that has become particularly pressing in the context of debates around multiculturalism, where the question of what multiculturalism is for has major implications for the way we address women's equality. When the case for multicultural policies is conceived primarily within the framework of recognition, this suggests that the object is to ensure to all cultural groups – regardless of their majority or minority status – the recognition of their equal worth. Societies, that is, should not presume that one culture is superior to another, should not impose on one cultural group the practices that have become normal for another, and should stop treating cultural minorities as alien or backward. The problem immediately arises: what if this recognition of a previously marginalized or despised cultural group makes it harder for women within that group to secure their own equality? What if the prevailing values of the group include the expectation that women should be secluded in their father's or husband's household? What if the marriage practices of the group include polygyny? What if they include divorce regimes that permit the unilateral divorce of a wife but not the unilateral divorce of a husband?

As the burgeoning literature on feminism and multiculturalism testifies (e.g., Okin, 1998; 1999; 2002; Shachar, 2001; Spinner-Halev, 2001), the claims cultural groups make for greater recognition within their wider society can come into sharp conflict with the rights and autonomy of individual women. Otherwise well-intentioned moves towards recognizing the diversity and legitimacy of a multiplicity of cultures can encourage public authorities to turn a blind eye to coercive practices that institutionalize women's subordination; can strengthen the power of self-styled community leaders – almost always male – who represent a very partial view of "their" community's most cherished traditions; and can lead to a paralyzed relativism that puts sensitivity to cultural difference over the rights or needs of women.

One way to tackle this – I think this is indeed a crucial element – is to approach more carefully the meanings we attach to "culture," "cultural community," and "cultural group." No culture is static, no cultural group homogeneous. Some of the claims made on behalf of cultural groups are pretty blatantly opportunistic; some reflect the vested interests of those exercising internal power. What Uma Narayan (1998; 2000) describes as processes of "selective labeling" often identify particular practices and values as core constituents of a group's identity – those whose modification would fundamentally damage the group – and yet combine this with a relaxed tolerance of the way other practices have evolved. Where such labeling selects out as essential practices that have been particularly damaging to women, we are entitled to some degree of skepticism about the nature of these cultural claims.

The deconstruction of "culture" and "cultural group" provides one crucial way forward for tackling these moments of conflict. The other key element, I think, is to stand back and reflect on what multiculturalism is for. If multicultural policies are conceived primarily as a way of meeting a group's legitimate claims for cultural recognition, then even after the appropriate deconstruction, we may still find instances where claims for recognition come into conflict with the claims of sexual equality. Apart from an a-priori commitment to either sex equality or cultural recognition, there then seems no obvious way of settling which trumps the other. But what if we think of multiculturalism, instead, as a way of meeting legitimate equality claims, or – as Jacob Levy (2000) has recently suggested – as a way of redressing cruelty and violence? Multicultural policies would still be a pressing objective, necessary to address the unequal treatment of minority cultural groups and the "culture-racism" to which so many are exposed. If, however, the object is to promote equality or eliminate cruelty, then an inequality of or cruelty towards women enters immediately on the same terrain.

When he discusses examples of coercion or violence towards women, Jacob Levy argues that if "multiculturalism is properly grounded in the avoidance of these evils [cruelty, that is, or coercion or violence] rather than in any distinctive moral status of cultural groups, then there isn't any particular moral difficulty (whatever practical difficulties there may be) in restraining such practices" (2000: 51). Alternatively, one might draw on arguments from equality, for if multiculturalism were properly grounded in the need to redress the unequal treatment of minority cultural groups, there would not be any particular moral difficulty (whatever the practical ones) in insisting that it be pursued in ways that also secure women's equality. I am not suggesting that either of these approaches gives us an easy metric with which to resolve all outstanding disputes – these are difficult issues, not to be wished away in such airy fashion. But the treatment of women figures more centrally in a discourse of equality or cruelty than in one that revolves around the "recognition" of cultural groups; and we might have more chance of formulating a multiculturalism that works for women if we stopped talking about recognition.

This, in a sense, is what Fraser is moving towards in her opening essay in this volume when she differentiates between the identity and status models of recognition, and recasts recognition struggles, not as claims about collective identities, but as seeking to establish the subordinated individuals as full partners in social life. The key move here is to distance recognition politics from the groupiness of group recognition: recognition no longer requires any assertion about the validity of the group identity, for it is the individuals who are to be recognized as full partners rather than the groups to which they belong. I have suggested that in one way this may go too far, and that some of the struggles for political voice may require a strong assertion of group agency even if not necessarily a strong assertion of group distinctiveness and worth. In another way, however, I worry that Fraser's reformulation does not go far enough. Perhaps we now need to be tougher on what is implied in the notion of recognition, more worried by what it threatens to validate, and less swayed by its initial appeal.

The essays in this volume deal with the dynamic interplay between claims for respect and claims for social justice. In linking the language of recognition to social movements contesting citizen exclusion, they simultaneously problematize and extend the original meanings attached to the term. The stress on self-organization provides a particularly compelling way of linking what have been regarded as potentially distinct arenas of redistribution and recognition, shifting the emphasis from an either/or opposition and towards struggles for inclusion and political voice. This fits well with Fraser's increasing emphasis on the lack of agency and denial of participation as a central part of what misrecognition involves. But given how "recognition" is wielded in other parts of the literature – and given especially the impact it can have on debates about multicultural citizenship – we may want to be even more circumspect in our future use of the term.

"Recognition struggles" and process theories of social movements

Carol Mueller

Introduction

The present collection offers an unusual opportunity to examine process theories of social movements in light of a rich diversity of chapters on "recognition struggles." The present theorizing represents sustained attention to one of the central concerns of social movement theory: the frequently adversarial process of gaining and losing recognition for identities in the course of a wide range of collective actions. That most of the "action" recorded here shows the intersection of the discursive and the political serves to expand social process theories further in the incorporation of identity framing and construction. The concept of collective identities represents the bridge between these two forms of theorizing. The chapters encompass a diversity of mobilizations that occur as identities become the objects as well as the means of struggle. They are particularly concerned with ascribed or antecedent identities that are renegotiated in the context of collective action.

In the language of process theories of social movements, "recognition struggles" concern the intersection of collective identities and the entire field of collective action. Yet, even now, social movement theory has far more to say about "struggles" than how they are aided or hindered by recognition of the identities of participants, beneficiaries, interested bystanders, and adversaries. Although most theorists will agree that the framing of identities is a necessary but potentially hazardous task for any social movement, there is considerable disagreement about the degree to which existing, "natural," or inherited identities form the basis of mobilization, solidarity, and continuity for struggles over time. Current social movement theory has not resolved the issue of whether the role of collective identities in a process of mobilization is primarily one of rediscovery of traits suppressed by a system of cultural and political domination or is solely the result of a creative process based in the ongoing interpretive work of the movement (della Porta and Diani, 1999: 94). Most likely, it is both, but how much of each and under what circumstances? This lack of resolution does not imply that collective identities have not figured in contemporary theorizing, but that there is not a strong consensus from which to approach the contributions in the present volume. This is, to some extent, a result of the particular way in which issues of identity entered contemporary process theories of social movements.

European scholars were the first to insist on the centrality of collective identities to the study of social movements (Pizzorno, 1978; Touraine 1981; Melucci 1980; 1985; 1989; 1995; 1996), although Tilly's concept of "catnet" (1978) had recognized the foundation of collective action in social networks characterized by categorical meanings. In the 1970s and 1980s, most North American students of social movements had embraced the assumptions of Olson's (1963) rational actor model and cast off questions of meaning and symbolism as dangerously associated with the irrational assumptions embedded in mass society and much of collective behavior theory (McPhail, 1991). Preoccupied with questions of why social movements succeed or fail, they developed resource mobilization (McCarthy and Zald, 1973; 1977) and political opportunity paradigms (McAdam, 1982; Tarrow, 1989). The European challenge combined with an increasingly postmodern academic environment moved North Americans towards a "cultural turn" (Morris and Mueller, 1992; Larana, Johnston, and Gusfield, 1994; Johnston and Klandermans, 1995) which has resulted in increasingly integrated approaches (della Porta and Diani, 1999; McAdam, Tarrow, and Tilly, 2001).

The "discovery" of collective identities by US theorists proceeded slowly from its origins in European new social movement theory. It has been introduced into North American work through local traditions in social psychology, symbolic interactionism, and framing, broadly conceived as social construction. These approaches place a major emphasis on the negotiated relationship between the individual and various collective levels of social movements. They examine the construction of identities as one of the ongoing processes of collective action. The focus has been primarily on collective identities generated through collective action rather than the great variety of antecedent identities such as ethnicity, nation, religion, and class. Like its European predecessors, the US approach has focused almost exclusively on identities created *in toto* within social movements. With the increasing attention to mobilizations organized around "antecedent identities" in the last ten years, theorizing has begun to reflect more systematically the problematics of *recognition struggles* as they are understood in the present volume. While incorporating much of social constructionism, more recent work reflects additional issues that arise from mobilizations based on identities that have at least some portion of their origins in the history, myths, symbols, and collective memories associated with antecedent social locations. My purpose here is to focus on the issues raised by four of the major theorists and their associates working on issues of collective identity in Europe and North America. The studies in this volume are then queried for new directions to address the issues.

Identization and the construction of social movement identities

Alberto Melucci

Of the Europeans theorizing contemporary social movements through collective identities, Alberto Melucci has been the most influential in bringing the concept to international attention and the most persistent in insisting on the "newness" of these movements (1989; 1996). Based on his field theoretic approach to research in Italy, Melucci's concept of collective identities is all encompassing. For him, the collective identity is the movement and the movement itself is process. The process is that of becoming a social actor, of becoming a player on the stage of world history. At one point, he recommends that the process be indicated by the verb, to *identize*, rather than the noun, identity (1995). The verb represents the process. While not denying that movements operate in an environment of constraints and resources, he is most impressed by the indeterminacy of the movement as a social actor that lacks the coherence its ideologues and antagonists attribute to it. His understanding of collective identity as a verb reflects this highly contingent status.

The identity consists of the contingent definitions of means, ends, and fields of action that exist in a state of tension arising from a system of social relationships as well as systems of meaning. Tensions are accentuated in a time of crisis when the unity of the actor is tested and people fight not only for concrete and symbolic objects, but also for "the possibility of recognizing themselves and being recognized as subjects of their action" (1995: 48). Through collective identities, social actors recognize each other, are recognized by others, set boundaries, determine criteria for membership, select members, and provide continuity over time.

Melucci (1980; 1985; 1989) argued for over twenty years that because these movements are not based in traditional identities of class or ethnicity, but rest on opposition to new forms of domination, the processes of collective identities are uniquely important and, by creating new social actors, constitute major outcomes of social movements. Contending that contemporary movements mark a historical departure in the extent to which they target civil society, make claims that are largely directed towards cultural systems, and recruit adherents from constituencies where social movement participation lacks the solidarity of working-class or ethnic communities, he takes issue with resource mobilization and political process approaches that ignore the expressive outcomes of social movements, most notably the creation of viable collective identities.

Systematic attention to collective identities came to North America largely through Melucci's work, stimulated by Jean Cohen's special issue of *Social Research* in 1985. Despite wide disagreement about the "newness" of contemporary movements, his work on collective identities has been widely appreciated in both Europe and the USA. Attention to the processes by which identities are created through collective action marked a major departure in the mid-1980s. Despite the major preoccupation of US social movement scholars at that time with resource mobilization and political process issues, both social psychologists and scholars from symbolic interaction traditions were adapting Ervin Goffman's (1974) *Frame Analysis* to help understand how participants in social movements create meanings to interpret their situation (see particularly Gamson et al., 1982; Klandermans, 1984; Ferree and Miller, 1985; Snow et al., 1986). Soon this work was joined with the emerging interest in collective identities. The two principal scholarly groups here are David Snow, Robert Benford, and their colleagues concerned with the framing tasks faced by social movement organizations and Gamson and his colleagues working on media framing of social movements and issue campaigns. Where Melucci's identization encompasses the movement's very existence as a social actor, North American scholars have isolated more delimited characteristics of movements.

David Snow and Robert Benford

Snow, Benford, and their colleagues argue that a frame is "an interpretive schemata that simplifies and condenses the 'world out there' by selectively punctuating and encoding objects, situations, events, experiences, and sequences of actions within one's present or past environments" (Snow and Benford, 1992: 137). As they have elaborated their framing paradigm, they have identified three tasks faced by social movement organizations: diagnostic framing that defines a condition as problematic and in need of amelioration as a result of human agency; prognostic framing that outlines a program for redress of problematic conditions, including targets, strategies, and tactics; and motivational framing that keynotes vocabularies of motive to activate participation (Hunt et al., 1994). Diagnostic and prognostic framing impute motives and identities to antagonists or targets of change while motivational framing involves the construction of motives and identities of protagonists. All three forms of framing involve the construction and negotiation of collective identities. As an interactive interpretive process, framing is thought of in terms of rhetorical strategies working recursively to influence future courses of action while at the same time reflecting interpretations of previous actions.

Within the context of these rhetorical framing strategies, most of Snow and Benford's effort is focused on differentiating the identity fields for the three types of social movement actors. Although most work on collective identities focuses on the collective identities of protagonists, Hunt et al. (1994) expand use of the concept to encompass imputed identities for the major actors involved in social movements as framed by protagonists. That is, protagonists construct identities for their adversaries as well as the bystanders they would like to recruit or neutralize. Their interesting idea of an identity "field" conveys the impression of a multiplicity of similarly situated actors.

Like most students of collective identities (see also Verta Taylor and Whittier, 1992; 1995), Snow and his colleagues argue that boundary-markers and symbols of continuity are critical for framing of identities. Boundary-markers are meanings that delineate the field of the movement protagonists and their supporters from adversaries by drawing on appropriate cognitive and evaluative cultural materials interpreted through the lens of relevant events. For the religious, peace, and anti-nuclear movements they study, Hunt et al. demonstrate convincingly that the organizations' tactics, strategies, and targets are influenced by collective identities assumed by or ascribed to the three types of social actors. Because protagonists have a certain self-conception (i.e., identity) some courses of action are open while others are closed – apparently regardless of resources or political opportunities. Similarly, the identities they impute to their adversaries and to bystanders influence their choice of tactics and strategies. This emphasis on the strategic concerns of social movement organizations parallels the emphasis of resource mobilization and political process on the strategic preoccupations of social movements, particularly through organizations as actors. They argue that collective identities are constructed from available cultural material by social movement organizations and have a major influence on the course of collective action. Although the processes studied by Hunt et al. are recursive, the types of movements they study fail to consider the role of antecedent identities.

William Gamson

Based in a very different research agenda on the media framing of issues and movements, Gamson (1992b; 1995) also discusses identities in terms of framing, but is the first of the theorists here to consider antecedent identities that precede collective action. He argues that "the locus of collective identity is cultural; it is manifested through the language and symbols by which it is publicly expressed. We know a collective identity through the cultural icons and artifacts displayed by those who embrace it. It is manifested in styles of dress, language, and demeanor" (1992a: 60).

He begins with Snow et al.'s (1986) concept of collective action frames, which he characterizes in terms of injustice, agency, and collective identities. The first refers to the issues addressed by a social movement and the second and third to the movement as social actor. Of the three, collective identity refers to the process of defining the "we" who take action, usually in opposition to some "they" who have different interests or values (1995: 99). Like Hunt et al., collective identities for Gamson are adversarial; "we" is partially defined by opposition to some "they," even when the adversary is a cultural form or social practice.

While Snow and his colleagues look at the framing of identity fields for diverse actors, Gamson includes antecedents by differentiating the collective identities of protagonists in terms of three embedded layers: organization, movement, and solidary group based on social location (1995). The first layer refers to the identity of movement organizations such as unions, affinity groups, consciousness-raising groups, national organizations, etc., although any single individual may belong to more than one organization within a social movement, each with a somewhat different identity. The second level is the identity of the movement as a totality, like the peace movement, women's movement, environmental movement, etc. Finally, he refers to the identity associated with an individual participant's social location, for example, as worker, woman, African, all of these. The three layers of identity may be differently valued by an individual. Gamson gives the example of many working-class Americans who identify with "working people" (their social location) but not with their union or with a "labor movement" they perceive as historically dated. The most successful social movements, he argues, provide powerful links between the participant's sense of self and all three layers of movement identity.

Because his focus is on the role of the media, Gamson's research examines the imperfect way that the media convey the three layers of identity to external audiences including allies, adversaries, observers, and targets of action. Protagonists' styles of dress, language, demeanor, and modes of discourse provide material for answering the question "who are these people?" to Hunt et al.'s general audience, but they are mediated and transformed in the process. Because Gamson's embedded identities reflect social location as well as the movement and its organizations, he comes closer to reflecting the tasks of recognition struggles addressed here.

Donatella della Porta and Mario Diani

In one of the latest integrations of European and American traditions for studying social movements as process, della Porta and Diani (1999), validate this cross-fertilization, drawing on the US tradition of framing and social construction and the European tradition emphasizing Melucci's concept of collective identities as process or identization. Placing the processes of identity production, maintenance, and revitalization at the center of their social movement analysis, they follow Hunt et al. in enumerating the same three sets or fields of collective identities and in arguing that boundary construction is the major mechanism through which action "constitutes" identities.

Based on Lofland's work on movement culture (1995: 192ff.), they argue that identities are developed and sustained through models of behavior, objects, and narratives combined in specific ritual forms, as well as artifacts, events, and places that have symbolic significance for sustaining an identity. Identities are formed and reformed through reconfiguration of these types of cultural elements, frequently in public, but in some cases ritual enactments of identities are reserved for the internal life of the group. These ritual experiences are particularly important for casting and recasting individual identities (see also Taylor and Whittier, 1995). Through these processes of meaning construction, identities activate and reflect relationships of trust and antagonism as well as providing the major sources of continuity linking experiences and events over time and space for both individuals and organizations.

Having argued that the process of constituting identities is also the process of collective action through which movements seek to achieve their goals, della Porta and Diani get to the crux of the matter for present purposes. Namely, how are antecedent identities incorporated into the identities of social movements? To start, they argue that "the identity of a movement almost inevitably ends up being described by its militants as 'natural'" (1999: 93). Through collective action, people discover or rediscover their likenesses, which are considered as a natural result of sharing a condition of deprivation. Thus, pre-existing identities, like nationalism, are reworked for movement service in terms of both the past and the present through the course of acting together (1999: 94–95). Although elements of the past (national, ethnic, or gender histories, for example) are incorporated into the new identity, new elements must be added to warrant a sense of urgency and collective action. Because identity construction is an adversarial process, however, antagonists are at pains to demonstrate either the artificiality of the current construction or to denigrate the original identity. Indeed scholars such as Benedict Anderson (1991) and Hobsbawm (1993) claim that ethno-nationalist movements draw on myths of a largely non-existent past in the course of "inventing tradition" (Hobsbawm and Ranger, 1983).

And finally, della Porta and Diani find that, instead of a single homogenizing identity, there is instead, a "multiplicity of identities and allegiances among militants and movement groups" (1999: 100). Only rarely is a dominant identity able to integrate all of the others, and even then not in a hierarchical structure. Instead, "what is cursorily termed 'movement identity' is, in reality, largely a contingent product of negotiations between collective images produced by various actors and various organizations" (1999: 101). This multiplicity leads to what della Porta and Diani refer to as the paradoxes of collective identities (1999: 86): (a) identities provide a source of continuity over time while, at the same time, they are subject to constant redefinition; (b) identities provide participants with an organizing principle for defining allies and adversaries, but these alliance systems are themselves subject to constant negotiation and redefinition; and (c) as identities are linked with values and symbols, they seem close to emotional lines of action, yet many scholars invoke identities as a way of explaining collective action in rational terms.

Della Porta and Diani's integrative social process approach to the study of social movements brings us full circle back to Melucci and to the centrality that collective identities occupy in his work. Not without cause, Tarrow (1998) refers to Melucci's *Challenging Codes: Collective Action in the Information Age* (1996) as the "locus classicus" of collective identity theory (1998: 224, note 14). For Melucci, more than any other theorist, the construction of collective identities is the major work of social movements. In it, he sees the major task of explanation: "The empirical unity of a social movement should be considered as a result rather than a starting point, a fact to be explained rather than evidence" (1995: 43). To take any other position, he warns, is to accept a monolithic and metaphysical idea of collective actors.

Identization and recognition

The present volume offers a rich collection of studies illuminating and extending the preliminary work of social process theorists on collective identities. While rarely demonstrating the strategic uses of identities by social movement organizations, they nonetheless give compelling evidence of the processual nature of constructing, maintaining, and revitalizing

identities in the course of social movements and issue campaigns. Geographically dispersed, they encompass an intriguing set of studies ranging
from the center to the periphery of major industrial democracies. The diversity of their academic discourse offers perspectives that are alternately
historical, comparative, and transnational. And, despite a central concern
with issues of gender and sexual identities, they encompass multiple social
locations that have become both subject and object of "identization."

   In using these cases to expand social process theories of collective identities, I will start with issues on which there has been considerable consensus and move to concerns that have been brought to light by the richness
of the "recognition struggles" represented here. Social process theorists,
as well as the current authors, place at the center of their work: processes
of boundary creation and maintenance in adversarial environments; the
role of identities in providing social movements with continuity over time
and space; and, less frequently, the role of political institutions in supporting some identities and denying others.

   Like most of the social movement literature, the authors here find that
boundaries are sustained and transformed largely through adversarial
relationships. The chapters here indicate, however, the lack of autonomy enjoyed by social movements as they attempt to create identities in
adversarial environments. They also describe the continuity sometimes
provided by collective identities and their representations, but due to
the complexity of political cultures coupled with the uneven processes
of diffusion, they find that discontinuity over time and space is perhaps
more likely. Transnational perspectives demonstrate the interpretive role
of multiple modes of communication. Finally, many chapters indicate a
central role for formal political institutions in ratifying and/or transform-
ing identity claims that have seldom received the attention warranted.

Boundary maintenance/adversarial relationships

Most of the chapters here examine the standing or recognition of some
delimited category of people indicating social location and/or a political
identity including that of social movements. For Ferree, it is "women"
in the USA and Germany; for Valiente, it is "mothers" against drugs in
Spain; for Szalai, it is the Roma in Hungary; for Williams, it is the black
and migrant women of Europe; for Kulick and Klein, it is "travestis" in
Brazil; and for Hobson, it is differences in the recognition of "women" as
well as "feminists" in Sweden and Ireland. In each case, a politically
unrecognized or misrecognized identity (in Fraser's terms) is associated with a powerless or quasi-powerless position denying relevant actors
the capacity to address critical redistributive needs. As Lake points out,

"recognition struggles are provoked by domination, and the perceived nature of the domination shapes and sharpens the resulting assertion of identity." That is, the assertion of identity is coupled with claims for re-distribution. Even in Lake's discussion of fractured identities in Australia, conflict over who is authentically Aboriginal involves material goods like scholarships and foreign travel. The political and material consequences of failed recognition are clear.

And how is a challenging identity constituted? For most authors, it is a discursive representation with material consequences. Or, as Hobson puts it, these are struggles based on discursive resources played out on "symbolic terrains." For instance, Williams's discussion of the Black and Migrant Women's Project Report by the European Forum of Left Feminists, Hobson's exploration of Swedish laws on home care and widows' pensions, the conventions, campaigns, referenda, and initiatives that characterized multiethnic, gender, and political struggles in turn-of-the-century Oklahoma (Sainsbury), the translations and popular magazines in Hungary discussed by Gal, academic monographs, journal articles, and even newspaper advertisements in Australia (Lake), Ferree and Gamson's account of media discourse on court decisions and legislation in the USA and Germany, and state policies as well as popular myths and legends of the Roma in Hungary (Szalai). For women in Ireland (Hobson), the boundary-making process has been one of continually challenging the male-breadwinner norm that has sacrificed women's economic and political rights. Only rarely are the representations of identity dramatized in practices so rich in symbolism as the travestis' "scandals" so vividly described by Kulick and Klein.

Yet the forms of representation only modestly attest to the lack of control that protagonists exert over their identities. Williams's black and migrant women cannot speak for themselves but must rely, instead, on leftist feminists to bring their case before the European Women's Lobby, who, in turn, have consultative status to the European Union (EU). Similarly, the Roma in Hungary have little control over the terms in which their identity is constituted in public policy or popular culture. And, although "women" in Germany have standing to be recognized in the national media on abortion issues, they cannot decide the terms in which the abortion debate takes place (Ferree). Women in the USA have less standing in the press, but more influence over the terms of debate – as long as it is constructed from familiar discourse on individual rights. Hungarian translations of Western feminist writing are subject to the capricious whims of a system of clientelism in terms of what gets translated and from what perspective. Both Native Americans and African-Americans in frontier Oklahoma must make the choice of embracing an identity based on

standards of "civilization" established by the dominant Eurocentric culture, making it difficult to point out the injustices that flow from that
culture (Sainsbury). Women in Sweden may have achieved the ideal society as worker citizens, but identities as wife and mother are suspect
as the basis for public policy (Hobson). Travestis may scandalize clients
by proclaiming their sexual proclivities to the world, but they may also
get killed in the process. Surprisingly, it is these scandalous, but risky,
performances of Brazilian travestis that stand at one end of an autonomy
dimension, compared, at the other end, to Roma in Hungary or black,
ethnic minority, and migrant women in Europe who have little control
over the representation of their identities.

The lack of autonomy that many protagonists experience in controlling
their identity portrayal is just one reflection of the degree to which they
are embedded in adversarial and mediated relationships of long standing. Identity challenges spring not only, as expected, from targets of opposition, but frequently from allies and other actors sharing at least one
salient identity. In Hungary, the Roma are at the bottom of the ethnic
hierarchy in terms of recognition and services from the state, but among
themselves, they are also divided in terms of the "struggles and mutual
prejudices" between Beás, Oláh, and Romungro groups in terms of who
is a *real* Gypsy. Travestis, in Brazil, are alternately celebrated for their
beauty and vilified for the ambiguity of their sexual identity – not only by
police, politicians, and the Church, but, to a lesser extent, by gays and
lesbians with whom they make common cause on some issues (Kulick
and Klein). Black, migrant, and ethnic minority women in Europe not
only lack political standing to speak for themselves, but they fail to receive
a favorable hearing from the white, middle-class women who make up
the European Women's Lobby (Williams). In Australia, claims by white
women that they have been ignored in a male-centered history of their
country are challenged by women of African ancestry whose claims are
contested, in turn, by Aboriginal women. Szalai says for the Hungarian
Gypsies, "it is obvious that the striking of a balance, the representation
and institutionalization of the values of identity, are the most pressing
internal affairs facing the Roma community in our time."

For Lake, these are the "dialogic implications of recognition struggles,"
where categories of identity are destabilized and, in the case of feminists,
delimited. Similarly, in rejecting a politics of difference, Gal argues that
feminists must accept a politics of particularity as opposed to claims of
universal inclusiveness. Otherwise, like Sainsbury, Gal finds that "in every
assertion of difference we can find the implicit homogenization of those
newly identified as a category of the different." In Oklahoma, the division
between "Indian" and "settler" subdivides into "civilized" and "savage"

Indians versus European, African, Asian, and Hispanic settlers. Before the Civil War, African settlers were further subdivided into free and slave. For the suffrage movement, gender further divided all of these.

Yet the threat of "infinite recursivity" identified by Gal is played out in the real world of politics and movement mobilization by social actors who see opportunities and liabilities in claiming or repudiating identities. The challenges described here by actors who are similarly situated reflect the inevitable overlap of under-represented identities among those who have traditionally occupied relatively powerless social locations. It is rarely the case that misrepresentation and maldistribution are unidimensional. Women, for instance, have ethnic, religious, nationality, class, and political identities, just to name the most obvious. For each of these identities, the individual receives variable degrees of recognition and distributive rewards. In the past, social movements created identities such as "feminist" or "socialist" to subsume these diverse sources of meaning into a master identity designed to monopolize the sense of self. Hobson's description of the gender neutral worker citizen in Sweden, created by the labor movement in the nineteenth century, points to one of the most successful social movement identities in accommodating a multiplicity of changing policy issues and historical circumstances.

Identity as the basis of social movement continuity

Theorists such as Melucci and della Porta and Diani have argued that social movement identities are a major, if not *the* major source of social movement continuity. However, many of the studies described here document a remarkable variability in the negotiation and construction of identities over time and space. Continuity of identities seems to be associated with polar extremes of success and failure in mobilization. Hobson's discussion of the Swedish "worker citizen" is illustrative of successful mobilization over much of a century, as is Ferree's description of "women's" increasing media standing on the abortion issue in Germany and the USA over a much shorter period. Women's ongoing mobilization in both countries around the abortion issue has enhanced their media standing, which serves as a source of continuity reflecting the movements' success.

Hobson's study of women's issues in Sweden demonstrates the overwhelming success of the early framing of identities legitimated in terms of class by the labor movement of the late nineteenth century. Looking at women's political positioning over the course of the twentieth century, she shows the "path dependent" nature of identity framing for women within this political discourse. After gaining suffrage in 1920, most women in

Sweden were assimilated into the Social Democratic Party on the basis of a gender neutrality that had characterized the discourse of the early labor movement and continued throughout most of the century despite the fact that many issues of concern to women could not be accommodated. Recent repudiation of widows' pensions and allowances for women to care for their own children in the home have continued to validate a universal, class-based identity for women, like men, as workers, parents, and citizens. Contemporary feminist mobilizations have served to increase women's political role in the government and the party, but it has been difficult to address the concerns of immigrant women, women's unpaid work, and their low pay in service occupations. It would appear that electoral success institutionalizing adversarial relationships can serve to provide the continuity of a social movement identity over the long term.

Paradoxically, a similar result is achieved through long-term failure in achieving redistributive rewards coupled with repression, as the Roma have experienced. Yet the Roma described here by Szalai also share the identity of "victims" who are the objects of mobilization by others on their behalf. It appears that, like the black and migrant women on whose behalf leftist feminists lobby the EU (Williams), the ethnic identity is not a sufficient basis for mobilization in the face of multiple sources of deprivation.

The second set of issues involves a more traditional set of concerns, the difficulties in creating, maintaining, and defending a social movement identity over time and space in a hostile environment and from external challenges. Gal, for instance, describes the difficulties of creating a "feminist" identity in East Central Europe after the end of state socialism. She points out how politically marginal feminists responded to charges of "alien" or "foreign" influences by searching for origins in the history of late nineteenth- and early twentieth-century Hungary. Unfortunately for contemporary Hungarian feminists, these historical excavations have unearthed a further charge of "alien," as early suffrage campaigns for women have been linked to attempts to win the vote for ethnic minorities. Even the identity of "mothers," which served as the basis for mobilization in Spain, underwent continual challenge as they sought to support their drug-dependent children. At first they banded together for support and then to transfer some of their respectability as mothers to their children who were characterized as criminals. As Valiente describes it, their "standing" was questioned again by university professionals who challenged their expertise in treating drug dependency.

The discussion above on the contested nature of boundaries indicates just how difficult it is to maintain the authenticity of movement identity over time against challenges from within the category (e.g., woman, homosexual, or Hungarian). These internal challenges to authenticity, so richly described in the chapters here, deserve a more prominent place in social movement theories. Also, while movement theorists have previously indicated the importance of identity construction for protagonists, antagonists, and bystander publics, the papers here indicate that the objects of social movements' attentions (their beneficiaries) also have social identities that should be considered.

Political context and the construction of identities

At a time when the USA has experienced an unprecedented terrorist attack, apparently from Islamic fundamentalists, and conflict still rages between Catholic and Protestant in Northern Ireland, Palestinian and Israeli in the Middle East, Pakistani and Indian in Kashmir, it is obvious that categorical identities provide a major line of contestation within and between states. In addition, supranational political entities are mirrored by supranational identity movements ranging from feminists to fundamentalists of various persuasions. It is also obvious that states and their policies reflect political configurations elevating some identities and repressing others. Policies of subordination and oppression are reflected in the long-term victimization of peoples because of their identities. Domestic and foreign policies of national and emerging supranational political entities influence the forms of identity victimization as well as mobilization potential. Sainsbury's study of the Oklahoma suffrage movement a century ago, surprisingly, illustrates the degree to which local recognition struggles and movement mobilization have long been influenced by the imperatives of national politics.

East Central Europe has experienced the collapse of one supranational political configuration, state socialism, that had dominated the region since the end of World War II, and now faces the increasing influence of another supranational entity in the EU. The aftermath of state socialism in East Central Europe has opened those regions to influence from Western Europe regarding the treatment of identity groups, but the chapters here indicate the moderation of that influence by political configurations arising from both the immediate and the distant past. Gal, for instance, describes a political arena that has been masculinized in Hungary as an assertion against the discredited emphasis of state socialism on "equality" and "liberation," leaving no political space for women's mobilization as women. Although non-governmental organizations (NGOs) representing Western governments provide a space where feminist discourse and women's participation is encouraged, Gal finds that this language is discredited as alien and foreign. The very real problems women face of domestic violence, pornography, and sexual harassment must be addressed without recourse to feminist discourse or mobilization in that guise.

In further consideration of the aftermath of state socialism in Hungary, Szalai describes how Hungary's recent accession to the European Council has led to a policy on minorities designed to satisfy Western legal norms, but at the same time has set precedents that will advantage the larger number of ethnic Hungarians living beyond state borders. Because the national minorities in Hungary are quite small and well assimilated and the largest minority, the Gypsies, is poorly organized, the Minority Law of 1993 could afford to be "relatively generous" in determination of minority entitlements. Ethnic Hungarians living beyond the borders could then "bring to the table" these precedents, perhaps even gaining political representation in Romania, Slovakia, the Ukraine, and Yugoslavia. As Szalai describes the symbolic politics of the new law, it is not surprising that the diaspora community of Roma was considered least of all in its creation, and its "entitlements" are of little use to them. In this political context, with increasing evidence of segregation and discrimination, and their poor internal organization, Roma are increasingly engaged in sporadic, low-level mobilizations such as radical self-defense, protest campaigns, calls for statutory intervention, and extremist attacks. Her call for a Hungarian social science that could provide a non-patronizing rationale for supporting the Roma might serve as the basis for a broader social movement.

The role of the European Union in providing a forum for the greater recognition of women's rights has provided new political opportunities as well as a new focal point for women's mobilizations. This is apparent in Williams's discussion of mobilizations on behalf of black and migrant women in Europe and Hobson's treatment of assistance that women in the Republic of Ireland have received from the conditions set down for EU membership. For black and migrant women, the intercession of leftist women with the Women's Lobby of the EU offered political opportunities that were not available in member states. For Irish women, the monolithic hold of the Catholic Church and the state that encode essential gender differences in familialism and nationalism was to some extent broken when criteria for EU membership forced changes in rights to work in 1973. These changes could build on the increasing mobilization of Irish women that was accelerated by a 1967 United Nations' directive to NGOs to create official national organizations to lobby governments for gender equality. By 1995, the resulting Irish Council for the Status of Women had become the official National Women's Council of Ireland, representing over eighty women's organizations.

Despite their increasing importance in influencing political opportunities for recognition struggles, supranational political entities have not taken the place of national level politics. Two of the chapters here point to different phases in the struggle to establish what Hobson calls the cultural coding of citizenship or collective identities as they become embedded in political policies and culture. Hobson's chapter on the long-term hegemony of gender-neutral framing by the Swedish labor movement that persisted throughout much of the twentieth century demonstrates the power of identities created by successful social movements. In the Swedish case, this was an identity based on the recognition struggles around gender issues. Thus, public policy gradually incorporated gender differences so that women won the right to vote, to equal responsibility with their husbands for the care and support of their children, to secondary schooling, to work in the civil service, and to income maintenance when fathers failed to pay their support. In what she terms "path dependency," this channeling of the relationship between gender and citizenship created a false universalism in which women were incorporated into the polity on the same basis as men. Path dependency or an over-determined set of political identities that failed to acknowledge disparities in men's and women's life course and choices led to the threat of a separate women's party by the end of the century.

While the success of the Swedish labor movement's universalistic model of the worker-parent-citizen illustrates the way in which a hegemonic identity shaped recognition struggles for much of the twentieth century, Sainsbury's study of the suffrage movement in Oklahoma indicates how a multiplicity of recognition struggles were influenced by the changing opportunities defined by national politics: a civil war in which Native Americans made the mistake of siding with the South in the Civil War; the punishing aftermath of that choice for Native Americans and former slaves; party alignments defined by the war; shifting criteria for citizenship and for statehood; federal definitions of individual as opposed to communal property rights; and constitutional tolerance for state segregation laws. Despite this largely negative political context, the variety of recognition struggles provided opportunities in which the only state with a slave and confederate legacy granted full suffrage to women prior to passage of the federal constitutional amendment. A series of territorial and state conventions served to mobilize women among Native Americans, blacks, socialists, populists, and Euro-American settlers. With the largest socialist vote in the USA, Oklahoma early enacted progressive legislation legalizing the referendum and initiative which served as the means by which women were gradually able to increase the margin of support for suffrage.

Conclusions

McAdam, Tarrow, and Tilly (2001) argue in their work on contentious politics that there is a fine line at most between social movements and the politics of everyday life. It is within the context of social movements, however, that the indeterminacy of culturally embedded identities is heightened and new possibilities are explored. The centrality of processes for negotiating and constructing identities that lie at the heart of contemporary studies of collective action tends to emphasize fluidity and openness. Yet these processes occur within contexts of enduring political cultures as well as varying political opportunities. Although there are shades of meaning and interpretation that open multiple avenues of collective action for East and West German; for Protestant and Catholic in Northern Ireland; for Israeli and Palestinian in the Middle East; for Serb, Croat, and Albanian in the former Yugoslavia, the historical continuities attached to these identities (some of very short duration) preclude an infinite variety of conceivable actions.

The McAdam, Tarrow, and Tilly approach which emphasizes universal processes of contention across the modern period is contrasted with Melucci's (1994; 1995; 1996) continuing assertion that the contemporary period calls forth an unusually strong emphasis on the negotiation, construction, and deployment of collective identities, in short, recognition struggles. His claim that their agents seek recognition for identities as much as achievement of material and symbolic objects still awaits more rigorous tests.

This treasury of case studies provides an impressive legacy for the continuing study of collective identities. Like Melucci, they define recognition struggles as an ongoing process at the heart of social movements. Like Melucci, they richly illustrate that a collective identity is not a "thing"; it is a set of activities. Yet, also like della Porta, Diani, Gamson, Snow, Benford, Taylor, Whittier, and their collaborators, they repeatedly describe a set of recurring activities of negotiation and construction of boundaries that is consequential for redistribution in a context strongly influenced by national and supranational politics. So central are collective identities to social movements that these activities can take over other processes of networking, solidarity, and strategic planning in a field of variously situated actors. Melucci's conceptual solution is in referencing a verb, identization, by which he refers to "this increasingly self-reflexive and constructed manner in which contemporary collective actors tend to define themselves" (1995: 51).

None of the theorists cited or the papers here meet Melucci's call for recasting the entire study of social movements. He continued to argue through his last publications that current approaches are too top down, too political, and too superficial. By taking the movement at its word that it is a legitimate actor, he argued, the analyst ignores the most important questions related to the negotiation and construction of social actors. While not embracing Melucci's entire agenda, the present volume points us in new directions: the centrality of adversarial relationships in the negotiation and construction of identities, and, thus, the lack of autonomy that most collective actors face in being understood in the way they understand themselves; the potential of identities as a source of continuity for movements over time and space, yet the highly contingent nature of meanings when movements fail to be successfully institutionalized; and, finally, the often ignored role of the state in reinforcing or suppressing identities that might serve as foci of mobilization – a more cultural way of understanding its more familiar role in opening and closing political opportunities. Each of these themes moves the struggle for recognition closer to the center of social movement theory.

Notes

INTRODUCTION

1. There is much scholarly debate on what is new about "new social movements" (see Larana, Johnston, and Gusfield, 1994); Melucci (1995) makes a strong case for newness of current struggles in terms of their repertoires or action and the framing of claims. But our research suggests that what is new in recognition struggles is our analytical tools for interpreting them.
2. A fuller discussion of contested social movement theorizing can be found in Carol Mueller's epilogue in this book, in which she highlights the ways in which the articles of our book challenge and extends social process theorizing on collective identities.
3. Sydney Tarrow (1996) argues that one should distinguish cultural opportunities from political opportunities.
4. The discussion of the Saami is based on discussions of the doctoral research of Dave Lewis, who was a participant in this research project.

1. RETHINKING RECOGNITION: OVERCOMING DISPLACEMENT AND REIFICATION IN CULTURAL POLITICS

1. Actually, I should say "*at least* two analytically distinct dimensions" in order to allow for the possibility of more than two. I have in mind specifically a possible third class of obstacles to participatory parity that could be called *political*, as opposed to economic or cultural. Such obstacles would include decision-making procedures that systematically marginalize some people even in the absence of maldistribution and misrecognition, for example, single-district winner-take-all electoral rules that deny voice to quasi-permanent minorities (Guinier, 1994). The possibility of a third class of political obstacles to participatory parity brings out the extent of my debt to Max Weber. In the present essay, I align a version of Weber's (1958) distinction between class and status with the distinction between distribution and recognition. Yet Weber's own distinction was tripartite not bipartite: "class, status, and party." Thus, he effectively prepared a place for theorizing a third, political kind of obstacle to participatory parity, which might be called *political marginalization or exclusion*. I do not develop this possibility here, however. Here I confine myself to maldistribution and misrecognition, while leaving the analysis of political obstacles to participatory parity for another occasion.

2. In this essay, I deliberately use a Weberian conception of class (Weber 1958), not a Marxian one. Thus, I understand actors' class positions in terms of their relation to the market, not in terms of their relation to the means of production. This Weberian conception of class as an *economic* category suits my interest in distribution as a normative dimension of justice better than the Marxian conception of class as a *social* category. Nevertheless, I do not mean to reject the Marxian idea of the "capitalist mode of production" as a social totality. On the contrary, I find that idea useful as an overarching frame within which one can situate Weberian understandings of both status and class. Thus, I reject the standard view of Marx and Weber as antithetical and irreconcilable thinkers.

2. THE GENDERING OF GOVERNANCE AND THE GOVERNANCE OF GENDER: ABORTION POLITICS IN GERMANY AND THE USA

Thanks are extended to Lisa Brush for the alliterative title phrase, and to Lisa Brush, Jürgen Gerhards, Dieter Rucht, and Barbara Hobson and the other members of the Recognition Struggles group for their substantive comments

1. By "Germany" we mean West Germany between 1970 and 1990 and unified Germany thereafter. While abortion law and practices in East Germany are also important, they are beyond the scope of this paper. See Ferree and Maleck-Lewy (2000) and Harsch (1997) for analyses of how abortion was debated in East Germany both before and after unification.
2. To be precise, two years from the 1960s (1962 and 1967) were included from the *New York Times* and the sample from the *Los Angeles Times* began in 1972, reflecting the different availability of indexing in the papers. See the fuller description of methods as well as reports of related findings in Ferree et al. (2002b).
3. The statistics we report later are based on weighted numbers, corrected for sampling fraction differences between the two countries and among years. These are the actual sample sizes, which establish the weights for significance testing and indicate the statistical power of our analysis.
4. Briefly, the eight frames are: (a) the fetus as a human life; (b) the conflict between the fetus and the woman; (c) gender and the rights and roles of women; (d) the relation between the individual and the state; (e) judgments of morality; (f) social consequences of legal abortion; (g) the pragmatic balance of costs and benefits of legalization; and (h) social injustices in restriction for specific groups.

3. RECOGNITION STRUGGLES IN UNIVERSALISTIC AND GENDER DISTINCTIVE FRAMES: SWEDEN AND IRELAND

A special note of thanks to Roísin Flood for her expertise, research input, and running commentary on the Irish case. I would also like to thank Rianne Mahon and Diane Sainsbury for their comments.

1. The Liberal Party shifted its position towards daycare, but preferred family daycare rather than the publicly financed daycare model that became the

norm in Sweden. In the past decade, there has been a dramatic rise in coop-
erations, but family daycare is uncommon.

2. Two prominent feminists were given key positions on the Commission Study
   of Power and Democracy (Hernes, 1988; Hirdman, 1987).
3. Both Norway and Finland have adopted a form of care allowance, neither of
   which aroused the same bitter contests over gender equality (Liera, 1998).
4. The case is still being considered by the European Court of Human Rights,
   despite the fact that the benefits were reinstated.
5. Racism surfaced in the media exposure of several politicians from other political parties, whose racist slurs were captured on hidden tape recorders at
   election campaign booths.
6. It has also been publicly criticized by other immigrant men in the community
7. They can be found on a website: www.genus.org.se
8. Gudrun Schyman resigned as party leader after a series of articles appeared
   in the press about her misuse of tax deductions.
9. Prostitution politics have been part of the Swedish debate since the 1970s,
   with several commissions, but the campaign to criminalize the client took off
   in the late 1980s and 1990s.
10. The construction of the family within the Constitution required a referendum
    on divorce reform, which was passed in 1995. Ireland is one of only six coun-
    tries within the Council of Europe which gives Constitutional recognition
    of the family as a unit based on marriage (Lynch, 1996).
11. The Matrimonial Home Bill would have given women some claim to rights
    to the home/farm where she spent her adult life, but this was ruled un-
    constitutional. The formal reasoning was that it challenged property rights,
    but it also has been interpreted by feminist scholars as a reinforcement of
    the notion that households are headed by male breadwinners (Galligan,
    1998).
12. The law was interpreted as violating chapter 119 of the Treaty of Rome.
13. See http//www.iol.ie
14. Even though the benefit was stopped, women still were able to make claims
    during the 1984–1996 period and over 70,000 women claimed and were paid
    an estimated 260 million pounds (Coakley, 1997: 188).
15. Only five countries in the EU have not instituted paid parental leave: Ireland,
    the UK, Portugal, Greece, and the Netherlands (Bruning and Plantenga,
    1999).
16. See the case involving midwives and technical workers around equal pay for
    work of equal value appealed to the EU Court twice by the Swedish equality
    ombudsmen (*JämO v. Örebro länsting*, "Equal Pay for Work of Equal Value,"
    Case C-236/98 European Union Court of Justice).

4. MOVEMENTS OF FEMINISM: THE CIRCULATION OF DISCOURSES ABOUT WOMEN

1. As Nancy Fraser (1995; 1997a; this volume) notes, economic disadvantage
   and cultural disrespect are often intertwined. It is also true that there are many
   differences among movements lumped together as based on "recognition"
   and among those called "redistributive." My point is a different one: the

distinction identifies not so much a difference in movement types and demands as in forms of self-understanding and self-justification. The attention to such meta-concerns is a return to issues of subject formation and justification that motivated the classic discussions of Marx, Durkheim, and Freud.

2. In an earlier essay (Gal and Kligman, 2000a), Gail Kligman and I argued that this complaint is particularly odd in the face of a dearth of mass feminist movements anywhere in the world. What "counts" as feminism is also at issue.

3. For studies of feminism in individual countries see Cott (1987), Joan Scott (1996), and Jayawardena (1986); Mueller and Katzenstein (1987) compare several women's movements. The literature on comparative welfare states and comparative women's movements includes Koven and Michel (1993) and Hobson and Lindholm (1997). Among feminist critics of post-colonial discourse I have found Moghadam (1994), Grewal and Kaplan (1994) and Mohanty, Russo, and Torres (1991) useful.

4. See Heitlinger (1999) and Rupp and Taylor (1999) for recent work on the history of international feminism. When I started this project in 1995 there was not yet any wide-ranging discussion of the structure of cross-national activism, although Christian missionary activity, which provides a model, has an enormous literature (see Keck and Sikkink, 1998).

5. My discussion of intertextuality relies on Bakhtin (1981), and my definition of texts and of recontextualization draws on the work of linguistic anthropologists: Bauman and Briggs (1990), Silverstein and Urban (1996), and Irvine (1996); this line of work is especially stimulating for the analysis of circulation. It is a considerable departure from approaches to textuality in the work of Ricoeur and anthropologists such as Geertz. Most discussions of transnational "flows" focus on migrants and commodities, only rarely attending to ideas and social movements, but see Appadurai (1996) and Lee (2001). Derrida's (1977) notion of iterability is also relevant here. An example rarely called "flow" is Benedict Anderson's (1991) "modular" nationalism, whose actual movements, however, remain unanalyzed. The term "traveling discourse," that I use later, comes from Edward Said (1983). In an essay on "traveling theory," he argued that the same literary theory, developed in a different historical context, necessarily becomes quite a different artifact.

6. A useful collection of essays on translation is Venuti (1995), see also Lefevere (1992). See Silverstein (2000) for the distinction between translation of sense meaning and pragmatic meaning. For a further discussion of language ideologies and the recursions of "foreign vs. ours" mentioned here, see Gal and Irvine (1995) and Irvine and Gal (2000).

7. For the argument about experience and political categories I have found useful the work of Joan Scott (1988) and Phillips (1991), as well as the Eastern European writers discussed in this chapter.

8. Although it is difficult not to use the terms "East" and "West," note that these are shifting boundaries that are actually constructed, in part, by the sort of movements and translations I am describing in this section (see Gal, 1991).

9. It might also be true, as Fodor (1997) has argued, that when comparing themselves with their own mothers' circumstances, and with the relatively more constrained opportunities of women in Austria, Hungarian women perceived they had a comparative advantage. Nevertheless, the informal

recognition of sex discrimination among Hungarian women that Fodor also reports suggests this perception is not the whole story.

10. Note that the conditions I am describing are most relevant to Budapest. The centralization of the publishing industry is evident in all parts of the world (see, for example, Schiffrin, 2000, for the American case.)

11. My thanks to Anna Kende, who performed the first step of the survey. For East Central Europe before 1989 there was not the familiar American distinction between professional and popular journals. The political commitments of journals established since 1989 are more diverse and overt than for older papers, making a survey of positions easier to accomplish. Among the professional journals included there were ones that predate 1989, as well as ones created after 1989. We included ones that are decisively liberal or innovative in spirit, as well as conservative ones. Also surveyed were the popular intellectual publications not divided by discipline, often with strong political commitments and commentaries. Among these more general-audience magazines, I made an effort to include journals with demographically and politically contrasting audiences. Women's magazines were also included.

12. A noteworthy contribution to the lexicon is the coining of the term "nőtudomany," literally the "science of women," in order to render "women's studies" in Hungarian. But there are difficulties. In English, "women's studies" fits into a paradigm that includes "science studies," "cultural studies," and "ethnic studies" among others, and stands in contrast to greco-latinate disciplinary terms such as psychology, anthropology, and physics. The "studies" forms signal a relatively new enterprise that is multidisciplinary and not a science but rather a more humanistic form of scholarship, for example "cognitive studies" vs. "cognitive science." In Hungarian, as in German, there is no lexically marked distinction between the natural and humanistic sciences: "tudomany" covers them all. Hence "nőtudomany" does not stand against disciplinary endeavors – as in the English case – but if anything is rather in parallel to "nyelvtudomany" (language science, i.e., linguistics) and "orvostudomany" (medical science), and inadvertently has the flavor of putting women under a microscope.

13. The dilemma is familiar to French scholars who are often astounded at what passes for French feminism in the USA. In my discussion I have assumed that my audience is familiar with American feminist debates and have not explicated those. See Fassin (1999) for a view of French–American mutual misunderstandings.

14. My thanks to Viola Zentai for an exchange of views on the events described here.

15. Other views on the difficulties of liberal feminism in the region include Watson's (1997) analysis of the "masculinization of politics."

16. The accusation that feminism is a dangerous Western import is widespread in the region, as in many other parts of the world (see Jayawardena, 1986).

17. NGOs had this effect on men as well as women, and on a broader range of NGOs than I am discussing here. See Sampson (1996) for a trenchant critique.

18. Keck and Sikkink (1998) discuss in historical detail how and why the issue of domestic violence has been so successful, and in general the features of issues that "travel" well.

5. CONTESTING "RACE" AND GENDER IN THE EUROPEAN UNION: A MULTILAYERED RECOGNITION STRUGGLE FOR VOICE AND VISIBILITY

1. I have called the series of political interventions I describe a "campaign" even though they were not as coordinated as the word campaign suggests.
2. This history is discussed by Hoskyns (1996), Stolz (1994), and Knokke (1995). I am indebted in particular to Hoskyns's account. The account given here brings it up to October 1998 and is based upon European Commission (CEC) documents, newsletters of the European Forum of Left Feminists (EFLF), and interviews or discussions with five women activists involved in different ways in "race" and gender politics in the EU. All were originally based in England and three were of Asian or African descent. They were Emma Franks, a journalist based in Britain and commissioned by the European Forum of Left Feminists to convene the Report from the Black and Migrant Women's Project (EWL, 1995); Martha Osamor, a law center worker from North London who has been active in the Black Women's European Network and the Migrants' Forum of the EU and was, when interviewed, its vice-president; and Jyostna Patel, a social worker who moved to Brussels in the early 1990s and was, until recently, employed by the European Women's Lobby. She subsequently completed a study of good practice projects combating racism and sexism in EU member states commissioned by the CEC (EWL, 1999). Catherine Hoskyns, a member the project team, also commented on a draft of the paper, for which I am very grateful, as I am for the discussions with Jane Pillinger, the England contact for the European Forum of Left Feminists. Like Catherine and Jane, I was a white English member of the European Forum of Left Feminists during the period of the Black and Migrant Women's Project and attended conferences which discussed interventions in the European Women's Lobby (Williams, 1990). The analysis I provide reflects this background. While any mistakes and interpretations are my responsibility, I nevertheless dedicate this chapter to these women as a mark of respect for their tireless determination.
3. It should be noted that the term "multiculturalism" has not carried the same meaning in the USA and Canada as it does in the UK and Europe (see Hesse, 2001).
4. See Williams (1999) for an application of the politics of "recognition" and "redistribution" to the politics of welfare in the UK.
5. Elsewhere in her analysis, Fraser refers to participatory parity involving all *adults*. However, the social construction of "adult" is itself often exclusionary of, for example, children, people with learning disabilities, and people with mental health problems. It would be possible for participatory parity, in these terms, to coexist with the continuing physical abuse of children.

6. The numbers in brackets are the old Article numbers as they were referred to before the Treaty of Amsterdam in 1997. This consolidated the earlier Treaties of Rome and Maastricht, with the consequent renumbering of all Articles.

7. This was subsequently opened up further in the discussion and implementation of the three Action Programmes from the late 1980s to early 1990s. The Fourth Action Programme on Equal Opportunities for Women and Men, 1996–2000, has concerned itself with the relationship between work life and family life, sexual harassment, care, and homeworking (CEC, 1997).

8. In the early 1990s, the policy of "mainstreaming" was recommended to ensure that a gender perspective was included in all areas of work (Cockburn, 1997).

9. Interestingly, the EWL took the view that this umbrella approach to inequalities and discrimination weakened the case against sex discrimination and would have preferred separate provision for sex discrimination (Catherine Hoskyns, personal communication)

10. Most sources used cite lack of specific data on different categories of women as a deficiency in employment statistics.

11. The Project Team was Sumita Dutta, Catherine Hoskyns, Martha Osamor, Vasugee Pillay, Kate Thompson, Enise Yaylali, Emma Franks, Marika Mason, Erika Paez, Ruth Raymond, and Anna Ward. The England group carried out the collection and compilation of data. Emma Franks was appointed as a researcher and she brought more black women activists into the team.

12. Their reluctance was overcome only after a black woman worker in the EWL had persuaded the European Parliament to publish the original version of the report as an external research report. The Parliament did a reprint but then encountered opposition from some Belgian MEPs who felt their country had been misrepresented.

13. It would be insulting to refer to minority ethnic groups in UK as "migrants" just as it would be inappropriate to refer to Turkish women in Europe as "black."

14. Ackers (1999) points to the issue of transferability of qualifications and the implications of this for paid employment which affects internal and external migrants; likewise, they both have similar experiences in caring for family in the country of origin. Issues of lack of informal practical and emotional support are also shared.

15. Interview June 6, 1999.

16. I am grateful to Catherine Hoskyns for emphasizing this point.

17. When citizens and undocumented women are added together the total of minority ethnic women of third-world origin was calculated at 5 million – the same as the population of Denmark (EWL, 1995).

18. Whilst "race" and gender issues tend to be treated separately, the issue of migration is often considered as a single issue and not one which affects internal and external migrants differently.

19. Interview October 10, 1998. Nevertheless, some black women felt their place was in the Forum as it was addressing more pressing political issues around

racism. In 1998, the Forum was researching the economic, social, political, and cultural contributions made by black and migrant women in the EU in order to counter the "victim" image that has accompanied discussion about the women.

20. The information for the Report was collected through analysis of EU documents; interviewing activists, experts, and officials; analyses of questionnaires sent to relevant organizations for black and migrant women in the EU; and commissioning country-wide profiles.

21. Such ideas have been put into practice in Northern Ireland – see, for example, the report of UNISON/Impact Conference on Social Care held in Belfast in 1997 (Pillinger, 1997).

22. Interview June 1, 1999.

23. The Project Team, whilst acknowledged as a collective, is mentioned in name only on the very last page.

24. Interview October 10, 1998.

25. Much of the following information and the details on the development of the campaign since 1995 were obtained in Brussels in interview in October 1998 with Jyostna Patel who is Coordinator of the Good Practice Project described here (EWL, 1999).

26. Martha Osamor also emphasized the importance of building self-esteem as part of grassroots political work of the Migrants' Forum.

27. Campaigns around state violence have sometimes found direct and indirect support beyond minority ethnic communities, for example, in the demonstrations against police brutality following the killing in September 1998 of Semira Adamu, a twenty-year-old asylum seeker from Nigeria, during forcible expulsion from Belgium. She had resisted being flown back to Nigeria because of her refusal to go through with a forced marriage. The subsequent demonstrations in support of the refugees' and asylum seekers' civil rights organized by women's and immigrants' organizations found significant support among white Belgian people. In addition, unions representing airline staff said they would not take expelled refugees, and the families of the children murdered by a pedophile network attended Semira's funeral. This case of pedophilia in 1996 had highlighted corruption and brutality in the Belgian police and it was these anti-corruption and violence discourses which generated support for asylum seekers and refugees.

7. US WOMEN'S SUFFRAGE THROUGH A MULTICULTURAL LENS: INTERSECTING STRUGGLES OF RECOGNITION

1. The abolition of slavery brought the suffrage issue to the fore. Woman suffragists hoped that the revision of the Constitution would confer the right to vote to all citizens. Their hopes were dashed by the fourteenth amendment, which referred to male inhabitants and their right to vote. After the disenfranchisement of African-Americans in the south during the 1890s, many southerners opposed woman suffrage because they feared it would jeopardize white political supremacy (Flexner, 1975).

2. Although the Seminoles are often included as one of the five civilized tribes, they fall outside this discussion.
3. This discussion draws heavily upon Perdue (1998). However, there were important variations in women's status across the tribes.
4. Grandfather clauses were used to circumvent laws prohibiting discrimination on the basis of race, color, and previous servitude. In this case, the amendment introduced a literacy test and a grandfather clause. The clause exempted those eligible to vote on or before January 1, 1866, their descendants, Native Americans, and foreign immigrants. As a result, only African-Americans were subject to the literacy test.
5. By 1914, Oklahoma had the strongest socialist party organization in the USA; and that year the party won over 20 percent of the votes (Green, 1978).
6. The *History of Woman Suffrage* (HWS) contains no account of women's endeavors to win the vote at the Sequoyah convention.
7. Previously only the Oregon suffrage organization had launched initiative campaigns; and the right to the initiative for constitutional amendments existed in relatively few states (Banaszak, 1996).
8. Only in six states (two of them territories) was woman suffrage gained in a single try (Wyoming, Idaho, Arizona, Montana, Alaska, and Nevada). In Arizona and Montana, the legislature repeatedly refused to put a suffrage amendment to the voters, but once on the ballot the voters gave it their approval.

8. CONFLICTING STRUGGLES FOR RECOGNITION: CLASHING INTERESTS OF GENDER AND ETHNICITY IN CONTEMPORARY HUNGARY

1. Although the minority communities are given the right to select nominees for the various positions in the local minority government, it is, however, the right of the entire electorate to actually vote for them. In other words, the majority has a strong (sometimes decisive) say in approving or disapproving the personal political choices of the minority. Some of the serious conflicts that follow from such controversial regulations of the law will be discussed later.

9. SCANDALOUS ACTS: THE POLITICS OF SHAME AMONG BRAZILIAN TRAVESTI PROSTITUTES

Our biggest thanks go to the other contributors to this volume, especially its editor, Barbara Hobson, for crucial feedback, criticism, and suggestions. Don Kulick has read versions of this text at invited seminars held in various departments at the Universities of Bergen, Dublin, London, Manchester, Uppsala, Northwestern University, and New York University. He would like to thank everyone present on those occasions for their questions and critical comments.
1. Besides ambivalence – or rather, another dimension to ambivalence that makes it possible for travestis to interfere in the identity constructions of others – is the fact that they are taboo, in the Freudian sense of being rejected and prohibited by ideology, and, at the same time, therefore, desired. As Freud discusses, anyone who has violated a taboo becomes taboo himself "because

he possesses the dangerous quality of tempting others to follow his example: why should *he* be allowed to do what is forbidden to others? *Thus he is truly contagious* in that every example encourages imitation" (Freud, 1950: 42; first emphasis in original, second added). Georges Bataille's (1986) development of Freud's thoughts on taboo can also be mentioned here, since according to Bataille, and with clear relevance for the dynamics of travesti scandals, the shame associated with the breaking of sexual taboos is engendered as female.

2. As Darwin noted in his discussion of shame and guilt, shame is raised not by one's sense of guilt, but, rather, by "the thought that others think or know us to be guilty" (1965: 332).

3. Although homosexual political organizations and organized movements are a relatively recent phenomenon in Brazil – as well as the world more generally – Brazil has a long history of homosexual subcultures and social spaces (Green, 1999; Mott, 1989; Parker, 1999; Trevisan, 1986). It is interesting to note that during the late 1970s and early 1980s, most activists used the term "homosexual" rather than "gay" to describe their liberation movement, whereas in the later 1980s and 1990s "gay" was used increasingly by participants to describe themselves and their political movement.

4. On the connection of the stigmas associated with AIDS and homosexuality in Brazil, see Costa, 1992; Daniel, 1989; Daniel and Parker, 1990; Galvão, 1985; 1992; Klein, 1996; Moraes and Carrara, 1985a; 1985b; Terto, 2000.

5. During the dictatorship, Herbert Daniel participated in the underground resistance before leaving Brazil as a political exile. Upon returning to Brazil, and before becoming a noted AIDS activist, he worked primarily on gay and environmental issues. Daniel died of AIDS-related complications in March 1992.

6. Like many AIDS-NGOs during this period, and paralleling epidemiological realities (e.g., men who have sex with men were the largest category of people with HIV/AIDS in Brazil at this time), most of the participants at *Pela VIDDA* in its first years were gay-identified men.

7. Other *Pela VIDDAs* were established in São Paulo, Curitiba, and Goiânia in the early 1990s. *Pela VIDDA*-Rio de Janeiro's National Conference of People Living with HIV/AIDS, which has been held annually since 1991, has also played a critical role in promoting visibility and political voice among people living with HIV/AIDS.

8. The Brazilian federal government was required to allocate an additional $90 million of its own in order to receive the $150 million loan, bringing the total project to approximately $240 million dollars.

9. Grants from a second and smaller loan from the World Bank, "AIDS II," began to be dispersed to community-based organizations in early 1999.

10. Two of the most dramatic examples of the cross-fertilization between AIDS prevention activities and the emergence of gay communities in Brazil are the "Prevention of AIDS for Men who Have Sex with Men" project in Rio Janeiro and São Paulo, which was established in May 1993 by three prominent AIDS-NGOs (*Pela VIDDA*-Rio de Janeiro, ABIA, and *Pela VIDDA*-São Paulo) (see Parker, 1999; Terto et al., 1995; 1998), and the "Men at Night" project, which began in 1995 under the direction of Nuances, Porto Alegre's principal

gay group (Klein, 1999). These projects involved active collaboration between AIDS/NGOs, gay groups, and gay commercial establishments and situated AIDS prevention within discussions around sexuality/sexual identity and homosexual collectivities at local, national, and global levels.

11. Appointed members to the National AIDS Commission have included longtime gay activist Luiz Mott (head of the *Grupo Gay da Bahia*), a representative of the Rio de Janeiro based gay group *Acro-Íris* (Rainbow Group), and representatives of two AIDS-NGOs with histories of working with gay and travesti populations (GAPA/Rio Grande do Sul and GAPA/Belo Horizonte).

12. There are several reasons for this. One is that even though the overwhelming majority of travestis do use condoms with their clients, condoms can burst or slip off and remain inside a travesti's anus after intercourse. There are also travestis who are less careful about using condoms, either because they know or suspect themselves to be HIV+, or because they are desperate for money and a client offers to pay them more if they agree to be penetrated (or even to penetrate him) without a condom. Astonishingly, these kinds of clients remain common (for some interesting analysis and interviews with clients who say they do not use condoms when they visit male prostitutes, see Veneziani and Reim, 1999: 199–252). A final reason why HIV remains a grave threat to travestis is because condoms are almost invariably dispensed with entirely in a travesti's private relationship with her boyfriend(s). Using a condom with a man one loves would be treating him like a client, and it is well documented that one of the ways prostitutes (not just travestis) mark the status of their partner as special is to not use condoms during sex (see Kulick, 1998: 242, note 3 for a discussion).

13. See Larvie (1998), who has argued that international and national governmental agencies who work on AIDS issues (e.g. the World Health Organization, the Brazilian National AIDS Program) have played a critical role in the very creation of categories (e.g. sex professionals, men who have sex with men, transgendered people, street youth) around which travestis and other disempowered groups often organize.

14. This active involvement of non-travestis in travesti political organizations is mirrored in AIDS-NGOs as well. For example, GAPA/RS's travesti groups have nearly always been led by non-travestis.

15. Similarly, the travesti groups at the Support Group for AIDS Prevention in Porto Alegre, although organized primarily to promote HIV prevention and to improve the qualify of life of travestis with HIV/AIDS, spend much of their time on violence, personal safety, discrimination, and gender/sexual identity issues (Klein, 1996, 1998, 1999).

16. For example, in August 1994 approximately thirty travestis and fifty of their "Open-Minded" supporters staged a protest march through the streets of downtown Porto Alegre in response to the killing of the travesti Cris Loira (a GAPA group participant) by a client on the streets of Porto Alegre's main travesti prostitution zone (Klein, 1996; 1998).

17. There is a substantial and growing literature, mostly by geographers, on "queering public space." All scholars who write on this make the point that the mass appearance of gays, lesbians, and/or transgendered persons in public

space "queers" it: i.e., it (a) reveals that public space thought to be unmarked or neutral in regard to sexuality is in fact heavily saturated with *heterosexuality* (hence the common reaction to such manifestations as scandalous and unseemly); and (b) it reterritorializes the space to be space that can host queers (see, for example, Bell and Valentine, 1995; Nancy Duncan, 1996; Hubbard, 2001; Nast, 1998)

18. We are indebted to Roger Lancaster's formulation of a similar point in his discussion of this ethnographic data, which comes from Klein (1998) (Lancaster, 1998: 270). We have augmented Lancaster's observations with our own to foreground the notion of shame.

19. Žižek makes a useful distinction between political acts that "remain within the framework of existing social relations," and what he calls the "political act proper." A political act or intervention proper "is not simply something that works well within the framework of existing relations, but something that *changes the very framework that determines how things work*" (1999: 199, emphasis in original)

20. The anthropologists Hélio Silva and Cristina de Oliveira Florentino estimate that the Rio de Janeiro equivalents of daily tabloids like the British *Sun* or *Daily News* feature articles about travestis, on average, twice a week (1996: 107).

21. This had been a major bone of contention between travesti groups and the Ministry of Health since the Ministry financed and published a text called *Manual do Multiplicador – Homosexual* [The Manual for Multipliers – Homosexuality, BMOH, 1996]; a "multiplier" is the Ministry's term for engaged persons who develop educational methods and practices in specifically targeted communities. The Manual explained homosexuality for people who work with HIV prevention programs. The part of the Manual that concerned travestis, authored by the then-president of the Gay Group of Bahia, Luiz Mott, discussed travestis in ways many of them found deeply offensive. For example, the text designates travestis as *rapazes de peito* (boys with breasts) and asserts in lurid language that they are part of "the same subculture (*subcultura*) of violence that dominates the subculture of prostitution" (BMOH, 1996: 26). This text led to heated protests from travesti groups and demands that future official texts about travestis be written in consultation with travesti representatives.

10. MOBILIZING FOR RECOGNITION AND REDISTRIBUTION ON BEHALF OF OTHERS? THE CASE OF MOTHERS AGAINST DRUGS IN SPAIN

This book and my chapter are part of the research project on Gender, Political Identities and Recognition Struggles in Contemporary Societies directed by Barbara Hobson and sponsored by the Comparative Gender Studies Research School at Stockholm University and the Bank of Sweden Tercentenary Foundation. I would like to thank all of the members of the aforementioned research group and Gracia Trujillo for their invaluable comments on an earlier draft of this paper. In addition, Myra Marx Ferree and Fiona Williams gave me very useful recommendations regarding secondary literature. The empirical research was partly financed by the Women's General Directorate of the Madrid Regional Government (*Dirección General de la Mujer de la Comunidad Autónoma de Madrid*), whose support is acknowledged here. This paper is dedicated to the Spanish Mothers Against Drugs in token of my respect for their endless mobilization in favor of their drug addict children and other dependent people.

1. This is my reading of Pardo's study on the mobilization of two groups of women in California, although Mary Pardo (1995) seems to draw a positive assessment of the motherist groups that she studies.
2. The exception to this pattern are human rights groups.
3. 1995 data. Data for Spain and the European Union are provisional or estimated.
4. Mothers' groups differ in terms of other characteristics, for instance, religiosity and political beliefs.
5. Compulsory health insurance was introduced in Spain for low income industrial workers in 1942. Successive reforms extended the population covered under health schemes and the range and scope of benefits. The process of universalization of public health care was completed legislatively by a decree passed in 1989. For more information about health care policies in Spain, see Guillén, 1999.
6. The unemployment rate is the proportion of registered unemployed in the active population (the employed and the registered unemployed).
7. This book also contains many complaints of severe police mistreatment of drug users from some deprived areas who were arrested or imprisoned.
8. It is important to note that even in mothers' groups, some people believe that some mothers are partially responsible for their children's drug addiction (interview #1). Some psychologists and other professionals occasionally also blame mothers for the drug addiction of their children (interview #10).
9. In March 2000, 21 percent of those self-declared Catholics stated that they attend religious services (excluding social events such as weddings, first communions, or funerals) almost every Sunday or on religious feast days, and around 3 percent do so various days a week (Centro de Investigaciones Sociológicas, Study Number 2387).
10. The movement of worker priests first appeared in France in the mid-1940s under Cardinal Emmanuel Suhard and then spread to other countries, including Spain. These priests tried to organize parishes along non-hierarchical and participatory lines. Members of the congregations were encouraged to actively take part in religious activities and ceremonies. Worker priests were not so aware (or almost completely unaware) of other types of inequality, for instance gender inequality. The worker priests movement received support from the hierarchy of the Catholic Church after the Second Vatican Council (1962–65), but was later criticized and marginalized by the hierarchy.
11. The expression "the soup and the hug" was used by a professional working in the association FANTID in Madrid in a phone conversation with the author of this paper on May 31, 1999.

12. In some cases, when programs for parents ended, some mothers felt that they needed further interaction with relatives of drug addicts; this laid the basis for one association, ADELFA – Association of Parents, Relatives and Friends of Drug Addicts of the Municipal Districts of Arganzuela, Centro, Salamanca, Retiro, Chamberí and Moncloa (*Asociación De Padres, Familiares y Amigos de Drogodependientes de los Distritos de Arganzuela, Centro, Salamanca, Retiro, Chamberí y Moncloa.*) "ADELFA" is the Spanish word for oleander, a kind of flower or bush.

13. In Spain, grandmothers often take care of their grandchildren, for instance when mothers are in employment.

14. Without doubting that the most effective way for former drug addicts to reject the temptation of taking drugs again may be to avoid any contact with the drug problem, other factors may explain why this is the course of action strongly recommended to Spanish drug addicts. Given the high rates of unemployment, professionals (psychologists, social workers, and others) have defined themselves as the true experts on the problem of drug abuse. It is highly unlikely that these professionals will allow former drug addicts to define themselves as experts too, since this definition will dramatically increase the already very tough competition for jobs.

References

Acker, Joan. 1992. "Två diskurser om reformer och kvinnor i den framtida välfärdsstaten" [Two discourses on reform and women in the future welfare state], in *Kvinnors och mäns liv och arbete* [Women's and men's life and work], Stockholm: SNS Förlag, pp. 280–309.

Ackers, Louise. 1999. *Shifting Spaces: Women, Citizenship and Migration within the European Union*, Bristol: The Policy Press.

Acsády, Judit. 1997. "A huszadik század asszonyá: A századforduló magyar feminizmusának nőképe" [Woman of the twentieth century: images of women in Hungarian feminism at the turn of the century], in Béata Nagy and Margit S. Sárdi (eds.), *Szerep és alkotás: Női szerepek a társadalomban és az alkotóművészetben* [Role and creation: images of women in society and the arts], Debrecen: Csokonai Kiadó, pp. 243–53.

Act LXXVII. 1993. *Törvény a magyarországi nemzeti és etnikai kisebbségek jogairól*, Budapest: Parliament of the Republic of Hungary.

Agassi, Judith Buber. 1989. "Theories of Gender Equality: Lessons from the Israeli Kibbutz," *Gender & Society* 3(2): 139–58.

Allen, Susan L. 1988. "Progressive Spirit: The Oklahoma and Indian Territory Federation of Women's Clubs," *Chronicles of Oklahoma* 66(1): 4–21.

Alvarez, Sonia. 1990. *Engendering Democracy in Brazil: Women's Movements in Transition Politics*, Princeton University Press.

Åmark, Klas. 1992. "Social Democracy and the Trade Union Movement: Solidarity and the Politics of Self-Interest," in Klaus Misgeld, Karl Molin, and Klas Åmark (eds.), *Creating Social Democracy*, University Park, PA: Pennsylvania State University Press, pp. 67–96.

Amenta, Edwin. 1998. *Bold Relief*, Princeton University Press.

Anderson, Benedict. 1991 [1983]. *Imagined Communities: Reflections on the Origins and Spread of Nationalism*, London: Verso.

Anderson, Bridget. 2000. *Doing the Dirty Work? The Global Politics of Domestic Labour*, London: Zed Books.

Ang, Ien. 1995. "I'm a Feminist but... 'Other' Women and Post-national Feminism," in Barbara Caine and Rosemary Pringle (eds.), *Transitions: New Australian Feminisms*, Sydney: Allen and Unwin, pp. 57–73.

Appadurai, Arjun. 1996. *Modernity at Large: Cultural Elements of Globalization*, Minneapolis: University of Minnesota Press.

Attwood, Bain, and Andrew Markus (eds.). 1997. *The 1967 Referendum, Or When Aborigines Didn't Get The Vote*, Canberra: Australian Institute of Aboriginal and Torres Strait Islander Studies.

Bail, Kathy (ed.). 1996. *DIY Feminism*, Sydney: Allen and Unwin.

Bakhtin, Mikhail. 1981. "Discourse in the Novel," in Michael Holquist (ed.), *The Dialogic Imagination*, Austin, TX: University of Texas Press, pp. 259–422.

Banaszak, Lee Ann. 1996. *Why Movements Succeed or Fail: Opportunity, Culture and the Struggle for Woman Suffrage*, Princeton University Press.

Bárány, Anzelm. 1998. *Média, nyomda és könyvszakmai privatizáció, 1988–1998* [Media, publishing and the book industry's privatization], Budapest: Állami Privatizációs és Vagyonkezelő Rt.

Bataille, Georges. 1986 [1957]. *Erotism: Death and Sensuality*, San Francisco: City Light Books.

Bauman, Richard, and Charles Briggs. 1990. "Poetics and Performance as Critical Perspectives on Social Life," *Annual Review of Anthropology* 19: 59–88.

Behabib, Seyla. 2002. *The Claims of Culture: Equality and Diversity in the Global Era*. Princeton University Press.

Behrendt, Larissa. 1993. "Aboriginal Women and the White Lies of the Feminist Movement: Implications for Aboriginal Women in Rights Discourse," *Australian Feminist Law Journal* 1(1): 27–44.

Bell, David, and Gill Valentine (eds.). 1995. *Mapping Desire: Geographies of Sexuality*, London: Routledge.

Benjamin, Walter. 1968. "The Task of the Translator," in Harry Zohn (trans. and ed.), *Illuminations*, New York: Harcourt & Brace, pp. 69–82.

Bergman, Helena, and Barbara Hobson. 2002. "Compulsory Fatherhood: The Coding of Fatherhood in Sweden," in Barbara Hobson (ed.), *Making Men into Fathers: Men, Masculinities and the Social Politics of Fatherhood*, Cambridge University Press, pp. 92–124.

Bergqvist, Christina (ed.). 1999. *Equal Democracies? Gender in the Nordic Countries*, Oslo: Scandinavian University Press.

Bernstein, Mary. 2002. "The Contradictions of Gay Ethnicity: Forging Identity in Vermont," in David S. Meyer, Nancy Whittier, and Belinda Robnett (eds.), pp. 85–104.

Bhavnani, Reena. 1994. *Black Women in the Labour Market: A Research Review*, Manchester: Equal Opportunities Commission.

Blanchard, Dallas. 1994. *The Anti-Abortion Movement and the Rise of the Religious Right: From Polite to Fiery Protest*, New York: Macmillan.

BMOH (Brazilian Ministry of Health). 1996. *Manual do multiplicador – homosexual* [The manual for multipliers – Homosexuality], Brasília: Ministério da Saúde.

Bordin, Ruth. 1981. *Woman and Temperance: The Quest for Power and Liberty 1873–1900*, Philadelphia: Temple University Press.

Bordo, Susan. 1995. "Are Mothers Persons? Reproductive Rights and the Politics of Subjectivity," in Susan Bordo (ed.), *Unbearable Weight: Feminism, Western Culture and the Body*, Berkeley: University of California Press, pp. 71–97.

Bourdieu, Pierre. 1984. *Distinction: A Social Critique of the Judgement of Taste*, Cambridge, MA: Harvard University Press.

Brewster, Anne. 1996. *Reading Aboriginal Women's Autobiography*, Sydney University Press.

Browning, Barbara. 1996. "The Closed Body," *Women and Performance: A Journal of Feminist Theory* 8(2): 1–18.

Bruning, Gwennaëie, and Janneke Plantenga. 1999. "Parental Leave and Equal Opportunities: Experiences in Eight European Countries," *Journal of European Social Policy* 9(3): 195–209.

Brush, Lisa D. 2003. *Gender and Governance: States and Social Policies Through a Gender Lens*, Lanham, MD: AltaMira Press.

Buhle, Mari Jo. 1981. *Women and American Socialism, 1870–1920*, Urbana, IL: University of Illinois Press.

Bunreacht NA Heireann [Constitution of Ireland]. 1937. Dublin: Government Publication Office.

Burbank, Garin. 1975. "Socialism in an Oklahoma Boom-town," in Bruce M. Stave (ed.), *Socialism and the Cities*, Port Washington, NY: Kennikat Press, pp. 99–115.

   1976. *When Farmers Voted Red: The Gospel of Socialism in the Oklahoma Countryside, 1910–1924*, Westport, CT: Greenwood Press.

Burns, E. Bradford. 1993. *A History of Brazil*, third edition, New York: Columbia University Press.

Butler, Judith. 1997. "Merely Cultural," *Social Text* 15(3/4): 265–77.

Byrne, Anne, and Madeleine Leonard (eds.). 1997. *Women in Irish Society: A Sociological Reader*, Dublin: Colour Books.

Câmara da Silva, Cristiana. 1993. "Triangulo Rosa: a busca pela cidadania dos Homossexuais" [Pink triangle: the search for citizenship for homosexuals], Master's Thesis, Universidade Federal do Rio de Janeiro, Brazil.

Castles, Stephen, and Mark J. Miller. 1993. *The Age of Migration*, London: Macmillan.

Catt, Carrie Chapman, and Nettie Rogers Shuler. 1969 [1926]. *Woman Suffrage and Politics: The Inner Story of the Suffrage Movement*, Seattle: University of Washington Press.

CEC (Commission for the European Communities). 1995. *Communication on Racism, Xenophobia and Anti-Semitism*, Brussels: COM 1995 653, December.

   1997. *The Magazine: Quarterly Magazine of the Medium-term Action Programme on Equal Opportunities for Women and Men 1996–2001*, Brussels: European Commission.

   1998. *An Action Plan Against Racism*, Brussels: COM 1998 183, March.

Christiansen-Ruffman, Linda. 1995. "Women's Conceptions of the Political: Three Canadian Women's Organizations," in Myra Marx Ferree and Patricia Yancey Martin, pp. 372–93.

Clark, Blue. 1970–71. "Delegates to the Constitutional Convention," *Chronicles of Oklahoma* 48(4): 400–15.

Clemens, Elizabeth. 1998. *The People's Lobby*, University of Chicago Press.

Coakley, Anne. 1997. "Gendered Citizenship: The Social Construction of Mothers in Ireland," in Anne Byrne and Madeleine Leonard (eds.), pp. 181–95.

Cockburn, Cynthia. 1997. "Gender in an International Space: Trade Union Women as European Social Actor," *Women's Studies International Forum* 20(4): 459–70.

Cohen, Jean (guest editor). 1985. "Social Movements," *Social Research* 52(4).

Connelly, Alpha (ed.). 1993. *Gender and Law in Ireland*, Dublin: Oak Tree Press.

Connelly, Alpha. 1999. "Women and the Constitution in Ireland," in Yvonne Galligan, Ellis Ward, and Rick Wilford (eds.), pp. 18–37.

Connelly, Anne. 1993. "The Constitution," in Alpha Connelly (ed.), pp. 4–27.

Connelly, Eileen. 1999. "The Republic of Ireland and the Equality Contract: Women and Public Policy," in Yvonne Galligan, Ellis Ward, and Rick Wilford (eds.), pp. 74–89.

Connolly, Linda. 2002. *The Irish Women's Movement. From Revolution to Devolution*, Houndsmills: Palgrave.

Constitutional Review Group. 1996. *Report of the Constitutional Review Group*, Dublin: Government Stationery Office.

Cook, Geoffrey, and Anthony McCashin. 1997. "Male Breadwinner: A Case Study of Gender and Social Security," in Anne Byrne and Madeleine Leonard (eds.), pp. 167–80.

Costa, Jurandir Freire. 1992. *A inocência e o vício: estudos sobre o Homoerotismo* [Innocence and vice: studies on homoeroticism], Rio de Janeiro: Relume-Dumará.

Cott, Nancy. 1987. *The Grounding of Modern Feminism*, New Haven: Yale University Press.

CQ. 1975. *Congressional Quarterly's Guide to US Elections*, Washington, DC: Congressional Quarterly.

CSO (Central Statistical Office). 1993. *A negyedévenkénti lakossági munkaerő-felmérés adatai* [Data of the quarterly manpower survey], Budapest: KSH.

2001. *Statisztikai évkönyv 2000* [Statistical Yearbook 2000], Budapest: KSH.

Curthoys, Ann. 1993. "Identity Crisis: Colonialism, Nation and Gender in Australian History," *Gender & History* 5(2): 165–76.

Daniel, Herbert. 1989. *Vida antes da morte* [Life before death], Rio de Janeiro: Jabotí.

1993. "The Bankruptcy of Models: Myths and Realities of AIDS in Brazil," in Herbert Daniel and Richard Parker (eds.), pp. 33–47.

Daniel, Herbert, and Richard Parker. 1990. *AIDS: a terceira epidemia* [AIDS: the third epidemic], São Paulo: Iglu Editora.

(eds.). 1993. *Sexuality, Politics and AIDS in Brazil*, London: The Falmer Press.

Darvishpour, Mehrdad. 1997 "Invandrarkvinnor utmanar männens rol. Maktfördelning och konfliktor i Iranksa familjier i Sverige" [Immigrant women challenge the role of men: power resources and conflicts in Iranian families in Sweden], in Göran Ahrne and Inga Persson (eds.), *Familj, makt och jämställdhet* [Family, power, and gender equality], Stockholm: SOU, pp. 262–92.

2002. "Många skyldiga bakom hedersmorden" [Many guilty in the family honor killing], *Aftonbladet* 24(1): 2.

Darwin, Charles. 1965. *The Expression of the Emotions in Man and Animals*, University of Chicago Press.

Daskalová, Krassimira. 2000. "Women's Problems, Women's Discourses in Bulgaria," in Susan Gal and Gail Kligman (eds.), 2000b, pp. 337–69.

Debo, Angie. 1941. *The Road to Disappearance*, Norman: University of Oklahoma Press.

de Castro, Enrique. 1985. *¿Hay que colgarlos? Una experiencia sobre marginación y poder* [Should they be hanged? An experience on marginalization and power], Bilbao: Desclee de Brouwer.

1972 [1940]. *And Still the Waters Run: The Betrayal of the Five Civilized Tribes*, Princeton University Press.

della Porta, Donatella, and Mario Diani. 1999. *Social Movements: An Introduction*, Malden, MA: Blackwell Publishers.

Derrida, Jacques. 1977. "Signature Event Context," in *Limited, Inc.*, Evanston, IL: Northwestern University Press, pp. 1–24.

Dixson, Miriam. 1976. *The Real Matilda: Women and Identity in Australia 1788 to 1975*, Melbourne: Penguin.

Duncan, Nancy. 1996. "Renegotiating Gender and Sexuality in Public and Private Places," in Nancy Duncan (ed.), *Bodyspace: Destabilizing Geographies of Gender and Sexuality*, London: Routledge, pp. 127–45.

Duncan, Simon. 1996. "Obstacles to a Successful Equal Opportunities Policy in the European Union," *European Journal of Women's Studies* 3(4): 399–427.

Eduards, Maud. 1991. "Toward a Third Way: Women's Politics and Welfare Policies in Sweden," *Social Research* 58(3): 677–705.

1992. "Against the Rules of the Game – On the Importance of Women's Collective Actions," in Maud L. Eduards (ed.), *Rethinking Change – Current Swedish Feminist Research*, Uppsala: Swedish Science Press (HSFR), pp. 83–104

Einhorn, Barbara. 1992. *Cinderella Goes to Market: Citizenship, Gender, and Women's Movements in East Central Europe*, London: Verso.

Eklund, Ronnie. 1996. "The Swedish Case – the Promised Land of Sex Equality?" in Tamara Hervey and David O'Keefe (eds.), *Sex Equality Law in the European Union*, New York: John Wiley and Sons, pp. 337–56.

Elman, Amy. 1995. "The State's Equality for Women: Sweden's Equality Ombudsman," in Dorothy McBride Stetson and Amy G. Mazur (eds.), *Comparative State Feminism*, Thousand Oaks, CA: Age, pp. 237–53.

El Mundo, 1999. December 24. Madrid: 6–7.

Elzo, Javier, Francisco A. Orizo, Juan González-Anleo, Pedro González, María T. Laespada, and Leire Salazar. 1999. *Jóvenes españoles 99* [Spanish Youth 1999], Madrid: Fundación Santa María.

Epstein, Steven. 1998. *Impure Science: AIDS, Activism, and the Politics of Knowledge*, Berkeley: University of California Press.

Esping-Andersen, Gösta. 1990. *The Three Worlds of Welfare Capitalism*, Princeton University Press.

European Commission. 1998. *Social Portrait of Europe*, Luxembourg: Office for Official Publications of the European Communities.

EWL (European Women's Lobby). 1995. *Confronting the Fortress: Black and Migrant Women in the European Union*, Brussels: European Parliament, Directorate General for Research.

1999. *Overcoming Discrimination: Good Model Practice for Black, Minority Ethnic and Migrant Women*, Brussels: European Women's Lobby.

Fábri, Anna. 1999. *A nő hivatása: szemelvények a magyarországi nőkérdés történetéből, 1777–1865* [Woman's calling: selections from the history of the Hungarian woman question], Budapest: Kortárs Kiadó.

Farkas, János, and Ágnes Vajda. 1990. "Housing," in Rudolf Andorka, Tamás Kolosi, and György Vukovich (eds.), *Social Report 1990*, Budapest: TÁRKI.

Fassin, Eric. 1999. "The Purloined Letter: American Feminism in a French Mirror," *French Historical Studies* 22(1): 113–38.

Ferge, Zsuzsa. 1997. "Women and Social Transformation in Central-Eastern Europe: The 'Old Left' and the 'New Right,'" *Czech Sociological Review* 5(2): 159–78.

Fernandes, Rubem Cesar. 1994. *Privado porém público: o terceiro setor na América Látina* [Private yet public: the third sector in Latin America], Rio de Janeiro: Relume-Dumará.

Ferree, Myra Marx. 1987. "Equality and Autonomy: The Women's Movements of the United States and West Germany," in Carol Mueller and Mary Katzenstein (eds.), pp. 172–95.

1995. "Patriarchies and Feminisms: Two Women's Movements in Post-Unification Germany," *Social Politics* 2(1): 10–24.

Ferree, Myra Marx, and Elaine Hall. 1996. "Rethinking Stratification from a Feminist Perspective: Gender, Race and Class in Mainstream Textbooks," *American Sociological Review* 61(6): 929–50.

Ferree, Myra Marx, and Eva Maleck-Lewy. 2000. "Talking about Women and Wombs: Discourse about Abortion and Reproductive Rights in the GDR During and After the 'Wende,'" in Susan Gal and Gail Kligman (eds.), 2000b, pp. 72–117.

Ferree, Myra Marx, and Patricia Yancey Martin (eds.). 1995. *Feminist Organizations: Harvest of the New Women's Movement*, Philadelphia: Temple University Press.

Ferree, Myra Marx, and Frederick Miller. 1985. "Mobilization and Meaning: Toward an Integration of Social Psychological and Resource Perspectives on Social Movements," *Sociological Inquiry* 55(1): 38–61.

Ferree, Myra Marx, William A. Gamson, Jürgen Gerhards, and Dieter Rucht. 2002a. "Four Models of the Public Sphere in Modern Democracies," *Theory and Society* 31(3): 289–324.

2002b. *Shaping Abortion Discourse: Democracy and the Public Sphere in Germany and the United States*, New York: Cambridge University Press.

Finkel, Lucila. 1997. *El reparto del trabajo doméstico en la familia: la socialización de las diferencias de género* [The division of domestic work within the family: the socialization of gender differences], Madrid: Confederación Española de Asociaciones de Padres y Madres de Alumnos.

Fitzsimmons, Yvonne. 1991 "Women's Interest Representation in the Republic Ireland: the Council for the Status of Women," *Irish Political Studies* 6: 6–49.

Fletcher, Ruth. 2000. "National Crisis, Supra-National Opportunity: The Irish Construction of Abortion as European Service," *Reproductive Health Matters* 8(16): 35–44.

2001. "Postcolonial Fragments: Representations of Abortion in Irish Law and Politics," *Journal of Law and Society* 28: 568–89.

Flexner, Eleanor. 1975. *Century of Struggle: The Women's Rights Movement in the United States*, Cambridge, MA: The Belknap Press of Harvard University Press.

Florín, Christina. 1999. "Skaten som befriar: hemmafruar mot yrkeskvinnor in 1960-talets särbesattningsdebatt," [The tax shall make you free: the housewife versus the working woman] in Christina Florín, Lena Sommerstad, and Ulla Wikander (eds.), *Kvinnor mot kvinnor: Om systerskapests svärigheter* [Women against women: on the difficulties of sisterhood], Stockholm: Nordstets, pp. 106–35.

Florín, Christina, and Bengt Nilsson. 1999. "Something in the Nature of a Bloodless Revolution . . . How New Gender Relations Became State Policy in Sweden in the 60s and 70s," in Rolf Torstendahl (ed.), *State Policy and Gender System in the Two German States and Sweden 1945–1989*, Uppsala: Opuscula Historica Uppsaliensis no. 22, pp. 11–78.

Fodor, Éva. 1997. "Power, Patriarchy, and Paternalism: An Examination of the Gendered Nature of State Socialist Authority," PhD dissertation, University of California, Los Angeles.

Foner, Philip S., and Sally M. Miller. 1982. *Kate Richards O'Hare: Selected Writings and Speeches*, Baton Rouge: Louisiana State University Press.

Foucault, Michel. 1979. "Governmentality," *Ideology & Consciousness* 6(5): 5–21.

Franklin, Jimmie Lewis. 1982. *Journey Toward Hope: A History of Blacks in Oklahoma*, Norman: University of Oklahoma Press.

Fraser, Nancy. 1995. "From Redistribution to Recognition? Dilemmas of Justice in a 'Postsocialist' Age," *New Left Review* 212: 68–93.

1997a. *Justice Interruptus: Critical Reflections on the "Postsocialist" Condition*, London and New York: Routledge.

1997b. "A Rejoinder to Iris Young," *New Left Review* 223: 126–29.

1998. "Heterosexism, Misrecognition, and Capitalism: A Response to Judith Butler," *New Left Review* 228: 140–49.

2003. "Social Justice in the Age of Identity Politics: Redistribution, Recognition, and Participation," in Nancy Fraser and Axel Honneth 2003.

Fraser, Nancy, and Axel Honneth 2003. *Redistribution or Recognition? A Philosophical Exchange*, London: Verso.

Freud, Sigmund. 1950. *Totem and Taboo*, New York and London: W. W. Norton.

Funk, Nanette, and Magda Mueller (eds.). 1993. *Gender Politics and Postcommunism: Reflections from Eastern Europe and the Former Soviet Union*, New York: Routledge.

Gaines, Kevin K. 1996. *Uplifting the Race: Black Leadership, Politics, and Culture in the Twentieth Century*, Chapel Hill, NC: University of North Carolina Press.

Gal, Susan. 1991. "Bartók's Funeral: Representations of Europe in Hungarian Political Rhetoric," *American Ethnologist* 18: 440–58.

1997. "Feminism and Civil Society," in Joan Scott, Cora Kaplan and Debra Keates (eds.), pp. 30–45.

Gal, Susan and Judith T. Irvine. 1995. "The Boundaries of Languages and Disciplines: How Ideologies Construct Difference," *Social Research* 62(4): 967–1001.

Gal, Susan, and Gail Kligman. 2000a. *The Politics of Gender After Socialism: A Comparative-Historical Essay*, Princeton University Press.

(eds.). 2000b. *Reproducing Gender: Politics, Publics, and Everyday Life After Socialism*, Princeton University Press.

Galligan, Yvonne. 1998. *Women and the Politics in Contemporary Ireland: From the Margins to the Mainstream*, London: Pinter.

Galligan, Yvonne, Ellis Ward, and Rick Wilford (eds.). 1999. *Contesting Politics: Women in Ireland, North and South*, Boulder, CO: Westview Press.

Galvão, Jane. 1985. "AIDS: a 'doença' e os 'doentes'" [AIDS: the "sickness" and the "sick"], *Comunicações do ISER* 4: 42–47.

1992. "AIDS e imprensa: um estudo de antropologia social" [AIDS and the press: a social anthropology study], MA Thesis, Programa de Pos-Graduação em Antropologia Social do Museu Nacional da Universidade Federal do Rio de Janeiro.

1997. "As respostas das organizações não-governamentais brasileiras frente à epidemia de HIV/AIDS" [The response of Brazilian non-governmental organizations to the HIV/AIDS epidemic] in Richard Parker (ed.), *Políticas, instituições e AIDS: enfrentando a epidemia no Brasil* [Politics, institutions and AIDS: confronting the epidemic in Brazil], Rio de Janeiro: Jorge Zahar Editor/ABIA, pp. 69–108.

Gamson, William A. 1992a. "The Social Psychology of Collective Action," in Aldon D. Morris and Carol Mueller (eds.), pp. 53–76.

1992b. *Talking Politics*, New York: Cambridge University Press.

1995. "Constructing Social Protest," in Hank Johnston and Bert Klandermans (eds.), pp. 85–106.

Gamson, William A., and David Meyer. 1996. "Framing Political Opportunity," in Doug McAdam, John D. McCarthy, and Mayer N. Zald (eds.), pp. 275–90.

Gamson, William A., Bruce Fireman, and Steven Rytina. 1982. *Encounters with Unjust Authority*, Homewood, IL: Dorsey Press.

Gardiner, Frances. 1999. "The Impact of EU Equality Legislation on Women," in Yvonne Galligan, Ellis Ward, and Rick Wilford (eds.), pp. 38–54.

Gelb, Joyce. 1989. *Feminism and Politics: A Comparative Perspective*, Berkeley, CA: University of California Press.

Glatz, Ferenc, and István Kemény (eds.). 1999. *A cigányok Magyarországon* [Gypsies in Hungary], Budapest: MTA.

Goble, Danney. 1980. *Progressive Oklahoma: The Making of a New Kind of State*, Norman, OK: University of Oklahoma Press.

Goffman, Ervin. 1974. *Frame Analysis: An Essay on the Organization of Experience*, Boston, MA: Northeastern University Press.

Gordon, Ann D. (ed.) with Betty Collier-Thomas, John H. Bracey, Arlene Voski Avakian, and Joyce Avrech Berkman. 1997. *African American Women and the Vote 1837–1965*, Amherst, MA: University of Massachusetts Press.

Gordon, Linda. 1994. *Pitied But Not Entitled: Single Mothers and the History of Welfare*, New York: Free Press.

Graham, Sara Hunter. 1996. *Woman Suffrage and the New Democracy*, New Haven, CT: Yale University Press.

Green, James N. 1999. *Beyond Carnival: Homosexuality in Twentieth Century Brazil*, University of Chicago Press.

Green, James R. 1978. *Grass-Roots Socialism: Radical Movements in the Southwest 1895–1943*, Baton Rouge: Louisiana State University Press.

Greskovits, Béla. 1998. *The Political Economy of Protest and Patience*, Budapest: Central European University Press.

Grewal, Inderpal, and Caren Kaplan (eds.). 1994. *Scattered Hegemonies: Post-modernity and Transnational Feminist Practices*, Minneapolis, MN: University of Minnesota Press.

Grieve, Norma, and Ailsa Burns (eds.). 1994. *Australian Women Contemporary Feminist Thought*, Melbourne: Oxford University Press.

Grimshaw, Patricia. 2002. "Federation as a Turning Point in Australian History," *Australian Historical Studies Special Issue Challenging Histories* 118: 25–41.

Grimshaw, Patricia, Marilyn Lake, Ann McGrath, and Marian Quartly. 1994. *Creating a Nation*, Melbourne: Penguin.

Grunberg, Laura. 2000. "Women's NGOs in Romania," in Susan Gal and Gail Kligman (eds.), 2000b, pp. 307–36.

Guidry, John A., Michael D. Kennedy, and Mayer N. Zald (eds.). 2000. *Globalizations and Social Movements: Culture, Power and the Trans-National Public Sphere*, Ann Arbor: University of Michigan Press.

Guillén, Ana M. 1999. "Improving Efficiency and Containing Costs: Health Care Reform in Southern Europe," *European University Institute Working Papers* 99/16. Florence: European University Institute.

Guinier, Lani. 1994. *The Tyranny of the Majority*, New York: The Free Press.

Gustafsson, Gunnel, Maud Eduards, and Malin M. Rönnblom (eds.). 1997. *Towards a New Democratic Order? Women's Organizing in Sweden in the 1990s*, Stockholm: Publica.

Gutmann, Amy (ed.). 1994. *Multiculturalism: Examining the Politics of Recognition*, Princeton University Press.

Habermas, Jürgen. 1994. "Struggles for Recognition in the Democratic Constitutional State," in Amy Gutmann (ed.), pp. 107–48.

Halley, Janet. 1999. "Culture Constrains," in Susan Moller Okin (ed.), pp. 100–04.

Haraszti, Miklós. 1987. *The Velvet Prison: Artists Under State Socialism*, Princeton University Press.

Harsch, Donna. 1997. "Society, the State and Abortion in East Germany, 1950–1972," *American Historical Review* 102(1): 53–85.

Havasi, Éva. 2002. *Szegénység és társadalmi kirekesztettség a mai Magyarországon* [Poverty and social exclusion in contemporary Hungary], Budapest: KSH.

Havelková, Hana. 1997. "Transitory and Persistent Differences: Feminism East and West," in Joan Scott, Cora Kaplan, and Debra Keates (eds.), pp. 56–64.

Heitlinger, Alena (ed.). 1999. *Emigré Feminisms: Transnational Perspectives*, University of Toronto Press.

Helfferich, Barbara, and Felix Kolb. 2001. "Multi-level Action Coordination in European Contentious Politics: The Case of the European Women's Lobby," in Doug Imig and Sydney Tarrow (eds.), *Contentious Politics: Protest and Politics in an Emerging Polity*, Lanham, MD: Rowan and Littlefield, pp. 143–62.

Henriques, Julian, Wendy Hollway, Cathy Unwin, Couze Venn, and Valerie Walkerdine. 1998. *Changing the Subject: Psychology, Social Regulation and Subjectivity*, second edition, London: Routledge.

Hernes, Helga. 1988. "The Dimensions of Citizenship in the Advanced Welfare State," in *The Study of Power and Democracy*, English Series Report 15, Stockholm: Maktutredningen.

Hertha, 1938. "Kvinnans Ratta Plats ar i Folkhemmet!" vol. 4: 98.

Hesse, Barnor (ed.). 2001. *Un/settled Multiculturalisms: Diasporas, Entanglements, Transruptions*, London: Zed Books.

Higginbotham, Evelyn Brooks. 1993. *Righteous Discontent: The Women's Movement in the Black Baptist Church 1880–1920*, Cambridge, MA: Harvard University Press.

Hinnfors, Jonas. 1992. *Familjepolitik: samhällsförandringar och partistrategier, 1960–1990* [Family politics: societal change and political party strategies], Stockholm: Almqvist & Wiksell.

Hirdman, Yvonne. 1987. *The Swedish Welfare State and the Gender System: A Theoretical and Empirical Sketch*, The Study of Power and Democracy, English Series Report 9, Stockholm: Maktutredningen.

  1989. *Att lägga livet till rätta. Studier I sventsk folkhems politik* [Put your life in order: studies in the politics of the Swedish people's house], Stockholm: Norstedts.

  1998. *Med Kluven Tunga: LO and Genusordningen* [Forked tongue: LO and the gender order], Stockholm: Atlas.

Hobsbawm, Eric. 1993. *Nations and Nationalism since 1780*, New York: Cambridge University Press.

Hobsbawm, Eric, and Terence Ranger (eds.). 1983. *The Invention of Tradition*, New York: Cambridge University Press.

Hobson, Barbara. 1993. "Feminist Strategies and Gendered Discourses in Welfare States: Married Women's Right to Work in the United States and Sweden during the 1930s," in Seth Koven and Sonya Michel (eds.), pp. 396–430.

  1994. "Solo Mothers, Social Policy Regimes and the Logics of Gender," in Diane Sainsbury (ed.), *Gendering Welfare States*, London: Sage, pp. 170–87.

  1999. "Women's Collective Agency, Power Resources and the Framing of Citizenship Rights," in Michael Hanagan and Charles Tilly (eds.), *Extending Citizenship, Reconfiguring States*, Lanham, MD: Rowan and Littlefield, pp. 149–78.

  2000a. "Economic Citizenship: Reflections through the European Policy Mirror," in Barbara Hobson (ed.), *Crossing Borders: Gender and Citizenship in Transition*, Basingstoke: Macmillan, pp. 84–116.

  (ed.). 2000b. *Gender and Citizenship in Transition*, London: Routledge.

Hobson, Barbara, and Marika Lindholm. 1997. "Collective Identities, Women's Power Resources, and the Making of Welfare States," *Theory and Society* 26: 475–508.

Hoggett, Paul. 2000. *Emotional Life and the Politics of Welfare*, London: Macmillan.

Honneth, Axel. 1992. "Integrity and Disrespect: Principles of a Conception of Morality Based on the Theory of Recognition," *Political Theory* 20(2): 187–201.

  1995a. *The Fragmented World of the Social: Essays in Social and Political Philosophy*, Albany, NY: State University of New York Press.

  1995b. *The Struggle for Recognition: The Moral Grammar of Social Conflicts*, Cambridge, UK: Polity Press.

Horváth, Ágota. 1995. "Törvény és anarchia avagy törvényes anarchia: A Szociális Törvényről és az önkormányzati szociális rendeletekről" [Law and anarchy or lawful anarchy: on the Welfare Act and the local-level welfare regulations], in Edit Landau (ed.), *Az államtalanítás dilemmái: Szociálpolitikai kényszerek és választások* [Dilemmas of "state desertion": constraints and choices in social policy], Budapest: ATA, pp. 240–61.

Horváth, Ágota, Edit Landau, and Júlia Szalai (eds.). 2000. *Cigánynak születni* [Born Gypsy], Budapest: Új Mandátum–ATA.

Hoskyns, Catherine. 1991. "The European Women's Lobby," *Feminist Review* 38: 67–70.

  1996. *Integrating Gender: Women, Law, and Politics in the European Community*, London: Verso.

Hubbard, Phil. 2001. "Sex Zones: Intimacy, Citizenship and Public Space," *Sexualities* 4(1): 51–71.

Huber, Evelyn, and John Stephens. 1998. "The Internationalization and the Social Democratic Model: Crisis and Future Prospects," *Comparative Political Studies* 31(3): 353–97.

Huggins, Jackie. 1994. "A Contemporary View of Aboriginal Women's Relationship to the White Women's Movement," in Norma Grieve and Ailsa Burns (eds.), pp. 70–79.

Hunt, Scott A., Robert D. Benford, and David A. Snow. 1994. "Identity Fields: Framing Processes and the Social Construction of Movement Identities," in Enrique Larana, Hank Johnston, and Joseph Gusfield (eds.), pp. 185–206.

HWS. *The History of Woman Suffrage*. Vols. 1 to 3, 1881, 1889, edited by Elizabeth Cady Stanton, Susan B. Anthony, and Matild Joslyn Gage, Rochester. Vol. 4, 1902, edited by Susan B. Anthony and Ida Husted Harper, Rochester: Susan B. Anthony. Vols. 5 and 6, 1922, edited by Ida Husted Harper, New York: NAWSA.

Irvine, Judith T. 1996. "Shadow Conversations," in Michael Silverstein and Greg Urban (eds.), pp. 131–59.

Irvine, Judith T. and Susan Gal. 2000. "Language Ideology and Linguistic Differentiation," in Paul Kroskrity (ed.), *Regimes of Language: Ideologies, Polities, and Identities*, Santa Fe, NM: School of American Research, pp. 35–84.

Jackson, Nuala. 1993. "Family Law: Economic Security," in Alpha Connelly (ed.), pp. 109–29.

James, Louise Boyd. 1978–79. "The Woman Suffrage Issue in the Oklahoma Constitutional Convention," *Chronicles of Oklahoma* 56(4): 379–92.

Janky, Béla. 1999. "A cigány nők helyzete" [The situation of Gypsy women], in Tiborné Pongrácz and István György Tóth (eds.), *Szerepváltozások: Jelentés a nők és férfiak helyzetéről 1999* [Changing roles: report on the situation of men and women – 1999], Budapest: TÁRKI – SZCSM, pp. 217–39.

Jaquette, Jane S. (ed.). 1994. *The Women's Movement in Latin America: Participation and Democracy*, second edition, Boulder, CO: Westview.

Jaquette, Jane S., and Sharon L. Wolchik (eds.). 1998. *Women and Democracy: Latin America and Central and Eastern Europe*, Baltimore, MD: Johns Hopkins University Press.

Jayawardena, Kumari. 1986. *Feminism and Nationalism in the Third World*, London: Zed Books.

Johnston, Hank, and Bert Klandermans (eds.). 1995. *Social Movements and Culture*, Minneapolis, MN: University of Minnesota Press.

Kaplan, Gisela. 1992. *Contemporary Western European Feminism*, New York University Press.

Kaplan, Temma. 1982. "Female Consciousness and Collective Action: The Case of Barcelona, 1910–1918," in Nannerl O. Keohane, Michelle Z. Rosaldo, and Barbara C. Gelpi (eds.), *Feminist Theory: A Critique to Ideology*, Brighton: Harvester Press, pp. 55–76.

1997. *Crazy for Democracy: Women in Grassroots Movements*, New York and London: Routledge.

1999. "Luchar por la democracia: formas de organización de las mujeres entre los años cincuenta y los años setenta" [Fighting for democracy: forms of women's organizing between the 1950s and 1960s], in Anna Aguado (ed.), *Mujeres, regulación de conflictos sociales y cultura de la paz* [Women, social conflict regulation, and peace culture], Valencia: Universitat de València, pp. 89–107.

Keck, Margaret, and Katherine Sikkink. 1998. *Activists Beyond Borders: Advocacy Networks in International Politics*, Ithaca, NY: Cornell University Press.

Key, Ellen. 1912. *The Woman Movement*, New York: Putnam.

Kingston, Beverley. 1975. *My Wife, My Daughter and Poor Mary Ann*, Sydney: Nelson.

Kis, János. 1997. "Roma jogok – magyar érdekek" [Roma rights – Hungarian interests], *Népszabadság 55*, December 31: 20–23.

Klandermans, Bert. 1984. "Mobilization and Participation: Social-Psychological Expansions of Resource Mobilization Theory," *American Sociological Review* 49: 583–600.

1999. "'The Ghetto Is Over, Darling': Emerging Gay Communities and Gender and Sexual Politics in Contemporary Brazil," *Culture, Health, and Sexuality* 1(3): 239–60.

Klein, Charles H. 1994. "Para onde caminham as NGOs na luta contra a AIDS" [What is the future of NGOs in the fight against AIDS?], *HIVeraz* 2: 7–8.

1996. "AIDS, Activism and the Social Imagination in Brazil," PhD Dissertation, Department of Anthropology, University of Michigan.

1998. "From One 'Battle' to Another: The Making of a *Travesti* Political Movement in a Brazilian City," *Sexualities* 1: 329–43.

Kligman, Gail. 1998. *The Politics of Duplicity: Controlling Reproduction in Ceausescu's Romania*, Berkeley, CA: University of California Press.

Knokke, Woukko. 1995. "Migrant and Ethnic Minority Women: The Effects of Gender-Neutral Legislation in the European Community," *Social Politics* 2(2): 225–38.

Kochanowicz, Jacek. 2000. "Leviathan Exhausted: Ideas on the State of the Post-communist Transformation," *ECE/ECE* 27(1): 1–19.

Korpi, Walter. 2000. "The Faces of Inequality: Gender, Class, and Patterns of Inequalities in Different Types of Welfare States," *Social Politics* 7(2): 127–91.

Korpi, Walter, and Joakim Palme. 1998. "The Paradox of Redistribution and Strategies of Equality and Poverty in Western Countries," *American Sociological Review* 63: 661–87.

Kovács, Mária. 1994. "A magyar feminizmus korszakfordulója" [A turning point of Hungarian feminism], *Cafe Babel* 14(1–2): 179–84.

Koven, Seth, and Sonya Michel. 1990. "Womanly Duties: Maternalist Politics and the Origins of Welfare States in France, Germany, Great Britain, and the United States, 1880–1920," *The American Historical Review* 4: 1076–108.

(eds.). 1993. *Mothers of a New World: Maternalist Politics and the Origins of Welfare States*, New York: Routledge.

Kraditor, Aileen S. 1981 [1965]. *The Ideas of the Woman Suffrage Movement, 1890–1920*, New York: W. W. Norton.

Kuczi, Tibor, and Ágnes Vajda. 1992. "Privatizáció és második gazdaság" [Privatization and the second economy], *Holmi* 3(1): 38–52.

Kulick, Don. 1998. *Travesti: Sex, Gender and Culture Among Brazilian Transgendered Prostitutes*, University of Chicago Press.

Kyle, Gunhild. 1979. *Gästerbetskerka in mannsamhället* [Female guestworkers in a male society], Stockholm: Liber.

Kymlicka, Will. 1995. *Multicultural Citizenship: A Liberal Theory of Minority Rights*, Oxford University Press.

1999. "Liberal Complacencies," in Susan Moller Okin (ed.), pp. 31–34.

Lake, Marilyn. 1994a. "Between Old World 'Barbarism' and Stone Age 'Primitivism': The Double Difference of the White Australian Feminist," in Norma Grieve and Ailsa Burns (eds.), pp. 81–101.

1994b. "Personality, Individuality, Nationality: Feminist Conceptions of Citizenship, 1902–1940," *Australian Feminist Studies* 19: 25–38.

2000. "The Ambiguities for Feminists of National Belonging: Race and Gender in the Imagined Australian Community," in Ida Blom, Karen Hagemann, and Catherine Hall (eds.), *Gendered Nations, Nationalisms and Gender Order in the Long Nineteenth Century*, London: Berg, pp. 159–76.

2001. "Citizenship as Non-Discrimination: Acceptance or Assimilationism? Political Logic and Emotional Investment in Campaigns for Aboriginal Rights in Australia, 1940 to 1970," *Gender, Citizenships and Subjectivities* 13(3): 566–92.

Laky, Teréz. 1995. "A magángazdaság kialakulása és a foglalkoztatottság" [Employment and the emerging private economy], *Közgazdasági Szemle* 43(7–8): 28–44.

1999. *A munkaerõpiac keresletét és kínálatát alakító folyamatok* [Processes shaping supply and demand on the labor market], Budapest: Munkaügyi Kutatóintézet.

Lancaster, Roger. 1998. "Transgenderism in Latin America: Some Critical Introductory Remarks on Identities and Practices," *Sexualities* 1(3): 261–74.

Landim, Leilah (ed.). 1988. *Sem fins lucrativos: as organizações não-governamentais no Brasil* [Not for profit: non-governmental organizations in Brazil], Rio de Janeiro: ISER.

(ed.). 1993. *Para além do mercado e do estado? Filantropia e cidadania no Brasil* [Beyond the market and the state: philanthropy and citizenship in Brazil], Rio de Janeiro: ISER/Série Textos de Pesquisa.

Lang, Sabine. 1997. "The NGOization of Feminism," in Joan Scott, Cora Kaplan, and Debra Keates (eds.), pp. 101–20.

Larana, Enrique, Hank Johnston, and Joseph Gusfield (eds.). 1994. *New Social Movements: From Ideology to Identity*, Philadelphia, PA: Temple University Press.

Larvie, Sean Patrick. 1998. "Managing Desire: Sexuality, Citizenship and AIDS in Contemporary Brazil," PhD Dissertation, University of Chicago.

1999. "Queerness and the Specter of Brazilian National Ruin," *GLQ* 5(4): 527–58.

Lee, Benjamin. 2001. "Circulating the People," in Susan Gal and Kathryn Woolard (eds.), *Languages and Publics: The Making of Authority*, Manchester: St. Jerome's Press, pp. 164–81.

Lefevere, André (ed.). 1992. *Translation, History, Culture: A Sourcebook*, New York: Routledge.

Lengyel, László. 1998. "Levél a sajtószabadságról" [Letter about the freedom of the press], in Mária Vásárhelyi and Gábor Halmai (eds.), *A nyilvánosság rendszerváltása* [The transition of the public sphere], Budapest: Új Mandátum, pp. 35–40.

Lenihan, Brian. 1964. *Dáil Debates*, December 2, 1937 (213): 336.

Lentin, Ronit. 1998. "'Irishness' in the 1937 Constitution and Citizenship: A Gender and Ethnicity View," *Irish Journal of Sociology* 8: 5–24.

Lessenich, Stephan. 2000. "The Southern Image Reversed: The Dynamics of 'Transition Dynamics' in East Central Europe," *ECE/ECE* 27(1): 21–35.

Levy, Jacob T. 2000. *The Multiculturalism of Fear*, Oxford University Press.

Lewis, Dave. 2002. "Ethnic Mobilisation: The Case of Indigenous Political Movements," in Kristina Karppi and Johan Eriksson (eds.), *Conflict and Cooperation in the North*, Umeå, Sweden: Universitetsförlaget.

Lewis, Jane. 1992. "Gender and the Development of Welfare Regimes," *Journal of European Social Policy* 2(3): 159–73.

Liera, Arnlaug. 1998. "Caring as a Social Right: Cash for Childcare and Daddy Leave," *Social Politics* 5(3): 362–78.

Lipsky, Michael. 1970. *Protest in City Politics*, Chicago, IL: Rand-McNally.

Lister, Ruth. 1997. *Citizenship: Feminist Perspectives*, London: Macmillan.

Littlefield, Daniel F., Jr. 1978. *The Cherokee Freedmen: From Emancipation to American Citizenship*, Westport, CT: Greenwood Press.

Lofland, John. 1995. "Charting Degrees of Movement Culture: Tasks of the Cultural Cartographer," in Hank Johnston and Bert Klandermans (eds.), pp. 188–216.

Luker, Kirsten. 1984. *Abortion and the Politics of Motherhood*, Berkeley, CA: University of California Press.

Lutz, Helma. 1996. "The Limits of European-ness: Immigrant Women in Fortress Europe," paper presented at the Conference on Women and Citizenship, University of Greenwich, London, July 16–19.

Lutz, Helma, Ann Phoenix, and Nira Yuval-Davis (eds.). 1995. *Crossfires: Nationalism, Racism and Gender in Europe*, London: Pluto Press.

Lynch, Kathleen. 1996. "Appendix to Constitutional Review Group," *Report of the Constitutional Review Group*, Dublin: Stationery Office.

MacRae, Edward. 1990. *A construação da igualdade: identidade sexual e política no Brasil da "Abertura"* [Constructing equality: sexual identity and politics in Brazil during the "Transition" to democracy], Campinas, Brazil: Editora de UNICAMP.

1992. "Homosexual Identities in Transitional Brazilian Politics," in Arturo Escobar and Sonia Alvarez (eds.), *The Making of Social Movements in Latin America*, Boulder, CO: Westview Press, pp. 185–203.

Mahon, Evelyn. 1995. "From Democracy to Femocracy: The Women's Movement in the Republic of Ireland," in Patrick Clancy, Sheelagh Drudy, Kathleen Lynch, and Liam O'Dowd (eds.), *Sociological Perspectives*, Dublin: The Irish Sociological Association, pp. 675–704.

Mahon, Rianne. 2002. "Sweden's LO: Learning to Embrace the Differences Within?" in Fiona Colgan and Sue Ledwith (eds.), *Gender, Diversity and Trade Unions: International Perspectives*, London: Routledge, pp. 48–72.

Maleck-Lewy, Eva. 1995. "Between Self-Determination and State Supervision: Women and the Abortion Law in Post-Unification Germany," *Social Politics* 2(1): 62–75.

Manchin, Róbert, and Iván Szelényi. 1986. "Szociálpolitika az államszocializmusban. Piac, redisztribúció és társadalmi egyenlőtlenségek a kelet-európai társadalmakban" [Social policy under state socialism: market, redistribution, and social inequalities in the societies of Eastern Europe], *Medvetánc* 4(2–3): 69–113.

Marilley, Suzanne M. 1996. *Woman Suffrage and the Origins of Liberal Feminism in the United States, 1820–1920*, Cambridge, MA: Harvard University Press.

Marklund, Staffan. 1992. "The Decomposition of Social Policy in Sweden," *Scandinavian Journal of Social Welfare* 1: 2–11.

Marody, Mira. 1993. "Why I am not a Feminist: Some Remarks on the Problem of Gender Identity in the United States and Poland," *Social Research* 60(4): 853–64.

Marshall, Thomas H. 1950. *Citizenship and Social Class and Other Essays*, Cambridge University Press.

Martín, Manuel. 1996. *Informe juventud en España 1996: avance de resultados (Septiembre 1996)* [Report on youth in Spain 1996: preliminary results (September 1996)], Madrid: Instituto de la Juventud.

Maxwell, Amos. 1950. "The Sequoyah Convention," *Chronicles of Oklahoma* 28: 161–92, 299–340.

McAdam, Doug. 1982. *Political Process and the Development of Black Insurgency, 1930–1970*, University of Chicago Press.

McAdam, Doug, John D. McCarthy, and Mayer N. Zald (eds.). 1996. *Comparative Perspectives on Social Movements: Political Opportunities, Mobilizing Structures and Cultural Framings*, Cambridge University Press.

McAdam, Doug, Sidney Tarrow, and Charles Tilly. 2001. *Dynamics of Contention*, Cambridge University Press.

McCarthy, John D. and Mayer N. Zald. 1973. *The Trends of Social Movements in America: Professionalization and Resource Mobilization*, Morristown, NJ: General Learning Press.

1977. "Resource Mobilization and Social Movements: A Partial Theory," *American Journal of Sociology* 82(6): 1212–41.

McLaughlin, Eithne, and Nicole Yeates. 1999. "The Biopolitics of Welfare in Ireland," *Irish Journal of Feminist Studies* 3(2): 49–66.

McLoughlin, William G. 1993. *After the Trail of Tears: The Cherokees' Struggle for Sovereignty 1839–1880*, Chapel Hill, NC: University of North Carolina Press.

McPhail, Clark. 1991. *The Myth of the Madding Crowd*, New York: Aldine de Gruyter.

Meaney, Geraldine. 1991. *Sex and Nation: Women in Irish Culture and Politics*, Dublin: Attic Press.

Melucci, Alberto. 1980. "The New Social Movements: A Theoretical Approach," *Social Science Information* 19(2): 199–226.

1985. "The Symbolic Challenge of Contemporary Movements," *Social Research* 52(4): 789–816.

1989. *Nomads of the Present*, London: Hutchinson Radius.

1994. "A Strange Kind of Newness: What's 'New' in New Social Movements," in Enrique Larana, Hank Johnston, and Joseph R. Gusfield (eds.), pp. 101–30.

1995. "The Process of Collective Identity," in Hank Johnston and Bert Klandermans (eds.), pp. 41–63.

1996. *Challenging Codes: Collective Action in the Information Age*, Cambridge University Press.

Meyer, David S. 2002. "Opportunties and Identities: Bridge-Building in the Study of Social Movements," in David S. Meyer, Nancy Whittier, and Belinda Robnett (eds.), pp. 3–24.

Meyer, David S., Nancy Whittier, and Belinda Robnett (eds.). 2002. *Social Movements, Identity, Culture and the State*, Oxford University Press.

Mihesuah, Devon A. 1993. *Cultivating the Rosebuds: The Education of Women at the Cherokee Female Seminary 1851–1909*, Urbana, IL: University of Illinois Press.

Miles, Angela R. 1996. *Integrative Feminisms: Building Global Visions, 1960s–1990s*, New York and London: Routledge.

Miner, H. Craig. 1976. *The Corporation and the Indian: Tribal Sovereignty and Industrial Civilization in Indian Territory, 1865–1907*, Columbia, MO: University of Missouri Press.

Mishra, Ramesh. 1984. *The Welfare State in Crisis: Social Thought and Social Change*, Brighton: Wheatsheaf Books.

Moghadam, Valentine. 1994. "Introduction: Women and Identity Politics in Theoretical and Comparative Perspective," in Valentine Moghadam (ed.), *Identity Politics and Women: Cultural Reassertions and Feminisms in International Perspective*, Boulder, CO: Westview Press, pp. 3–26.

Mohanty, Chandra, Ann Russo, and Lourdes Torres (eds.). 1991. *Third World Women and the Politics of Feminism*, Bloomington, IN: Indiana University Press.

Molnár, Emilia, and Kai Schafft. 2003. "A helyi roma/cigány kisebbségi önkormányzatok az ezredfordulón" [Local Roma/Gypsy minority governments at the turn of the millennium], *Szociológiai Szemle* 12(4): 00–00.

Molyneaux, Maxine. 1985. "Mobilization without Emancipation? Women's Interests, the State, and Revolution in Nicaragua," *Feminist Studies* 11(2): 227–54.

Montanari, Ingalill. 2000. "From Family Wage to Marriage Subsidy and Child Benefits: Controversy and Consensus in the Development of Family Support," *Journal of European Social Policy* 10(4): 307–33.

Moraes, Cláudia, and Sergio Carrara. 1985a. "Um mal de folhetim [Tabloid misfortune]," *Comunicações do ISER* 4: 20–27.
    1985b. "Um vírus só não faz doença" [It takes more than a virus to make a disease], *Comunicações do ISER* 4: 5–19.

Moreton-Robinson, Aileen. 2000. *Talkin' Up to the White Woman: Indigenous Women and Feminism*, St Lucia, Australia: University of Queensland Press.

Morgan, Sally. 1987. *My Place*, Fremantle, Australia: Fremantle Arts Press.

Morris, Aldon, and Carol Mueller (eds.). 1992. *Frontiers in Social Movement Theory*, New Haven, CT: Yale University Press.

Morris, Jenny. 1999. *Pride Against Prejudice: A Personal Politics of Disability*, London: Women's Press.

Morris, Lynette. 1996. "Black Sistas: Indigenous Women and the Welfare," in Kathy Bail (ed.), pp. 198–210.

Mott, Luiz. 1989. *O sexo proibido: virgens, gays e escravos nas garras da inquisição* [Prohibited sex: Vigins, gays, and slaves in the grasp of the inquisition], Campinas, Brazil: Papirus.

Mršević, Zorica. 2000. "Belgrade's SOS Hotline for Women and Children Victims of Violence: A Report," in Susan Gal and Gail Kligman (eds.), 2000b, pp. 370–92.

Mueller, Carol, and Mary Katzenstein (eds.). 1987. *The Women's Movements of the United States and Western Europe*, Philadelphia, PA: Temple University Press.

Mulinari, Diane. 2001. "Race/Ethnicity in a Nordic Context: A Reflection from the Swedish Borderlands," in Anna Johansson (ed.), *Svensk genusforskning i världen* [Swedish gender research in the world], Gothenburg: Nationella Sekretariet för Genusforskning, pp. 6–27.

Muncy, Robyn. 1991. *Creating a Female Dominion in American Reform, 1890–1935*, New York: Oxford University Press.

Mushaben, Joyce. 1989. "Feminism in Four Acts: The Changing Political Identity of Women in the Federal Republic of Germany," in Peter Merkl (ed.), *The Federal Republic of Germany at Forty*, New York University Press, pp. 76–109.

Mushaben, Joyce, Sara Lennox, and Geoffrey Giles. 1997. "Women, Men and Unification: Gender Politics and the Abortion Struggle Since 1989," in Konrad Jarausch (ed.), *After Unity*, Providence, RI: Berghahn, pp. 137–72.

Myrdal, Alva. 1941. *Nation and Family*, London: Routledge, Kegan and Paul.

Myres, Sandra L. 1982. *Westering Women and the Frontier Experience 1800–1915*, Albuquerque, NM: University of New Mexico Press.

Nandy, A. 1983. *The Intimate Enemy: Loss and Recovery of Self Under Colonialism*, Delhi: Oxford University Press.

Narayan, Uma. 1998. "Essence of Culture and a Sense of History: A Feminist Critique of Cultural Essentialism," *Hypatia* 13(2): 86–106.

2000. "Undoing the 'Package Picture' of Cultures," *Signs* 25(4): 1083–86.

Nast, Heidi. 1998. "Unsexy Geographies," *Gender, Place and Culture* 5(2): 191–206.

NAWSA Proceedings. Selected years. *Proceedings of the Annual Convention of the National American Woman Suffrage Association*, Washington, DC and Warren, OH.

Neményi, Mária. 1994. "A kötelező heteroszexualitástól a kötelező feminizmusig" [From compulsory heterosexuality to compulsory feminism], *Cafe Babel* 14(1–2): 163–70.

O'Connor, Julia, Ann Shola Orloff, and Sheila Shaver. 1999. *States, Markets and Families: Gender, Liberalism and Social Policies in Australia, Canada, Great Britain and the US*, Cambridge University Press.

O'Connor, Pat. 1998. *Emerging Voices: Women in Contemporary Irish Society*, Dublin: Institute of Public Administration.

O'Hare, Kate Richards. 1906. "The Land of Graft," *International Socialist Review* 6(10): 598–604.

Okin, Susan Moller. 1998. "Feminism and Multiculturalism: Some Tensions," *Ethics* 108: 661–84.

2002. "'Mistresses of Their Own Destiny': Group Rights, Gender, and Realistic Rights of Exit," *Ethics* 112: 205–30.

Okin, Susan Moller (ed.) with respondents Joshua Cohen, Matthew Howard, and Martha C. Nussbaum. 1999. *Is Multiculturalism Bad for Women?* Princeton University Press.

Olson, Marcur. 1963. *The Logic of Collective Action*, Cambridge, MA: Harvard University Press.

O'Neill, William L. 1969. *Everyone Was Brave*, Chicago, IL: Quadrangle Books.

Orloff, Ann Shola. 1993. "Gender and the Social Rights of Citizenship: The Comparative Analysis of State Policies and Gender Relations," *American Sociological Review* 58(15): 303–28.

O'Shane, Pat. 1976. "Is There Any Relevance in the Women's Movement for Aboriginal Women?" *Refractory Girl* 12: 31–34.

Ostner, Ilona, and Jane Lewis. 1995. "Gender and the Evolution of European Social Policies," in Stephen Leibfried and Paul Pierson (eds.), *European Social Policy: Between Fragmentation and Integration*, Washington, DC: Brookings, pp. 159–93.

Palme, Olof. 1972. Speech at the Social Democratic Congress.

Pardo, Mary. 1995. "Doing It for the Kids: Mexican American Community Activists, Border Feminists?" in Myra Marx Ferree and Patricia Yancey Martin (eds.), pp. 356–71.

Parker, Richard. 1994. *A construção da solidariedade: AIDS, sexualidade e política no Brasil* [Constructing solidarity: AIDS, sexuality, and politics in Brazil], Rio de Janeiro: ABIA, IMS-UERJ, and Relume-Dumará.

    1996. "Empowerment, Community Mobilization, and Social Change in the Face of HIV/AIDS," *AIDS* 10 (suppl. 3): S27–S31.

    1999. *Beneath the Equator: Cultures of Desire, Male Homosexuality and Emerging Gay Communities in Brazil*, New York and London: Routledge.

Parker, Richard, and Veriano Terto, Jr. (eds.). 1998. *Entre homens: homossexualidade e AIDS no Brasil* [Among men: homosexuality and AIDS in Brazil], Rio de Janeiro: ABIA.

Peattie, Lisa, and Martin Rein. 1983. *Women's Claims: A Study in Political Economy*, New York: Oxford University Press.

Pedersen, Susan. 1993. *Family, Dependence, and the Origins of the Welfare State: Britain and France, 1914–1945*, New York: Cambridge University Press.

Perdue, Theda. 1980. *Nations Remembered: An Oral History of the Five Civilized Tribes 1865–1907*, Westport, CT: Greenwood Press.

    1998. *Cherokee Women: Gender and Cultural Change, 1700–1835*, Lincoln, NB: University of Nebraska Press.

Phillips, Anne. 1991. *Engendering Democracy*, University Park, PA: Pennsylvania State University Press.

    1995. *The Politics of Presence*, Oxford University Press.

    1997. "From Inequality to Difference: A Severe Case of Displacement?" *New Left Review* 224 (July): 143–53.

Phizacklea, Annie, and Carol Wolkowitz. 1995. *Homeworking Women*, London: Sage.

Pierson, Paul. 1994. *Dismantling the Welfare State,* Cambridge University Press.

Pillinger, Jane. 1997. *Partnership and the Risk for Peace*, The EU Special Report Programme for Peace and Reconciliation, Report of the Northern Ireland European Parliament Hearing, Northern Ireland: UNISON.

Piven, Francis Fox, and Richard A. Cloward. 1971. *Regulating the Poor*, New York: Vintage.

Pizzorno, Alessandro. 1978. "Political Exchange and Collective Identity in Industrial Conflict," in Colin Crouch and Alessandro Pizzorno (eds.), *The Resurgence of Class Conflict in Western Europe*, New York: Holmes & Meier, pp. 277–98.

Protokoll [Record of Proceedings] 1994/95: 9, 10, 43. Riksarkivet [Swedish National Archives].

Reese, Linda Williams. 1997. *Women of Oklahoma, 1890–1920*, Norman, OK: University of Oklahoma Press.

Reid, Madeline. 1990. *The Impact of Community Law on the Irish Constitution*, Dublin: Irish Centre for European Law.

Riemer, Jeremiah. 1993. "Reproduction and Reunification: The Politics of Abortion in United Germany," in Michael G. Huelshoff, Andrei Markovits, and

Simon Reich (eds.), *From Bundesrepublik to Deutschland: German Politics After Unification*, Ann Arbor, MI: University of Michigan Press, pp. 167–88.

Riley, Glenda. 1984. *Women and Indians on the Frontier, 1825–1915*, Albuquerque, NM: University of New Mexico Press.

Rito, Lucia. 1998. *Muito prazer, Roberta Close* [My pleasure, Roberta Close], Rio de Janeiro: Editora Rosa dos Tempos.

Róna-Tas, Ákos. 1997. *The Great Surprise of the Small Transformation: The Demise of Communism and the Rise of the Private Sector in Hungary*, Ann Arbor, MI: University of Michigan Press.

Rosenberg, Tina. 2000. *Queerfeministisk agenda*, Stockholm: Atlas.

Ruggie, Mary. 1984. *The State and the Working Woman: A Comparative Study of Britain and Sweden*, Princeton University Press.

Rupp, Leila, and Verta Taylor. 1999. "Forging Feminist Identity in an International Movement," *Signs* 2(2): 363–86.

Ryan, Edna, and Anne Conlon. 1975. *Gentle Invaders: Australian Women at Work*, Ringwood, Australia: Penguin.

Said, Edward. 1983. "Traveling Theory," in Edward Said (ed.), *The World, the Text, and the Critic*, Cambridge, MA: Harvard University Press, pp. 224–47.

Sainsbury, Diane. 1996. *Gender, Equality and Welfare States*, Cambridge University Press.

Sampson, Steven. 1996. "The Social Life of Projects: Importing Civil Society to Albania," in David Kideckel (ed.), *Civil Society: Challenging Western Models*, Boulder, CO: Westview Press, pp. 159–78.

Sauer, Birgit. 1995. "'Doing Gender': Das Parlament als Ort der Geschlechterkonstruktion" [Doing gender: Parliament as a locus for the construction of gender], in Andreas Dörner and Ludgera Vogt (eds.), *Sprache des Parlaments und Semiotik der Demokratie* [Parliamentary language and the semiotics of democracy], Berlin: Walter de Gruyter, pp. 172–99.

Scales, James R., and Danney Goble. 1982. *Oklahoma Politics: A History*, Norman, OK: University of Oklahoma Press.

Scheper-Hughes, Nancy. 1992. *Death Without Weeping: The Violence of Everyday Life in Brazil*, Berkeley and Los Angeles: University of California Press.

Scherer-Warren, Ilse, and Paulo J. Krischke (eds.). 1987. *Uma revolução no cotidiano: os novos movimentos sociais na América Latina* [A revolution in everyday life: new social movements in Latin America], São Paulo: Editora Brasiliense.

Schiffrin, André. 2000. *The Business of Books*, London: Verso.

Schirmer, Jennifer. 1993. "The Seeking of Truth and the Gendering of Consciousness: The CoMadres of El Salvador and the CONAVIGUA Widows of Guatemala," in Sarah A. Radcliffe and Sallie Westwood (eds.), *'Viva': Women and Popular Protest in Latin America*, London and New York: Routledge, pp. 30–64.

Schlytter, Astrid. 1993. *Om rättvisa i barnsomsorgen* [Justice in child welfare], Stockholm: Nalkas Boken Förlag.

Schrems, Suzanne H. 2001. *Across the Political Spectrum: Oklahoma Women in Politics in the Early Twentieth Century, 1900–1930*, Lincoln, NB: Writers Club Press.

Schyman, Gudrun. 2002. Speech to the Left Party Congress.

Scott, James. 1990. *Domination and the Arts of Resistance: Hidden Transcripts*, New Haven, CT, and London: Yale University Press.

Scott, Joan. 1988. *Gender and the Politics of History*, New York: Columbia University Press.

1996. *Only Paradoxes to Offer: French Feminists and the Rights of Man*, Cambridge, MA: Harvard University Press.

Scott, Joan, Cora Kaplan, and Debra Keates (eds). 1997. *Transitions, Environments, Translations: Feminisms in International Politics*, New York: Routledge.

Second Commission on the Status of Women. 1993. *Report to the Government*, Dublin: Government Stationery Office.

Sedgwick, Eve Kosofsky. 1993. "Queer Performativity: Henry James's 'Art of the Novel,'" *GLQ* 1(1): 1–16.

Seidman, Gay W. 1999. "Gendered Citizenship. South African's Democratic Transition and the Construction of a Gendered State," *Gender and Society* 13: 287–307.

2000. "Adjusting the Lens: What do Globalizations, Trans-nationalism and the Anti-Apartheid Movement Mean for Social Movement Theory?" in John A. Guidry, Michael D. Kennedy, and Mayer N. Zald (eds.), pp. 339–58.

Seidman, Steven. 1997. *Difference Troubles: Queering Social Theory and Sexual Politics*, Cambridge University Press.

Sewell, William, Jr. 1980. *Work and Revolution in France: The Language of Labor from the Old Regime to 1848*, Cambridge University Press.

Shachar, Ayelet. 2001. *Multicultural Jurisdictions: Cultural Differences and Women's Rights*, Cambridge University Press.

Sheridan, Susan. 1995. *Along the Faultlines: Sex, Race and Nation in Australian Women's Writing 1880–1930s*, Sydney: Allen and Unwin.

Sík, Endre, and István György Tóth (eds.). 1997. *Az ajtók záródnak (?!)* [Do the doors close?!], Budapest: TÁRKI-BKE Szociológia Tanszék.

Šiklová, Jiřina. 1997. "Feminism and the Roots of Apathy in the Czech Republic," *Social Research* 64(2): 258–80.

Silva, Hélio R. S., and Cristina de Oliveira Florentino. 1996. "A sociedade dos travestis: espelhos, papéis e interpretações" [Travesti society: mirrors, roles, and interpretations], in Richard Parker and Regina Maris Barbosa (eds.), *Sexualidades brasileiras* [Brazilian sexualities], Rio de Janeiro: ABIA/IMS-UERJ/Relume-Dumará.

Silverstein, Michael. 2000. "Translation, Transduction, Transformation," Unpublished manuscript. Presented at a conference on Translation in Germany.

Silverstein, Michael, and Greg Urban (eds.). 1996. *Natural Histories of Discourse*, University of Chicago Press.

Sjöberg, Ola. 2000. *Duties in the Welfare State: Working and Paying for Social Rights*, Stockholm: Swedish Institute for Social Research.

Skidmore, Thomas E. 1988. *The Politics of Military Rule in Brazil 1964–85*, Oxford University Press.

Skocpol, Theda. 1992. *Protecting Soldiers and Mothers: The Political Origins of Social Policy in the United States*, Cambridge, MA: Harvard University Press.

Skocpol, Theda, Marjorie Abend-Wein, Christopher Howard, and Susan Goodrich Lehmann. 1993. "Women's Associations and the Enactment of

Mothers' Pensions in the United States," *American Political Science Review* 87(3): 686–701.

Smith, Dorothy. 1974. "Women's Perspective as a Radical Critique of Sociology," *Sociological Inquiry* 44(1): 7–13.

Smyth, Ailbhe. 1993. "The Women's Movement in the Republic of Ireland, 1970–1990," in Ailbhe Smyth (ed.), *Irish Women's Studies Reader*, Dublin: Attic Press, pp. 245–69.

Snitow, Ann. 1995. "Feminist Futures in the Former East Bloc," in Marina Blagojević, Daša Duhaček, and Jasmina Lukić (eds.), *What Can We Do for Ourselves?* Belgrade: Center for Women's Studies, pp. 141–54.

Snow, David A., and Robert D. Benford. 1992. "Master Frames and Cycles of Protest," in Aldon D. Morris and Carol Mueller (eds.), pp. 133–55.

Snow, David A., Burke E. Rochford, Steven Worden, and Robert Benford. 1986. "Frame Alignment Processes, Micromobilization, and Movement Participation," *American Sociological Review* 51: 464–81.

SOU (Statens Offentliga Utredningar) [State Public Commission]. 1997. *Om fördelning av ekonomisk makt och ekonomisk resurser mellan kvinnor och män*, reports 83, 87, 113, 114, 115, 135, 136, 137, 138, 139.

Spalter-Roth, Roberta, and Ronee Schreiber. 1995. "Outsider Issues and Insider Tactics: Strategic Tensions in the Women's Policy Network," in Myra Marx Ferree and Patricia Yancey Martin (eds.), pp. 105–27.

Sperling, Liz, and Charlotte Bretherton. 1996. "Women's Policy Networks and the EU," *Women's Studies International Forum* 19(3): 303–14.

Spinner-Halev, Jeff. 2001. "Feminism, Multiculturalism, Oppression, and the State," *Ethics* 112: 84–113

Staggenborg, Suzanne. 1991. *The Pro-Choice Movement*, New York: Oxford University Press.

Standing, Guy. 1997. "The Folly of Social Safety Nets: Why Basic Income Is Needed in Eastern Europe," *Social Research*, 64(4): 1339–81.

Stark, Agneta. 1997. "Combating the Backlash: How Swedish Women Won the War," in Ann Oakley and Juliet Mitchell (eds.), *Who's Afraid of Feminism? Seeing Through the Backlash*, London: Hamish Hamilton, pp. 224–44.

Steinberg, Marc W. 1999. "The Talk and Back Talk of Collective Action: A Dialogic Analysis of Repertoires of Discourse Among Nineteenth Century English Cotton Spinners," *American Journal of Sociology*: 105(3): 736–80.

Stiglmayer, Alexandra (ed.). 1994. *Mass Rape: The War Against Women in Bosnia-Hercegovina*, Lincoln, NB: University of Nebraska Press.

Stolz, Pauline. 1994. "Black and Migrant Women in the European Women's Movement," paper presented at the Crossing Borders – International Dialogues on Gender, Social Politics, and Citizenship Conference, Stockholm, Sweden, May 27.

Subirats, Joan (ed.). 1999. *¿Existe sociedad civil en España? Responsabilidades colectivas y valores públicos* [Does civil society exist in Spain? Collective responsibility and public values], Madrid: Fundación Encuentro.

Summers, Anne. 1975. *Damned Whores and God's Police: The Colonization of Women in Australia*, Melbourne: Penguin.

Sundström, Marianne. 1987. *A Study in the Growth of Part-time Work in Sweden*, Stockholm: Swedish Centre for Working Life (ALI).

Svanström, Yvonne. 2003. "Criminalising the John – a Swedish Gender Model," in Joyce Outshoorn (ed.), *The Politics of Prostitution: Women's Movements, Democratic States and the Globalisation of Sex Commerce*, Cambridge University Press.

Sydney Morning Herald, 1998. October 17.

Sykes, Roberta. 1975. "Black Women in Australia: A History," in Jan Mercer (ed.), *The Other Half: Women in Australian Society*, Ringwood, Australia: Penguin, pp. 313–21.

Snake Dreaming: Autobiography of a Black Woman, 3 volumes:
1997. *Snake Cradle*, Sydney: Allen and Unwin.
1998. *Snake Dancing*, Sydney: Allen and Unwin.
2000. *Snake Circle*, Sydney: Allen and Unwin.

Szalai, Júlia. 1991. "Some Aspects of the Changing Situation of Women in Hungary in the Process of Transition," *Signs* 17(1): 152–71.
2000. "From Informal Labor to Paid Occupations: Marketization from Below in Hungarian Women's Work," in Susan Gal and Gail Kligman (eds.), 2000b, pp. 200–24.

Szelényi, Iván. 1992. *Harmadik út? Polgárosodás a vidéki Magyarországon* [Is there a third road? The process of embourgeoisement in rural Hungary], Budapest: Akadémiai Kiadó.

Takahashi, Mieko. 2003. *Gendered Dimensions in Family Life: A Comparative Study of Power in Sweden and Japan*, Stockholm: Stockholm Studies in Sociology.

Tarrow, Sidney. 1989. *Democracy and Disorder: Protest and Disorder in Italy, 1965–1975*, New York: Oxford University Press.
1996. "States Opportunities: The Political Restructuring of Social Movements," in Doug McAdam, John D. McCarthy, and Mayer N. Zald (eds.), pp.
1998. *Power in Movement: Social Movements, Collective Action, and Politics*, second edition, New York: Cambridge University Press.

Taylor, Charles. 1994. "The Politics of Recognition," in Amy Gutmann (ed.), pp. 25–75.

Taylor, Judith. 1999. "Case X: Irish Reproductive Policy and European Influence," *Social Politics: International Studies of Gender, State and Society*. 6 (2): 203–30.

Taylor, Quintard. 1998. *In Search of the Racial Frontier: African Americans in the American West, 1538–1990*, New York: W. W. Norton.

Taylor, Verta, and Leila J. Rupp. 1993. "Women's Culture and Lesbian Feminist Activism: A Reconsideration of Cultural Feminism," *Signs* 19(1): 32–61.

Taylor, Verta, and Nancy Whittier. 1992. "Collective Identity in Social Movement Communities: Lesbian Feminist Mobilization," in Aldon D. Morris and Carol Mueller (eds.), pp. 104–29.
1995. "Analytical Approaches to Social Movement Culture: The Culture of the Women's Movement," in Hank Johnston and Bert Klandermans (eds.), pp. 163–87.

Terborg-Penn, Rosalyn. 1998. *African American Women in the Struggle for the Vote 1859–1920*, Bloomington, IN: Indiana University Press.

Terto, Veriano, Jr. 2000. "Male Homosexuality and Seropositivity: The Construction of Social Identities in Brazil," in Richard G. Parker, Regina Maria

Barbosa, and Peter Aggleton (eds.), *Framing the Sexual Subject: The Politics of Gender, Sexuality and Power*, Berkeley and Los Angeles: University of California Press, pp. 60–78.

Terto, Veriano, Jr., Edgar Merchán-Hamann, Kátia Guimarães, Maria Eugênia Lemos Fernandes, Murilo Mota, Vagner de Almeida, and Richard Parker. 1998. "Projeto Homossexualidades: a prevenção de AIDS de homens que fazem sexo com homens no Rio de Janeiro e São Paulo" [The Homosexualities Projects: AIDS prevention among men who have sex with men in Rio de Janeiro and São Paulo], in Richard Parker and Veriano Terto Jr. (eds.), pp. 111–18.

Terto, Veriano, Jr., Richard Parker, Murilo Mota, Katia Guimarães, and Renato Quemmel. 1995. "AIDS Prevention and Gay Community Mobilization in Brazil," *Development* 2: 49–53.

Thompson, E. P. 1963. *The Making of the English Working Class*, New York: Vintage Books.

Tilly, Charles. 1978. *From Mobilization to Revolution*, Reading, MA: Addison-Wesley.

Timár, János. 1994. "A foglalkoztatás és a munkanélküliség sajátosságai a posztszocialista országokban" [Some peculiar features of employment and unemployment in the postcommunist region], *Közgazdasági Szemle* 42 (7–8): 46–63.

Tingsten, Herbert. 1973. *The Swedish Social Democrats: Their Ideological Development*, trans. Greta Frankel and Patricia Howard-Rosen, New Jersey: Bedminster Press.

Todorova, Maria. 1997. *Imagining the Balkans*, New York: Oxford University Press.

Tolson, Arthur L. 1972. *The Black Oklahomans, A History: 1541–1972*, New Orleans: Edwards Printing Company.

Touraine, Alain. 1981. *The Voice and the Eye*, Cambridge University Press.

Trevisan, João Silvério. 1986. *Perverts in Paradise*, London: GMP Publishers.

Tsing, Anna Lowenhaupt. 1997. "Transitions as Translations," in Joan Scott, Cora Kaplan, and Debra Keates (eds.), pp. 253–72.

Turner, Brian. 1993. *Citizenship and Social Theory*, London: Sage.

Vajda, Ágnes. 1997. "A legális munkahelyeken kívül végzett munkák az 1980-as évek végén, az 1990-es évek elején" [Work done outside the web of registered workplaces at the turn of the 1980s and 1990s], in Edit Landau (ed.), *Az államtalanítás dilemmái: munkaerőpiaci kényszerek és választások* [Dilemmas of "state desertion": constraints and choices on the labor market], Budapest: ATA.

Vallinoto, Tereza Christina. 1991. "A construção de solidariedade: um estudo sobre a resposta coletiva à AIDS" [Constructing solidarity: a study on collective organizing in response to AIDS], Master's Thesis, Escola Nacional de Saúde Pública.

Ványai, Judit, and Erzsébet Viszt. 1995. "A szolgáltatások növekvő szerepe" [The increasing role of the service sector], *Közgazdasági Szemle* 43(7–8): 45–62.

Vásárhelyi, Mária. 1998. "Újságírói autonómia és sajtószabadság" [Freedom of the press and the autonomy of journalists], in Mária Vásárhelyi and Gábor

Halmai (eds.), *A nyilvánosság rendszerváltása* [The transition of the public sphere], Budapest: Új Mandatum, pp. 303–16.

Veneziani, Antonio, and Riccardo Reim. 1999. *I mignotti: vite venduti e storie vissute di prostitute, gigolò e travestiti* [Whores: lives sold and stories lived by prostitutes, rent boys, and transvestites], second edition, Rome: Castelvecchi.

Venuti, Lawrence. 1995. *The Translator's Invisibility: A History of Translation*, New York: Routledge.

Wachter, Ruth. 1962. "Kvinnosakens dilemma," *Tiden* 1962: 413.

Wadensjö, Eskil. 1997. "Invandrarkvinnoranas arbetsmarknad" [The immigrant women's labour market], in Inga Persson and Eskil Wadensjö (eds.), *Glastak och glasväggar: den konssegregerade arbetsmarknad* [Glass ceilings and glass walls: the sex-segregated labor market], SOU 137: 195–212.

Watson, Peggy. 1997. "Civil Society and the Politics of Difference in Eastern Europe," in Joan Scott, Cora Kaplan, and Debra Keates (eds.), pp. 21–29.

Weber, Max. 1958. "Class, Status, Party," in Hans H. Gerth and C. Wright Mills (eds.), *From Max Weber: Essays in Sociology*, Oxford University Press, pp. 180–95.

Weekend Australian, 1998. October 24.

White, Deborah Gray. 1999. *Too Heavy a Load: Black Women in Defense of Themselves, 1894–1994*, New York: W. W. Norton.

Williams, Fiona. 1989. *Social Policy: A Critical Introduction, Issues of Race, Gender and Class*, Cambridge: Polity Press.

1990. "A Report of the Fifth Annual Conference of the European Forum of Socialist-Feminists, Gothenburg," *Critical Social Policy* 28: 96–102.

1999. "Good-Enough Principles for Welfare," *Journal of Social Policy* 28(4): 667–87.

Wilson, Tikka Jan. 1996. "Feminism and Institutionalised Racism: Inclusion and Exclusion at an Australian Feminist Refuge," *Feminist Review* 52: 2–10.

Winkler, Celia. 2002. *Single Mothers and the State*, Lanham, MD: Rowan and Littlefield.

Wrench, John. 1996. *Preventing Racism in the Workplace*, Dublin: European Foundation for the Improvement of Living and Working Conditions.

Wright, James R., Jr. 1973–4. "The Assiduous Wedge: Woman Suffrage and the Oklahoma Constitutional Convention," *Chronicles of Oklahoma* 51(4): 421–43.

Yeates, Nicole. 1997. "Gender and the Development of the Irish Welfare System," in Anne Byrne and Madeleine Leonard (eds.), pp. 145–66.

Young, Iris Marion. 1990. *Justice and the Politics of Difference*, Princeton University Press.

1997. "Unruly Categories: A Critique of Nancy Fraser's Dual Systems Theory," *New Left Review* 222: 147–60.

2000. *Inclusion and Democracy*, Oxford University Press.

Yuval-Davis, Nira. 1997. *Gender & Nation*, London: Sage.

Žižek, Slavoj. 1999. *The Ticklish Subject: The Absent Center of Political Ontology*, London and New York: Verso.

Index

ABGLT, *see Associação Brasileira de Gays, Lésbicas and Travestis*
Aboriginal and Torres Strait Islander Commission (ATSIC), 159
Aboriginal women
  crises in identity, 157–58
  life stories or autobiographical narratives of struggle, 155–57
  and making and dissolution of identities, 159–60
  recognition struggles, 145–46, 160
  relevance in the women's movement, 148–49
"Aboriginal Women and the White Lies of the Feminist Movement," 149
abortion politics in Germany and the USA, 35–63
  challenging gender of governance, 46–52
  challenging governance of gender, 52–60
  comparison of, 35–44
  data and methods, 44–46
Abortion Rights Action League, *see* National Abortion and Reproductive Rights Action
ACLU, *see* American Civil Liberties Union
Action Information Motivation (AIM), 80
Action Plan Against Racism, 135
African-Americans
  recognition struggles, 162, 163–65, 169–73, 180–81, 185
  self-doubt/self-hatred, 184
AIDS activism, 226–27, 228–33
AIM, *see* Action Information Motivation
American Civil Liberties Union (ACLU), 42
Amsterdam Treaty, 84, 127
Anderson, 281
Ang, Ien, 157
Anti-Discrimination Pay Act, 85
Associação Brasileira de Gays, Lésbicas and Travestis (ABGLT, Brazilian

Association of Gays, Lesbians, and Travestis), 232–33
Association of Social Democratic Women, 43
ATSIC, *see* Aboriginal and Torres Strait Islander Commission
Australia, Women's Liberation movement in, 146–48
Australian Feminist Law Journal, 149
authority, and abortion politics, 36–37, 39
autonomy, and abortion politics, 35–36, 37–39, 57–60
Axel Springer, 103

Baby, Jovana, 220–21, 233
Bandler, Faith, 153
Barnard, Kate, 174, 177–78
Behrendt, Larissa, 149
Benford, Rob, 277–78
Bertelsmann Corporation, 103
Biggers, Kate, 178
Black and Migrant Women's Project, 130–31, 141–42
Black and Migrant Women's Project Report by the European Forum of Left Feminists, 131
black minority
  see also Aboriginal women; African-Americans; race and gender in the EU
  destabilization of category "black," 152–55
  political and historical representations made on behalf of and about "women," 148–52
  recognition struggles, 145–46, 160
"Black Women in Australia – A History," 148
boundary-making, 74–77
Bourdieu, Pierre, 105
Branstetter, Winnie, 175

331